Tarnow; The Life and Destruction of a Jewish City
(Tarnów, Poland)

Translation of
Tarnow; Kiyuma ve-Hurbana Shel Ir Yehudit

Volume II

Original Book Edited by: Dr. Avraham Chomet

Originally published in Tel Aviv 1954 - 1968

A Publication of JewishGen, Inc.
Edmond J. Safra Plaza, 36 Battery Place, New York, NY 10280
646.494.5972 | info@JewishGen.org | www.jewishgen.org

©JewishGen, Inc. 2023. All Rights Reserved
An affiliate of New York's Museum of Jewish Heritage – A Living Memorial to the Holocaust

Tarnow; The Life and Destruction of a Jewish City (Tarnów, Poland)
Translation of *Tarnow; Kiyuma ve-Hurbana Shel Ir Yehudit*

Copyright © 2023 by JewishGen, Inc. All rights reserved.
First Printing: November 2023, Kislev 5784

Editor of Original Yizkor Book: Dr. Avraham Chomet
Project Coordinator: Jill Leibman
Project Coordinator Emerita: Ann Drillich
Cover Design: Rachel Kolokoff Hopper
Layout: Jonathan Wind
Name Indexing: Stefanie Holzman
Reproduction of photographs: Stefanie Holzman

This book may not be reproduced, in whole or in part, including illustrations in any form (beyond that copying permitted by Sections 107 and 108 of the U.S. Copyright Law and except by reviewers for public press), without written permission from the publisher.

JewishGen Inc. is not responsible for inaccuracies or omissions in the original work and makes no representations regarding the accuracy of this translation. Digital images of the original book's contents can be seen online at the New York Public Library website or the Yiddish Book Center website.

Library of Congress Control Number (LCCN): 2022947276
ISBN: 978-1-954176-62-1 (hard cover: 480 pages, alk. paper)

About JewishGen.org

JewishGen, an affiliate of the Museum of Jewish Heritage - A Living Memorial to the Holocaust, serves as the global home for Jewish genealogy.

Featuring unparalleled access to 30+ million records, it offers unique search tools, along with opportunities for researchers to connect with others who share similar interests. Award winning resources such as the Family Finder, Discussion Groups, and ViewMate, are relied upon by thousands each day.

In addition, JewishGen's extensive informational, educational and historical offerings, such as the Jewish Communities Database, Yizkor Book translations, InfoFiles, Family Tree of the Jewish People, and KehilaLinks, provide critical insights, first-hand accounts, and context about Jewish communal and familial life throughout the world.

Offered as a free resource, JewishGen.org has facilitated thousands of family connections and success stories, and is currently engaged in an intensive expansion effort that will bring many more records, tools, and resources to its collections.

Please visit https://www.jewishgen.org/ to learn more.

Executive Director: Avraham Groll

About the JewishGen Yizkor Book Project

Yizkor Books (Memorial Books) were traditionally written to memorialize the names of departed family and martyrs during holiday services in the synagogue (a practice that still exists in many synagogues today).

Over the centuries, as a result of countless persecutions and horrific atrocities committed against the Jews, Yizkor Books (Sefer Zikaron in Hebrew) were expanded to include more historical information, such as biographical sketches of famous personalities and descriptions of daily town life.

Following the Holocaust, the idea of remembrance and learning took on an urgent and crucial importance. Survivors of the Holocaust sought out other surviving residents of their former towns to memorialize and document the names and way of life of those who were ruthlessly murdered by the Nazis. These remembrances were documented in Yizkor Books, hundreds of which were published in the first decades after the Holocaust.

Most of these books were published privately, or through landsmanshaftn (social organizations comprised of members originating from the same European town or region) that still existed, and were often distributed free of charge. Sadly, the languages used to document these crucial histories and links to our past, Yiddish and Hebrew, are no longer commonly understood by a significant percentage of Jews today. As a result, JewishGen has undertaken the sacred responsibility of translating these books into English so that the culture and way of life of these communities will be preserved and transmitted to future generations.

In 1986, a group of farsighted JewishGenners started a project to pool their efforts together in groups based upon their ancestors from each town and donate money to get the Yizkor books of their ancestral towns translated into English. As the translated material became available, it was made accessible for free at www.JewishGen.org/Yizkor. Hardcover copies can be purchased by visiting https://www.jewishgen.org/Yizkor/ybip.html (see below).

It is our hope that the translation of these books into English (and other languages) will assist the countless Jewish family researchers who are so desperately seeking to forge a connection with their heritage.

Director of JewishGen Yizkor Book Project: Lance Ackerfeld

About JewishGen Press

JewishGen Press (formerly the Yizkor Books-in-Print Project) is the publishing division of JewishGen.org, and provides a venue for the publication of non-fiction books pertaining to Jewish genealogy, history, culture, and heritage.

In addition to the Yizkor Book category, publications in the Other Non-Fiction category include Shoah memoirs and research, genealogical research, collections of genealogical and historical materials, biographies, diaries and letters, studies of Jewish experience and cultural life in the past, academic theses, and other books of interest to the Jewish community.

Please visit https://www.jewishgen.org/Yizkor/ybip.html to learn more.

Director of JewishGen Press: Joel Alpert
Managing Editor - Jessica Feinstein
Publications Manager - Susan Rosin

Notes to the Reader

The images in the original book were reproduced from photographs from the time of the first edition. These reproductions were already of poor quality, being pre-war and at least 30 or more years old. As a result, the images in the book are the best achievable.

A reader can view the original scans of the book on the websites listed below.

The original book can be seen online at the Yiddish Book Center website:

https://www.yiddishbookcenter.org/collections/yizkor-books/yzk-nybc314331/tarne-kiem-un-hurbn-fun-a-yidisher-shtot-vol-2

OR

at the New York Public Library Digital Collections website:

https://digitalcollections.nypl.org/items/656e8bd0-166c-0136-71fc-2d55e79793ab

To obtain a list of Shoah victims from Tarnow (Tarnów, Poland), the reader should access the Yad Vashem web site listed below; one can also search for specific family names using family name option. These lists are continually updated by Yad Vashem, so it is worthwhile to periodically search these lists.

There is more valuable information (including the Pages of Testimony, etc.) available on this website: https://yvng.yadvashem.org/

For additional Tarnow information, please visit: https://kehilalinks.jewishgen.org/tarnow/

A list of all books available from JewishGen Press along with prices is available at: https://www.jewishgen.org/Yizkor/ybip.html

Photo Credits

Front Cover:

Photo:
Tarnow Poland, The Great Synagogue, before the war. Copyright Yad Vashem Photo Archive. 2986/32. Used with permission CAS-470473.

Front Cover Background Photo: *Wild Grasses* by Rachel Kolokoff Hopper.

Back Cover:

Photos:
Top Left - *Ruza Meszel with her little daughter Nina. [Page 378].*
Top Right - *Mina and Eli Sommer, 1928.* Courtesy of Henry Sommer.
Bottom Left - Front row: *Scheindl Sommer and Chaim Joseph Sommer with their grandchildren Zofia and Blanca Messinger. Back row: Eli Sommer, Mina Sommer Messinger, Marcus Messinger, Moses Sommer.* Courtesy of Henry Sommer.
Bottom Right - *Dr. Henryk Faber, a doctor in the Jewish Hospital, with his daughter, Francziska, in the Tarnow Ghetto.* Courtesy of Arie Avigor.

Back Cover Quote: *Chamber of the Holocaust, Jerusalem-Mount Zion. [Page 369].*

Project Coordinator Introduction

Close your eyes for a moment and imagine walking through the streets of Tarnow in 1936 when 25,000 Jews lived there – about half of the total population. Picture a time before the vibrant Jewish life in Tarnow was silenced forever. In the 400 years of its existence, Tarnow served as a major center of Jewish life, a place where Hasidism, Zionism, and Enlightenment thrived, where progressive and observant Jews walked side by side on the ancient streets and where Jewish shopkeepers, doctors, town leaders, lawyers, factory owners, clothing tradesmen, and porters made up the varied fabric of the once thriving community.

Imagine that for one afternoon you are walking through the streets and narrow alleyways of Grabowska, the Jewish district. As you pass the yeshivas with their myriad of pious students, the sound of prayer and communal learning fill the air. Rushing by you that afternoon are children on their way from school to their afternoon sports clubs or after school yeshivas and mothers heading to the Rynek to shop at the stores and pushcarts. Without even noticing, you have passed patients heading to the Jewish Hospital, porters delivering goods, or perhaps the everyday workers, such as the tailors, the knife sharpeners, the hatmakers, the cobblers diligently plying their trades on the bustling streets. As you walk the streets of Jewish Tarnow, you will surely pass the Old Synagogue built in 1581, the majestic New Synagogue completed in 1908, small synagogues known as shteibels, study houses and yeshivas.

Night falls and the sounds of the Jewish shopkeepers closing their stores and the Hasidim speaking Yiddish to each other as they rush to evening prayers abound. Jewish representatives on the town council hurry to city meetings, intellectuals head to the Jewish library and young adults gather at Zionist activities.

Soon, the bustling Jewish neighborhoods will be quiet once again. No one could have imagined that the future would hold a forever silence.

The Tarnow Yizkor books tell the stories of a magnificent and vibrant Jewish community, one in which our relatives coexisted as neighbors, friends, business associates and congregants in the synagogues. They led fulfilling and productive lives in a town filled with Jewish communal institutions and charities, sports organizations, Jewish schools, and a myriad of religious and social institutions. Until they didn't…..

The Tarnow Yizkor book volume 2 was published in 1968 with stories in Yiddish and Hebrew. It includes details of the annihilation of the Jewish community and the destruction of the monuments of Jewish heritage, as well as documents the names of the precious souls lost in the Holocaust.

This Yizkor book starts at the end, immediately before the forces of evil systematically terminated the vibrant Jewish community that had existed for hundreds of years. The first few chapters describe Jewish life immediately before the war. This volume then chronicles the subsequent destruction and devastation of Tarnow's Jewish institutions and synagogues and the deportation and death of most of its 25,000 Jewish residents.

The Yizkor book remembers...those who died and those who were saved by righteous gentiles, the children in the ghetto who snuck out to obtain food for their families and the heroes who participated in the Tarnow Ghetto uprising. It describes the Jewish social organizations that attempted to provide sustenance to the hungry, the doctors who attended to the sick despite the shortages of medicine in the ghetto and the faith of the doomed rabbis.

The last chapters of this Yizkor book tell of new beginning after the war – in Tarnow and around the world. There are accounts of life in the post-war Tarnow Jewish community, descriptions of the few pre-war Jewish landmarks that remained intact and details of the activities of the post-war Jewish Committee in Tarnow.

In the final pages of this volume, there is a partial list of the Tarnow Jews who perished (al kiddush Hashem) a martyr's death at the hands of the Nazi murderers. This list was compiled before 1968. A new necrology supplement was prepared in 2020-2021 and added to the Yizkor book so that more families could submit the names of their Tarnow relatives who were killed in the Holocaust.

One of the greatest challenges in remembrance is the loss of the eyewitnesses to describe the rich lives our ancestors lived in Tarnow. The survivors have written down their remembrances and documented them in this Yizkor book in order to ensure that those precious memories are never lost. The translation of this Yizkor book into English, and its publication, now guarantee that these remembrances will be available to future generations and the legacy of Jewish Tarnow will never disappear.

Jill Leibman Kornmehl

Acknowledgements

It has been a journey to complete the Tarnow Yizkor book translation and this accomplishment would not have been possible without the help and support of so many others.

I would first and foremost like to pay tribute to my in-laws, Nathan and Frances Leder Kornmehl, survivors who inspired me to become more involved in remembrance of their home town of Tarnow, Poland. It is the preservation of their memories, and those of other survivors, that was the impetus for me to take on this project.

As I become more involved in the Yizkor book project, I connected with other Tarnow descendants and activists for Jewish remembrance. Our amazing and dedicated Polish activists, Adam Bartosz, Magda Michal Bartosz and Natalia Gancarz have been instrumental in preserving the sites of Jewish interest in Tarnow mentioned in the Yizkor book. They have also provided unique historic photographs from their personal collections and archives that are included in the book.

The Tarnow Yizkor book translation project was first coordinated by Dr. Ann Drillich, and I am grateful to her for all her efforts. We were fortunate to have an exceptional team of paid and unpaid translators. Their tasks went beyond translating words and I was impressed by their efforts to make the translations accurate, which involved delving into resources, checking spellings of names and streets and consulting Yiddish language experts for obscure words. Deepest thanks to translators Gloria Berkenstat Freund, Miriam Leberstein, Daniel Kochavi, Mark Alsher, David Schonberg, Hannah Hochner, Gil Stamberger, Nancy Bassel, Leonard Bland, Barbara Blaustein, Philip Frost and Natanya Nobel. My appreciation to Gerald Pragier for his work on the updated necrology list.

This project was made possible by JewishGen and its staff. We appreciate Mr. Avraham Groll, for his strategic vision, dedication and oversight of the organization. Thank you to Lance Ackerfeld, who provided much needed guidance for the Tarnow Yizkor book chapter translations. I would like to acknowledge the efforts of Jonathan Wind, Rachel Kolokoff Hopper and Stefanie Holzman of the JewishGen Press team.

Special thanks to a wonderful group of people whose support and contributions to Jewish remembrance have been remarkable and have inspired my own interest and involvement in the Tarnow Yizkor book project. My deepest thanks to Elizabeth Szancer, a descendant of a family deeply rooted in Tarnow, for being such a wonderful role model for remembrance. Thank you to Dr. Dan Oren, for his exceptional leadership and involvement in protecting and commemorating the surviving sites of Jewish heritage in Tarnow. My gratitude to Russ Maurer for so many contributions, including the fantastic job he did coordinating the Necrology index, an invaluable addition to the Tarnow Yizkor book. My appreciation to Howard Fink, for demonstrating to me the importance of safeguarding a shared history and making sure that descendants have access to this information.

Lastly, I would like to express my deepest appreciation to my family – my husband, Bernard Kornmehl, and our sons, Jason, Adam and David Kornmehl – whose love and support make all things possible. I could not have reached this milestone without them. Their interest in the publication of the Tarnow Yizkor book as a legacy of their survivor parents and grandparents has been remarkable. The completion of the chapter translations and the publication of the Tarnow Yizkor book will ensure that future generations of our family, and others, will have this legacy forever.

Jill Leibman Kornmehl

Geopolitical Information

Tarnów, Poland is located at 50°01' N 20°59' E and 154 miles South of Warsaw

	Town	District	Province	Country
Before WWI (c. 1900):	Tarnów	Tarnów	Galicia	Austrian Empire
Between the wars (c. 1930):	Tarnów	Tarnów	Kraków	Poland
After WWII (c. 1950):	Tarnów			Poland
Today	Tarnów			Poland

Alternate Names for the Town:

Tarnów [Pol], Tarnau [Ger], Tarna [Yid], Tarnov [Rus], Tarniv [Ukr], Tarnuv, Torne, Tornen, Turna

Nearby Jewish Communities:

Radłów 7 miles NW
Wojnicz 8 miles WSW
Żabno 9 miles NNW
Tuchów 9 miles SSE
Dąbrowa Tarnowska 10 miles N
Ryglice 11 miles SE
Gromnik 12 miles S
Zakliczyn 13 miles SW
Radgoszcz 14 miles NNE
Pilzno 14 miles ESE
Rzepiennik Strzyżewski 15 miles SSE
Ciężkowice 16 miles S
Szczurowa 16 miles WNW
Brzesko 17 miles WSW
Jodłowa 17 miles SE
Radomyśl Wielki 18 miles NE
Czchów 18 miles SW
Dębica 19 miles E
Opatowiec 20 miles NW
Szczucin 20 miles N
Nowy Korczyn 21 miles NNW
Uście Solne 21 miles WNW
Koszyce 21 miles WNW
Brzostek 21 miles ESE

Bobowa 22 miles S
Biecz 23 miles SSE
Wampierzów 23 miles NNE
Nowy Wiśnicz 24 miles WSW
Kołaczyce 24 miles SE
Bochnia 25 miles W
Przecław 25 miles ENE
Gorlice 26 miles SSE
Grybów 27 miles S
Wiślica 27 miles NNW
Mielec 27 miles NE
Pacanów 27 miles N
Rzochów 27 miles NE
Nowe Brzesko 28 miles WNW
Kazimierza Wielka 28 miles NW
Ropczyce 28 miles E
Jasło 28 miles SE
Wielopole Skrzyńskie 29 miles E
Stopnica 29 miles N
Nowy Sącz 29 miles SSW
Sadkowa-Góra 30 miles NNE
Oleśnica 30 miles N
Borowa 30 miles NNE

Jewish Population: 12,586 (in 1900)

Map of Poland showing the location of **Tarnów**

Table of Contents

Preface	Editorial board	3

A. Past Eras

There Was Once a Jewish City Tarnow	Ahron Szporn	5
Tarnow "In The Old Days" [H]	Dr Z. Kasif	7
Tarnow - My Old Home	Avraham Zinger	13
To My Beloved Town That Is No More [H]	Yaakov Fleisher	18
Contribution to the History of Jews in Tarnow	Dr. Avraham Chust (Comet)	24
Adolf Rudnicki – A Jew from Tarnow	Menashe Unger	35
The Way of Life of the Village Jews in Tarnow County	Dr. Yeshayahu Fajg (Fagi)	38
What I Remember of Jewish Tarnow	Yitzhak Blazer	40
Information About the Jewish Cemetery in Tarnow	Dr. Avraham Chomet	52
Our First Steps	Dr. Naftali Szwarc	60
The "Hashomer Hatzair" Movement in Tarnow [H]	Mink	66
From My Memories	Josef Hayman	69
A Polish Poet Tells of Jewish Tarnow	Abraham Chomet	74

B. In Memory of the Departed

Yoseph Umanski z"l – devoted to Hebrew language [H]	Ben–Tzion Uman	77
Dr Shmuel Szpan of blessed memory (z"l)	Yaakov Fleisher	78
Daniel Leibl of blessed memory	Krassel	80
Zev Bloch (Webtchyu) z"l [H]	Y. Fleisher	81
Dr Naftali Szwarc z"l	A.Kh.	81
In memory of Ehud Shachar (Schwarz) [H]	A.Kh.	82

C. Fragments of Tarnow's Jewish Community of the Past

In Pictures		86

D. The Holocaust

The Road of Pain and Suffering	Yosef Kornilo	116
The Trial of Wilhelm Heinrich Rommelmann, may his name be erased		144
A Mother's Prayer [H]	Nathan-Ari Ginzberg	153
Tarnow Rabbis Who Perished *oyf Kiddush haShem*	Menashe Unger	157
The ADMOR [Hasidic rabbi] of Grudzisk [H]		166
About the Heroic Role of the Jewish Children During Nazi Rule	Ahron Szporn	167
Children Accuse		172

A Collection of Memories of the Hitlerist Hell	Ruchl Goldberg-Klimek	175
Memories of the Uprising in the Tarnow Ghetto	Hela Bornsztajn-Ross	181
How Miriam Korn Heroically Died	Yakov Kener	182
Memories of Those Terrible Times	Lily–Wider Rozenberg	184
Belzec, the Place of Death of the Tarnow Jews	Yerzy Bergman	186
The Belzer Rebbe Gave Me His Blessing	Dr. Yeshayahu Hendler	189
The Social Aid in Jewish Tarnow During the German Occupation	Dr. Avraham Chomet (Khumit)	191
Christians Who Saved Tarnow Jews	Dr. Avraham Chomet, Josef Kornilo	206

E. After the Holocaust

What Remained of Our Jewish Tarnow	Yosef Kornilo	217
The "Bund" and its Activities in the Jewish Committee Tarnow after the Holocaust	Ahron Szporn, Montreal, Canada	229

F. Tarnow Jews in Israel and Abroad

10th of Tevet, General Day of Kaddish and Remembrance of the Community of Tarnow [H]	Zvi Ezrachi (Matt)	232
The Activity of the Tarnower Landsmanschaft in Montreal	Ahron Szporn	233
From the Landsmanschaft in Toronto	Abraham Singer	236
From the Tarnow Landsmanschaft in New–York	L. Gottleib	238
From the Tarnower Landsmanschaft in Paris	Abraham Chomet	239
From the Tarnower Landsmanschaft in Israel [H]	Abraham Chomet	240
List of Holocaust victims		242
Memorial Pages		291

G. Miscellaneous

Tarnow Book Index	356
Tarnów Necrology Supplement	392
English Edition Name Index	425
Appendix	445

Tarnow; The Life and Destruction of a Jewish City (Tarnów, Poland)

Volume II

50°01' / 20°59'

Translation of
Tarnow; Kiyuma ve-Hurbana Shel Ir Yehudit

Published in Tel Aviv, 1954-1968

Acknowledgments

Project Coordinator:

Jill Leibman

Ann Drillich (emerita)

This is a translation from: *Tarnow; kiyuma ve-hurbana shel ir yehudit;*
(The Life and Destruction of a Jewish city (2 vols)),
Editors: A. Chomet, Tel Aviv, Association of Former Residents of Tarnow, 1954-1968
(H, Y, 1381 pages)

Note: The original book can be seen online at the NY Public Library site: Tarnow (1954)

This material is made available by JewishGen, Inc. and the Yizkor Book Project for the purpose of fulfilling our mission of disseminating information about the Holocaust and destroyed Jewish communities.
This material may not be copied, sold or bartered without JewishGen, Inc.'s permission. Rights may be reserved by the copyright holder.

JewishGen, Inc. makes no representations regarding the accuracy of the translation. The reader may wish to refer to the original material for verification.

JewishGen is not responsible for inaccuracies or omissions in the original work and cannot rewrite or edit the text to correct inaccuracies and/or omissions.

Our mission is to produce a translation of the original work and we cannot verify the accuracy of statements or alter facts cited.

Volume II

Yiddish TOC translated by Gloria Berkenstat Freund

Hebrew TOC translated by Yocheved Klausner

[Page 7, Volume 2]

Preface

by Editorial board

Translated by David Avraba

In the memorial book (*Yizkor book*): *Tarnow– The Life and Destruction of a Jewish Town* Volume 1 that was published in 1954, the life of the Jews of Tarnow of the past was broadly described. Not every aspect of life in Jewish Tarnow was described in this memorial book. In particular, there are only few chapters with details of the destruction of our past community. In these new chapters comprising Volume 2, the travails and the terrible tortures that the Jews of Tarnow suffered in the ghetto and the death camps are more fully documented.

In writing a second volume, our goal was to fill a void by presenting more testimonies of the surviving Jews from our town who were miraculously saved from the Nazi hell and by sharing additional information and facts relating to the life, the travails and the joys of Tarnow's Jewish community.

Besides this, we felt it necessary to use materials that were left over from the earlier edition and this we have brought afresh, thereby giving the possibility to describe more clearly the nature of the Tarnow Jewry of the past.

We have also taken into account the fact that our holy martyrs were not given a Jewish burial and they do not have *matzeivot* [gravestones], for in mass graves and gas chambers their dear souls departed aloft. This was one of the significant factors that brought us to the decision to prepare this second volume of the *Tarnow* memorial book, and thereby to provide the few remnants of Tarnow Jewry left alive the opportunity to memorialize in a second volume their relatives who perished in the Holocaust. And finally, we also prepared– according to our best potential and limited knowledge– a partial list of Tarnow Jews who perished (*al Kiddush Hashem*) a martyr's death in the terrible Holocaust, at the hands of the Nazi murderers.

There is no doubt that this list is not a full one– it contains only a small portion of the Jewish community of Tarnow that numbered before their destruction around twenty-five thousand souls.

We have taken upon ourselves a heavy burden and a great responsibility. If we have been able to carry out this work successfully, this goal was achieved due to the great assistance received from the Tarnow associations in Montreal, Toronto and New York, and in particular due to the efforts and help of public figures, our townsmen, in those places; Aaron Shporn, Abraham Singer, Abraham Wenger and Leon Gottlieb.

We see it as a duty also to mention here our young townsman, Jerzy Bergman, who lives in Tarnow with his family. He helped us obtain documents and pictures of the past Jewish community of Tarnow.

To all– many thanks and *yasher koach* – congratulations!

[Page 15, Volume 2]

Past Eras

There Once was a Jewish Town, Tarnow

by Ahron Szporn (Montreal, Canada)

Translated by Miriam Leberstein

Ahron Szporn

During the horrors of the Second World War, when the Nazi genocide and war criminals wreaked total destruction on the Jewish people, the Jewish community of Tarnow, like all of Polish Jewry, was also destroyed.

Our hearts are broken, and in the memories of the survivors of Tarnow there is etched the nightmare of the era of extermination. We see before us the horrifying images of those who gave up their dear souls and were killed in the mass graves and gas chambers.

A quarter of a century has passed since those horrific events. A new generation has grown up, one that did not witness the Holocaust and that is unable to comprehend that in the twentieth century Jews were burnt alive and gassed in crematoria. It is therefore our task, the obligation of the handful of survivors from Tarnow, not to allow the pain and suffering and the horror of the Holocaust to be forgotten or fall into the abyss of oblivion.

In our memories we always return to our former Tarnow home, one that no longer exists and to our tormented parents and siblings who perished in such a terrible way. And who can forget our dear little children, whose heads the German murderers bashed against stone walls, the merciless German beasts who in their murderous fury would hurl the poor children out the windows?

[Page 16, Volume 2]

We, the remnants of Tarnow Jewry who were fortunate to miraculously survive the Holocaust, must remember and remind others never to forget and not to forgive.

Let every gravestone, every monument that we erect in the memory of our annihilated community serve as an eternal light whose flickering flames will penetrate the hearts of the Tarnow survivors, scattered over the entire world, and remind us of our obligation to sustain the eternal memory of Tarnow, which took such pride in its impressive personalities who distinguished themselves in the realms of science, art and literature

A section of the old "Jewish Street" in Tarnow

[Page 17, Volume 2]

Our Jewish Tarnow had an abundance of outstanding Jews who created an entire array of exemplary organizations and institutions in all areas of political, socio-economic and cultural life. Driven by friendly competition, every political group made the greatest efforts to increase its activity to create ever more useful institutions in the Jewish community. Pure idealism and self-sacrifice were embedded in the nature of the Jews of Tarnow, shared by every community activist, no matter their party affiliation.

Everything has disappeared, has been erased. The Nazi torturers and executioners barbarically destroyed it all, without leaving a trace.

So it is the obligation of the survivors to observe:

Yizkor [memorial prayer for the dead] for our Tarnow Jews who died as holy martyrs

Yizkor for our martyrs who fell in battle against the greatest enemy of mankind

Yizkor for the heroic ghetto and partisan fighters who exalted the honor and dignity of the Jewish people.

Our Tarnow martyrs were not spared the tragic fate of the Jews annihilated upon the sacrificial altar and ruins of Europe.

[Page 18, Volume 2]

Tarnow "In The Old Days"

by Dr Z. Kasif (Tel Aviv)

Translated by Daniel Kochavi

Introduction

Fragments of memories, that I am putting down on paper, belong to a distant past that is completely different from present days. They belong to "days of yore" when I lived in Tarnow: until 1920 (the end of WWI and the beginning of independent Poland) as well as the years 1927-1932, when I was the principal of the gymnasium (Jewish high school) for boys and girls run by the "Safa Berura" (clear language) Society in Tarnow.

My intention is not to describe fragments of original sources of the Tarnow history, but to bring out memories from the forgotten depths that, in the opinion of the author, are important in a book dedicated to the people of Tarnow who are still alive. One cannot avoid being subjective when telling these stories. Since members of my family took part in various public activities in the last ten years of the existence of the community, my personal memories are connected sometimes with several community events in Tarnow.

Childhood

My earliest memories are connected to the religious atmosphere around me, I remember clearly the "shtiebel" of the "Lomde Torah" (Torah scholar) society (located at 12 Lwowska Street) where our family members prayed: my grandfather, my uncle and I. In this "Shtiebel" I was the only child dressed in European clothes, without side locks, which were traditional among the "Hassidim". "Lomde Torah" members hid their resentments in our case- since my grandmother's father' R. Zecharia Mendel Aberdam was one of founders and eminent scholars of the "Shtiebel".

[Page 19, Volume 2]

My mother tongue was Yiddish with a southern-Russian accent (my mother was from Berdichev). However most of the children in the city garden (called the Garden of the Marksman) "Ogrod Sterzelecki" spoke Polish among themselves. I still remember today how isolated I felt due to the lack of a "common language" with the neighboring children.

An orphan

I became an orphan when my father passed away (see below). The very strict members of the "Lomde Torah" considered my maternal grandfather (R' Zalman Chodorov from Berditshev, who lived at that time in Tarnow) as responsible for the education of the young Orphan. My mother, however, decided *not* to send me to the religious school (cheder) before the official compulsory age of six. When I reached the age of six I began learning "Hebrew in Hebrew". I started studying the Bible (Chumash) with the book of Genesis (rather than Leviticus) and "Gemara for beginners", a modern book by the standards of those days – all explained in *Hebrew* (and not in Yiddish).

The Hebrew high-school, "Safa Berura", was expanding at that time. I took private lessons with one of its young teachers -the most religious among them- R' Yosef Omanski, z" l, every Tuesday -all in Hebrew. The Hasidim in the "shtiebel" complained severely to my grandfather for allowing my mother to submit me to what they felt was a "forced conversion", God forbid, by a Zionist, Hebrew teacher. But my mother, of blessed memory, Mrs. Reizel Zilberfenig, who was a 25-year-old widow, stood her ground as far as my education was concerned and I remained R' Omanski's pupil until the age of 15-16. People of Tarnow remember that R' Yosef Omanski, who was an outstanding scholar, remained until the end of his life devoted to Judaism and to Hebrew. He passed away at the ripe old age of 91 two years ago in Israel. May his memory be a blessing.

Youth

After I learned modern Hebrew my mother insisted that I study the traditional six books of the Gemara and the traditional Rabbis' commentaries with R' Abaeli Hirsh, a scholar well known among "Torah scholars", but with ideas more accepting of the new generation.

As I mentioned before, I first spoke in Yiddish, read and wrote in Hebrew and only *afterwards* did I study Polish privately. My teachers were Miss Pinna and, later, Maria Gleicher, who were members of "Miriam", a Zionist organization. So even the Polish I studied had a Zionist flavor.

[Page 20, Volume 2]

My mother had both a strong and quiet personality and made sure that the educational goals she had set for me – in Judaic or secular studies - were adhered to. She wanted me to get a complete secondary and academic education- but, as far as possible, within the framework of a Judaic home and a traditional family- without mixing with "gentiles (goyim)". Therefore, I attended public school only after seventh grade (in Polish high school) and afterwards eighth grade (in an Austrian High school in Vienna). While attending these schools I never attended classes on Shabbat to ensure that I would not get used to violate Shabbat prohibitions (writing, traveling etc.). In Austria I was officially excused from attending classes on Saturday. At the Polish Royal High School there was no legal way to exempt me from attending school on Shabbat. Therefore, my Uncle had to bribe the class educator (Klitovski) with several kilos of flour (this was during the period right after WWI). And so, the absence periods "disappeared" from the class log or were "excused".

Teaching and Education

To follow up on this: several years after I evaded attendance at the Polish school on Shabbat I became the first principal of the Jewish High school known as "Safa Berura" in Tarnow. It was of course, closed on Shabbat. Its main goal was a special secular education and the study of Hebrew by the youth of Tarnow.

The formation the "Safa Berura" high school was a decisive turning point in my life but was also the beginning of small revolution in the education of Jewish youth in Tarnow. Once Jews in Galicia gained equal rights before the law, Jewish parents who wanted their children to get a general education, started sending them to public high schools (Austrian and Polish), which were free. From the Jewish point of view these schools had a negative influence on the Jewish youth. Jewish students became assimilated among Polish students, absorbed foreign culture but also suffered open and hidden anti-Semitism.

For various reasons Polish and Galician Jews never contemplated the founding of schools with Hebrew teaching (of the "cultural "type) [author's note – more secular]. However, in large and medium-size towns in central and southern Poland, Jewish high schools were created where a third of the curriculum (2 hours per day) was dedicated to Jewish studies and two-third (4-5 hours a day) to general studies in Polish. This also happened in our town. The "Safa Berura" Society existed before WWI and taught only "classes" or "courses", as well as basic Hebrew classes in the afternoon. After WWI, however, the "courses" and Hebrew lessons were moved to the culture (Tarbut) union building that was founded in Tarnow, while the "Safa Berura" Society opened a school; starting with kindergarten in the 1920's and expanding to a bilingual elementary school with 4 classes. Later, in 1927, the first class of the high school "Safa Berura" was opened.

In those days every high school consisted of 8 grades including "ours" where additional classes were added yearly until, in 1935, when the first senior class graduated.

[Page 21, Volume 2]

Volume 1 of the Tarnow book includes many details about "Safa Berura" that won't be repeated here.

I'll just point out that the overall operation for the "Safa Berura" High School was the responsibility of the heads of the society - R' Haim Nigar and Dr Shmuel Shafan, who worked tirelessly to develop the institution. From 1927-1932 the author of this chapter was its principal. From 1932 to 1939 it was headed by Dr Rozenbush.

Five classes graduated from "Safa Berura" High School before the start of WWII. Being one of the founders of the school I'd rather not "toot my horn". This institution is carved in my heart as a dynamic school, whose teachers had great educational influence, not only in their classrooms but also in the Jewish community and the Zionist youth movement in Tarnow. A large percentage of the Holocaust survivors, who live in Israel today, drew, one way or the other, their Zionism from "Safa Berura" HS in Tarnow. One of the Righteous Gentiles was the official supervisor from the Polish District, Mr Wladyslaw Wierzbicki, during the first years of its existence.

To open a new HS was a daring enterprise on the part of the founders of the school and the principal, who had just finished his studies at the University, given the conditions in Poland at that time. The Catholic supervisor treated the new institution in a fatherly manner and often overlooked the formal faults committed by the school in the beginning.

Family Memories

The Aberdam family: my Hebrew name is Zecharia. I was named after R' Zecharia Mendel Aberdam, father of my grandmother- who was a wise and outstanding scholar, devout leader, his whole being immersed in scholarship. I remember well his wife, Mrs. Hana Mindel Aberdam, my grandmother's mother: a wrinkled elderly woman, wearing a black head ornament with fine cloth. She was a strong woman who managed a successful bank and ruled all who surrounded her. I remember clearly the old office, grey and dusty, from which (sic:great) grandmother "ruled". She would sit behind a large desk and behind her was a heavy steel box [editor note: safe]. In front was another separate desk used by Mr Pinchas Fenichal," a jack of all trades" in the office. He was the bookkeeper, confidential advisor, "communication officer" a kind of "factotum". I remember with sympathy the various characters who traipsed into this office. They belonged to a world that sank and disappeared. I recall them from afar with fondness. They included money agents, delivery agents, the daytime-eating "young man (i.e. the yeshiva students who ate with different families each day). The grandchildren and great-grandchildren were part of the atmosphere of my (sic: great) grandmother's office. They sniffed freely around the office, played with the various sealing stamps, examined the strange telephonic instrument and were impressed by the numerous copies of letters created by the hand-operated duplicating machine.

[Page 22, Volume 2]

A visit to my grandmother also included traditional treats: cake and an orange from Israel, a luxury in those days that only the "leaders'" children got to enjoy.

My (sic: great) grandmother lived during a long peaceful time and trusted in a peaceful future. At a later time, her family (and later her heirs) complained that the old woman leased a large part of her house to a local well-to-do resident, Baron Gatz (from Okutzim) on a long-term basis, 20 years, at fixed rent. WWI started shortly after my (sic: great) Grandmother's death and was followed by a runaway inflation. The same agreement that had guaranteed security was not even worth the paper it was written on.

The generations after Hana Mindel Aberdam no longer entered into long term agreements.

Memorial stone dedicated to R' Yeshayahu Silberberg, z"l
erected by his children who survived the Holocaust

[Page 23, Volume 2]

Weksler family: After my (great)grandmother' death the grey and dark bank office passed on to her son in law R' Israel Weksler. "Uncle Israel" was not able to develop this business and to adapt to the period between the two world wars but only maintained it. His sons were not interested in this business- they married and moved far away. WWII brought an end to the Aberam-Weksler bank.

Wolff-Silberfenig Family: My father. R' Benyamin Zev (Wolf) Silberfenig, z" l, passed away on Shemini Atseret (22 Tishri) 5667 (1907). He caught a cold followed by a lung inflammation (pneumonia). Antibiotics did not exist in those days. My father did not recover- he was only 27 when he died.

When I grew older, friends of my father (Benny Bernshtater, Rubin, R' Haim Nigar and others) told me that his home was among the first Zionist homes at a time when most Tarnow Jews were fanatic Hassidim and very few assimilated. Young men, who were ousted in shame from the Kloyz (Ed note: religious learning community) because they showed interest in "enlightenment", poured their heart out to father. So, did men whose place in the "Beth Midrash" was literally trashed because of their interest in Zionism. In my father's home, they strategized on how to remove the stigma of people who assimilated and who also dominated the Jewish public establishments in Tarnow.

The anti-Zionists knew of my father's activities but they did not dare attack or hurt him because he belonged to an established and respected family. He also maintained a traditional appearance. I still see clearly my father's appearance: a bushy beard, dressed in a long silk coat on Shabbat, wearing a "velvet brim Polish hat" (his father came from Plonsk, a small town near Warsaw where Ben Gurion also came from). When I grew older I saw his beautiful handwriting and enjoyed his great style in several languages. There were two large (book)cases in his room. The first was filled to the brim with Hebrew literature both ancient and rabbinical, mostly large Six Sedarim (Talmud) from Vilna printed on parchment. The second bookcase contained all the Hebrew books that came out in his days, mostly "how to" and other similar books.

After my father's death, my mother preserved the character of the "home" (see above) and my sister Hinda, z"l, followed in my parents' footsteps. They both perished during the great slaughter of Tarnow in June 1942.

R' Yeshayahu Haim Silberfenig, my father's brother was the most outstanding personality in our family. Many readers of this book will recall "Shaya" (his nickname among Tarnow old timers) from the time of his downfall, after he was socially and physically destroyed. I, however, remember him well at the peak of his greatness, a radiant figure in the streets of Tarnow, generous and kind hearted, ready to empty his pockets, take off his shoes and give them to a needy person he encountered on his way (this really happened!) He was a great public speaker, devoted Zionist and "urban" public figure. He was a brilliant businessman-in industry as well as commerce. He also could lead the service on the major high holidays. An atmosphere of nobility and culture reigned in his luxurious home. For many years he hired an excellent private Hebrew teacher (Shimon Koplanski) who taught my aunt and her three children Hebrew and Hebrew literature at the highest level.

[Page 24, Volume 2]

But, before WWI, fate intervened and the house of Yeshayahu Silberfenig "fell apart". At the outbreak of WWII his family was scattered to all corners of the world and, as a result, his two daughters and his son survived – but the parents perished during the Holocaust. My aunt Mrs. Golda Mozel my father's sister, also perished.

An entire generation of this wonderful family almost disappeared. The remaining descendants of the family are scattered to-day over four continents: from Israel to the USA and from Australia to Brazil.

Section of an old street "the Yiddishe street" (Zydowska Street) in Tarnow

Tarnow – My Old Home

by Avraham Zinger (Toronto – Canada)

Translated by Gloria Berkenstat Freund

Avraham Zinger

I was still very young when I left my dear home-city of Tarnow. The events of my young years were deeply etched in my memory… The images from the past Jewish life in Tarnow run by as in a film.

With a tremble in my heart, I undertook the refreshing of my memories that were connected to that life and to recreate Tarnow Jewry, which perished so terribly *al kiddish haShem* [in the sanctity of God's name – as martyrs]. Therefore, I will strive, within the framework of my abilities, to provide details of my Jewish Tarnow as I saw them and as I still remember them today.

Jewish life in Tarnow was effervescent. Jews, there, always toiled for their livelihood, each in his own way, according to their intentions and capabilities, as industrialists, as workers or employees, as wholesale merchants or shopkeepers. The economic significance of Tarnow was due to Jewish diligence and industriousness… Thanks to the entrepreneurial spirit of the Tarnow Jews, the city became an important center of trade and industry that contributed greatly to the rise of the entire Tarnow County. In another spot, in the first volume of the memorial book, *Tarnow*, we find mentioned the most important names of Tarnow Jews who laid the foundation for the great trade and industrial enterprises, where a large number of Jewish and non-Jewish workers and employees were employed.

[Page 26, Volume 2]

The Szancer-Bornsztajn steam mill – in Tarnow – today belonging to the state

An extensive, diversified clothing industry developed strongly during the era between the two World Wars that was entirely in Jewish hands and employed approximately 3,000 Jewish workers… They created this strong professional organization in Tarnow that consistently kept watch over their work interests. These Jewish toilers saved money to build their own worker house, a magnificent building named after the Bundist leader, B. Michalewicz. The offices of the trade unions of the various branches were housed there; the communal institutions, which were created and supported by Jewish workers who found themselves under the influence of the Bund, had a place there. It should be remembered here that at the construction of this workers house, Friend Avraham Herszkowic of New York, an activist in the trade union movement there, contributed a significant sum of money.

* * *

Tarnow Jews led modest lives. The majority of Tarnow Jews earned their livelihood with great effort and from this difficult life the Tarnow Jews built magnificent cultural institutions, medical and philanthropic institutions.

[Page 27, Volume 2]

Zydowska Street known as "The Jewish Street" On the right near the pile on the ground was the entrance to the courtyard of the Old Synagogue

Tarnow Jews understood how to overcome their daily concerns and in their eternal thirst for education and knowledge reached higher scholarly and economic levels. Tarnow Jews always searched for ways to a new future and helped lay the foundations for [their] national and social ascent. Jewish life in Tarnow had thousands of allures and joys… Jewish children sang *Halutz* [pioneer] songs somewhere on the green grass in Szenkl's field or in the fields outside the castle on the mountain and danced the *hora* [Israeli dance] impetuously.

On a *Shabbos* [Sabbath] or on another day of rest, the sounds of the revolutionary and Yiddish freedom songs from the Jewish workshops, from the modest union halls of the Jewish working people, from the young workers called for struggle and devotion to the ideals of worker unity.

Therefore, our thoughts always turn back to the way of life in in our old home town that possessed so much "*Yiddishkeit*" of all kinds – so much suffering and joy.

[Page 28, Volume 2]

No trace remains of the effervescent life in Tarnow… Everything was destroyed by the Nazi murderers… Everything created in the city by the Tarnow Jews over the course of generations was erased, wiped away.

Nothing more than ruins remain of our magnificent Old and New Synagogues… of the houses of study where Tarnow Jews would study day and night… of the modern Temple Synagogue with the organ… of the small synagogues, the centers for a strict, Orthodox congregation of Jews… of the dozens of *minyonim* [groups of 10 men required for prayer] and *shtiblekh* [one-room houses of prayer]…

And where is the exemplary Jewish hospital in Tarnow with its capable doctors and devoted nurses?...

Where is our Jewish orphanage with the orphaned children who found such a warm and good home there?...

Where are the Hebrew schools in Tarnow?... Where are our very rich libraries... and where are the Jewish cultural and sport-gymnastic unions and institutions?...

Everything was totally annihilated... Our Jewish Tarnow was destroyed in the flood of the general destruction of Jews in Poland.

The ruins of the New Synagogue on Nowa Street in Tarnow, which was destroyed by the Gestapo during the Nazi occupation

[Page 29, Volume 2]

Our old Tarnow home had its characteristics that differentiated it from other Jewish communities in Poland. Yet our Jewish Tarnow was so well-known among Polish Jewry thanks to its great sons, scholars and scribes, writers and columnists, artists and scientists... We had no reason to be ashamed of our Jewish Tarnow, which for centuries was a source of *Yiddishkeit*, of higher morality with its communal customs, with deep understanding and fraternal readiness to help the needy. We are proud of our honored place in the Zionist and Socialist movement... How magnificent were all of our youth organizations of various beliefs.

* * *

By the light of civilization in the 20th century, by the cold-blooded silence and frequent assistance of the Jew-hating circles among our neighbors, with whom we lived together during the centuries and with whom we often fought together for their and our freedom... the German murderers annihilated our Tarnow Jewry in a bestial manner...

There were exceptions... there were Christians who helped... who risked their own lives to save Jews... There were several such noble Christians in Tarnow... We can count them on the fingers of one hand.

The former Nowa Street. "New houses have been built there now…" The new house, marked by the arrow, is located on the land of the destroyed New Synagogue

[Page 30, Volume 2]

A fragment of the former Nowa Street (bordered by Koszarowa Street). A three-story house (indicated by the arrow and where the municipal national council is located today) on the spot where the building of the Jewish *kehila*" [Jewish Community administrative offices] stood before the Holocaust (the block of the Devora Weksler houses)

* * *

These Christians were accepted with great honor into the group of the Righteous Among the Nations, the chosen from the nations of the world, which was erected in the memorial monument, Yad Vashem, in Jerusalem.

Polish as well as Tarnow Jewry was annihilated with the total silence of the large and small nations. Everything… Everything… that once was in Jewish Tarnow has disappeared like a dream. The Nazi hurricane turned over, cut out and tore out the many-branched Tarnow Jewish tree by its roots… Today the Jewish streets have disappeared in Tarnow… The Jewish houses… The Jewish ruins already have been cleared in Tarnow… New houses have now been built, new streets have been paved in the city where Tarnow Jews lived and toiled through the centuries.

Only the cemetery remains in Tarnow…

[Page 31, Volume 2]

To My Beloved Town That Is No More

by Yaakov Fleisher (Rechavia, Israel)

Translated by Daniel Kochavi

Where have you gone? Years of my youth and golden dreams, years of naive childhood, warm hearts and eternal friendships. Nights of discussions, evenings spent studying the language of the homeland we yearned for [Israel]. Where are you near and dear opinionated sons of the Youth Movements – each with its own ideological view of a future full of glory?

Hikes in the Tatra hills and Carpathian forests, Shabbat hikes under the group flag, nights by the bonfires in the woods in unfriendly surroundings where our bewitched spirits soar to the new homeland, to a society built on a life of creation and longings, a society physically and spiritually struggling to rebuild after a thousand year of ruin and creates new stones for a nation's house. Although some friends, relatives, brothers and parents rejected these ideas, the sun shone on the horizon and the stars beckoned from above…. youth convoys streamed on, echoing joyful songs upon departure, trains packed and seaports crowded with Halutzim from all over Europe, with faithful sons eager to rebuild the beckoning homeland. Oh!!! How worthy the years, how joyful was the soul yearning for great accomplishments, to embrace the world, to conquer deserts and subdue all resistance.

Group of Tarnow Shomrim in 1920

Seated from left: Engelhart Artek, Traum Sigmund–now in Australia, Handler Yeshayahu (now a doctor in Tel Aviv), Kaufman Mordecai, (–), Zaltz Yaakov
Standing from the left: Zimmerman; Manek Rodner; Speizer Yaakov; Margolit Leon; Koperman Israel; Swartz Artek (now in Kibbutz, from Rechavia); Eisenberg

[Page 32, Volume 2]

"Hashomer Hatzair" in Tarnow year 1921 – Troop "Zev" (trans. Wolf)

Sitting from left in order: 7–Zemel, 8–Ressler, 9–Vachtel Hayim (today a Doctor in Tivon)
Standing: 1–Tornheim, 2– Pris Milk,3–Stein,4–Lintser,5–Omanski Yaakov,6–Brown Henek
(now in Tarnow)
In the middle: Kornilo Yoseph (now in Israel)

Poland, the adopted motherland and enchanted country, its beauty drew the soul and relieved the longing for rest. The abundance of the country satisfied physical needs but did not bring rest to the soul. An eternal flame burned deep in our heart and drove a search for the uncertain tomorrow, pulled the spirit and promised to fill an inner void.

Individual longings became the longings of the society. Societies and groups were created, organized youth grew into a social way of life, created sign–posts, an unending struggle between the individual and the society but in the end the movement won, one for all and all for one, only external barriers seem to separate them. So, my beloved town; cradle of childhood and dreams, its rich and glorious past was abandoned like a lover betraying his beloved for a creation of new dreams and longing.

[Page 33, Volume 2]

To Israel To Fulfill Dreams

The snow melted, the sun shone and spring arrived. Friends, members of the [Zionist] movement, left in droves. "Will we meet again?" cried the sons. The ships sailed over stormy seas to distant shores that were so close to the heart and soul. Fear of the unknown grew; can the will and strength endure? The land ate her sons. Years of hunger and disappointments went by. The reality was far removed from the ideal. The limited ability was far from the aspiration. Weak bodies and broken spirits yielded to the cruel realities. Fresh graves appeared suddenly here and there hidden in the shadow of eucalyptus trees in cemeteries, the name of a friend or acquaintance from the town memorialized the person who was disillusioned in his long travel. Many felt they found their way back to a past that had been left behind and forgotten as if they had returned "home". They felt that they had overcome their despair and were pursuing their previous path and so could follow history; – however history quickly changed their fate forever….

Meeting of Halutzim from Tarnow after their release from prison in 1924
(they were caught during their illegal entry to Israel)

Seated first on top row from the left: Yitzchak Kornilo (now in Israel)
Seated below in the middle: Friedman Bear

[Page 34, Volume 2]

Meeting of Tarnow Halutzim in Eretz Israel in 1925

Sitting from the left: Sturm Pinchas (now in Israel); Klapholtz Ezra (now in Israel) ;(–), (–), Rubin Yaakov (now in Israel); Shreiber Zvi
Standing from the left: Shanhoff Moshe, (–),Faust Shmuel, (–), Levanoni Zev (now in Israel), Frankel, Kornilo Yitzchak (now in Israel), Pintshoski

The years of hardship and disappointment in the chosen land [Israel] passed and a period of flourishing and prosperity followed. New kibbutzim and settlements conquered the desert, widened the frontiers and fortified the people of the book. Remarkable agricultural achievements ensured the stability of their new home in Israel. Cities grew, industry flourished. But then the Holocaust threatened everything that was left behind. The community once enlisted bodily and spiritually in the defense of Israel, the homeland. Then they turned around to join the war against the Nazi invader that was prepared to destroy everything.

Awareness of the Shoah

Slowly the news trickled in, the news of the Shoah reached us. The unbelievable became fact. The Nazi beasts managed to destroy the pride of the Jewish community in Europe, six million victims died through no fault of their own. Historical horrors exceeded any imaginable scale. After great hardship, the survivors reached Eretz Yisrael and the cruel truth came to light. The glorious past had been wiped out in no time and only a few survived. Flowering Jewish towns and communities in Europe had disappeared, entire families were torn away from the Jewish tree. My beloved town, the joy of my life, betrayed her purpose. Tarnow, a town and mother in Israel, with thousands of Jews, rich and poor, was decimated. This holy, glorious and active community was desecrated by the Nazi troops. The heart of her youth stopped beating. On the other hand, the non–Jews remained seemingly whole with their looted riches. They did not suffer much but inflicted much pain. The glorious New Synagogue in the heart of the Jewish community with its high dome that seemingly competed with the towers of the Christian churches was sacrificed for the idol of destruction and racial hatred. The only remainder of the New Synagogue's once great past and its grand building is a single scorched column that was rescued and serves as a monument over the large common grave in the ancient Jewish cemetery. One of the survivors, a stone mason, carved words of deep meaning into the column – "And the sun shone and was not ashamed – 25000 Jewish martyrs are buried here, innocent human beings, sacrifices to the Nazi beasts. The tombstone enclosed all those killed here" – All this happened in 1942, in the 20th century, a century of scientific and technical achievements, a century of highest values and ideas in the world.

[Page 35, Volume 2]

Survivors of the Tarnow Jewish community at a memorial near the common grave of Jews killed in the Buczyna forest in Zbylitowska Góra (outside Tarnow) in 1967

[Page 36, Volume 2]

The Future

History quickly passed over the Shoah. The State of Israel was created. Many survivors of the sword [Nazis] found a home there. The state flourished in spite of many obstacles and attacks. It created a faithful and secure home for Am Israel (people of Israel) living in the Diaspora.

Years have passed and gone – the glorious past is long gone. But a flame hissed for generations in my beloved and lost town of Tarnow, and hundreds of similar communities in the Diaspora. This flame became a strong fire that destroyed generations. But it led to the foundation of Medinat Israel (the State of Israel)!

My sacred Tarnow community! May your memory be blessed and entwined in the creation of the homeland [State of Israel]. And your cherished sons and daughters, brothers and sisters, tortured sons and mothers who collapsed on the long and hard road to the new homeland and are no longer with us, you will remain forever in our hearts!

[Page 37, Volume 2]

Contribution to the History of Jews in Tarnow
(Facts and Events)

by Dr. Avraham Chust (Comet), Israel

Translated by Gloria Berkenstat Freund

Dr. Avraham Chust

Blood Libel in Tarnow in 1844

    A periodical, an impartial weekly of Jewish interests, entitled *Algemeine Zeitung des Judentums* [*General Newspaper of Judaism*], was published in the first half of the 19th century in the German city of Leipzig in the German language edited by Dr. Ludwig Philippson. From time to time, correspondence from Tarnow was published in this periodical, which makes it possible for us to become acquainted with the life and achievements of Tarnow Jewry in that era.

    Thus we learn from a correspondence from Tarnow that was published on the 29th of April 1844 (no. 18) about a blood libel in Tarnow that unsettled the entire Jewish population in the city. According to what is reported in the correspondence, an 11–year–old Christian boy disappeared on the 25th of April 1844. Suspicion fell immediately upon the Jews, that they had grabbed the boy in order to slaughter him for Passover. On the same evening, the local police with the help of military members, searched all of the Jewish houses for the disappeared boy. In addition, help was called for from the peasants in two neighboring villages, with the task of searching the suburbs of Tarnow. All of the streets on which Jews lived were guarded and the house and residence of the rabbi was thoroughly searched. There were searches of the butchers and the bakeries where the matzos were baked. The flour there even was sifted… As we read in the above–mentioned correspondence, all of the people who were employed in making matzos were investigated and, after the investigations, everyone of them was searched to see if they were carrying blood–filled vials.

[Page 38, Volume 2]

And although it was shown after a thorough search that the suspicion that had fallen on the entire Jewish population was completely groundless, and despite how the correspondent from Tarnow emphasized it [that the suspicion was unfounded], the Christian population retained its belief that the Jews had murdered the boy to make use of the Christian blood.

It was fortunate that several days later the boy was seen in a locality near Tarnow… The correspondent said that there is no doubt that he [the boy] had been hidden so that the agitated mood would not dissipate too soon.

Priests Attack Jewish Merchants Near the Castle Hill…

In 1965 a collection of monographs about Tarnow and its history, entitled *Ziemia Tarnowsa* (*The Tarnow Earth*) was published by the provincial committee in Krakow in its publication. A treatise entitled *Fun der Fargangenheit fun Tarner Erd* [*From the Past of Tarnow Earth*] was written by the young Polish historian, Josef Duczik, who writes that "an interesting case took place in 1629, when priests beat Jewish merchants who would come to Tarnow not far from the holy Martin–Berg (Castle Hill – ed.) because they did not give the priests the appropriate respect. (p. 27)."

About Improving the System of Teaching the Jewish Religion in the Middle Schools in Tarnow

As is reported in the previously mentioned *Algemeine Zeitung des Judentums*, in a correspondence from Tarnow on the 17th of December 1855 (no. 51) – the Galician state government demanded that the managing committee of the Jewish *kehila* in Tarnow announce a competitive test for teachers of Jewish religion for Jewish students in the *gymnasia* [secondary school] and the Real School in Tarnow. In connection with this decree, the newspaper mentions that the subject of the Jewish religion in the Tarnow *gymnasia* [secondary school] was taught in a completely unsatisfactory manner. It was very sad that one of the largest *kehila* in Galicia, which could be considered an important Jewish cultural center, had to be asked with serious words by the officials in power to take an interest on behalf of its own and its fathers' faith. The correspondent emphasized that credit should be given to the then Tarnow *kehila* managing committee that "It instantly and energetically went to work."

[Page 39, Volume 2]

The correspondent appealed to the then head of the Tarnow *kehila*, Y. B. Goldman, that, "He not let himself be led off the path by various party schemes or other petty motives." In addition, a separate warm thank you to Petri, the then director of the Kaiser Royal *gymnasia* [secondary school] in Tarnow, at whose initiative the entire matter was raised.

Tarnow Jews Want to Establish a German–Hebrew School

From a correspondence from Tarnow that was published in the Leipzig *Algemeiner Zeitung des Judentums* of the 21st of December 1858 (no. 52), we learn that about 500 Tarnow Jews signed a petition to the Jewish *kehila* [*kehila* = committee of elected officials managing Jewish affairs] with a request to establish a German–Hebrew school in Tarnow.

It is worthwhile to mention that these schools were strongly opposed by the Orthodox Jewish circle that also opposed this request from the enlightened Jews to create a secular school. This happened in the era when the Austrian reaction increased in strength and which had as its purpose the annulment of the achievements of the revolution of 1848.

The Jewish hospital in Tarnow in 1939

[Page 40, Volume 2]

The Jewish Hospital in Tarnow in 1860

Tarnow Jewry could already take pride in its social–communal institutions in the first half of the 19th century. Jewish Tarnow was especially proud of the Jewish Hospital that was erected in 1842 and in the course of later years grew into one of the best medical institutions in all of western Galicia.

In the previously mentioned newspaper article from Leipzig of the 24th of April 1860 (no. 17), an account was printed that the administration of the Jewish hospital in Tarnow had published [about its work] during the period of 1858–1859.

According to this report, in the course of the 17–year existence of the hospital, approximately 10,000 sick people were taken care of and, in addition, it is interesting that among 486 patients who were there under medical treatment were 12 Italian soldiers who were wounded in the Italian–Austrian War.

As was reported in the mentioned account, the rise of the Jewish hospital in Tarnow was possible thanks to the sacrificial work of the hospital managing committee of that year, to which belonged Chaim Leib Fajgenbaum, Yisroel Avraham Kaminer, Mendl Keller and Menka Weksler, in addition to the main doctor (prescriber), Dr. Yaacov Szicer, who simultaneously was the main doctor in the civilian Christian hospital. In the course of many years, he was active in these two hospitals, without harm to his private medical practice and without any reward. As a sign of respect on the part of the entire population, he was awarded the honored title of Freeman of the city of Tarnow.

[Page 11, Volume 2]

The City Managing Committee of Tarnow and its Demand to Recreate a Ghetto for the Jewish Residents

The first rays of civic and political equal rights appeared for the Jews in Galicia with the freedom movement in the Austrian state in 1848. The Polish *mieszczanie* [townspeople], whose representatives ruled on the managing committees of the Galician cities, aspired to maintain with all possible means the earlier limitations in regard to the Jewish population and when in Austria in the first years of the second half of the 19th century, the reaction returned to power, the local government organs in the cities and *shtetlekh* at once began to suppress the few equal rights the Jews had received in the era of the "people's spring."

The Tarnow city managing committee was particularly distinguished in this area. As we learned from a correspondence from Tarnow that was published in the Leipzig *Algemeiner Zeitung des Judentums* of the 24th of April 1860 (no. 17), in the second half of 1858, the Tarnow city managing committee took as its responsibility the established privilege of 1764 of Polish King Stanislaw August that required the recreation of a Jewish ghetto in Tarnow. Hence, the representatives of the Jewish *kehila* in Tarnow undertook action against the attempt to annul the previously acquired right of the Tarnow Jews to live outside the ghetto area in the city. As a result of this attempt of the then Tarnow *kehila*–parnesim [elected Jewish community members], the county leader in a decree of the 8th of January 1859 ordered the Tarnow city managing committee to protect and to respect the civil rights of the Jews and not permit the disturbance of the current peaceful living together of the Jewish and Christian population of the city and that it not damage the development of the city, which was thanks in the greatest part to the commercial and industrial activity of the Jewish population.

The county leader added to this declaration, supporting the ministerial decree of the 13th of September 1858, where also at the order of the Galician national government of the 11th of October 1858, the active and passive voting rights to the city managing committee and to the municipal board could under the same legal conditions be obtained by the Jewish as by the Christian residents and in that connection the county leader made the Tarnow city managing committee aware that it was obligated to restrain itself from every principally negative attitude concerning this right.

[Page 42, Volume 2]

The municipal organs of power in Tarnow had to give up their aspirations to recreate a Jewish ghetto in Tarnow in the second half of the 19th century.

Bloody Attacks on Jews in Tarnow in 1866

From time to time in the first tens of years in the second half of the 19th century, bloody excesses against the Jewish population took place in Tarnow.

From a correspondence from Tarnow that was published in the previously mentioned Leipzig *Algemeiner Zeitung des Judentums* of the 22nd of May 1866 (no. 22), we learn that on the 6th of May drunk recruits appeared on the road to the Jewish neighborhood in Tarnow, who called out, "*Bić Żydów*" [murder Jews]. Every Jew they encountered was bloodily beaten and robbed. At the same time, panic broke out in the Jewish neighborhood… Jews in great haste hammered shut the doors and shutters of the shops… closed the gates of the houses.

Alas, there were those who did not escape in time and close the shops… Not only were they murderously beaten by the bandit–like recruits, who came to the marketplace, all of their goods in the shops were stolen… With luck, several esteemed Christian citizens of the city persuaded the city leader that he should intervene with the local military commandant and to ask him to put an end to the violent actions of the hooligan attacks.

They did not have to ask the acting Austrian general for very long and as is reported in the above cited correspondence, he himself appeared in the Jewish neighborhood with a division of soldiers and sent out patrols, which drove away the mob and arrested the main attackers. They were punished in the presence of the general and military patrols guarded the streets of the city all night. Calm reigned the next day in the city.

[Page 43, Volume 2]

*

We have written in detail about the bloody pogrom against the Jews in Tarnow in 1870 in the first volume of the *Tarnow Yizkor Book* (in the article about the history of the Jews in Tarnow).

Jewish Societies and Institutions in Tarnow in the Second Half of the 19th Century

The *Bikur Cholim* Society

In addition to the Jewish hospital in Tarnow, about which we wrote in the previous lines, in the second half of the 19th century, a very useful activity developed with the establishment of the *Bikur Cholim* Society [Society for Care for the Sick], whose task was to give free medical help to the poor Jews as well as cover a part of the expenses for their medicines.

As we learned from a correspondence from Tarnow that was published in *HaMagid* [*The Preacher*] of the 22nd of January 1873, this society was founded in Tarnow in 1872 and in the month of January 1873 already had about 700 members who supported the activity of the society with all their possible strength. Devoted communal workers such as Reb Berish Maszler, Reb Pesakh Bibelman, Reb Shlomo Trinc, Reb Berl Dankowicz, Reb Avraham Klajnhendler and Reb Yisroel Mendl Keler belonged to the society's managing committee.

Noyse–haMita v Menakhmi baOylim

This society [of those who carry the dead on the mita or bed to the cemetery and the consolers of the mourners], which was very prominent in the Jewish neighborhood in Tarnow in the 1930s, has already been described in the first volume of the memorial book, *Tarnow*. It numbered 800 members in 1932 and had as its purpose supporting the poor and sick Jews by assisting them in moving the deceased from the house to the cemetery. This society was founded in Tarnow in 1891 and in time grew to be a very important social institution in the city.

[Page 44, Volume 2]

As we learned from a correspondence from Tarnow that was published in *HaMagid* on the 10th of February 1893, this society opened a kitchen for the poor at the beginning of the year where everyone who "stuck out their hand" received a cup of tea and bread in the morning for one *zloty* (one *Kreuzer* – two pennies) and a bowl of soup and bread for two *Kreuzer* for lunch.

The work of this society on behalf of the poor strata of the Jewish population in Tarnow took on a very wide scope during the winter months. Until the month of March, every poor Jew received bread and coal for all seven days of the week. A great campaign to collect money from the rich middle class in the city was carried out every year for this purpose. This campaign was led by the then community activists, Skharye Mendl Aberdam, Ahron Safir, Mordekhai Dovid Brandsztatter, H. Hajman and occupied with distributing the bread and coal were Pesakh Bibelman, Shlomo Klajner, Pinkhus Moshe Goldwaser, Yosef *haKohen* [member of the priestly class] Ejzenberg. As was described in the previously mentioned correspondence, 1,200 loaves of bread and 600 kilograms [about 1,322 pounds] of coal were distributed during one week (in the month of February 1893).

As we see, the number of the poor in the Jewish neighborhood in Tarnow was not small.

The Great Aid Action by the Tarnow Jews on Behalf of the Jewish Community in the Neighboring *Shtetl* of Zabno After a Fire in 1888

On a Friday afternoon at the end of April 1888, a fire broke out in the neighboring town of Zabno near Tarnow, which engulfed the entire *shtetl* from one corner to the other. Almost all of the houses were burned and the entire Jewish population in the *shtetl* remained without a roof over its head. There also were human victims and as we learned from a correspondent from Tarnow in *HaMagid* of the 6th of May 1888 (no. 17), several Torah scrolls and rare religious books were burned. As the correspondent writes, on the same evening as the fire, Tarnow Jews sent bread to the fire victims in Zabno and on the next day, *Shabbos*, wagons of bread left for Zabno so that the Zabno Jews would not suffer from hunger.

[Page 45, Volume 2]

Headstone of Reb Mordekhai Dovid Brandsztatter, of
blessed memory, and his wife, Shprinca, of blessed memory

An aid action on behalf of the Zabno Jews was simultaneously organized with the then leader of the *kehila*, Herman Merc, at the head.

F. Grosbard, the head of the Zabno *kehila*, issued an appeal at the conclusion of *Shabbos* [Sabbath], in which he described the sad situation of the Jewish population in the burned *shtetl*, where in addition to the fact that almost all of the residences were burned, no survivors remained of all of the houses of prayer with their Torah scrolls and treasure of holy books.

[Page 46, Volume 2]

The appeal ended with an impassioned call for immediate help for those in the Jewish community in Zabno who had suffered from the fire.

The *Shavei Tzion* Society in Tarnow in 1893

As we learned from a correspondence from Tarnow that was published in *HaMagid* on the 20th of October 1893 (no. 32), the Shavei Tzion Society [Returners to Zion] was founded there with the purpose of buying land in Eretz Yisroel and sending one of the members there from time to time; this fate fell upon around 100 members who decided to emigrate to Eretz Yisroel. The society first numbered forty members at its founding and the founders undertook a campaign to recruit members from other cities in Galicia.

The Jewish Community in Tarnow in 1897–98 and 1913–14

When writing the treatise, *The History of the Jews in Tarnow*, we did not have the opportunity to make use of a series of sources and information concerning the facts that have a connection to the history of the Jews in Tarnow and which we received later, afterï¿½the first Tarnow memorial book had already had been printed. The various information that we provide here are a significant contribution to the history of the Jews in Tarnow. We have taken it from a *Calendar for Israelites*, published by the former Austrian union, Austrian–Israelite Union in Vienna. In this calendar, published in the German language, we found facts about almost all of the Jewish *kehila* in the entire Austro–Hungarian monarchy.

Let us be permitted at this point to express a hearty thanks to the Tarnow *landsleit* [people from the same town] and Friend Chaim Keller, who today lives in Vienna with his esteemed wife and son and before the Holocaust occupied a distinguished place in the clothing industry in Tarnow and was among the active leaders of the local *Mizrakhi* [religious Zionists] movement, for his efforts and help in obtaining the above–mentioned calendars for several years.

The Tarnow *kehila* in the Budget Year 1897–98

The head of the *kehila* [organized Jewish community] at that time was Yosef Maszler and his representative was Ahron Safir. Avraham Aberdam, Mordekhai Dovid Brandsztatter, Borukh Jakubowicz, Yakov Maszler, Moshe Ornsztajn, Naftali Ruvin, Artur Szancer, Moshe Weksler, Hirsh Witmaier, Dovid Cinz belonged to the advisory council. The representative of the rabbinate was Naftali Rubin and the rabbinate's assessors were Naftali Goldberg, Moshe After, Shlomo Yosef Kurc, Yehuda Arszicer, Yoel Etinger. Yosef Ejzenberg, Shlomo Dovid Baran were at the head of the Chevra Kadisha [burial society] and Berish Maszler and Borukh Jakubowicz belonged to the managing committee of the Jewish hospital.

[Page 47, Volume 2]

The Jewish *kehila* in Tarnow in the Budget Year 1913–14

Barely six years passed and the Jewish community in Tarnow had gone through a significant ascent. Close to the outbreak of the First World War, in the budget year of 1913–14, 17,000 souls were registered with the Tarnow *kehila* and there were 850 *kehila* taxpayers. Berish Maszler was then the head of the *kehila* and his representative was Eliyahu Baran. Yosef Maszler (the older one) and Leon Szwanenfeld belonged to the restricted *kehila* managing committee. Avraham Aberdam, Dr. Eliash Goldhamer, Yakov Geldwirt, Mordekhai Dovid Hercig, Mendl Hercbaum, Borukh Jakubowicz, Ignaci Maszler, Dr. Herman Pilcer, Dr. Edvard Rapaport, Herman Soldinger, Yoel Szpigel, Dr. Shlomo Febus, Lazar Szpira, Ayzyk Safir, Avraham Tarn, Dovid Cinz belonged to the comprehensive managing committee. Reb Avraham Abela Sznur was the city rabbi. *kehila* secretary: L. Lerhaupt. There were Jewish societies active then in Tarnow: *Noyse–haMita* [society of those who carry the dead from the house to the cemetery], *Yad HaRutsim* [Orthodox workers organization], *Mishnius* [Society for studying the Torah], *Kiddushin* [Torah innovations], *Rodfei Tzedek* [Pursuers of Justice], *Chevra Yoledet* [society to help pregnant women] and *Kallahï¿½* [society to assist poor brides]. It was also mentioned in the previously cited calendar for this budget year that 40 prayer groups [*minyonim*] existed in Tarnow.

A Rabbinical Conference in Tarnow in 1927

For the voting to the third Sejm [Polish parliament], which took place in 1928, the National Union of the Zionist Party in western Galicia joined the Zionist National Union in eastern Galicia and both proposed a joint list [of candidates] under the name, the Unification of Jewish Parties in Lesser Poland [historical area with Krakow as its capital], when a minority bloc was organized in Congress Poland which encompassed only some of those from the non–Jewish and also from the Jewish national minority. In addition to the two blocs, another was created, the third election unification of the Folkists and the Orthodox *Agudah* in the Jewish neighborhood.

[Page 48, Volume 2]

Headstone of Reb Yoakhim Maszler, of blessed memory – member of the *kehila* managing committee in Tarnow in 1897–98

An independent Jewish policy was one of the main slogans of all three groups.

Taking a stand for this election were also the camp of the Galicianer rabbis, who fought all Jewish national movements, even those in agreement with *Agudah* [organization founded by Orthodox rabbis].

[Page 49, Volume 2]

Headstone of Reb Artur Szancer, of blessed memory – member of the *kehila* – the managing committee in Tarnow in 1897–98

As Dr. Yitzhak Szwarcbard writes in his book, *Tsvishn Beyde Velt Milkhomes* [*Between the Two World Wars*], (page 230) – 35 rabbis held a conference in Tarnow on the 5th of December 1927 and 281 rabbis were called again to a similar conference in Lemberg on the 27th of December 1927 and a policy of supporting the government without conditions was declared at both conferences.

[Page 50, Volume 2]

[On the right is] the headstone of Dr. Herman Pilcer, of blessed memory, and his wife Lucia – [he] was a member of the kehila [organized Jewish community] managing committee in Tarnow in 1913–14.

[On the left is] the headstone of Dr. Shlomo Merc, of blessed memory – court council and member of the city council in Tarnow until the outbreak of the First World War.

These two rabbinical conferences also are mentioned in the collection, *Di Yidn in Videraufgeshtanenem Poyln* [*The Jews in Newly Reconstituted Poland*], edited by Dr. Yitzhak Sziper, Dr. A. Tartakower and Aleksander Haptka (p. 11), in which is described the decision on the resolution that was adopted at the conference in Tarnow, in which it was clearly emphasized that "The conference speaks out against actions which are not in accord with the wishes of the [government] authority because it is our duty to carry out a policy of loyalty to the government."

This policy– as reported by A. Haftka in the cited collection – was confirmed at the conference of the 281 rabbis in Lemberg on the 27th of December 1927.

Novi Dziennik [*New Daily Paper*] from Krakow from the 11th of December 1927 (no. 328) also published the news about this rabbinical conference, where it was reported that a meeting of some 20 rabbis from eastern and western Lesser Poland took place in the residence of Reb Leyzer Lezerin of Tarnow on the 5th of December 1927 about an agreement concerning the elections. According to this information, the chairmanship of the convention was held by the rabbi from Krakow and the conference unanimously declared itself against the spread of the Pilsudski decree concerning democratic elections to the *kehila* [organized Jewish community].

[Page 51, Volume 2]

Headstone of Reb Ayzyk Safir, may his memory be blessed – member of the *kehila* managing committee in Tarnow in the years 1913–14. On the right (the X mark) a memorial tablet to the memory of his wife, Klara, may her memory be blessed, perished in the Tarnow ghetto in 1942.

Headstone of the Tarnow city rabbi before the First World War, Reb Avraham Abela Shneur, may the memory of a righteous man be blessed

On another day – the 12th of December 1912 – a retraction was published in *Novi Dziennik* (no. 329) that reported that the Tarnow rabbinical conference did not have any connection to election matters because, in general, elections were not debated and resolutions were not adopted there [at the conference] and the conference had been called only to consult about creating a union of rabbis in Lesser Poland. In addition, on the 27th of December 1927, it was decided to call a separate conference in Lemberg about this matter [a union of rabbis].

[Page 53, Volume 2]

Adolf Rudnicki – A Jew from Tarnow

by Menashe Unger, New York

Translated by Gil Stamberger

Edited by Erica S. Goldman-Brodie

One of the greatest writers in Poland today is Adolf Rudnicki. Adolf Rudnicki however is not a Polish writer, but explicitly a Jewish writer writing in Polish. I would say the main Jewish writer in today's Poland, not only because his whole theme is Jewish, because all the heroes in his novels and stories derive from Jews, but because he is today the advocate of the Jewish lament in Poland.

Adolf Rudnicki is the modern Job, the Jewish mourner, who complains and cries about our great destruction, about the disappearance of the most colorful part of the whole Jewish people in the last thousand years, about the three million Jews in Poland and about the loss of the six million who have been cut off by the Germans, may their name be obliterated.

I am connected with Adolf Rudnicki with a number of threads from (the life of) my youth. And immediately when I came to Warsaw, I started to look for his telephone number, and when I connected with him by phone, he did not believe that it was me he was talking to and quickly agreed to come to see me at the "Grand Hotel" where I was staying.

And after an hour of waiting, the bell of my room rang, and at my door stood a tall and handsome "mensch" with a head of curly black hair, a longish nose and with a timid gloom in his eyes.

We embraced each other, wiped off our tears quietly and, as if by a magic wand, the 40 past years were swept away and we both were transformed into two young children.

We were quiet the first few moments and soon Adolf Rudnicki felt at home and threw himself on my bed in his coarse woolen sweater and stayed lying on my bed until the middle of the night.

In order to be able to understand the mystery how it happened that the son of a Rabbi became a Polish writer with a typical Polish name like Rudnicki I have to reveal the secret that the real name of the famous Polish writer, Adolf Rudnicki, is Aharon Hirschhorn and he is the youngest son of Rav Itshe Hirschhorn, who was the chief Gabbay at my father's beit din (rabbinic court), זצ"ל (may the memory of the Tzaddik be blessed) at the time when my father ate chestnuts with his father-in-law, the Rozvadover Rebbe, Reb Moshe Horovitz.

[Page 54, Volume 2]

Afterwards Reb Itshe travelled with my parents to Żabno, got married there and became Gabbay in the court of the Rebbe. He went with my parents to Vienna where during the First World War the Rebbe's court was re-established.

Reb Itshe, the Gabbay has been very faithful to our home and especially my father, זצ"ל. He prayed the Shacharit prayer in front of the pulpit, he had a nice voice and knew the Rofshitzer and Rozvadover nussach (prayer method) and the Rofshitzer and Rozvadover specific nigunim (religious songs).

Reb Itshe Gabay has strongly taken care of the health of my father זצ"ל and he did not want my father would to have a heartache because the youngest son of the Rebbe had left the right path. I remember an episode which has carved itself strongly into my memory, how Reb Itshe Gabbay has protected the honor of the Rebbe's youngest son.

This has happened in the years around 1917/18. In Tarnow there already was a Hebrew school "Safa Berura", the Jewish youth (movements) of "Hashomer Hatzair" and Poalei Zion and other organizations. I was more attracted to the Poalei Zion youth, even though in the big "kloyz" (religious study house) where I learned for a while together with Avraham Wald (Ya'ari), today the famous bibliographer and culture researcher in Jerusalem[1], who sympathized more with the "Hashomer Hatzair" and with his younger brother Yudke Wald (today the famous Hebrew writer Yehuda Ya'ari in Israel), who was a member of "Hashomer Hatzair". But I was carried away by the PoaleiZion movement.

At this time a young man with the name Itshe Schiper, who was called Itshe Kapelushnik lived in Tarnow. He was a relative of the famous Jewish historian Dr Yitzhak Schiper ה״ד (May Hashem avenge his blood). By profession he was a hatmaker and he liked to write articles in the party newspapers. Itshe Kapelushnik also had a love for the Yiddish theatre and he had decided to perform Peretz's "In Polish oyf der Keyt" (chained in the synagogue's anteroom). As I had been pulled into this play, I remember that I have been very enthusiastic in the rehearsals. Peretz has been very close to me from my youth and especially as this specific drama "a dream of a sinful kloyzenik" (Ed. note kloysznik, a student in a small synagogue) has been somewhat symbolic for the life of my youth at that time.

[Page 55, Volume 2]

And once, on a Sunday afternoon the hall of "Safa Berura" was packed with Jewish youth, I was below the stage and the main hero, the "sinful kloyzenik" had been made up as I looked (then), he also borrowed my kaftan und my broad rabbi's velvet hat and the actor, made up in a longish pale face with black, curly side curls like little bottles and a black round little beard around his tender face called from the stage; "inside me a rose has flashed up … will no one punish me?"

I was sitting dressed only in my Talit Katan (Ed note: small tallit, undergarment) behind the stage in the wardroom and imagined that it was me who said this from the stage.

And suddenly …. The sinful kloyzenik says passionately from the stage: "my soul drips out, drop by drop….."

I hear a huge turmoil in the hall …. At the entrance policemen appeared. Someone has complained who did not want that this drama should be performed. The theatre youth has been dispersed and the main hero, the "sinful kloyzenik" and the second hero Reb Berchiye have been arrested and led on the Walowa Street to the police (office).

When the Jews of the Walowa Street saw this young man, "the sinful kloyzenik" being led away, a rumour started to spread that the youngest son of the rabbi had been arrested, and soon, "at the gate", small groups of Jews already said that they had heard that the son of the Rabbi had asked to make an effort to free him.

And I was lying behind the stage in big trouble, I did not have my kaftan and did not have my broad rabbi's velvet hat. I put on a simple cloth jacket which was hanging in the wardrobe and a hat made from cloth and ran quickly out of "Safa Berura". I ran in one breath through the backstreets to the "Holtz" Square, to the house of Reb Itshe Gabbay. There they dressed me in a kaftan and a different Rabbi's hat and I still managed to get home in time for the afternoon-evening Prayer and Reb Itshe Gabay told everyone that someone had posed as the son of the Rebbe and that the youngest son of the Rebbe had been in his home the whole afternoon.

[Page 56, Volume 2]

This is how Reb Itshe Gabbiy has saved my honour.

Also, a second episode has engraved itself in my memory many years later. This happened when I returned from Palestine to Warsaw in the middle of the 1930's.

I wanted to see my mother, may peace be with her, who lived in Tarnow with my brother, the Żabner Rebbe Rabbi Elazar, may God avenge his blood, who succeed my father after my father's death, (may the memory of the Tzaddik be blessed).

My mother was already old and I knew that in my attire I would not manage to get in to visit her. I had a beard as required (at this time I was also a vegetarian) and a kaftan could be acquired in Tarnow, but what to do with side curls, how could I appear before my mother without side curls?

The Jewish cultural activist, Seinfeld in Cracow, the brother-in-law of the poet Imber, had procured a large hat and to the hat two small curly side curls had been attached and when I dressed in the kaftan and the skullcap with the velvet hat, I again looked like the religious young man from the past … Like this I travelled from Cracow to Tarnow and went to the home of Reb Itshe Gabbay. There I changed clothes and went to the house in Lwowska Street 24 where my brother and my mother lived.

But a mishap took place; it was a hot summer day and I gave a push to the hat on my head and the two side curls which were attached to the skullcap were pushed aside as well; one side curl now hung behind an ear and the second almost in the middle of my forehead. Reb Itshe Gabay immediately noticed this and gave a turn back to the skullcap and the side curls returned to their correct location and my mother, may peace be with her, who already was old and did not see well did not notice this at all.

When I now told the memories to "Elyusha" (this was the nickname of the son of Reb Itshe Gabbay) he asked me to talk more about his father and about his and my home, as he wanted to refresh his youthful-memories which were buried deep in his brain…..

[Page 57, Volume 2]

But so that we should not just talk chit chat Adolf Rudnicki returned to his permanent subject, the killing of the Jews in Warsaw, the Warsaw ghetto uprising and the huge catastrophe which had hit us.

* * *

Adolf Rudnicki was a profound lyricist (writing) in prose. He had published his first novel "Rats" in 1932 about the psychological and moral situation of the Jews who lived in a shtetl, better: his shtetl.

In the year 1933, his second novel, "The Soldiers" appeared, where the human values of the individual were described. Before the war, several more novels were published and in 1939, he was drafted into the Polish army; he participated in the army in the downfall of Poland. The first period of the Hitlerian occupation he spent in Lemberg (Lwow, now Lviv in Ukraine) and the most difficult years he stayed in Warsaw where it was his destiny to be a witness and a chronicler of the slaughter of the Polish Jewry. His literary creations are based on his own experiences and memories.

Adolf Rudnicki tells in his short story "Passover" how in those days, during the ghetto rising in Warsaw he came disguised as an Aryan next to the ghetto wall and met there a young lonely Jewish woman. "We used to recognize each other among strangers through our eyes, in which suddenly a warm, familiar spark appeared" – Rudnicki writes there – "and when passing each other we used to call to each other, without a word, pointing to each other their and our destiny … the young women now did not only shake, she choked on her tears …. they die, she whispered quietly, they die and no trace will remain of them except ruins, fire and vague memories nothing will remain from so many lives, love, suffering, customs and memories ….. may it though be described, strongly emphasized as well, that it may remain a memory of their multicolored life and inhuman and so beautiful death. If even only one will remain, may it be possible to describe all of this, so that people may one day come from behind the seventh sea and cry as we cry today"…

Adolf Rudnicki remained true to this testament until today. All his themes in his novels and short stories revolve around the murdered six million Jews.

[Page 58, Volume 2]

- Do you plan to travel to Israel – I suddenly inserted into my long chatter, in order to interrupt the depressed mood.
- I cannot leave this place, where the great disaster happened. I cannot and do not want to run away from our huge tragedy. Here in Warsaw, in Poland our destruction happened, here a whole people disappeared, here I must stay.
- Come with me one morning to the ruins of the ghetto – he continued to talk with sadness – you will see how from the mounds of bricks from the destroyed ghetto houses one hears a quite crying … these are the little children with their mothers who cry, who have been buried alive under the ruins …. This is the crying of the ghetto heroes who had asked for help, for guns, but no help came; here I have to stay and for always express my pain and sadness.

And what could I answer him? I only asked him, that he should at least travel for a visit to Israel and he agreed to do so in the close future…

A damaged house in the Zydowska Street of Tarnow (the board with the writing Ulica Żydowska remained)

Footnote:

1. In the year 1953 he received the Ussishkin prize and several years later the Bialik prize he passed away and soon afterwards

[Page 59, Volume 2]

The Way of Life of the Village Jews in Tarnow County

by Dr. Yeshayahu Fajg (Fagi), Haifa

Translated by Miriam Leberstein

I was born in a village near Tarnow, where my father was in the dairy business. So I learned about the life of the Jews in the village, which was located not far from the town. Their lives were hard, not only because it was hard to make a living, but also because of the difficulties of living a traditional Jewish life.

How, actually, did the village Jews earn a living? They would buy agricultural products from the peasants, and sell the peasants manufactured goods. Those peasants who were better off and who had their own horses would transport their own products to the town, in the belief that they would get a better price there. But even in the village itself, there was commerce in string, thread, cheap wool and knitted products, which were often exchanged for eggs, poultry, rabbit skins, vegetables, potatoes or other village products. Sometimes, a glazier would come from town to repair the broken panes, and would be paid in either money or goods.

The village had a tavern that was run by a Jewish lessee. There were also a mill and another dairy dealer [in addition to my father]. In a number of neighboring villages lived Jews who cultivated a few acres of land. There were also rich Jews who owned a lot of land, but they themselves lived in town and they would lease their estates to Jews or non-Jews, or for political reasons (anti-Semitism), would hire a Pole as manager.

Village Jews lived far from settlements with many Jews and in most cases couldn't gather the necessary *minyan* [quorum of ten) required for communal prayer, even when Jews from three villages got together. There was never a *minyan* consisting entirely of adult, married men. They had to resort to bar–mitzvah boys and young unmarried men, and you can imagine how proud these were, because without them the *minyan* would not have been possible.

There was also a serious problem in providing Jewish education for children in the village. It is true that they could attend the Polish school, but who would provide them with the necessary little bit of Jewish learning. Where would they get that? The village had a *cheder* [religious school for young children], but only when one of the Jews would provide a room for a whole semester for use as a classroom. For a teacher, they would bring in a *belfer* [helper in a *cheder*] from the town, who would pound the Torah into the children's heads. Few Jews would pay tuition for such a *cheder*; rather they would make a symbolic payment as a way of earning a *mitzvah* [credit for a good deed], and the money barely sufficed to support the *cheder*.

[Page 60, Volume 2]

When the high holy days came, the question arose of how to provide for communal prayer in the village. There wasn't the necessary number of adult married men to make up a *minyan* during the Days of Awe. They were confronted with two choices: They could invite guests from the town, along with the cantor brought in from town, to make up the *minyan*. Or, they could travel to town along with their entire household for the period of Rosh Hashanah and Yom Kippur. Both solutions posed difficulties. Bringing in a cantor cost money, and the cantor also required them to pay for the chorus that accompanied him. They could raise the required money only by having all the village Jews make a contribution, but that wasn't so simple to do.

Nor was it easy to travel to town, which entailed harnessing up the horses to wagons and loading up the children and one's meager possessions. But most people chose this second option. Every Rosh Hashanah and Yom Kippur you could see horse–drawn wagons loaded with people and baggage, carrying Jews who had moved into town in order to serve God during the high holy days. They made do by sleeping on floors with relatives who lived in town, or in rented accommodations. In this way, they got to hear a good cantor. But they were never free from worry and fear over the houses they had left behind in the village.

The village Jews were always concerned for their children's educations. They strived to give them a Jewish secular education in town. But few sent their children to *gymnasium* [academic high school]. Others apprenticed their children to craftsmen in town, so they could learn a trade.

I want to take this opportunity to mention the names of those Jews who left the villages to live in Tarnow and who later played a distinguished role in Jewish communal life there.

Yankev Blat came from the village Pleshno. An expert in classical languages (Greek, Latin), he was a very talented philologist, who, had he not been a Jew, would have had an impressive career in university. While still in the 4th class in *gymnasium*, he was already reading the Greek *Iliad* and *The Odyssey*. He got the highest grades in school. He later became director of a high school in Drohobitsh. Engineer Borgenicht came from the village Biale. Zev Bloch came from the village Koshitse, and as soon as he graduated from gymnasium in Tarnow, made aliyah to Israel, where he was one of the founders of Kibbutz Bet Alfa.[1] Lawyer Dr. Zayden was from the village Skusheshuv. The brothers Layman. The brothers Vestraykh finished gymnasium in Tarnow; one of them, Avrom, died in India and the other, Dovid, emigrated to America.

[Page 61, Volume 2]

In general, there was a strong tendency among village Jews to move to town, both because of the difficulties mentioned above and also because of external pressures, that is, anti–Semitism and persecution. This occurred as early as the time of Austrians, after the election in Warsaw in 1907, during which the Jews helped campaign for the Socialist candidate in opposition to the anti–Semitic candidate of the Endecja [National Democrats, a right–wing, nationalist party]. When the Socialist won, that became a fresh reason for anti–Semitic actions, especially in the villages, where the Jews mostly did not live in their own houses, but rather rented houses or leased taverns or dairies.

Jews were also driven out of the villages by economic pressures. The priests called for a boycott of Jews, telling people not to buy from or sell to Jews. The peasants were swayed by the priests' sermons and didn't want to deal with the village Jews, but they still maintained business relationships with the Jews in town. The priests and anti–Semites caught on to this, and set up their own shops, organized into so–called agricultural circles. These new stores paid a much cheaper price for agricultural products.

At that time, I moved with my family to Tarnow. Although the movement to make the Polish villages "free of Jews" had abated somewhat, in 1918 it regained strength, just when Poland became independent. Then came the laws regarding redistribution of land. This law about the redistribution of land was postponed from year to year regarding land owned by the Polish nobility, but it was quickly and with great severity passed in regard to land owned by Jews in villages. In this way Jews were completely removed from the villages.

Footnote:

1. He died in 1966.

[Page 62]

What I Remember of Jewish Tarnow

By Yitzhak Blazer, Haifa

Translated by Gloria Berkenstat Freund

Yitzhak Blazer

Much has already been written of the spiritual story of Tarnow Jewry, about the specific Jewish way of life that was deeply rooted in the Jewish endeavors in Tarnow from its rise until its tragic destruction, about the Tarnow of Torah giants, about the Tarnow synagogues, about the numerous charity institutions, about the Love of Zion [Palestine, now Israel] of the Tarnow Jews and about the effervescent political and communal life of Tarnow Jewry.

However, Jewish life in Tarnow was so rich and colorful that without a doubt, the pride that Jewish Tarnow possessed has not yet been fully described. Therefore, in providing a bundle of memories of my old Tarnow home, I will strive to not be repetitious.

Concerning the Age and importance of the Jewish Community in Tarnow

The Jews [living] there played an extraordinary important role in the general development of the city of Tarnow. If the poor *shtetl* [town] of Tarnow, which over many centuries was a private possession of the Polish noble magnate families, grew into an important trade center in Lesser Poland into, one of its largest cities, this was exclusively thanks to the activities and industriousness of its Jewish residents.[a]

[Page 63]

Tarnow Jews were an important source of income for the nobles, for the owners of the city. The Tarnow Jews were pioneers who led the city to its then central trade position and, therefore, contributed to the economic ascent of the city for the city population, for the non–Jewish town dwellers.

However, despite this, the life of the Tarnow Jews was not always a bed of roses. Historical research concerning the existence of the Jews in Tarnow before the 17th century did not provide any great results and only on the basis of conjectures and signs, on the basis of legends that were passed from generation to generation and on the basis of ancient headstones at the Tarnow cemetery can we come to the conclusion that Tarnow Jews suffered more than once from bloody excesses and blood libel trials that took place there.

In connection with this, I remember a fact from my childhood, which is engraved in my memory. My oldest brother Yisroel, of blessed memory, once showed me a book of Jewish history written in the German language (today I do not remember the name or the author); today I only remember that my brother received the book from Reb Wolf Krapner, of blessed memory, who was administrator at Kwadratsztajn's house on Holc Platz. Several crates of Hebrew, Polish and German books were located in an attic room of this house.

As I remember, there were books there that provided details about the terrible blood libel trials against Jews in Tarnow and about bloody excesses that took place in Tarnow for hundreds of years before the total destruction of the Tarnow Jewish community and during which innocent Jewish blood was shed.

Not far from the entrance at the cemetery, opposite the mass grave of the martyrs who perished at the hands of the German killers, there were ancient headstones from before the First World War (I doubt they still exist today), with erased letters. According to the conjecture that would be repeated by the older generation of Tarnow Jews, the graves of the martyrs who perished during the anti–Jewish persecutions and excesses against the old Tarnow community were to be found in this area of the Tarnow cemetery.

Before the destruction, there also were signs of the lively spiritual development of past Tarnow Jewry. First must be remembered the Old Synagogue that stood from the second half of the 16th century.[1] In time this synagogue building sank significantly and in order to enter the actual holy place, one had to walk on the Jewish Street through the large courtyard or from Fisz Platz, one had to go down several steps to get to the synagogue entrance hall.

[Page 64]

A fragment of the area at the Tarnow cemetery where the oldest headstones stood
[Photographed by Y. Bergman in 1965]

The gate to the entrance to the synagogue courtyard in front of the destroyed old synagogue coming from the Jewish neighborhood
[Photographed by Y. Bergman in 1966]

[Page 65]

The Old Synagogue in Tarnow, built in 1581 [the front of Fisz Platz]

We would hear sermons and novel interpretations of actual religious problems in this Old Synagogue in which Tarnow rabbis and Torah scholars studied for hundreds of years and along with such Torah giants as the Rabbi Yehuda Leib *haKohan Maimon*, may the memory of a righteous man be blessed, the first Minister of Religion in the Land of Israel, as well as the Rabbi Meir Szapira, the Lubliner Rebbe [who was] the founder of the *Yeshiva Khakhmei Lublin* and of many other rabbinic societies.

The Old Synagogue building was blown up by the German vandals one day along with the other houses of prayer including the New Synagogue and tens of other synagogues, *minyanim* [10 men needed for communal prayer: in this case, the places in which the *minyanim* met] and *kloyzen* [private houses of study].

[Page 68]

The interior of the Jubilee (New) Synagogue

The unadorned Torah reading table of the old synagogue, now overgrown with grass, remained undamaged after the explosion and still stands today in the place, protected by the city managing committee as a "historical memorial"… In addition to the cemetery in Tarnow, this reading table is today the only remnant of the magnificent Jewish community and it gives witness to the tragic fate of Tarnow Jewry and its sacred cultural treasures.

[Page 67]

Copy of the picture, "The Talmudists" by Professor F. Wilenberg

Hasidism and Hasidim in Tarnow

Hasidism [Hasidic philosophy] planted its roots in the Jewish streets of Tarnow very early. Deep faith, the study of Torah with insight and ingenuity, this was the fundamental foundation of Tarnow Hasidism that in time, thanks to this doctrine, became very strong and won wide circles of Tarnow Jewry.

[Page 68]

There are written details about the great influence of Sanzer Hasids in the Jewish neighborhood in Tarnow and about the great center of this version of Hasidism in the Sanzer *kloyz* [private house of study] in Tarnow in the first volume of the Tarnow Yizkor Book. I will only emphasize that hundreds of young men studied day and night in this large *kloyz*. During the winter months, it was difficult to find a place to study in the morning.

Many Tarnow Hasidim studied in the Sanzer house of prayer, which had a rich collection of expensive and rare religious books.

There was no lack of students in the Belzer *shtibel* [one–room synagogue] and in the two small Bobower *kloyzen*. Among others who studied in the Belzer *shtibel* was the martyr, Efroim Sztiglic, of blessed memory, about whom my brother, Ahron Blazer, may he live long, (today a lawyer of Haifa) who studied there with him, said that he had the mind of a genius and an extraordinary memory. While in general, the Sztiglic family in Tarnow produced great scholars, it is enough to remember Reb Alter Sztiglic, the great scholar, a brother of Efroim, who authored many important books and innovative interpretations of the Talmud and *Halakah* [religious law]. The *magid hashiur* [person who teaches a class on a page of Talmud] at the Belzer synagogue then was the religious judge, Mikhl Holender, of blessed memory.

A large number of scholars always were found in the Dzikower *kloyz*. Such gifted young men as Yissokher Wakspres, Yehosha Fracht, the Klener brothers, the Hertzog brothers, the children of Reb Yeshayale Rozner, Yehosha Szlisl, Grinbaum, Kaufman and many other talented young men who were brutally murdered by the German hangmen had all studied [there] with great diligence.

And how boisterous the Boyaner *shtibel* always was and with what zealousness did they study with the rabbis from Szczuczyn, Paszowic, Grodzisk and Żabno…

Or with Reb Yisroel Yosele Unger, of blessed memory, and in tens of other houses of prayer in the Jewish center of Tarnow…

Torah scholars, such as Reb Moshe Wolf Reb Avrahamele Gewelb, Reb Mendl Hofman, Reb Meir Malter, Reb Wolf Weksler and many, many other dear scholarly Jews who excelled with their insight and expertise emerged from these *kloyzen* and rabbinic *shtibelekh*.

Brilliant young men who were considered as future great men of Torah of their generation came out of these *yeshivas* [religious secondary schools], among many others: Yakov Holender, Leibish Szajner, Abush Szwarc, Shaul Brener, Nafatli Mehr, Borukh Rinder, Moshe Rik, Eliezer Templer, Kalman Halbersztam, Moshe and Meir Weksler, Yeshaya Orszicer, Borukh Tajtlbaum… All of the dear, young men, tortured by the Nazi murderers, perished *al Kiddush haShem* [as martyrs – in sanctification of God's name].

[Page 69]

The active scholars famed for spreading Torah and Hasidism among young Jewish men were not only in the *yeshivas*. But finally at the end of the 19th century, several Torah scholars, who gave private lessons in the Torah, *Gemora* [Talmudic commentaries] and supplements to the Talmud, also taught worldly subjects.

One of the most important such teachers was Reb Ayzik Wrubel, of blessed memory, who taught Dr. [Salo] Sholem Wittmayer Baron, famous today as a professor at Columbia University in America, the son of Reb Eliyahu Baron, the head of the *kehila* for many years and a communal activist in Tarnow (his wife Mina, may her memory be blessed, was descended from the esteemed Wittmayer family in Tarnow). It is worthwhile also to remember Reb Ayzik Wrubel's son, the young Dr. Zvi Wrubel–Ankori, who after graduating from the Hebrew *Safa–Berura* [pure language] *Gymnazie* in Tarnow in 1938 emigrated to Israel, where he received his doctorate from Hebrew University and today is a professor at this college in Jerusalem.

* * *

If the Tarnow Sanzer *kloyz* grew into a weighty center of Hasidus in Tarnow, it was in thanks to the great spiritual influence of the Sanzer Rebbe, Reb Chaim Halberstam, may the memory of a righteous man be blessed, an extraordinary personality who occupied an honored place among the geniuses of his generation. In addition to this, he was the author of many books on Torah and Hasidism. Thanks to his intelligence and insight, he was a true guide in the lives of his Hasidim, who had the fullest confidence in their rebbe. They asked his advice on every important matter and followed his instructions fully. Therefore, it is no wonder that the rebbe was drawn to the Hasidic city of Tarnow, which lay not far from Sanz. His oldest son, the Szinewer Rebbe, Reb Yehezkiel Halberstam, may the memory of a righteous man be blessed, was known as one of the greatest *Admorim* [abbreviation of *Adoneinu Moreinu v"Rabeinu* – our master, our teacher our Rabbi] and geniuses. He had a negative position toward the *Hovevi Zion* [Lovers of Zion] movement in Galicia. When the founding meeting of the *Hovevi Zion* society took place in Tarnow on the 22nd of Tevet, the 27th of December 1896, and the managing committee elected the Tarnow Szinewer Hasid, Reb Zakhria Mendl Aberdam, as the treasurer of the society, among others Reb Yehezkiel Halberstam convinced them that Reb Zakhria Mendl Aberdam had not accepted the election and declared that he [Reb Zakhria Mendl] had no connection to the *Hovevi Zion* in Tarnow.[2]

[Page 70]

Headstone of Reb Fibel Blazer,
of blessed memory, died in 5691 [1931]

Reb Leibish Halberstam, may the memory of a righteous man be blessed, the son of the Szinower Reb, a grandson of the founder of the Sanz dynasty, Rebbe Reb Chaim Halberstam, may the memory of a righteous man be blessed, had a close attachment to Tarnow Hasidim. He was the rebbe at the largest Tarnow *kloyz*, he was a great scholar and God–fearing person. He always placed an emphasis on learning Torah. His doctrine of Hasidism distinguished itself with its moderation and characteristic of avoiding noise and boisterous forms of expression. He was not a great believer in lavishly receiving his followers at his table or with accepting *kwitlekh* [notes requesting the rabbi's intervention with God for a marriage for a child, a child for a barren woman, etc.] and so on. I remember a case from my youth when I had the opportunity to be able to study near the great scholar. My father, of blessed memory, had the habit of spending time with the rebbes for the Days of Awe. I was still a young man when my father, may he rest in peace, once took along my younger brother, Mendl, may his memory be blessed, and me to Rebbe Reb Leibish Sanzer. The rebbe was just then teaching and did not permit anyone to disturb him and, therefore, it was difficult to approach him. However, he made an exception for my father, may he rest in peace, and the rebbe welcomed us. He sat at a heavy book and when my father, may his memory be blessed, turned to him with a request, that he should bless us – my brother Mendl and me – that we should be good Torah students. The Rebbe, Reb Leibish, first declared that he could not have an influence on us to become good students of Torah and emphasized that if we studied with diligence, we would be good students. He finally gave us a blessing.

[Page 71]

My brother Mendl, may he rest in peace, in later years graduated from the well–known Hildesheimer *yeshiva* [religious secondary school] and received his doctorate and ordination as a rabbi. He fell as a martyr at the hands of the German murders in the Tarnow ghetto.

The Bobover Rebbe, Reb Ben–Zion Halberstam, may the memory of a righteous man be blessed, son of Reb Shlomo Halberstam, may the memory of a righteous man be blessed, a grandson of the author of *Divrei Chaim* [*Writings of Chaim*], the Sanzer Gaon [genius] and Rebbe, Reb Chaim Halberstam, had an influence on Sanzer Hasidism in the last years before the Holocaust. The main novelty of Bobover Hasidism was placing weight on the young generation. Bobover Hasidism had a large following in Tarnow and had two Bobover *shtibelekh* [one–room synagogues], where hundreds of young men studied, in Tarnow. During elections to the Tarnow *kehila* [organized Jewish community], the Bobover Hasidim would issue their own candidate list and their distinguished, publicly esteemed representative, Yisroel Wind, of blessed memory, always received the appropriate number of votes to be elected as a member of the Tarnow *kehila* council.

In order for the portrait of Hasidism in Tarnow to take in all the schools of thought and variants, I will provide in a general way several facts about such rabbinical authorities as the *gaonim* from Dzików, Żabno and Grodzisk because these martyred Tarnow rabbis are mentioned with more details and with more expertise and thoroughness by our Tarnower, Menasha Unger, in his important book, *Sefer Kedoshim* [*Book of Martyrs*], which was published in New York in 1967.

[Page 72]

The Dzikówer Rebbe, our teacher and master, Reb Alter Horowitz, may the memory of a righteous man be blessed, a grandson of Rebbe, Reb Naftali of Ropshitz [Ropczyce] and a son–in–law of the Wisznicer Rebbe, Reb Yisroel Hager, may the name of a righteous man be blessed, was one of the great Hasidic rabbis in Tarnow. The Rebbe, Reb Alter, was very well–known and beloved in the Hasidic circles and he was known far beyond the borders of Tarnow for his knowledge and intelligence. On the holidays, particular during the Days of Awe, Hasidim would come to Tarnow to spend it with the Dzikówer Rebbe. They came not only from other areas in Galicia, but also from the larger world, from England, from Belgium, Holland, etc. The names of the respected Tarnow Jews who belonged to the loyalist Hasidim of the Dzikówer Rebbe remain in my memory, such as Reb Abush Faust, may he rest in peace, Reb Eliyahu Gewirtz, may he rest in peace, my honorable father Reb Feywel Blazer, may he rest in peace, Reb Shimkhale Wakspres, may he rest in peace, Reb Yekele Faust, may he rest in peace, Reb Yeshayale and Dov Rozner, may they rest in peace, Reb Manish Kelner, may he rest in peace, Reb Toyva Grinbaum, may he rest in peace, Reb Zalman Guter, may he rest in peace, Reb Yeshayale Szpiro, may he rest in peace, Reb Yitzhak Aszchenazi, may he rest in peace, and many, many hundreds of devoted Jews who would take an active part in various community, humanitarian actions on behalf of the needy Jews in Tarnow.

All of the influential leaders of the Tarnow *Agudah* [association – organization founded by Orthodox rabbis] were concentrated around the Rebbe, Reb Alter, who was a follower of the *Agudah* organization and, above all, his influence was owed [to the fact] that the representatives in the *kehila* [organized Jewish community] in Tarnow worked together with the Zionist faction. During the last years before the Holocaust, as a result of an agreement, a representative of *Agudah* (Reb Elya Gewirc, may he rest in peace) stood at the head of the *kehila*–council and the office of the chairman of the *kehila* managing committee was from the Zionist block (Dr. Menderer and, during the last two years before the Holocaust, Dr. Avraham Chomet, long may he live).

At the table that would be led by Rebbe, Reb Alter on Friday nights in the presence of a large group of Hasidim, he would provide teachings and innovations as was the custom of his father, the Rebbe, Reb Yehosha, may the memory of a righteous man be blessed, the author of *Atarat Yehosha* [*Crown of Joshua*]. At the conclusion of the evening, the Hasidim glorified the evening with an ecstatic *rikud* [Hasidic dance]. The Dzikówer Hasidim also were known as great musicians and leaders of prayers, who brought in a breath of life and sweetness into their prayers. It is enough to remember our unforgettable Reb Abush Faust, may his memory be blessed, Reb Shmuel Eder, may his memory be blessed, and their magnificent, strong voices, as well as Shmuel Korn, long may he live (now lives in Israel), who possessed musical talent and a particularly beautiful voice. The Hasidic band of the Dzikówer young men with their Rochnitz– Dzikówer melodies were known in almost all Hasidic circles in Galicia.

[Page 73]

They studied in the Dzikówer *kloyzen* [plural of *kloyz* – private houses of study] in Tarnow with earnestness and zeal. The students could make use of a rich collection of Talmud books and post–Talmudic commentaries; in addition there were also books of responsa, philosophy and *Midrash* [early commentaries], books of Kabbalah and *musar* [ethics]. There were also rare, valuable copies of books in the well–organized book collection that had been published by the first Hebrew printer.

There were two separate rooms in the Dzikówer *kloyz*. Prayers took place in one room and instruction in the second one. I had the privilege of studying a page of *Gemora* [Talmud] and commentaries at the *Beis Dzików Yeshiva* for a time with my teacher and leader, Reb Moshe Ahron Brand, of blessed memory, who was a great scholar and sage, along with the two sons, Reb Meir, may God avenge his blood, and Reb Yekele, may God avenge his blood, of the Rebbe, Reb Alter. Both sons and their brother, Reb Mendl, may his memory be blessed, their father, Rebbe, Reb Alter, may the name of a righteous man be blessed, and his *rebbitzen* [rabbi's wife], the righteous, esteemed woman, Chava, the Wicznicer Rebbe's daughter, may she rest in peace, were tortured by the German murderers and perished *al kiddush haShem* [in sanctification of God's name – as martyrs].

The Dzikówer Rebbe's daughter, Dwoyrala, and his son, Reb Yehudale, who now live in Israel, survived through a miracle.

* * *

The Żabner Rebbe, Reb Eliezer Unger, may the memory of a righteous man be blessed, a grandson of the Rebbe, Reb Mordekhai Dovid Unger, may the memory of a righteous man be blessed, from Dombrowa, near Tarnow, also was among the great Jewish personalities in Tarnow. Reb Eliezer's father, Rebbe Sholem Dovid, may the memory of a righteous man be blessed, had lived in Tarnow before the First World War and was known as a *gaon* [genius]. After his death in 1923, his oldest son, Reb Eliezer, may the memory of a righteous man be blessed, who lived in Tarnow, became rebbe. He was esteemed and beloved by a great circle of Hasidim. During the German occupation, he did not want to leave the Tarnow Jews, although his Hasidim begged him to leave Tarnow for Żabno where they had prepared a hiding place in a secure bunker for him and his family.[3] He was savagely tortured by the Nazi murderers and he perished *al Kiddish haShem* in September 1942.

[Page 74]

The Grodzisker Rebbe, Reb Eliezer Horowitz, may the memory of a righteous man be blessed, a son of Rebbe, Reb Chaim Horowitz of Polaniec, who lived in Radomysl and in Rzeszów after the First World War, was known as a great sage in Jewish Tarnow. The Grodzisker Rebbe was a giant of Torah and had a great circle of Hasidim from Tarnow and, particularly, from Congress Poland. He led a yeshiva in his house of prayer where he taught many young men and he himself taught Torah lessons. He was tortured in the Tarnow ghetto in Kislev 5703 ([November–December 1942). As Menasha Unger, author of the book, *Sefer Kedoshim*, writes, "his shout of Shema Yisroel'[b] before the Germans shot him, created a shudder in the entire Jewish area."

The Pokszewicer Rebbe, Reb Yehiel Horowitz, may the memory of a righteous man be blessed, a son of *Imrei Noam* [Rebbe Meir Horowitz, author of the book *Imrei Noam* – a book of Torah commentary], may the memory of a righteous man be blessed, was well–known in the Hasidic world in Tarnow. A grandson of the great *gaon*, Reb Naftali Ropczicer, and a brother of the Dzikówer Rebbe. He left three sons who continued with Pokszewicer Hasidism. His son, Rebbe Naftali, settled in the city where his father had been rebbe, in Pokszewic. His second son, Reb Alter the last Pokszewicer Rebbe, and his younger brother, Reb Avraham, of blessed memory, were murdered by the Nazis.

Announcement on behalf of the council of the community of Tarnow in 1935 about the sermon of Rabbi Chaim Zwi Szotland at Reb Yeshayala's *minyon* [10 men needed for organized prayer] at the synagogue in Tarnow

[Page 75]

The Stucziner Rebbe, Reb Yitzhak Horowitz, may the memory of a righteous man be blessed, a son of the Rozwadower Rebbe, Reb Moshe, may the memory of a righteous man be blessed, and a grandson of Rebbe Reb Naftali of Ropshitz [Ropczyce], may the memory of a righteous man be blessed, was among the rebbes with great influence in the Hasidic world. More facts about this great scholar and righteous man are in the first volume of the Yizkor Book, *Tarnow*, where other giants of Torah and the righteous Jews who lived in and had an influence in Tarnow are mentioned.

* * *

Can I forget the effervescent Jewish life in my former Tarnow home… in the home where a God–fearing community of Jews, who day and night lived their lives in the study of Torah… where a large group of toiling Jews lived, who worked hard for their income in order to live an honored Jewish life…

How cruel their pain must have been… how deep the abyss of their suffering… and what a horrible hell in which they found themselves living until the last day when there remained no trace of Jewish Tarnow…

I remember our magnificent communal–political activity in Jewish Tarnow… the dozens of political, humanitarian and cultural organizations… I remember, and I remember with pride, the high morale of Tarnow Jewish leaders… the deep understanding and fraternal spirit to help every needy Jew…

Can I forget the dear Tarnow Jews with their eternal thirst for Torah and knowledge?... I was in Tarnow, my city of birth, several times after the last war… Each time, my first step was to the place where the Dzikówer *kloyz* stood… No trace remains of it… even the devastation has been cleared away… Only an empty spot remains, without a holy ark, without bookcases that reached up to the balcony… filled with books…

The yeshiva young men were slaughtered – just as in all of the other Jewish communities… dear students of Torah… and my thoughts always returned back to this place, where the holy house of prayer once stood… where the Rebbe, Reb Alter, may the memory of a righteous man be blessed, would send his prayers with such ecstasy to the Creator of the world …

Translator's footnotes:

    a.   Lesser Poland was a division of the Polish–Lithuanian Commonwealth formed in 1569. Magnates in Poland were members of the wealthy and influential nobility.
    b.   "Hear O Israel," the opening words of the central prayer of Judaism; they are the last words a pious Jew says before death.

Footnotes:

1. It was built in the year 1581.
2. *HaMagid* [*The Preacher*], 1897, Issue 7.
3. *Sefer Kedoshim* [*Book of Martyrs*] – Menasha Unger – p. 159.

[Pages 76, Volume 2]

Information About the Jewish Cemetery in Tarnow

by Dr. Avraham Chomet

Translated by Miriam Leberstein

The cemetery in Tarnow is all that remains of its annihilated Jewish community. During their reign in Tarnow the German vandals used the cemetery as a place of execution of the Jewish population. There, too, they would bring the corpses of the Jews they had tortured and killed, to be buried in the mass graves they had prepared for them. The Nazi savages did not respect the sanctity of the holy place and neglect reigned over the cemetery during the horrific years of the Second World War.

German or Ukrainian and local brutes desecrated the cemetery, upending entire rows of tombstones, which they used to pave the main streets of town. There arose a bizarre new trade as many people were willing to buy the valuable marble gravestones which had stood at the graves of prominent Tarnow citizens.

A part of the Jewish cemetery in Tarnow, destroyed during the Holocaust

[Page 77]

Scattered and overturned gravestones at the Tarnow cemetery

* * *

In light of this disgraceful desecration, it is no wonder that they destroyed the part of the cemetery where there stood the graves of rabbis, religious scholars, and holy martyrs – victims of riots and pogroms – as well as the communal leaders who had contributed to the welfare of the town. On this piece of land, not far from the entrance to the cemetery, you could still find, before the Holocaust, old gravestones, even then almost completely sunken into the ground. Only here and there were the headings visible, or rarely, entire parts of stones, with letters that were difficult to read or completely erased.

The earliest reports about the Jewish cemetery in Tarnow are found in a Polish monograph entitled "Six Hundred Years of Tarnow," published in 1930 by a Christian resident of Tarnow, Aniela Pishawa, owner of the oldest printing shop in town. We read there, on page 209, that it wasn't possible to ascertain the date that the first Jewish cemetery in Tarnow was established. But, as Pishawa reports, on May 4, 1531, Konstantin Ostrogski, the prince of Ostrog and Zaslaw, owner of the town of Tarnow, gave the Jews in the town a "*list swabodni*", a letter of freedom, a kind of privilege, which decreed that no one could disturb the cemetery known as the "*kirkhof*", upon a penalty of 500 Polish zlotys.[1].

[Page 78]

From a second source, the book "Tarnow in the Time of the Lelevitn," written by Dr. Jan Leniek (published in 1911), we learn that the city of Tarnow owned a small village called Pogwizdow, which was located between the fields of the suburb Zawala and the village Grabowka. Tarnow had obtained this village from its founders, according to a document cited by Leniek (which is in the town archives,) which contains the text of a contract made in 1631 between the town leaders of Tarnow and the representatives of the Jewish population there, regarding their rights and obligations in regard to the use of the cemetery, which was already in existence in Pogwizdow.

The parties to the contract were: On the part of the town administration, the then–mayor, Baltazar Boykowitc, the council member of the district of Tarnow, and the sworn men of the town council; On the part of the Jewish residents, the signators were Zakhariah Lazarowitc and his brother in law Shloyme, the so–called "elders" of the Tarnow Jews. According to Leniek, the contract stipulated that since Jews had long had a cemetery in Podwizdow and since they had purchased an adjoining piece of land, and since a dispute had arisen over how the purchased land was to be used, both sides had agreed that in the future the Jews must pay for the use of the cemetery 8 Polish zlotys a year, in two installments, beginning in 1631. The town council was obliged to assure that the Jews would not be disturbed by the people of Pogwizdow or by the residents of Tarnow. (Dr. Leniek, "Tarnow," p. 137.)

[Page 79]

Tarnow Jews did in fact pay this fee, since, as Dr. Leniek continues in his above–mentioned monograph, he found in a *pinkes* [record book or register] in the Tarnow municipal archives, lists of income and expenses for the town for the period 1632–1633, and the list of income includes the sum of 8 Polish zlotys, 12 groshn in fees for the use of the cemetery in Podwizdow.

Dr. Leniek also cites a later ruling by the municipal government of May 15, 1763, according to which Jews had to pay for the cemetery 3 zlotys as "head tax" and in addition the manager of the cemetery, who lived there, had to pay 3 zlotys head tax and 16 zlotys as fees for the land which he used, and in addition had to provide 15 days of labor. (p.137)

* * *

Later, the owner of Tarnow, Prince Kazimierz Radziwill, in the Privilege of February 17, 1676, affirmed the above mentioned rights that the Jews had received from prior owners regarding maintenance and use of the cemetery, emphasizing the obligation of the town administration to assure that Jews not be beaten or attacked at the synagogue or cemetery.

In the course of time the town experienced significant growth. The number of Jewish residents increased yearly, and it became necessary to enlarge the cemetery. There were uncultivated plots of land nearby, and the representatives of the Jewish community always tried to acquire more and more additional land bordering on the cemetery. We have ascertained several such purchases on the basis of mortgage records in the Tarnow district court. For example, in 1840, 1893, and 1900, the leaders of the Jewish community bought land parcels bordering the cemetery. In 1924, they bought a larger piece of land in Podwizdow and later, in the years before the Holocaust, they made further efforts to buy additional land near the cemetery.

[Page 80]

An empty piece of land in the old Jewish cemetery in Tarnow which is believed to have once held the graves of martyrs, victims of anti–Semitic persecutions

* * *

As previously noted, the old gravestones in cemeteries are of significant value in researching the way of life in Jewish communities. Often they reveal legends and significant events in the community, which are also described in detail in the *pinkes* [records] maintained by the manager of almost every cemetery. An old gravestone was often the only remaining trace of a great personality or scholar.

By 1581,[2] the cemetery at Podiwzdow had existed for many years. The printshop proprietor already mentioned, Aniela Pishowa, in her monograph, "Six Hundred Years of Tarnow," noted that the earliest date that could be found on a gravestone at the cemetery was 1642.

[Page 81]

The question of the oldest grave stone is also addressed elsewhere in this yizkor book. According to Yitzhak Blazer's article, "What I Remember of Jewish Tarnow," not far from the entrance to the cemetery, across from the mass grave of the 20,000 martyrs killed by the Germans, you could still find, before the last world war, ancient gravestones with obliterated inscriptions.

According to the hypothesis circulating among the old generation, Blazer says, that was the site of the graves of martyrs killed in the anti–Semitic persecutions of the past.

Concerning this separate area for martyrs, we have information which confirms the hypothesis discussed above, in an article in the Tarnow "Yidishe Vokhnblat [Jewish Weekly) of January 31, 1931, entitled, "The Traces of Napoleonic Wars in the Cemetery in Tarnow," by a Tarnow resident, Yitzhak Shifer. The author, with the aid of the manager of the cemetery, Reb [respectful term of address] Shimon Apel, searched for old gravestones in 1931, and first of all determined that there was such a separate area for martyrs. As he wrote: "There is now (i.e. in 1931) an empty piece of field (*planka*) shaded by the huge crowns of an old tree, and the field is marked by a gravestone that has been dug up to form a shallow site from the joint grave of a couple, which was rare for the times in a Jewish cemetery, on which it is inscribed that they were buried on the area for martyrs."

According to Shifer, he heard from the old grave digger employed by the cemetery in 1931 that the grave digger had been told by his grandfather that the martyrs were murdered on St. Martin hill by bandits in Russian uniforms.

[Page 82]

In his efforts to elucidate the matter Shifer went through the cemetery *pinkes* which was located in the office, which had been kept for 250 years, and he found a notation in Polish, which he reported verbatim in his article, and which we reproduce here in Yiddish:

1. On the day of the holy Sabbath, which falls on the 4th day of Sukkot, there fell as a holy martyr Rabbi Reb Aron, the grandfather of Rabbi Reb Chaim, in Walbram, and he was buried Sunday (Hoshana Rabba) at the new cemetery.
2. The same day Reb Yitzhak fell as a martyr along with his brother Dovid and they were buried on Hoshana Rabba
3. The same day Reb Ezra fell as a martyr and was buried the same as the above.
4. The same day Reb Zelig Katz was killed as a martyr and was buried the same day as the others.
5. The same day Reb Mekhl fell as a martyr and was buried the same day as the above.

As the author of the article further notes, on the same page as the above–cited entries the year 5570 (1810) was written and on that basis the author concluded that the murders had to have occurred during the time that year that the Russian army was stationed in Tarnow, having come to the aid of the Austrian army in its war with Emperor Napoleon. In this regard the author also relies on information provided by a Christian official of the City Council, Professor Hertzig, in his monograph entitled, "The History of the Town of Tarnow," that was published in Tarnow in 1911, according to which Russian soldiers were in Tarnow by 1809.

Another part of the cemetery with broken and overturned gravestones

[Page 83]

* * *

Before the war the Tarnow Jewish cemetery was renowned for its exemplary orderliness. Thanks to its energetic manager Reb Shimon Apel, precise records were kept of the thousands of persons interred there and one could easily locate any gravesite one wished. The administration of the Tarnow Jewish community always gave special attention to the maintenance of the cemetery. In the years just before the outbreak of World War II, they were already making plans to restore and secure the old gravestones in the area near the entrance where the graves of the great scholars, rabbis and community activists were located. The horrific Holocaust disrupted these plans. The German barbarians did not take care of the cemetery. Valuable gravestones were taken to pave the streets. Many gravestones were broken and scattered.

[Page 84]

Only after a few Jews returned to Tarnow, either having survived Hitler's hell by 1000 miracles, or survived the war in the Soviet Union and were repatriated, were efforts made to build a new Jewish life upon the ruins. The first action of the postwar Jewish Committee was to retrieve the gravestone pieces from the streets, restore the stones in the cemetery that had fallen and repair the broken ones.

The ostensibly new Jewish life on the ruins of the Tarnow Jewish community did not last long. Gradually those Jews who had miraculously survived left Tarnow. A large number went to Israel. Many emigrated overseas. All that remains in Tarnow is the cemetery, along with a handful of Jews who survived the Holocaust.

An old gravestone at the cemetery in Tarnow

[Page 85]

An old gravestone at the cemetery in Tarnow
from the Hebrew year 5587 (1827), photo by Bergman, 1965

Two old gravestones in the form of medallions at the cemetery in Tarnow

On the one at the left we read: "Died 19 Kislev, 5568 (1808)."
On the right, "Died (same date)" but the year is no longer legible.
Clearly it is the same year as on the first gravestone.

[Page 86]

Without a doubt the last remnants of Jews still living in Tarnow will also leave. Then, what will happen to the cemetery? What will happen when the municipal government wants to implement the law in Poland, according to which a cemetery that remains unused for 25 years comes under the authority of the municipal government, which is free to use it as it sees fit?

We were able to obtain photos of some of the gravestones[3] in the cemetery, and in particular, we managed to get, from among the trees and overgrown grass, which covered the entire section near the entrance, pictures of some very old ones (on one the date 1808 is visible) with the inscriptions which are very hard to make out.

In November, 1961, the Tarnow Jews in Israel and in other countries received news that the cemetery was being broken up, that gravestones were being stolen and that the municipal government was planning to extend Szpitalna [Hospital] Street by cutting off a wide strip from the cemetery. Shocked by the news, the Tarnow *landsmanshafts* [organizations of fellow townspeople] in Israel, New York and Canada, made a written demand to the municipal government to cease the efforts to desecrate the cemetery and to combat the systematic theft of gravestones.

In the meantime, we have not heard about further desecrations. A handful of 10–15 Jews still live in Tarnow, who carry the torch of the destroyed Jewish community, and do not let it go out.

Original footnotes:

1. [*Kirkhof* is] an old Polish word derived from the German, denoting a cemetery.
2. The same year that the large old synagogue was built in Tarnow.
3. Thanks to the hard work of a young Tarnow student, Y. Bergman, who, despite having been born after the Holocaust, exhibits an exceptionally warm attitude to everything connected with Jewishness and a deep interest for research into the history of Tarnow Jewry, its suffering and tragic annihilation.

[Page 87, Volume 2]

Our First Steps

by Dr. Naftali Szwarc[1]

Translated by Gloria Berkenstat Freund

Dr. Naftali Szwarc,
of blessed memory

Our generation in Tarnow traveled a distant road. The city for us was the beginning of the road – into the unknown. However, the cradle of our ideals and dreams was in the distant and for us now empty city.

Tarnow was a vibrant city, full of effort and work by the Jewish population – but simultaneously, it also was the smithy where our generation forged its ideas. A generation that could not and did not want to assimilate; in general, the [Jewish] national and social ideal that in truth had now begun to crystalize stood before our eyes. We knew and felt that we were Jews, but as young people who had grown up and were educated in the Polish school, absorbing there at that time the idea of Poland's fight for independence – we were not very familiar with the concept of JEW. We knew Jew as an ethnic unit, saw Jewish customs and way of life in the houses and outside them. But at that time, we searched for something else.

It was stirring around us. An organized workers movement rose that fought for a better future and liberated people – whether these were Polish or Jewish people. We established as an axiom: in which direction to go? With which flow to go? None of us wanted to resign from his national membership; however, we also did not want to close our eyes to the embattled socialism.

[Page 88]

This problem, at the beginning of our conscious political thought, was an important question which we had to consider and also answer. In our subconscious, we were drawn to standing in the ranks of the builders and revivers of our people. We thought that the time would come when our people would return to their homeland and then we would be able also to realize the social ideal that so enticed us. Therefore, the young people of that time strove to deepen the content of both ideals – the Jewish people and socialism.

But for everyone, there was "*Yiddishkeit*" [a Jewish way of life]. We searched for some kind of new contents for this idea, searched and found an entire treasury of Jewish knowledge and faith. The Zionists were not disappointing and served as an inexhaustible source in this area from which we could draw a refreshing drink like a tired mountain climber from spring water. We began to read the works of [Theodor] Herzl, [Max] Nordau, Ahah-Ha'am [Asher Hirsch Ginsberg]. Herzl awoke in us the idea that there was a Jewish question. But [Leon Pinsker's *Auto-Emancipation*, which led us to the Jewish set of problems and also showed the way, had a particularly strong effect on the young during those years. Only Herzl's *Judenstaat* [*The State of the Jews*] gave the people an answer to the question concerning our tomorrow. This work, which arose during the dark days of the Dreyfus trial, spoke to us more strongly with its concise language than many volumes of scientific treatises and, for many young minds, the "old new land" became a real dream…

But these were the first steps. Because already at the start of this road, two things became clear: first, that we had to organize a so-called "circle," later a "community;" that we had to study together because we could do nothing alone. Second: we had to create an organization that would be capable of fulfilling all of the tasks.

The first circles were founded in the *gymnasia* [secondary school], but the teachers watched us and we had to obey all of the rules of conspiracy. Worse were our pupils and university students who had the answer to all Jewish hardships: assimilation. Our explanation that there was no nation that wanted to accept us did not help. The uniformed university students divided themselves into two camps: one, which drew a person to his own people; the second, which would adapt and identify with the Polish people. Thus, at our first step we were quickly in the struggle between the two powers: the synagogue and the assimilated comrades.

[Page 89]

We searched for a new foothold and content in Jewish life. Before our eyes stood the simple Jews of the street, whom Yitzhak Leibush Peretz described so beautifully. Martin Buber also spoke to the heart and spirit of the young people. His books revealed to us the Jewish person we were searching for – *der singender Jude* [the singing Jew], whom Buber brings out in one of his works. In our environment in Tarnow and in other cities and *shtetlekh* [towns] in Galicia, which was still a province of the Hapsburg Austrian-Hungarian monarchy, we found the simple Jew – the merchant, artisan, worker, educated, intelligentsia and Hasid – who spoke to God and observed the 613 *mitzves* [commandments]. This impelled us to visit the synagogue on Simchas Torah [holiday commemorating the completion of the yearly reading of the Torah and the start of the reading for the new year], or a rebbe's *shtibel* [one-room synagogue] and to uncover a new world filled with content, rapture and the Jewish way of life that was unknown to us until then. Thus we uncovered the bright road of Jewish knowledge and Jewish history. We wanted to know more about our people. Not only for ourselves, but also for the other young people who had begun to move closer to us.

Thus in Jewish history we found heroes around whom we could weave legends. The Jewish holidays were approaching. Understandably, the Chanukah candles left an unforgettable impression and our hearts were filled with pride for the heroic Maccabees. Or Passover – the holiday and symbol of freedom, the exit from Egyptian slavery.

We were not alone, just a few individuals. The majority of the Jewish young people of that era thought exactly like us. Thus a new type of Jew was fashioned in the years before the First World War, who was so beautifully described in the song of the Jewish-Czech poet, [Hugo] Zuckerman (fell at the front as an Austrian soldier): *Wir wollen Makkabäer sein* [We want to be Maccabees].

We lacked only the language. Only Hebrew would have opened the source of our old Jewish culture for us. The Yiddish language, which developed strongly during that time, could not give us what we found in *Ivrit* [modern Hebrew], the language of the Tanakh [the Five Books of Moses, the Prophets and the Writings]. This was a difficult task. Among the Polish culture, literature and language, in a strange land – finding the way to their own language. We began to learn Hebrew intensively at a special course, but not many succeeded in learning it.

[Page 90]

* * *

Now it is worthwhile to pause to consider the rise and development of the Jewish youth organization, *HaShomer* [The Watchmen], later, *Hashomer HaTzair* [The Young Guard – Labor Zionists], which was the central movement in the cities and *shtetlekh* [towns] in Galicia. Many of us, during the First World War, found ourselves in Vienna as refugees. A special Polish school for the children of the refugees existed in the capital of Austria, but mainly Jewish children studied there.

Even before the outbreak of the war, there was a Jewish scout organization in Vienna, led by Dr. Washitz. Simultaneously, Jewish self-education groups existed there, as a continuation of the student groups from Galicia. Since both movements – the scouts and the groups – carried out their activities among the Jewish higher education students and pupils and both were permeated with a national spirit, they united into one organization whose guide and model were the *Eretz Yisroel HaShomer* – for self-defense, for protecting Jewish lives, Jewish fields and possessions.

The directors of *HaShomer HaTzair* in Tarnow in 1918

Sitting from the left: Chana Ofner, Meir Man, Miriam Umanski, Sima Urmian (lives in Israel), Manek Engelhart
Standing from the left: Naftali Szwarc, Efroim Zagersztrom, Tulek Flancer, Lola Rutenberg, Kalek Fris (lives in Israel), Zeev Block (died in Israel, 1966)

[Page 91]

A group of comrades from *Hashomer HaTzair* in Tarnow in 1918

Sitting on the bottom, from the right: Leon Klar, Chaim Haber
Sitting from the right: Yakov Wandsztajn (today a doctor in London), Yakov Wajs, Naftali Szwarc, Yosef Hendler, Insler
Standing from the right: Gabriel Asterwajl, Yakov Klapholz (today a doctor in Israel), Nusan Haber, Leon Kampf (today an engineer in Israel), Shinagl Fredek (today in Israel), (–), Yosef Kornilo (today in Israel), Galicer, Kalman Goldberg (today in Israel)

The Vienna *HaShomer* carried out intensive activity in the areas of education, self-education and scouting, which later became the basis for the activity of *HaShomer HaTzair* in Galicia after the end of the war, in the years of Poland's independence. Several young people, who had left the city during the war years returned to Tarnow. They founded the *HaShomer*, at the head of which stood Meir Man, a student from the Vienna Polytechnical University. The beginning was modest, without a meeting place. The winning over of new young people was very difficult. We had a great deal of enthusiasm during the early years. This is not the place to describe the exact history of the creation of a circle of *HaShomer*. However, I will provide several facts here:

Only university students and pupils belonged to *HaShomer* at the beginning of its rise.

[Page 92]

This, as it turned out, shrank the frame of the organization for a designated circle of young people. We decided to expand this frame and recruit young workers for the movement. The results were good. After a few years, we were able to send several such young people to Eretz-Yisroel as the first *halutzim* [pioneers] from Tarnow. The two most important events were the making of contact with the Polish scout youth, the *Harcerstwo*. Helping to make contact was Adam Ciołkosz, later the distinguished leader of the Polish Socialist Party (*P.P.S.* [*Polska Partia Socjalistyczna*]).

The day is unforgettable when our organization marched through the Tarnow streets in our uniforms. For the first time in the history of Tarnow, Jewish organizations of young people in uniform went through the most important streets – from Krakowska to the train station, accompanied by several tens of guards who went as a delegation to the conference in Tarnow-Wisznia, near Turek.

Group of friends, *HaShomer HaTzair* in Tarnow in 1919

Sitting from left: Lula List, Tzila Zavorstrum, Hana Fris
Standing from left: Tziporah Fris, Lula Rotenberg, Sala Ladner
(today in Israel)

[Page 93]

Leaders of the *HaShomer HaTzair* group in Tarnow

Sitting from the left: Manek Engelhart, Milek Wajs (today a doctor in America), Chaim Hercman, Meir Man, (–)
Standing from the left: Naftali Szwarc, Kalek Pris (today a veterinarian in Israel), Zeev Bloch, Aleksander Wandersztajn, Bernard Krumhulc (veterinarian in Israel), Flancer Tulek

As is usual, at the beginning of every movement, there were many problems to resolve. First of all – deciding the concept and essence of a youth organization, its frame, purpose and task. A large number of us agreed quickly with the way of the German youth movement – *Der Wandervogel* [the wandering bird – German youth group that opposed industrialization by hiking in the country and enjoying nature]. Many passionate discussions were carried on. At the same time, we must not forget that these were the years after the October Revolution and of the Balfour Declaration, of the downfall of the Austro-Hungarian Empire and Kaizer Wilhelm's Germany and of Poland's independence. In the very excitement of all of the events, our young people established a central purpose: preparing *Halutz* [pioneer] cadres for *Eretz Yisroel*. An agricultural farm in one of the estates was created in Tarnow for this purpose to prepare our young people for agricultural work.

There were other problems. How to educate boys and girls together in one agricultural collective. The idea of separate groups had been discarded a long time ago.

[Page 94]

Thus ripened the new organization among the Tarnow Jewish young people. To be truthful, it was not the only one in the Jewish neighborhood. Little by little, various worker organization began to be created; the religious youth in their manner and with their ways, found the suitable organizational frame, but mainly supported themselves on the pattern of the older generation.

Years passed. Jewish Tarnow no longer exists; no trace has remained of its institutions, houses, and who knows how long the only remaining sign of the past Jewish life in the city – the cemetery – will remain. The only things from those years that remain are what we took with us when we left Tarnow. Everyone left on his own road. However, an idea often drills in my brain: will someone become interested in the *sturm und drang* [turbulent] period of the Tarnow Jewish youth, its strivings and ideals, its daily life, its holidays, when our generation of the beginners and guides are no longer among the living?!…

Original footnote:

1. Died in the month of November 1967.

[Page 95, Volume 2]

The "Hashomer Hatzair" Movement in Tarnow

by Mink

Translated by Daniel Kochavi

In the late afternoon, the large school yard of the "Safa Berura" school in Tarnow was crowded with Jewish children. But they were not students. A "Hashomer Hatzair" troop met in a small room there. Its magic attracted the best boys and girls from every corner of the city. They came from the poor Jewish sections, from the mixed Jewish-Christians quarter, from streets that included a small number of Jewish families (only the well-to-do assimilated families dared to reside there). The sons and daughters from all classes of the Jewish population of Tarnow joined the group.

Loud sounds burst from the large school yard and reached the street on one side and the monastery and city hall gardens on the other. Laughter, joy, Hebrew singing echoed all around. In the rooms beneath walls decorated with landscapes, the Shomer Hatzair-trainees listened attentively and absorbed thirstily the words of their leaders who were slightly older than them.

The Tarnow "Hashomer Hatzair" [editor note: Zionist Youth Movement] was typical of tens or hundreds of such groups scattered throughout Galicia and Poland 30 years ago.

"Hashomer Hatzair" youth group in Tarnow with seniors in 1922

seated from left: Gzashiv, Y. Zomer, Marmoor, Moshe Klapholz (presently a judge in Israel)
standing from the left: Shmuel Heller, Yaakov Shpyzer, Yeshayahu Hendler (presently a physician in Israel), Borganicht

[Page 96, Volume 2]

They joined the group beginning at the age of ten: workers' children, children of small business owners, of Jewish merchants and farmers, of the assimilated professional intelligentsia – from all corners of the Jewish diaspora they soaked up the atmosphere of rebellion against the existing order and the desire to transform it into a dream of renewal of the ancient-new homeland [Israel].

They were organized in small troops and large educational groups (regiments) that strived for their best personal and social experiences. Individually or as a group they acquired nationalistic [Zionistic] values, deepening the emotional and idealistic ties with events in Eretz Israel - this was the weaving of a rich and colorful tapestry they all longed for.

Among these young people - or more precisely apart from them – stood out a small boy who was too young to join any of the groups. With his twinkling eyes and constant laugh, he was loved by all. Shulek[1], a playful mischievous kid was part of every activity. He participated in many outdoor games such as hide and seek and others. When the group or the "regiment" met, in times of celebrations and holidays, when hiking and camping in the woods or mountains, he was always there. Beloved by all, Schulek became an integral part of the "Hashomer" group in Tarnow but I do not remember how. His father was the owner of a well-known restaurant in town. Many of the city's top Christians managers dined there. As his son, the young boy understood deeply the situation of his family and his people.

And so, while still a child, he became part of the troop. He absorbed the "Hashomer" Hatzair atmosphere and became an inseparable part of this fresh and growing spirit.

After several years he becomes the focus of the social activity of the troop. He organized hikes, trips and social gatherings. He was the editor of the regiment and troop papers- he became a leading personality within his age group. Eventually his group and his regiment did not satisfy his great enthusiasm. He wanted to widen his contact with people.

During the summer gatherings and other meetings with "Shomrim" brothers from other groups, he initiated the idea of an all-encompassing group circle that would eventually become a Kibbutz. He did not only initiate, but he established contacts, he visited other cities and in fact creates a new Kibbutz.

This how his young trainees knew him. First as the leader of the Hebrew gymnasium students and later as the leader of the larger regiment - leading all with his intensely active spirit.

His outstanding teaching talent knew no limits. Every idea and interest of his students, their large and small activities became parts of the life of this loving and beloved educator. No wonder his students worshiped him. Every utterance became "holy", every opinion an infallible ruling. Indirect contacts with his young people were not sufficient for him. He always wanted to know about their life styles – He spent much time with their parents to understand their background and to get the parents' support of his educational efforts. His trainees' teachers become well acquainted with him and respected this young man's ability to reach their students.

[Page 97, Volume 2]

Shulek Wachtel z"l in Kibbutz Yad Mordechai

He did not believe in the total "burning of bridges". "We have a duty to learn"- is his mantra to the rebels against the school educational regime. He demands serious learning and scolds those who despised the value of studies.

School education is not sufficient for him. He himself searched for every new book to broaden the interests and knowledge of his young group. He always kept up with Jewish and Christians events in the town and the state, and he involved others in his keen political interests.

He understands that it is not enough to conquer young hearts. The wide-open outdoor spaces called him. His teaching efforts extend to the woods and mountains. An athlete and scout, he becomes a personal example for the strengthening of his young trainees' character.

In his free time, he and his friends go on long hikes in the Tatras and Beskidis (Polish mountains) and he becomes an unrivaled brotherly helper.

This is how I knew him in the Hashomer troop in Tarnow at the time of the diaspora of Galicia.

When I met him again in the Kibbutz in Israel - his adult sense of responsibility and practicality added to the depth of his character.

Beloved by young and old he remained a faithful son of the Shomrim movement who devoted and sacrificed his life to its goals.

May he be of blessed memory.

Translator's footnote:

1. Wachtel (the editor). Uncertain transliteration to Shulek

[Page 98, Volume 2]

From My Memories

For an Oath
(Based on a true experience)

by Josef Hayman[a]

Translated by Gloria Berkenstat Freund

The late rabbi in Tarnow, Reb Meir Arak, may he rest in peace, the author of a series of scholarly books that, because of his great knowledge of Talmud also were known outside the borders of Poland, once let himself be convinced to discuss an episode from his life.

He had clearly explained the significance and essence of the oath from the standpoint of the rich Talmudic literature about the matter to his students, who would eagerly come and give him respect.

This rarely speaking thinker did not like to talk to those who would quickly decide to interrupt him with a question; therefore, we listened to him, concentrating on his words.

"On a hot July day in the year 191..." Rabbi Arak, may he rest in peace, said, "the priest from a village that lay several miles from Buczacz, my then residence, asked me to mediate an argument between him and a Jew – a village trader who lived in the same village. At my amazed question as to why he had come to me, he answered that the matter was of such a disturbing character that he saw no other way out.

"When I agreed that he could give the matter to me, the priest told me that for a very long time he had been in a completely satisfactory trade relationship with the above-mentioned Jew – until yesterday. But it seemed that the Jew had in an ugly way abused the trust which he had been given.

[Page 99, Volume 2]

Headstone of Yosef Hajman, of blessed memory

"Last night, as happened often, the priest through his window, which looked out onto a garden, called the Jew to talk to him about a matter on which it was necessary for him to mediate.

"While in a bit of a drawn-out conversation with the Jew, the priest was given the 5,000 *krone* in five banknotes of 1,000 *krone* that had arrived in the mail, which the priest lay on his desk.

"Soon the priest said that someone was waiting for him in the neighboring room. Sending away the Jew, he went to the nearby room and returning after a short time, he remembered that he had earlier left the money on his desk.

[Page 100, Volume 2]

"However, the money had disappeared.

"Knowing with certainty that beside the Jew no one had crossed the threshold of the room, he sent for him and categorically demanded the money back, adding that because of their long acquaintance, he would be quiet about the entire incident because he thought that the Jew had just experienced a "weak moment" in giving into the *yetzer-hara* [evil inclination].

"However, the Jew categorical maintained that he had not taken the money and because of this, it was understandable that he could not return it.

"The priest was very uncomfortable about turning to the court because he did not want the higher regime to know about the incident and knowing how much honor and respect – as he expressed it – my local co-religionists gave me, he resolved to entrust me completely with the determination and care of the unpleasant matter.

"I could not refuse his request and asking that he wait for me, I immediately sent for this Jewish acquaintance of mine who lived several kilometers from Buczacz and, informing him of the matter, I demanded an explanation and a prompt solution of this unpleasant incident.

"However, the Jew, very determined, argued that he had not taken the money; he so simply, fervidly and passionately assured me of his innocence that I faltered in my suspicion in regard to the truth of the priest's accusation and considered it necessary to come to a compromise in this matter.

"During long negotiations, the priest lowered his demand to 4,000 *krone* and the Jew finally decided to pay 2,000 *krone*, previously hearing from me that he would probably have to give an oath.

"Finally, the priest was satisfied with the sum of 3,000 *krone*. However, when the Jew declared that he would in no way give more, I told him categorically that there was no other way for him than to give an oath that would determine the outcome of the matter.

"However, before this happened, I gave the Jew several days to think, according to our obligatory rules.

"This had for its purpose the avoidance of the giving an oath under coercion and without long and conscientious contemplation of such an important step.

[Page 101, Volume 2]

"The oath was supposed to be given in the main synagogue in the presence of as many Jewish members of the *kehile* [organized Jewish community] as possible and the giver of the oath was supposed to be wearing his *talis* [prayer shawl] and *tefillin* [phylacteries].

"The Jew, hearing my words, became pale and declared that tomorrow he would say if he would give an oath and then we had to let the priest know about this.

"The same Jew, very worried, came early the next day and with sad and trembling words declared that he was ready to swear.

"Deeply moved by his words, I declared that in in the foreseeable future, I would designate a day for giving the oath.

"The priest came to me on the same day, confused, completely overwhelmed and said that he no longer requested an oath from the Jew because the money had been found in the meantime. A peasant from the parish had just brought him the entire sum of money… He had found it in the small garden near the parish.

"It probably went out through the window in a breeze that arose when the priest entered the nearby room to which he suddenly had been called. The peasant confessed that, at first, he had the desire to hide the money for himself…However, this had not given him any rest and he decided to give it to the priest who now considered it a mystery as to why the Jew wanted to give 2,000 *krone* even though had not taken the money…

"It probably was to avoid the oath, for which he [the Jew] literally trembled. However, why did he not want to give 3,000 *krone* and finally decided to give the oath?

"Understand," Rabbi Arak, may he rest in peace, said, "that I ordered that the Jew be brought to me. I told him everything that had happened in the meantime and asked him to give an oath on all of the questions.

"After a short interval, the deeply-moved Jew answered: 'In order not to swear and not to mention God unjustifiably, I, a destitute and ignorant Jew wanted to sacrifice my modest possessions.' In my haste, I superficially considered that my possessions totaled about 2,000 *krone*. Whereas, as I had to pay up to 3,000 *krone*, I wanted to precisely evaluate and calculate my worth in my home and, therefore, I declared that I would on another day announce if I was prepared to take an oath.

[Page 102, Volume 2]

"According to my calculations, my material situation did not permit me to give more than 2,000 *krone*… Therefore, I declared, although with a heavy heart that I was ready to give the required oath.

"Also present in the house was the priest who I asked to be called to the meeting with the Jew. Quiet reigned for a second. The priest ended it. Deeply moved, he took 2,000 *krone* out of his pouch and gave them to the Jew with the request that he take the money as a reward for the heavy suspicion and worry that he, the priest, had caused him.

"The Jew refused to take the 2,000 *krone* and said that with fervent prayers he thanked the Master of the World who, by a miracle, had freed him from giving an oath.

"The priest expressed his wish that the entire case of the oath would be kept quiet.

"He then did much good for the Jews. Not long ago I learned that he had died. Therefore, I first now speak about this case. May the name of the Lord be praised…"

II

The Synagogue *Shamas*

Once at dawn, walking through Zydowska Street, I met the short, blond *shamas* [beadle] who knocked on the gates of the houses with his wooden hammer and thus called on the pious to come to the morning prayers at the synagogue.

I confess that I have not met a synagogue *shamas* who does this above-mentioned work, for a long time. Surely, he had a very small sector "to knock on" because it is understandable that he could not do this in the entire city, where Jews now live all over.

This custom, it appears, was connected with the tradition of that time when the Jews lived in a ghetto and they needed to have a lot of time and great effort so that the only notice of this sort would reach all of the Jews in the city.

[Page 103, Volume 2]

In addition, the Jews, in their almost 2,000-year exile, had to consider the environment that above all only tolerated this and did not permit that they call their believers to prayer in a noisier way.

The meeting with the current *shamas* awakened memories in me of my young years when I heard the knocking on the gates of the Tarnow Jewish houses by the then *shamas* on Friday nights, as well as the words given from mouth to mouth: *Men klopt. In shul arein* [There is knocking. Go to the synagogue].

The Jews animatedly began closing their shops; they energetically ejected the customers present; the women began to prepare the candles, preparing the candlesticks and the menorahs and we children, who during the warm days at this time played in front of the houses, with resentment had to leave.

In our childish fantasy, this *shamas* – a tall, slightly stooped, gray Jew – appeared to be a religious zealot who disturbed our game with his early knocking on the gates. Therefore, we did not like him, nor his hammer and some of us were simply afraid of him, particularly during the Days of Awe when, long before daybreak, with his grave voice he would call the God-fearing Jews to perform *Selikhos* [penitential prayers]. His voice appeared to us as if from under the earth, like a bell that rings an alarm and it caused we children's hair to stand up and mostly we kept our heads under the featherbeds…

Yet our fear was only an exaggerated feeling of unease that worried us – as I convinced myself – as well as the older generation of Jews.

Over the course of the entire month of Elul [August-September], after the blowing of the *shofar* [ram's horn], an extraordinarily serious mood was noticed on the faces of the worshippers who, during the recitation of *Selikhos*, were transformed into oppressed, very agitated people. Their mood was similar to that of an accused person who needed to appear quickly for his judgement. Between Rosh Hashanah and Yom Kippur were heard from these men's hearts sighs and quiet moans whose source was the deep belief that Yom Kippur would decide the question of their life [and death] and that only with repentance, prayer and charity would they turn aside their bad fate.

[Page 104, Volume 2]

These were days of trembling and regret… At the close of Yom Kippur, after the liberating sound of the *shofar*, when the sacred fast day had ended, their hearts became full of hope and courage and mainly the belief that their fervent prayers had been heard.

Today it is hard to find such a deep belief, such hearts, full of repentance, such genuine, deep-hearted piety…

With the arrival of winter and the cold weather, the Jewish boys' feelings of antipathy toward the *shamas* were put to rest with a winter sleep. Not being able to play in the courtyard, we forgot about him during this time.

Before Purim, our games in front of the house resumed. One of our group of young boys had an ingenious idea to masquerade as a *shamas* for Purim. Masked, dressed in a *shtreimel* [fur hat worn by Hasidic men] and a long *kapote* [long black coat worn by pious men], he held a stick in one hand and in the other hand a wooden hammer used to bang out meat cutlets, he gave three knocks on the gate.

At first, he evoked astonishment – on the first night of Purim the Jews do not go to the synagogue – but then, general laughter. And when he knocked on the door of the *shamas*, the latter ran out of his house with his stick, annoyed that someone had laughed at God's worship… Understandably, the boy ran away.

My unfriendly, completely unjustified attitude toward the *shamas* also changed in later years.

On the eve of Passover, when I was already studying at the synagogue, the *shamas* came to my father with a request to write a plea for him to a very influential person about providing him help for the holiday.

He lamented, "For a poor person, this is the most difficult time of the year and the expenses in connection with preparing for Passover prevent me from sleeping for several weeks. My expenses for this holiday are proportionally greater than for a well-to-do person, if not a rich Jew."

The *shamas* answered my father's question about how he should understand this: "My apartment, although not large, must be plastered for the holiday and whitewashed – a well-to-do person does not need to do it because his room is painted. Once a year, that is for Passover, I must get fresh straw for the straw bag [for a bed] – someone well-to-do has a mattress.

[Page 105, Volume 2]

"For my five children – this is the average number of children in every poor Jewish home – I must order shoes and clothing because they have nothing to wear, while the well-to-do have [clothes] made throughout the year.

"Every pious Jew has holiday dishes [dishes for Passover] that are hidden in the attic after Passover. If, however, for me over the course of the year a dish broke and a pot became *treyf* [unkosher] and, as the way it is, money to buy the missing utensils is always lacking in the house, my wife would say to the child who was in the house: 'Go up to the attic and bring a plate or pot from the holiday dishes.' Understand, as the holiday approaches, the replacement is now needed – a well-to-do person does not have this [problem].

"The same earrings," the *shamas* lamented, "that my wife has had since our wedding usually are found in the pawnshop office and we have to redeem them on a holiday because the poor woman is ashamed to go to the synagogue on the holiday with bare ears; a well-to-do person does not have this expense.

"I do not speak of other necessary expenses, such as: matzos, eggs, wine, meat… Understand, the well-to-do also needs to have everything, but from where does one of limited means get the money for everything? Outside my scant salary, I only have pitiful side income. I make and sell braided candles for *Havdalah* [ceremony ending the Sabbath], but how often do I sell these? One piece lasts almost the entire year. My wife sells cooked chickpeas or kidney beans in the street. If she does not sell all the goods, it means leftovers and not earnings, and our always hungry children eat it up. So…

"Is it then any wonder that every year, from Purim to Passover, I almost never sleep because of the problems and worry?"

A sincere feeling of sorrow and shame then filled my heart.

I was ashamed that several years earlier I had wronged this poor man in my thoughts.

Original footnote:

> a. The memories of Josef Hajman, of blessed memory, the most praiseworthy Zionist leader and communal activist in Tarnow, who died in 1937 – were published in the weekly *Tygodnik Zydowski* [*Jewish Weekly*] and a portion of them already was published in the *Tarnow Yizkor Book*, published by the *landsmanschaft* [organization of people from the same town] of Tarnow Jews in the year 1954. We now publish the Yiddish translation of his further memories of Tarnow which in his time also were published in the above-mentioned *Tygodnik Zydowski*. (Ed.)

[Page 106, Volume 2]

A Polish Poet Tells of Jewish Tarnow

by Abraham Chomet

Translated by Mark Alsher

In 1961 there appeared in London in the "Veritas" Publishing House memoirs by Jan Bielatowicz titled "*Książeczka*" (The Booklet).

The author Jan Bielatowicz graduated from the Gymnasia in Tarnow and the Philosophy Faculty of the University in Cracow and had published a whole series of scientific treatises in the realm of language and literature research. He also wrote journalistic and literary articles. During the Second World War he saw combat in Poland, Italy and Libya and after the War he took part as an emigrant in various literary publications and edited several himself.

A large part of the Booklet contains the author's memories of the time that he was in Tarnow, and there he gives many interesting details both in regard to the city itself and also in regard to its inhabitants, their way of life in all of the aspects of the pre–War society.

Since the author dedicates warm words of memory to the Jewish residents of Tarnow, so we here provide a Yiddish translation from the Polish language of several fragments from the Booklet which pertain to the destroyed Tarnow Jewry.

Recalling the sports–gymnastics clubs in Tarnow, the author writes:

(Page 133)… Tarnow, one of the fortresses of Polish Zionism, raised up many groups of "Shomrim" [Guards] and sports. Besides "Samson" (Shimstarhon), Tarnow also had the Zydowska Młodzież Sportowa" (Z. M. S.) (Jewish Sport Youth), the "Jutszenka" (Bund Sport Club – ed.), "Dror," "Hakaddur," "Hagibbor," "Hapoel" [Freedom, The Ball, The Hero, The Worker – tr.] and others…

At 18 Urszulanska Street the enemy set up his "katownie"[1]. For five years – this was called the seat of the secret police – some 20 thousand men, women and children were brought in there, often locked in chains. Of these, two thousand did not come out alive. Some of them used to be brought out in bags so that the parts of their bodies would not scatter.

[Page 107, Volume 2]

"The gates of the modern Tarnow prison during this period held 50 thousand prisoners.

"Catching people was a separate thing... people from Tarnow were among the first prisoners of Oswiecim and the very first were the engineers of Moszcice.

"All of the Jews went into the gas ovens. Klar with his wife Rebecca, he of the postage stamps and the school implements... and Leyzer, he of the lemon and cream "lodis"[2] ... and Penichel of the old books and "bridges"[3]... Flatto of the cookies and those who used to sit in the "Secesie," "Avenue," and "Weiss" coffee houses and the students of the Hebrew gymnasia... and all of the residents of the alleys of "Szrudmieszczie"[4] and "Rynek," from the streets: Wekslarska, Kreta, Żydowska and "Hakaddur" and the gambler Mendel Kamm ... and the women who sold warm beans and cold bread–kvass... and Wachtel and Moritz – the experts in cooking fish "pa żydowsku" and the medical doctors and the lawyers, the booksellers.

"The cupola of the new synagogue which dominated the eastern horizon of the city — fell to ruins in the flames, all of the podiums of all of the old synagogues were burned...

The entrance gate to the prison building in Tarnow
Photo courtesy of Y. Bergman (1966)

Original footnotes:

1. torture place (ed.)
2. ice cream (ed.)
3. help workbooks for students
4. in the city center

B. In Memory of the Departed

In memory of the sons of Tarnow who fell for the motherland

Translated by Daniel Kochavi

In the first volume of the "Tarnow" memorial book we remembered the heroic members of our town, who fell during the Israeli War of Independence in 1948–1949.

Tarnow Jews also gave their precious lives in the Sinai campaign of 1956 and in the Six Days War in 1967.

Much to our regret we do not have the names of all the Tarnow soldiers, or of their parents, who fought and died on those fronts.

They all fought heroically….

Honor and praises to the Tarnow heroes!

Honor and condolences to their Tarnow parents!

[Page 113, Volume 2]

Yoseph Umanski z"l – devoted to Hebrew language

by Ben–Tzion Uman, Israel

Translated by Daniel Kochavi

Yoseph Umanski, of blessed memory (z"l), was born on the 28 of Teveth (1870) in Ukraine. He received a traditional Torah–based education as well as a wide ranging one in all Jewish and general knowledge. He became a Zionist in his youth and was very devoted to Eretz Israel and to Hebrew.

More than seventy years ago when still living in Russia he asked Dr Mandelshtam in Kiev for permission to emigrate to Israel. He received a negative reply because Dr Mandelshtam doubted that he could support his wife and child there.

In 1903 (63 years ago) he obtained a permit from the Russian authorities to open a licensed Hebrew school in his home in Dubnow (Uman district, Kiev province). A Jewish student named Krimeski taught arithmetic and Russian. This teacher was paid a salary but Umanski and two friends (David Weinstein, now in the USA, and Yoseph Wakselman who stayed in Russia) taught, free of charge, Talmud, literature, history etc. in Hebrew using the Berlitz method. He spoke only Hebrew to the 3 and 4 year-old children. In his home Hebrew was the main language spoken.

He hated the tsarists government and looked for ways to leave Russia. The opportunity came in 1906 when he was invited by the society of Hebrew teachers in Galicia and Bukovina to become a teacher and the principal of the Hebrew school in Vizhnitz, Bukovina.

Although he knew Yiddish, Russian and German he insisted on speaking only Hebrew with the Russian Jews from the day he left in 1906. He insisted that every Jew must learn Hebrew. In the years 1906–08 he taught Hebrew as a teacher and principal in the Vizhnitz school (Bukovina) near Lvov (in eastern Galicia). In 1908 he began teaching in Tarnow in Western Galicia. For a time, he was active in the "Ha Mizrachi" federation in Tarnow and in 1911 he was chosen as a representative to the world "Ha Mizrachi" council that took place in Vienna. During the years of WWI, he lived in Vienna and taught Hebrew to the refugee children. He returned to Tarnow in 1918 and remained there until he emigrated to "Eretz Israel" (Palestine) in April of 1934.

[Page 114]

For the first two years he lived in the "Genigar" settlement. There he taught Hebrew to the members' parents. His many students included professors, physicians, teachers and other well–known people who lived in Israel and in other countries.

While he was still in Russia he started writing about the "Amoraim" and published in 1896, in an anthology titled "Literary Treasure", a comprehensive article "Stories of Rav**". Later, while in Tarnow from 1929 until 1931, he published two books: "Levi Ben Sisi" and "Rav" that included the history of the "Amoraim" and their commentaries arranged alphabetically. In Israel the Rabbi Cook Foundation published in 1949–1951 two of his essays "Sages of the Talmud" that included all the Sages and detailed locations of where they appear in the Talmud. His other essays remained in his private papers.

He was very strict in observing the commandments, but respected people who had more liberal views. He lived a long and good life and was fortunate to see a fifth generation in Israel.

His memory will remain with us forever.

[Page 115, Volume 2]

Dr Shmuel Szpan of blessed memory (z"l)

by Yaakov Fleisher (From Rechavia)

Translated by Daniel Kochavi

We have lost one of our most revered members, an early Zionist in Galicia, beloved and respected by his friends and his rivals.

He was involved in Zionism from an early age, an exemplary leader– untouched by the pursuit of honors, dedicated totally to his public role– as a Zionist leader in western Galicia –and as an official and president of the Tarnow community.

Shmuel Szpan was a self–taught intellectual and lawyer.

Dr Shmuel Szpan, z"l

He loved people, and fought courageously for justice and the rights of people and the simple Jew.

He considered his work not just a profession but a mission to be accomplished with devotion and zeal.

From 1913 on he participated in every Zionist Congress as a representative from Western Galicia for many years. In that year (1913) he enjoyed his honeymoon in Eretz–Israel and, among other activities, he was involved in the founding of Rechavia.

[Page 116]

In 1927 he became a member of the Congsay court until the start of WWII, and chairman of the parents committee of the Shomer Hatzair in his town; he worked tirelessly for all Pioneer youth movements; he was among the founders of the Hebrew school in Tarnow; the Hebrew cultural center, the popular Zionist library, named after him, which included all the literature related to the movements in the town, sports organization and more.

His personal efforts led to the Zionist victory in the Tarnow election and he was appointed head of that community. In that position he was active in community activities, including the establishment of a Jewish hospital, a Jewish orphanage, sport organizations and various charitable organizations.

During all this time he never gave up his desire for self–fulfillment and emigration to Israel. At the height of his career he and his family emigrated to Israel (1934) and then began the hard struggle to survive. The veteran leader limited his activity to the "committee of Tarnow emigrants" in Haifa; he established funds to assist needy emigrants. He also initiated the publication of a wide–ranging memorial book of the Tarnow Jewish community.

At the same time, he engaged in a daring attempt to become a farmer in spite of his age. We watched him near his home in Givat–Ada raising chickens, lambs and calves– full of the joy of creating.

Dr S. Szpan passed away at the age of 86. He died when mourning a friend from the committee of Tarnow emigrants at his home in Haifa.

People from all corners of the country attended his funeral – intellectuals and simple folks, from cities, villages and Kibbutzim. They all came to honor their friend in his ultimate journey.

("Al Hamishmar" 14.3.67)

Daniel Leibel of blessed memory

by Krassel

Translated by Daniel Kochavi

Not long before best wishes for his 75th birthday came from all corners of the world, many of his admirers hoped that his scattered research would be gathered and published in one volume – but this was not to be.

Ten years ago, I met Daniel Leibel and a friend in the home of Prof Salo Shalom Baron, one of the great historians of our generation. I listened to a lively discussion about Tarnow (Tarnoff in Yiddish) where both grew up. He was born in Dembitz, the town mentioned in the memorial book that he edited. But his youth was spent in Tarnow, a town that in the days of the enlightenment (Haskalah) was illuminated by the personality of Brandstetter.

[Page 117]

He experienced the period of national awakening and practical Zionism at the close of the 1890s which included the "Ahavat Zion (Love of Zion)" Society and the founding of Machanayim.

The next generation of the national and Hebrew–Zionist awakening was a group of Yeshiva youth known has "Ha Shachar (The Dawn)", that concerned itself with the growth of Hebrew and Zionism. Members of "Ha Shachar" dispersed — some to Palestine as part of the second Aliyah (immigration in the 1920's) (Lofben and Dov Kimchi), some to "Chochmat Israel" (his childhood friend–I. Pris-Chour). But he was different. As the youngest member of the group he was attracted to the "Poale Zion" movement at a young age. The leaders were Yaakov Kenner and Yitzchak Shifer. As is well known, Tarnow was the cradle of the "Poale Zion"* movement in Galicia. However, those who were looking for wider horizons left and Leibel was one of them. He became active in the movement in Poland. Especially in writing – in polemic publications and editing – all in Yiddish. He abandoned his other research interests. Under the influence of Shifer he became interested in Yiddish research and a practical goal: developing a spelling system that he pioneered early on. In addition, he had a deep love of and wrote poetry (his Yiddish poetry was the main feature of a gathering in the early 1920s). Hence his interest in Bible tales and its treasures. In Poland, after WWI, he edited the "Poale Zion" newspaper and after the split in the movement he joined the leftist Poale Zion movement. He first met Bialik (a major Hebrew poet) in Berlin on his way to Palestine. They remained close friends until Bialik's death. His recollections of Bialik (in "Golden Chain") are the most wonderful one's ever published. Bialik influenced his participation in folklore. In Palestine he remained active in the leftist" Poale Zion" group and with the party he joined "Mapam" and then "United Labor "parties. While working with the newspaper "Davar" he participated in the Yiddish "Poale Zion" journals.

He published his own poetry as well as translated poetry under an assumed name; among those was a translation of "Anhali" by Slobetsky (first in as part of the "Mincha" volume and later separately in 5722) He always yearned for free time to engage in reading and language research. He was able to achieve this goal after his retirement from "Davar" (an Israeli newspaper) several years ago. He moved to Jerusalem and then published results of his research that included the "hidden megillot". These studies were remarkable in their innovation and deep understanding of the mysterious connection between the text and the language that seemed to be unrelated. He enjoyed discussing topics of language and Bible as well as current and past events. He was deeply interested in the many diverse topics connected by a common thread – Jewish roots with varied implications for both past and present.

("Davar" 11 Adar I–5727)

[Page 118, Volume 2]

Zev Bloch (Webtchyu) z"l

by Y. Fleisher

Translated by Daniel Kochavi

He passed away in Bet Alpha on 6/26/1963 at the age of 64.

He was born in a village near Tarnow, Galicia that nurtured his love of nature and people. His superior intelligence was apparent already at a young age. He completed his early education in religious class and the "Kloyz" school in Tarnow.

A graduate of the Tarnow gymnasium he was one of the founders of "HaShomer Hatzair" in town. He was the leader of the town group and one of the organizers of the Hagganah (defense troop) in Tarnow against the Polish thugs who ran wild when the new nation was founded at the end of WWI.

He was one of the first (and illegal) HaShomer Hatzair group of Olim (emigrants to Palestine) in January of 1920. He walked for a number of months through the Carpathians in Romania and reached Palestine on May 17, 1920.

Here he labored in road building, in the Galil in Upper Bethania. He was one of the founders of "Shomrei Rishon" kibbutz, Bet Alpha and the National Kibbutz. He went as an envoy to Romania and Poland. He was active in the National Kibbutz and in the Histadrut (worker organization) in the cultural and ideological areas. He lectured in Seminars, was a skilled publicist and wrote many articles and books. He was very devoted to the ideology of his movement.

Dr Naftali Szwarc z"l

by A.Kh.

Translated by Daniel Kochavi

He passed away in Tel Aviv at the age of 67 on November 18 1967. He was born in Tarnow to a family devoted to Zionism. A student in our town High School, he became acquainted with Judaism and Zionism.

After receiving a PhD in philosophy from the University of Vienna he went to work for a Jewish bank in Tarnow. After working as a banker, he moved to an Insurance company. His outstanding skills were quickly recognized and he became a senior member of insurance companies in Lvov and Warsaw.

Dr Naftali Szwarc was very active in the Zionist movement and various community affairs. During the debates in the 1930's concerning the merging of the "Histadrut" (Unity) and "Poale Zion" parties, Dr Szwarc was one of the major leaders in the "Histadrut" movement in eastern Galicia who was opposed to this merger and remained committed to the "Hitachdut" as envisioned by A.D. Gordon.

Dr Naftali Szwarc participated in several Zionist congresses and emigrated to Palestine in 1940. In Israel he worked at "Sneh" an Israeli insurance company.

[Page 119, Volume 2]

From the left: Naftali Szwarc, Shmuel Vandstein

After some time, he occupied an important position in this company. He published several books on insurance issues and was a lecturer at the "Insurance Institute".

Until his death Dr Naftali Szwarc was active in the National Council for the Prevention of Traffic Accidents and was a member of the Israel organization of insurance companies.

His friends and acquaintances valued his integrity and simplicity.

In memory of Ehud Shachar (Schwarz)

by A.Kh.

Translated by Daniel Kochavi

Ehud Shachar (Schwarz) was born in the year 5696 (1936) in Kibbutz Merchavia. His father Aron (Artek) Schwarz, a native of Tarnow, became an active member of "The Shomer Hatzair" after WWI in his native town. He emigrated to Palestine in 5685 (1925) and settled in Merchavia with his wife, Eliza, member of the Zaberski family, one of the founders of this Kibbutz.

Ehud studied at Merchavia Institute. He was, even as a youngster, "a mischievous and brave Tsabar (native Israeli)"[1]

In August 1954 he enlisted in Tzahal (Israel Armed forces). He was killed during the Gaza battle on 7 Adar 5715 (February 28 1955). He was 19.

His parents, relatives and friends in the Kibbutz mourn him deeply.

[Page 120]

Ehud Schachar (Swarch) z"l

His father–Artek recited the following at his funeral:

> Ehud, Ehud
> We raised and taught you
> We gave you all we could,
> We taught you to overcome the hardest trials,
> However, you overcame at much too high a price
> We are proud of you.
> You fell while doing your duty, as we taught you.
> They came from all parts of the land to honor you as befits you.
> You left us broken and shattered.
> For your sake, honor and memory we will go on living and working
> in the spirit that we taught you
> Goodbye dear son Ehud, rest in peace.[2]

His friends from the kibbutz also eulogized him: "Ehud was always the first to carry out the most difficult tasks required, with great joy, eagerness, devotion and great productivity".

Ehud was "a faithful member of the movement, devoted to the homeland, society, the Kibbutz, his family and his beloved group and all its members". [2]

His girl–friend from the Kibbutz wrote in the memorial pamphlet:

"He fell heroically and we are proud of him. We will continue our just fight to go on with life, and achieve the just peace we long for. Ehud will remain in our memories forever." [2]

We the people of Tarnow are also proud of Ehud Schachar (Schwarz), son of Artek Schwarz, a native of Tarnow.

Original footnotes:

1. From the eulogy by his friends at his burial (Pamphlet in memory of Ehud Schachar published by "Hashomer Hatzair" Merchavia)
2. From the memorial pamphlet mentioned above.

[Page 121, Volume 2]

C. Fragments of Tarnow's Jewish Community of the Past

– In Pictures–

Translated by David Schonberg

[Page 122, Volume 2]

The colorful and dynamic Jewish life of Tarnow has been well-described and in detail in a long series of articles and memories, both in the first volume and in this, the second volume, of the Tarnow memorial book (*yizkor-bukh*).

It would however be, without doubt, an exaggeration on our part to say that all aspects of the vibrant Jewish life in Tarnow have been fully described in these two volumes of the Tarnow memorial book.

Therefore, we thought it necessary to illustrate the various fragments of the past Jewish life in Tarnow with pictures that we have received from Tarnow Jews…

[Page 123, Volume 2]

The City

The market–place [Rynek] and the Municipality building prior to the Holocaust on a Sabbath

Wielke Schody Street– The 'Great Stairway' street

[Page 124, Volume 2]

Pilsner Gate Street– and its continuation (extension)– Lwowska (Lemberg) Street
Photograph. Bergman, 1964

Walowa Street
Photograph. Bergman, 1965

[Page 125, Volume 2]

Bernardyńska Street
Photograph. Bergman, 1965

Goldhammer Street
Photograph. Bergman, 1965

[Page 126, Volume 2]

Platz Wolnoszczi Street
At the time of the German occupation– it was called Magdeburg Square.
The house indicated with an X is where there previously was a bus station.
This square served as an assembly point for Jewish forced laborers and those awaiting deportation.
Photograph. Bergman, 1965

Train station
Photograph. Bergman, 1967

[Page 127, Volume 2]

The memorial stone that has remained undamaged until today, can be found in the house in Goldhammer Street. It was installed in honor of the founder of the 'credit company for business and industry' in Tarnow, Herman Merz z"l, the well-deserved public figure and head of the community (in the years around 1870). Thanks to his efforts a two-storied house was built and this credit institution took up the whole ground floor.

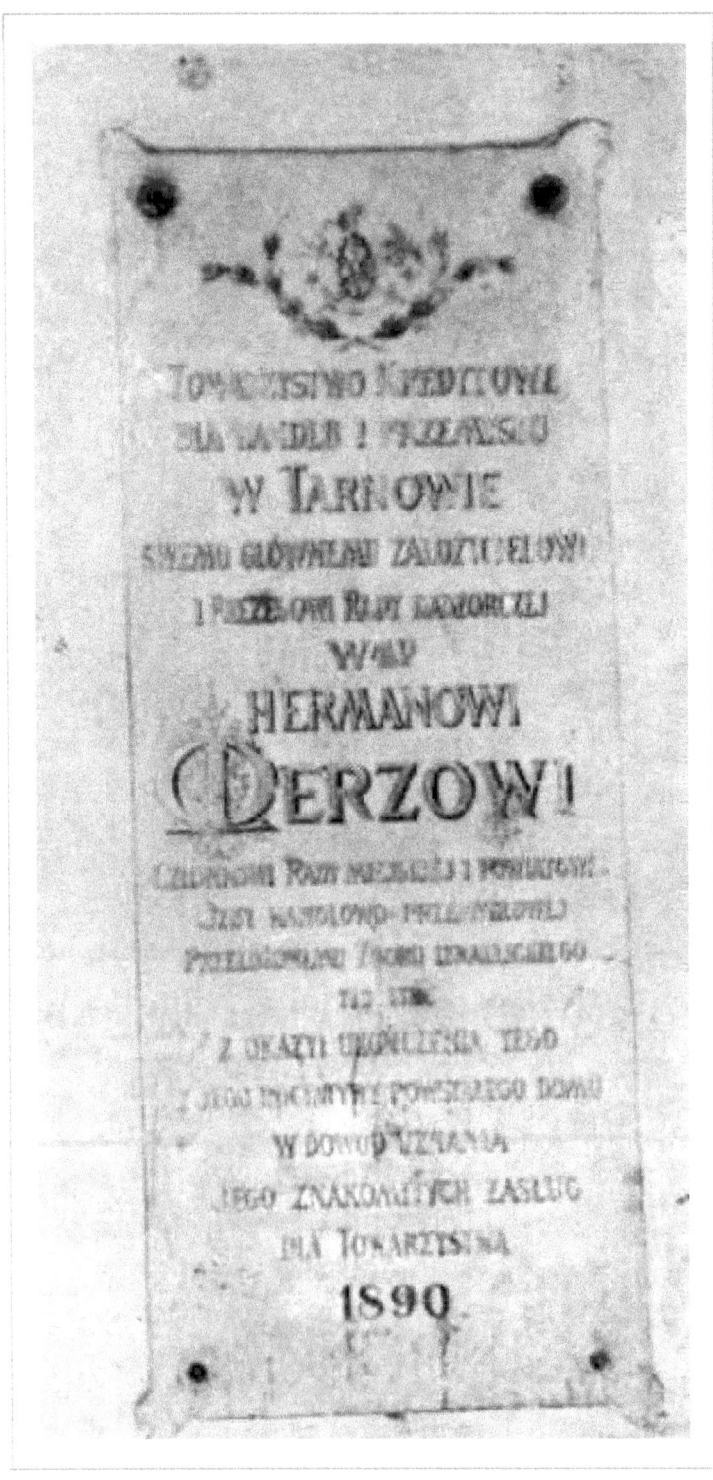

Photograph. Bergman, 1966

[Pages 128-129, Volume 2]

Fragments of Tarnow's Jewish Community of the Past – In Pictures {cont.}

From the Jewish life of Tarnow before the Holocaust

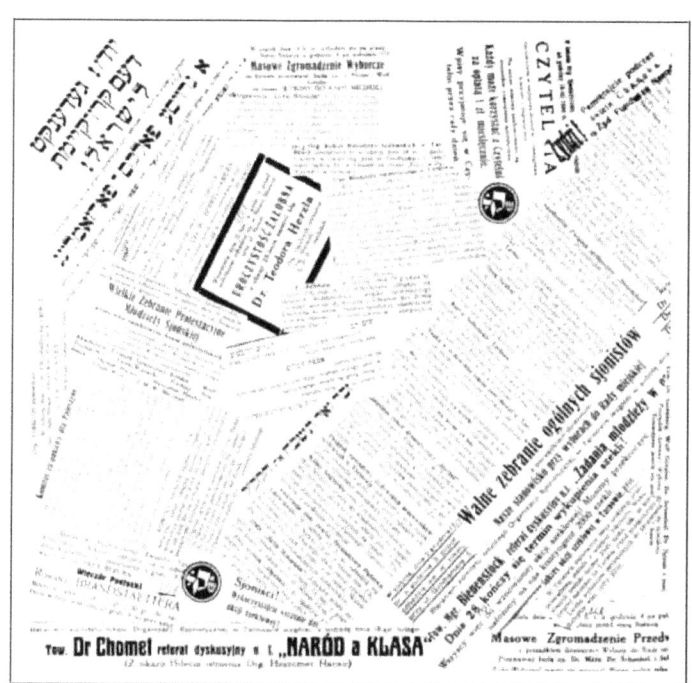 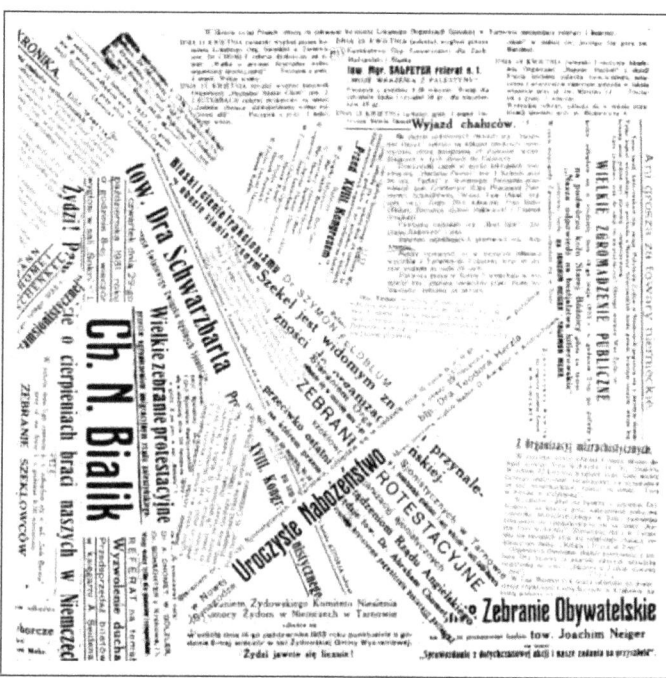

Tarnow Jewry from newspaper notices/ adverts – Tygodnik Zydowski *Jewish Wochenblatt* which appeared in Tarnow before the Holocaust

The Leadership of the Zionist youth group– *HaNoar HaZioni* in Tarnow, 1930

Sitting from left: Nahum Blumenkrantz (today in USA), Wysia Fingerman–Friman (today in Israel), Shlomo Yisrael (today in Canada)
Standing from left: Victor Weiss (today Attorney Levanoni, in Israel), Yaakov Bienenstock (today an attorney in Israel), Yosef Friman (today in Israel)

A group of Zionist youth on a trip in 1928

From the Socialist movement in Jewish Tarnow

1st May demonstration of youth– Bund– Zukunft [future] organisation, Tarnow, 1935

Young Poalei Zion' organisation in Tarnow, 1921

[Page 132, Volume 2]

Jewish officers from Tarnow in the Austrian army, at the time of the First World War

Standing from left: Betzalel Shpeizer, Yosef Uber, R. Wermuth, Dolek Lewinger, Zemel, Yisrael Feldstein, Koretz (lives in Canada), Margoliot Juliosh (lives in Israel), Emile Adler (lives in Israel), Wildstein, Lewinger Monek
Reclining: Dolek Eichhorn

[Page 133, Volume 2]

Friends' party

Sitting from left: Rottenberg, Weisman, Shtrobing, Yosef Israelowitz, Dolek Pomerantz, Avraham Yortner, Dr. Ignatz Goldfinger
In centre: Shlomo Eichhorn. Next to him, standing: Dr. Muskatenblit
Sitting from right: Grinfeld, Monek Katz, Olek Brand, Eichhorn, Yaakov Haber, Dr. Herman Pomerantz, Dr. Fenichel, Dr. Adolf Katz, Dr. Leibl

Football team of the *Shimshon* [Samson] sports organisation in Tarnow

The portrait of the well–known Tarnow philanthropist, Debora Wechsler z"l (who passed away in 1887). Until the outbreak of the Second World War it was hung in the reception area of the Jewish hospital in Tarnow. In her will the noble philanthropist bequeathed her two large houses in Tarnow– on Folwarczna and Nowa Streets - to the Jewish community, on condition that the income from the houses should go towards maintaining the Jewish hospital in Tarnow. Located in one of the houses on Nowa Street were the offices of the Jewish community. The portrait was found by our young Bergman in a Christian house in Tarnow.

[Page 135, Volume 2]

The community leadership call the Tarnow Jews to come to a special gathering in the synagogue 1.4.1924 (at 6pm) in connection with the opening of the Hebrew University in Jerusalem (and that shops should be closed at 6pm).

[Page 136, Volume 2]

Employees of the clothing factory of 'Zowder & Weinstock' in Tarnow before the Holocaust. Standing, third from the right is Abraham Singer – today in Toronto

Business school in Tarnow

Seated from the right: **Me'at–Ezrahi** (now a teacher in the Moriah school in Tel Aviv), Dr. Taube, Mrs. **Shnor**, Mrs. Einshpruch (director of school), Kleinhandler Anda, [–], Wildstein

[Page 137, Volume 2]

Business advertisements of Tarnow Jews

Photomontage– Dr. A. H. {Abraham Chomet}

[Page 138, Volume 2]

Fragments from the Tarnow cemetery

Matzeiva – tombstone on the grave of the great Rabbi (HaRav HaGaon) Meir Arak, zs"l
Photograph. Bergman, 1966

[Page 139, Volume 2]

Matzeiva – tombstone on the grave of the Rabbi, R' Leibishl Halberstam, zs"l

[Page 140, Volume 2]

Matzeiva – tombstone of R' Hermann Merz, z"l

Matzeiva – tombstone of R' Meyer Eckstein, z"l

Photograph. Bergman, 1966

[Page 141, Volume 2]

Matzeiva – tombstone of R' Ascher Shwanenfeld, z"l (1831–1896)

Matzeiva – tombstone of R' Shlomo Zalmen Shwanenfeld, z"l, son of R. Ascher Shwanenfeld, z"l, who died in 5681 (1921)

Photograph. Bergman, 1967

[Page 142, Volume 2]

Matzeiva – tombstone of R' Henryk Soldinger, z"l
– 5629– 5682 (1869–1922)

Matzeiva – tombstone of R' Simcha Keller, z"l
– died 5696 (1936)

Photograph. Bergman, 1966

[Page 143, Volume 2]

Matzeiva – tombstone of Rivka (Regina)
Komet (Chomet), z"l
– 5624– 5688 (1864–1928)

Matzeiva – tombstone of R' Shlomo (Salomon)
Komet (Chomet), z"l
– 5618–5693 (1858–1933)

Photograph. Dr. A.H. (Abraham Chomet), 1947

Matzeiva – tombstone of Dr. Emil Mutz, z"l – died 5684 (1924) and memorial plaque in memory of his brother Mgr. Leon Mutz, who died in Lwow, 1940

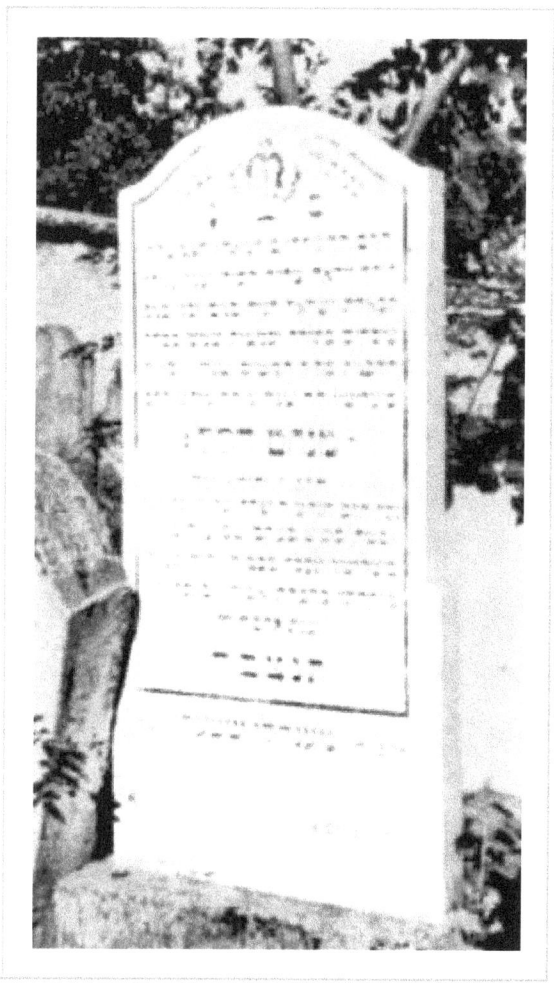

Matzeiva – tombstone on the kever of the Rabbi of Bielska, R' Menahem Hillel, z"l

Photograph. Bergman, 1966

[Page 145, Volume 2]

Matzeiva – tombstone of Dr. Emil Wieder, z"l and Dr. Maksymilian Rosenbusch, z"l who were murdered by the Nazis in the Holocaust

Matzeiva – tombstone of Mgr. Henryk Shpielman, z"l, who died in 1945

[Page 146, Volume 2]

The main entrance to the New Synagogue (*der nayer shul*) from the front – on Nowa Street

D. The Holocaust

[Page 149]

The Road of Pain and Suffering

by Yosef Kornilo, Ramat–Gan

Translated by Gloria Berkenstat Freund

Yosef Kornilo

On the eve of the war, at the end of August 1939, chaos already predominated in Tarnow. A timed–bomb exploded at the train station in Tarnow on August 28, 1939 at around 11 o'clock at night. Several people were murdered and many were wounded. The train station building was greatly damaged. This was a clear omen of the imminent outbreak of war with Hitler's Germany.

The German Army divisions crossed the Polish border on the 1st of September 1939. German tanks rolled on the Polish highways… Unhindered German bombers bombed Polish cities and *shtetlekh* [towns].

At the last minute, the Polish Army leadership made the greatest efforts in mobilizing large reserves in order to stop the raging march forward of the German Army.

I, too, a veteran sanitary officer, needed to appear at the Fifth Sanitary Battalion in Krakow. However, the train was no longer active… Masses of refugees arrived in Tarnow from Krakow and other localities… Jews ran in the eastern direction… [The] Polish Army division completely took control of the means of communication during the confusion to more quickly reach the San River.

[Page 150]

And when the Fifth Sanitary Battalion arrived in Tarnow, the entire division and I began to run to the east. The soldiers of my sanitary battalion, persecuted by the German bombers, ran away, hiding in the side fields and forest. I returned to Tarnow to my wife and two children through roundabout ways.

The Germans already were ruling the city.

Divisions of the German Army took Tarnow on the 8th of September 1939. A few days barely passed and the evil members of the Gestapo began their criminal activities. The *Kripo* (German criminal police), too. The *S.S.* and the Polish police, which was called *Granatowa policja* [Blue police] because they wore dark blue uniforms, immediately began to rule the city.

The first action by the Gestapo was the designation of a commissariat city managing committee to which only Poles belonged at first and after a time the managing committee was taken over by the Germans.

As Germans moved in, several officials took over the most beautiful Jewish residences in the city.

The "county chief" became the first ally of the Germans. The German occupiers immediately began to persecute the Jewish population. Commissar *treuhänder* [trustees] were placed in all Jewish enterprises and large businesses. Searches of Jewish residences were carried out daily, systematically, during which Jewish possessions were stolen. The Germans provided for their families in Germany and took everything from the Jews that had value and could be used by their wives and children in Germany.

The German rulers stole everything: expensive silver and gold items, crystal, rugs and rare furniture. They dragged me from my residence more than once and requisitioned me to take the stolen items of value to the store–houses.

Grabbing Jews in the streets, first from the circles of the Jewish intelligentsia, and forcing them to work at cleaning and sweeping the streets was a daily event. Young German *S.S.*–members with the *totenkopf* [skull and crossbones] on their hats

[Page 151]

ill–treated with cruel savagery the enslaved Jewish "street–cleaners" who, in addition, had to sing and dance under murderous blows.

On a cold, frosty winter day, the Germans forced me to work to clear away the snow.

– 2 –

On the 12th of September 1939 the first announcements appeared on the walls of the houses proclaiming that Jewish shops need to be identified with a white–blue *Mogen–Dovid* [shield of David – a Jewish star] insignia of 15 centimeters in diameter. In addition, not only the doors of the shops but the various signs also had to be identified that way. There was a very severe penalty for violating this order.

In order to undermine the financial existence of the Jewish population, all of the accounts, deposits and safes of Jews in the banks were blocked, according to an order of the 18th of September 1939. In addition, they had to deposit a sum of more than 2,000 *zlotys* in a "savings account," from which they could take out at most 250 *zlotys* a week.

It was the Jewish artisans who met the greatest number of different administrative restrictions, who had to struggle with the greatest of difficulties in order to maintain their workshops.

Thus, the needs of the Jewish neighborhood in Tarnow grew greater every day and poverty and hunger intruded into Jewish homes. Tarnow Jews began to sell their jewelry and other valuable things in order to be able to endure the difficult time. Those who did not have anything to sell were hungry and depended upon the help of their relatives and friends or of the Jewish community, which had only available a limited range of social support and activities.

– 3 –

On the 23rd of November 1939, a new edict was published that ordered all Jews of both sexes older than 10 years to wear a white band on the left arm, 10 centimeters [almost four inches] wide with a blue *Mogen Dovid* [Shield of David – Star of David] sewn on it. The members of the Jewish *Kehilla* [organized Jewish community] managing committee wore stiff armbands with an embroidered *Mogen–Dovid* so that they could be distinguished from other Jewish residents. Jewish doctors were permitted to wear another armband with the inscription *ARTZ* [doctor].

[Page 152]

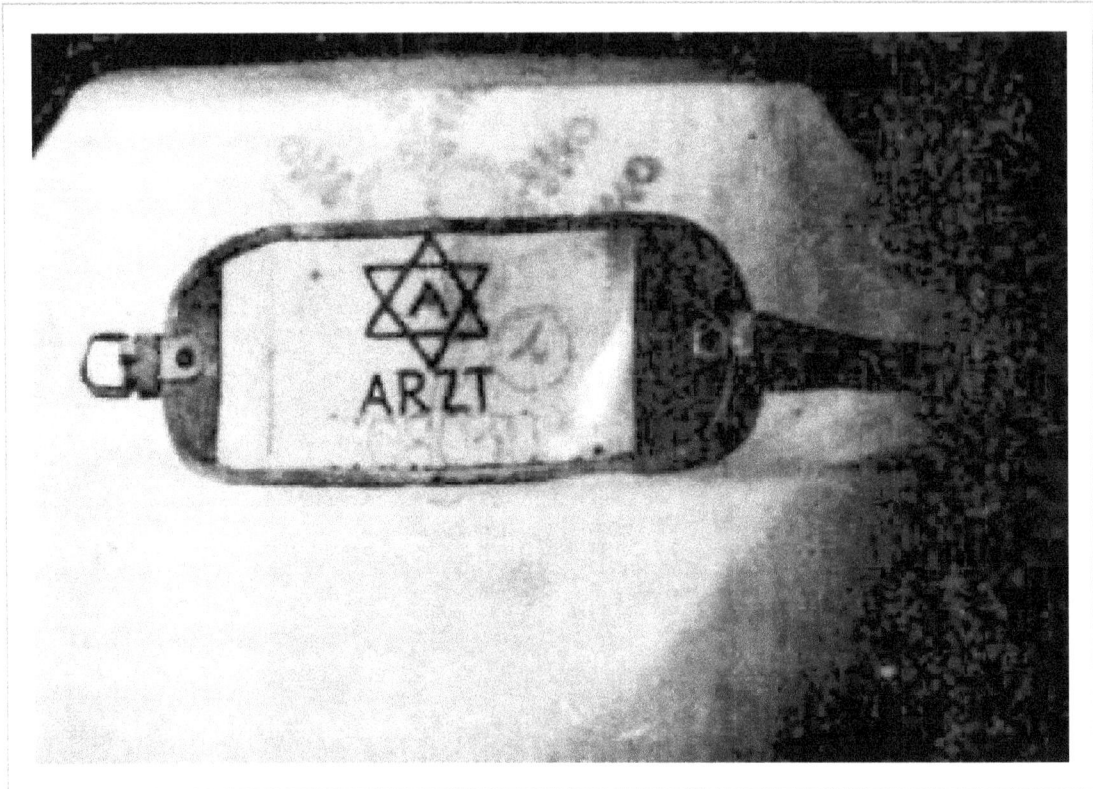

The armband with the inscription *ARTZ* [doctor]

The German regime officials as well as the Polish police placed great weight on the cleanliness of the armbands and there was a monetary penalty or arrest for several hours for a dirty armband. There was the threat of jail for not wearing the armband.

Converts to Christianity were on a par with all of the other Jews. Conversions were of no help and the converts shared the fate of the entire Jewish population in Tarnow. For example – when the Gestapo members [Gerhard] Grunoff and [Karl] Oppermann were in the residence of the convert Engineer Bester on Chopin Street 4, while they carried out the stolen things of value, they had the opportunity to notice that among those present in the residence, only one woman wore an armband. Oppermann did not hesitate… He drove all those present who were not wearing an armband out of the residence to the courtyard of the house and shot everyone. Only the woman with the armband remained alive.

[Page 152]

– 4 –

The lives of the Jewish population in Tarnow became more difficult with each day. Every cultural and communal activity ceased during the first weeks of the German occupation. Several Jewish schools and unions were closed. At every turn, the German rulers made us feel that our lives were dispensable. From day to day the violent acts became more barbarous. Meeting a German in the street, a Jew had to greet him and take off his hat from his head. Every German had the right to take a Jew for any work, even the most difficult. Day or night he could drag a Jew from his residence or shop or grab him in the street for this purpose. The German officers made use of us in carrying baggage, in cleaning their autos, in loading goods and heavy materials, in pulling porters' wagon, etc. In addition, we were pelted with curse words, such as *Jew die*, pig Jew, tough Jew. The wage for such work was a blow to the stomach or in the lower part of the back.

Jewish women who had learned household management well were assigned to work as servants to the high Gestapo and police officers.

And when Germans wanted to occupy themselves and ridicule the Jews, they would call two or more Jews on the street and order them to bloodily beat each other.

The torture and torment of the Jews often took on a larger scope. At every opportunity the Germans would threaten to shoot those Jews who were grabbed on the street or in their residences in order to watch with a sadistic joy the fear they evoked from their victims.

On a winter day at the end of 1939 – on the eve of the Christian holiday – the German murderers caught several Jews in the street and led them to the former cavalry barracks at Chiszower Street where the *S.S.* members now lived. There, all of the grabbed Jews were driven into a large room where they were ordered to stand with their faces to the wall. Then they were told to kneel and to hold their hands high. An *S.S.* man immediately came in and ordered everyone to say their confessions and he disappeared with the words, "These are your last minutes." After him appeared a broad–shouldered *S.S.* man in a long, white linen coat and with a butcher knife in his hand.

[Page 154]

It is easy to imagine the fear that fell on the people when the *S.S.* man took out the first of the row of kneeling Jews. After several minutes he returned and there were signs of blood on his linen coat and knife. He immediately led out the second of the rows and again returned immediately with a more bloodied linen coat and knife and he continued in this way until he had led out the last Jews in the house.

Each time he led a Jew into the neighboring house, the *S.S.* man in the white linen coat slaughtered a goose with the long knife and the captured Jew had to flick the feathers, clean and prepare the goose for a large meal that was to take place in the *S.S.* barracks. After more hours of this work, the Jews were freed. Such horrible cases, whose purpose was not only to make fun of and to deride the Jewish population, but also to debase them and to weaken their morale, were daily phenomena.

– 5 –

On the 4th of November 1939 new edicts were published: Jews were forbidden to work in state institutions, to trade with Aryans, to undergo treatment by Aryan medical personnel; Jewish *ARTZ* doctors were forbidden to take Aryan patients. Jews were not permitted to take seats in the front part of the Tarnow tramway. All Jews employed in the various offices were dismissed from work without any compensation.

A terrible panic and dread fell on the Tarnow Jews when on the 9th of November 1939, the German barbarians, under the pretext of [the Jews] not having paid the high tax [placed on them], set fire to all of the synagogues and houses of prayer in Tarnow. These various actions destroyed all of the synagogues in the Jewish neighborhood in Tarnow in a single day. Along with the religious books and the Torah scrolls, the ancient Old Synagogue and the houses of prayer, as well as the Devora Menkes Synagogue and the Struszina Synagogue were burned down. No trace remained of the small synagogues, of the *minyonim* [prayer groups of 10 men required for organized prayer] and the *shtiblekh* [one–room synagogues] that were supported by the Tarnow rabbis. The Tempel Synagogue with its organ and the Porters' Synagogue on Grabowka, where Jewish laborers and men of the people prayed, disappeared in smoke. The heavy brick walls of the New Synagogue were exploded with dynamite [and] the synagogue was completely burned. Only one lopped off column of the magnificent sacred building remained, which today stands in the Tarnow Jewish cemetery as a memorial over the mass grave of the exterminated Tarnow Jewry. On the spot on which the Old Synagogue stood, near Fisz–Platz, the Bima [Torah reading desk] from the synagogue remains standing.

[Page 155]

All efforts trying to get the Gestapo officers to stop the horrible annihilation actions were without success. On the contrary – it was strongly forbidden to undertake any means to put out the fire.

A feeling of insecurity and confusion entered our hearts after this extraordinary German annihilation action. In addition, the systematic capture of the Jews in the streets and the economic repression affected the spread of poverty into an even larger number of Jewish houses. Yesterday's rich men [today] began to wrestle with material worries. On the part of the social divisions at the Jewish *Kehila* [organized Jewish community], efforts were made to alleviate the need in the Jewish neighborhood, but the limited means of the then *Kehila* managing committee did not permit the development of wider aid action on behalf of the impoverished Jewish population.

Simultaneously, a Jewish curfew was introduced. According to the order of the 11th of December 1939, Jews were forbidden to leave their residences as well as appear on the roads, streets and squares from seven o'clock at night until five in the morning. Only the members of the *Kehila* managing committee and a number of medical personnel [ARTZ] received permission to be on the street at that time. However, they refused this privilege, not wanting to be exposed to various dangers.

– 6 –

On the 18th of September 1939 it was ordered that the armband be worn on the right arm instead of the left arm.

[Page 156]

The same month, the Germans created a *Judenrat* [Jewish council] with a "Jewish elder" at the head in place of the *kehile* managing committee. The seat of the *Judenrat* was located in the Jewish Community building of the Kehila at Nova Street 11, with the main entrance on Folwarczna Street, and its task was mainly carrying out the orders of the German regime thugs in all matters regarding the Jewish population. As a result, the administrators of the Jewish Hospital, of the old people's and orphan's houses and of other Jewish institutions belonged to the *Judenrat*.

At first, at the heads of the *Judenrat* were honest and esteemed communal workers who truly believed that they would be able to diminish the severity of the German anti–Jewish edicts with their influence. Among the first leaders of the *Judenrat* in Tarnow were the serious leaders who, immediately sensing the true intentions of the German power holders, refused this dubious "honor" or completely escaped from Tarnow. Or the Gestapo liquidated them at the Auschwitz death camp, as happened to the most devoted Zionist leaders, Dr. Szenkel and Dr. Goldberg and others. From 1940 until the complete annihilation of Tarnow Jewry, Folkman as the "Jewish elder" and Y. Lerhaupt as his representative, were the heads of the Tarnow *Judenrat*.

Sztub, Frenkel, Y. Fast and Klajnhendler among others now belonged to this *Judenrat*. Employed in the chancellery of the *Judenrat* were more officials, such as, among others, the previous *Kehila* officials: T. Laufer, Dora Sztram, the previous *kehila* officials E. Zauersztorm, Honig the *Magister* [holder of a university degree] and Reshka Faber.

Even earlier, the *Judenrat*, according to an order from the Germans of the 4th of November 1939, compiled a list of all Jewish residents in Tarnow. In addition, a separate list was made of the well–off and a separate list of the Jews capable of work. On the basis of such a list, the Gestapo men carried out a search of the well–off part of the Jewish population during which they stole every expensive thing that they found. During this plundering, the Gestapo members *Pan* [Mister] Malutki and Nowak excelled, and in addition they murderously beat the owners of the things they stole.

[Page 157]

A number of Jews were chosen daily from the list of those people capable of work, and were supplied to the Gestapo for various heavy labor on behalf of the Germans. Jews could buy themselves out of such work by paying the *Judenrat* [Jewish council] a certain sum of money from which some of the money would be provided to those who were sent to work in their place.

In the courtyard of the house in which the guard of the *Judenrat* was located stood a wooden cell that served as a temporary jail. I would often come to the office of the *Judenrat* to take care of various matters and at one such opportunity I saw a member of the Gestapo leading to the cell a Jew whom he had caught on the street, because he undoubtedly was not wearing an armband. And immediately afterwards one heard a shot from a revolver.

In this courtyard there always stood a corpse wagon and a group of Jews from the *Chevra Kadisha* [burial society] on duty, whose task was to bring the Jews shot in the streets to the cemetery and to bury them there.

The *Judenrat* had to take care that all of the demands of the higher Gestapo and police officers and make sure their families were satisfied. For this purpose an economic administrative division was created at the *Judenrat* whose task was to provide the German rulers with luxurious residences and club facilities, with the most expensive cosmetic articles, with rare delicacies and the most modern furniture. A special Jewish tailor and shoemaker workshop also was active that worked for the Gestapo and police officers. It should be understood that this was without any payment.

Jewish wagon drivers had to be prepared at all times to drive these German murderers around and observe their cruelty. Of all the Jewish wagon drivers of that time, [only] Yisroel Izak survives, who today lives in Israel.

The managing committee of the Jewish Hospital, which remained under the leadership of the pre–war director, Dr. Eugeniusz Sziper, also belonged to the *Judenrat*. He fulfilled his task with self–sacrifice along with a group of diligent and dedicated doctors, such as Dr.

Lustik, Dr. Marcin Block and his wife, Dr. Tessa, Dr. Chaim Wachtel, Dr. R. Hendler, Dr. E. Schochter and Dr. Ziegfried. During the most difficult occupation conditions the entire medical personnel, as well as nurses and all ancillary personnel, contributed to the survival of many patients in the Jewish hospital. It was an extraordinarily difficult struggle to acquire the necessary medicine for the sick and to acquire everything that was needed to continue permitting the activity of the hospital. In addition, helping the doctors and nurses were young medics, such as among others: Leon Rajch, G. Osterwejl, Chaim Faber . Many others worked with great fervor as medics, and, as has already been said, all of the nurses, who despite great danger, devotedly and courageously stood at their posts.

[Page 158]

In addition to the general medical facilities, a dental clinic also existed at the Jewish hospital.

The Jewish hospital received great help from a group of volunteer co–workers who did not spare any effort or strength in their work on behalf of the sick. Among this well prepared voluntary auxiliary the nurse Chaim Organd stood out as well as others employed as nurses: Mrs. Organd, Royza Wachtel, Langer and Mrs. Krumholc from Krakow.

The leaders of the general city hospital, with a Ukrainian at its head, tried to undermine the existence of the Jewish Hospital and in 1941 after a series of persecutions on the part of the German power organs, the Jewish Hospital was moved to the building adjacent, to the Jewish old age home building, which was remodeled with great effort and hardship and made appropriate to the needs of a hospital institution.

After the third deportation action, the Jewish Hospital was again moved to a house on Boznic Street. In addition, the Gestapo took almost all of the instruments and medicines during the relocation. A primitive Jewish hospital was again barely organized with great difficulty; the *S.S.* members during the final liquidation of the Tarnow ghetto, shot all of the sick who lay in the hospital and stole all of the remaining medical instruments and medicines.

[Page 159]

– 7 –

Our life was bitter and melancholy in 1940. Pressed together in a crowded residence, with constant insecurity and fear, seized for work or arrested without any reason, we had to struggle under the heavy burden of the new decrees.

On the first day of the German occupation, General Governor [Hans] Frank banned kosher slaughtering of meat and in October 1939 forced labor by the Jews was arranged for the entire area of occupied Poland.

Frank banned the use of trains by Jews with the order of the 26th of January 1940.

Jews were forbidden to leave their residences on the 17th of April 1940 in connection with some German celebration. A similar ban was made public on the 30th of April 1940 because of the 1st of May holiday. In addition, Tarnow Jews were not supposed to look out of their windows.

In order to throw fear into the Jewish population in Tarnow, a further group of esteemed Jews, among others the lawyers Dr. Emil Wider, Dr. Yitzhak Holzer, the director of the Hebrew school, Dr. Rozenbush, and the industrialist Yakov Schwartz were deported to Auschwitz at the beginning of 1940. Such Jews could be a hindrance for the annihilation plans of the German hangmen in relation to Tarnow Jewry. First, they had to be liquidated and annihilated.

At first it was permissible to help out Jews who were imprisoned in jail with food packages. However, this was also immediately forbidden. From time to time large transports of arrestees from the Tarnow jail were deported to Auschwitz. It was rare for someone to return alive from there. Later, the relatives would a receive a notice about the death of the deported arrestee. After paying a certain sum of money, the relatives received a canister of ashes of the burned corpse.

In 1940 the Tarnow jail already was overflowing. The Gestapo arrested Jews and Poles for transgressions of the orders from the large number of various edicts that made life difficult.

On the 14th of June 1940, a transport of over 700 prisoners in the Tarnow jail was deported to Oswiecim, which the German rulers gave the name Auschwitz. This was a transport of Jews and Poles from Tarnow and from a series of cities and *shtetlekh* in mid–Galicia, such as Rzeszów, Nowy Sacz and Nowy Targ; the majority, were people who had awakened some suspicion that they were hostile to the Hitlerist regime.

[Page 160]

The monument in front of the *mikvah* [ritual bath] – designated by the letter "v" – from which the first transport of arrested Tarnow citizens left for Auschwitz

The train of arrestees, a train of men, many of whom did not return to their families, left at dawn on that day from Boznic Street near the *mikvah* [ritual bath]. Among them were young and old men, exhausted from the terrifying investigations and horrible rack of torture by the Gestapo oppressors at Urulanska Street 18 – all from various trades, workers and apprentices, former officers in the Polish Army, lawyers, priests, merchants, peasants and students.

At that time it was quiet and empty on the Tarnow streets. A public warning had gone out several days earlier that on the 14th of June it was forbidden to appear on the street and one must not stand at the window of a residence. However, we were already awake and under the drapes at our window; we watched the train of the unfortunate ones, very many of whom, under the guard of the German police, were going on their last road.

[Page 161]

At the train station in Tarnow before loading of the arrested on the transport to Auschwitz

[Page 162]

The train went from Boznic Street to Pod Dębem Platz and from there to the freight train station where everyone was loaded into freight cars and the transport left in the direction of Auschwitz.

– 8 –

On the 25th of August 1940 a German "labor office" was opened in Tarnow, where all Jews age 12 and older had to register. The "labor office" gave out work cards with photographs, which everyone had to have with them at all times. Every month one had to appear at the "labor office" for a check, which often had a very tragic ending because young, healthy Jews would be deported directly to a labor camp in Pustkow (near Dembitz) or to Stalowa Wola from this office. In general, if Jews returned from these camps, they were broken and exhausted. Invalids, the old and sick, who had been through a medical examination and received a certificate that they were incapable of working, were freed from such forced labor. Their fate was already sealed.

During one of the murder actions in occupied Tarnow

[Page 163]

On the 15th of September 1940, Jews were forbidden to wear fur. All fur clothing, all fur items, mountain climbing shoes and radio apparatus had to be turned into the Gestapo storehouse at the Apollo movie theater. Jewish men and women stood in long rows for hours until they reached the German hangman and gave him the expensive fur clothing and radio apparatus – without any compensation. Those who did not turn in these items were threatened with the death penalty.

After completing the robbery action, searches were carried out in the Jewish residences. Woe to whomever was found with the least little bit of fur items.

In addition to the great wave of edicts, which made life difficult, there was the terrible plague of the constant seizing [of people] on the street, the baseless arrests and the frequent shooting of completely innocent people.

Every day the German murderers under the least pretext would drag Jews into the Gestapo office and after severe torture, they were taken from there, outside of the city, near the power station or to the Lipie forest to the castle mountain and even farther to Zbylitowska Mountain, where they would be shot. For the work of burying the bodies, the German police would seize Jews encountered by chance on the streets and take them to the execution sites to work digging mass graves. The Germans would place the Jews condemned to death along the dug out mass grave, order them to take off their clothes until nakedness. A German murderer would read the sentence. The crack of a machine gun salvo deafened the wailing of the victims. Their bodies fell into the open pit, which immediately was covered with dirt, and the Jews who were employed as diggers and were present during such horrible executions were strongly forbidden to describe what they had seen. So that they would not forget this order, the Germans, like angry animals, would beat them with murderous blows. Then they returned to their homes, bloodied, half alive.

The peasants who lived in the neighborhood of this mass grave would say that after the executions they would hear human moaning from under the ground. The Jews, covered alive with dirt, suffered horribly in their death throes until they exhaled their holy souls.

[Page 164]

It was very difficult for Jewish children who were suddenly torn from their home environment and with their compassion watched the fear of their parents, instinctively understanding the tragedy of their situation.

My 11-year-old daughter, Halinka [diminutive of Halina], often asked us various questions, from which it was clear that she had established and understood that it was the questions about a war against the Jews. She would always repeat: Sooner or later our turn will come.

My two children: Edit, of blessed memory; and may she have a long life, Halinka (today Mrs. Feingold in Paris)

[Page 165]

It was worse obtnaining coal for heat because it could only be bought on the black market at high prices. The death penalty was threatened for price gouging.

Therefore, it was impossible to buy life's necessities in the city or in the neighboring area at the free market. Even to appear at a confectionary or coffee house was forbidden to Jews.

Hunger, need and illness now reigned in Jewish houses.

– 9 –

The year 1941 began with new anti–Jewish edicts and atrocities by the German occupiers. The German regime became stricter in regard to the Jewish population. The German murderers prepared for the extermination actions in Jewish Tarnow with systematic forethought. At the beginning of February 1941 they accused the Jews in Tarnow, [claiming] that one of them had wounded *Pan* [Mr.] Malutki, a member of the Gestapo, while he was carrying out a search. Like wild animals, the Germans threw themselves at the Jews who by chance found themselves on the streets of Tarnow and they shot many of them.

At this time, a group of Jews who had escaped from Tarnow to Russian– occupied eastern Galicia at the outbreak of the war decided to return. The Gestapo immediately began [dealing with them] as soon as they arrived, searching their residences, accompanied with murderous blows. In addition, several of them were tortured in a beastly manner and others were arrested. Thus, Engineer Szif, the *ARTZ* [medical practioner] Dr. Holender, the rabbi of Biala near Bielko, Dr. Hirszfeld who, after the outbreak of the Second World War, returned from Switzerland from the Zionist Congress and stopped in Tarnow, were among the Jews who returned to Tarnow from the Soviet areas and were shot; the iron merchant, Osterwajl, and the owner of the hotel, Meir Wajs, were tortured. Arrested then was the former officer in the Polish Army, Dr. Betsalel Szpajzer, who returned from Lemberg and was imprisoned in the cellar of the Gestapo in Bergman's iron storehouse building at Urshulanska Street. He was murderously tortured during frequent investigations. At every investigation, the Gestapo members (mainly Grunoff and Oppermann) cut off a part of his body (ears, the nose, the fingers) until he was tortured to death.

[Page 166]

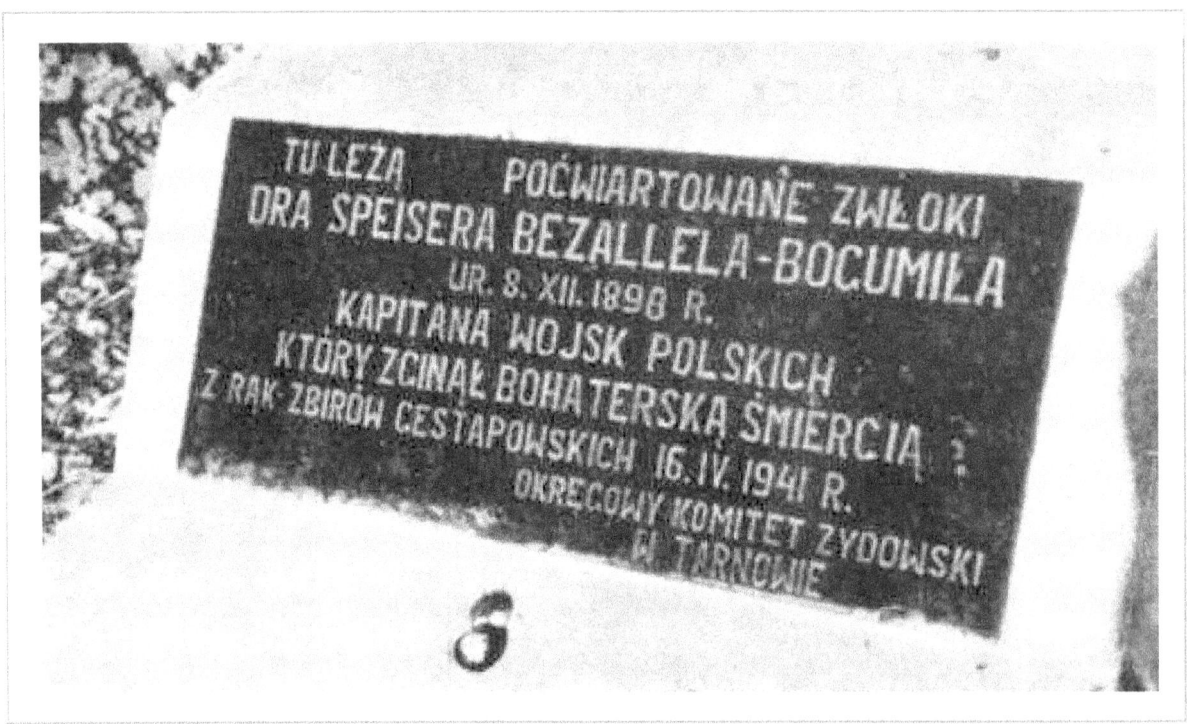

Headstone of Betsalel Szpajzer, of blessed memory, who was murdered by the Nazis in Tarnow in the year 1941

The Gestapo gave the cut–up body to the *Judenrat* in a basket.

At the time, Chaim Faber worked as a carpenter in the Gestapo building and, therefore had the ability to communicate with the unfortunate Dr. Szpajzer and also had precise news about the cruelties that took place in the Gestapo building. He actually spoke about the horrible suffering of Dr. Szpajzer and even turned to the *Judenrat* for help for him. He paid for this act with his life. He also was murdered in the Gestapo cellar. Both martyrs, Dr. Betsalel Szpajzer and Chaim Faber, were buried on the Tarnow cemetery. After the liberation of Tarnow, the Jewish Committee erected a headstone on the graves of both proud Tarnow Jews.

Starting with the 18th of February 1941, Tarnow Jews were not permitted to appear on the Tarnow streets and on the 20th of February the ban was expanded to include the trains and various and sundry other transportation means, such as autos, tramways and even simple wagons. Thus, for every train trip, a special permission from the county chief was necessary but was very difficult to obtain.

[Page 187]

Headstone of Reb Chaim Faber who was murdered at the hands of the Goths [Germans] in 5702 [1942]

On the 16th of October 1941 an order was published according to which it was forbidden for Jews to wear full beards and whiskers for "sanitary reasons." Under the same order, it was forbidden [for Jews] to walk on these streets: Krakowska (from the beginning of Komendatur Street), Walowa , Breyter, the market, Katedralna (including Kazimer Platz up to the market), the small and large staircases, Plac Rybny and Szlos Street (Zatkowa).

Jews were forbidden to stay and to walk in the area of the entire western part of Tarnow. In addition, at the same time the streets were indicated by which all Jews who still were living in the western area of the city could come to the eastern area of Tarnow.

[Page 168]

```
ANORDNUNG

1./ Aus sanitären Gründen ist den Juden das Tragen von Voll- und Backen-
    bärten verboten.

    Zuwiderhandlungen werden mit Geldstrafe bis zu 100 Zl und 14 Tagen
    Haft bestraft.

2./ Juden ist das Begehen:

    der Krakauerstrasse / von der Kommandanturstrasse ab/
    der Wallstrasse
    der Breite-Strasse
    der Marktstrasse
    der Kathedralstrasse einschliesslich Kasimir-Platz bis zum Ring
    der Kleinen und Grossen Treppe
    der Bastei-Treppe
    der Fischgasse
    und der Festungsgasse verboten.

3./ Auch das Begehen der Querstrasse zu diesen Strassen ist bis zu einer
    Entfernung von 100 m. verboten.

4./ Der Aufenthalt und das Spazierengehen ist den Juden im ganzen
    West-Stadtteil verboten.

5./ Die im West-Stadtteil wohnenden Juden können den Ost-Stadtteil auf
    der südlichen Gehwegseite der Narutowicz-Strasse oder auf der
    südlichen Gehwegseite der Linden und Mickiewicz-Strasse, die auf dem
    Ring wohnenden Juden können den Ostteil nur durch das Pilsener Tor
    erreichen.

6./ Der Zugang zu den Dienst- und Geschäftsgebäuden, die auf den verbote-
    nen Strassen gelegen sind, ist nur von der nächsten angrenzenden
    Querstrasse möglich.

7./ Zur Durchführung dieser Anordnung wird ein Ordnungsdienst beim Juden-
    rat errichtet. Er trägt eine Armbinde mit dem Judenstern und der
    Aufschrift "Ordnungsdienst beim Judenrat in Tarnow" und eine Dienst-
    nummer auf linker der Brustseite in Judensternform.

    Zuwiderhandlungen werden mit 100 Zl Geldstrafe bestraft.

    Diese Anordnungen treten sofort in Kraft.

                Tarnow, den 16. Oktober 1941.

                            Der Stadtkommissar:
                            Dr. Hein
```

The Nazi order of the 16th of October 1941, according to which Tarnow Jews were forbidden to wear beards and to walk on the main streets

To carry out these orders, an *Ordnungsdienst* [Jewish ghetto police] was created at the Tarnow *Judenrat* whose members had to wear armbands with a Mogen Dovid [Shield of David – a Jewish star) with the following inscription: *Ordnungsdienst* at the *Judenrat* in Tarnow, with the service number on the left side of the chest. Zigmund Miler was designated as the commandant of the *Ordnungsdienst* and Herman Waserman as his representative. Flugejzen, V. Lerner, Bajczer, Cymerman, Holender, Cimet, Traum and Gruszow, among others, belonged to the *Ordnungsdienst*. Cymerman was sentenced to death by the Tarnow Court after the war.

10

The year 1942 is recorded tragically in the history of Tarnow Jewry. The grabbing of Jews off the streets, shooting them without any reason and ordering the shrinking of the area where Jews could live, the robbery actions and the frequent driving of Jews from their residences – all of these forms of brutality were now daily events.

[Page 169]

The highpoint of the persecutions and murder actions of the German rulers was reached in the month of April 1942, after the outbreak of the German–American War. The out of control members of the Gestapo shot at every Jew they encountered on the streets of the city. The Gestapo members, [Wilhelm] Rommelmann, Grunoff, [Unger Otto] Jek, [Gerhard] Gaa, [Karl] Oppermann. Libor, Ilkow, Rommelmann and [Matthias] Kotruvan all of whom were sentenced to death by hanging by a Tarnow court after the war[a] were cruel with their sadistic, murderous vicious actions. The Gestapo commandant in Tarnow at that time was [Josef] Palten and the police commandant was the German officer Straus, who took part in all murder actions in Tarnow. His representative was the *Wachtmeister* [in charge of guard duty] Wunder.

At the beginning of 1942 we worked in the Tarnow *Judenrat* office with particular diligence. The carrying out of the registration of the Tarnow Jewish population according to which lists of the Tarnow Jews were assembled in great secrecy based on separate groups of those capable of working and those incapable of work, old people, invalids and those who received special help from the social divisions of the *Judenrat*.

A notation was made on the *meldkart* [registration card] of those incapable of work and of their families: "Incapable of work." Meanwhile, this group was left alone. They worked at their employment at home, not having any thought of what threat awaited them.

At the beginning of the month of June 1942, all registration cards were checked. At various places in the city, as well as at the Gestapo office, various commissions stamped the registration cards. A number of cards received a round stamp with the insignia of a swastika, the so–called "national emblem," and others received the printed letter "K." The significance of this insignia was understood in various ways.

Some said that the round stamp must signify "needed" for work and "on the contrary, the letter "K" must signify *krematorium* or *kaput* [broken].

[Page 170]

The fact was that all who had the comment "incapable" on their identification cards at the new registration now received the mark "K."

At the same time, the number of acts of terror and murder in Jewish Tarnow rose.

On the 10th of June 1942, announcements about the deportation of the Jewish population of Tarnow began to appear on the walls of the houses. A list, which had been put together by the labor office and contained the names of workers [considered] incapable of working, old and sick Jews, of women and children served as the basis for the deportation. Everyone recorded on the list of Jewish residents of Tarnow who were not able to work were informed by emissaries of the *Judenrat* to appear on the 11th of June 1942 at six o'clock in the morning at the gate the open ghetto around the Jewish residences . In addition, they were only permitted to bring with them 25 kilos of baggage.

On the 11th of June, all other Jews, who had not received such demands, were forbidden to leave their residences.

This day was difficult and tragic for Tarnow Jewry. Shooting was heard in the streets very early. A German gendarme division, S.S. members and Polish militiamen drove the frightened Jews, who already were waiting at the gates of their houses, in the direction of the marketplace. Jews from all corners of the city walked, confused, loaded with valises and bundles of supplies, including linens and even with work tools. With the butts of their rifles the German murderers beat Jews who had stopped for even a second to catch their breath. The marketplace immediately was filled with Jews. Under the hail of blows with rifle butts and whips, the Jews had to kneel, holding their heads bent to the ground. The Gestapo commandant [Josef] Palten was cruel and terrorized the assembled Jews with the help of his bandit–like members of the Gestapo and S.S. The entire murderous action was led by Martin Fellenz, the S.S. officer from Krakow, who was sent especially to oversee the deportation action in Tarnow.

The barbarity and the rampaging over the kneeling Jews at the marketplace by the vicious and uncontrollable members of the Gestapo and the Ukrainian bandit–like militiamen surpassed any human comprehension.

Jews, who appeared incapable of work in the eyes of the hangmen, all old people, the sick and children, were shot on the spot or were taken by trucks to be killed and buried within the mass graves at the Tarnow cemetery or at the Zbylitowska mountain. In the course of the day, trucks loaded with Jews who had been tortured and shot in the marketplace in Tarnow traveled back and forth on the road from the marketplace to the cemetery. One victim lay on top of the other [so that] the people on the street would not notice who was being taken.

[Page 171]

Jews, confused, loaded with valises and bundles, came from all corners of the city in the direction of the marketplace

The fate was cruel for the innocent, still very young children, whom the German and Ukrainian murderers, wild animals in human form, grabbed by their small feet and banged their heads on the cobblestones at the marketplace. The wails from women were heartrending when they were forced to tear themselves from their husbands… when they dragged the children from their mothers. The Jews remaining in the marketplace were grouped into a transport of thousands of Jews who walked down their last road in the direction of the train station under guard by the German gendarmes. There they were loaded 80 to 90 people into a one horse train wagon, which was then completely sealed. As we later learned, all transports that day went in the direction of Belzec.

[Page 172]

However, the bloodsucker Felenc still was not sated by Jewish blood. Several hundred Jews still were lacking in the number of victims who were needed to fill the gas ovens at Belzec. He immediately telephoned the *Judenrat* to supply a supplemental list of Jews who had not been deported. The employee of the *Judenrat*, Paul Reiss, a refugee from Germany who came to Tarnow during the Zbąszyń deportation, sat at the telephone. He categorically refused to prepare a list of Jews for the Gestapo.

The murderer Felenc immediately appeared in the *Judenrat* office and without any reason drove out every one of the Jews found there. Felenc shot the courageous Paul Reiss on the steps. He shot the remaining Jews from the *Judenrat* in the courtyard of the building. Such dear Tarnow Jews as Meir Rozenbaum, Pinkhas Trinczer, Hersh Eder and Chaim Traum perished then.

Now a bloody slaughter began in every house in the city in which Jews lived. Blood flowed from these residences. Whomever the Germans found there was shot.

The terrible murder action, which the German criminals labeled as aussiedlung [resettlement, actually deportations], lasted an entire week with short pauses. The tragic sum total of this first deportation in Tarnow in the month of June 1942 reached over 12,000 victims. Thousands of Jews were deported to the annihilation camps. Thousands perished in the Tarnow ghetto at the hand of the German and Ukrainian bloodsuckers.

– 11 –

After the end of the terrible murder action, the so–called aussiedlung, the German hangmen began to drive the surviving Tarnow Jews to work at cleaning the streets and erasing the signs of the bloody slaughter.

I, too, was assigned to this work, which consisted mainly of loading the dead Jews into peasant wagons that we pulled to the cemetery. Trucks and wagons loaded with dead Jews arrived there. Piles of corpses were placed right near the gates. Then the actual work began. First we removed the clothing from the dead bodies. The naked bodies were thrown into the prepared, open pits. The clothing was sent to the storehouses, which were located at the Szacki School.

[Page 173]

We often found among these bodies seriously wounded Jews who were still breathing. The Gestapo did a "favor" for these dying Jews and shot them to death.

Thus we worked hard for two days. We barely had ended our work at the cemetery when they gave us other employment: we had to carry out the possessions, the so–called *Judenguts* [Jewish goods] from the residents after the murder or the deportation of the Jews. Expensive items, carpets, paintings, silver and crystal service… We had to transfer everything to the special warehouses.

– 12 –

A feeling of fear and shock now reigned over the surviving Tarnow Jews. No one knew what was happening to their wife, children, parents or sisters and brothers and they looked for each other. There was not one family that had not mourned one of those who had perished.

However, there was no time for mourning. At once, on another day after the deportation, on the 19th of June 1942, the then county chief in Tarnow, [Gustav] Hackbarth, published an order creating a closed ghetto in Tarnow for Jews. The ghetto area began at the Pilzner gate on the left side and extended along the left side of Lwowska Street to Widok Street and finally along the right side of Koszarowa Street.

The internal area of the ghetto encompassed the streets: Folwarczna, Nowa, Boznic, Szpitalna, the old Dombrowska, Wolność Platz (called Magdeburg Square), as well as all of the alleys that bordered on these streets, such as Zamknienta, Drukarska, Polna and Josna.

A high fence was erected around the entire ghetto area, which was topped with barbed wire. Three gates led to the ghetto: two on Wolność Platz, of these one from Lwowska Street and the second from Szpitalna Street; a third gate was at Nowa Street, near the *Judenrat*. All three were guarded day and night on the outside by the Polish Granatower police [Blue Police – Polish police in German occupied Poland] and on the internal side by the Jewish militiamen of the *Ordnungsdinest* [Jewish ghetto police]. There was the threat of death for [leaving] the ghetto without special permission.

[Page 174]

Moving to the ghetto had to happen over the course of 48 hours. In addition, Jews were permitted to bring only the most necessary household items. Therefore, there remained in the Jewish residences outside the ghetto the expensive furniture and household items. Immediately after the transfer of the Jewish population to the new ghetto residences, these were taken to the storehouses at the Szacki School and to the house of Moler Haler at Nowa Dombrowska Street.

The remaining Jewish residences outside the ghetto were taken over by German families as well as by the Polish ones that had to leave their residences in the ghetto area.

Thus approximately 20,000 Jews, who remained alive after the first murder action, were pressed into the narrow area of the Tarnow ghetto. The normal condition was now several families living in one house.

These outlandish living conditions, the terrible crowdedness, the cases of primitive sanitary facilities in the residences and, in addition, the hunger that spread each day in the ghetto area – these were the causes that created the favorable conditions for the rise and spread of infectious epidemics.

On the road to the enclosed ghetto...

[Page 175]

The ghetto was no place for the sick. They were brutally and horribly exterminated. Despite the extreme crowdedness in the ghetto, transports of deported Jews would arrive from the neighboring *shtetlekh* and villages.

– 13 –

The Gestapo criminals Rommelmann, Grunoff, Oppermann, Jek would appear often in the ghetto and from time to time S.S. members would come too. They controlled the life and death of the ghetto resident.

The cruelest criminal in the ghetto was Rommelmann. He would coldly carry out his outrages with sadistic anger. His appearance in the ghetto would cause a deadly fear for everyone whom he met by chance. So well, he and his Gestapo friends would ridicule their victims in a horrible manner. Before carrying out a murder action, they would ask the frightened Jews in what position they wanted to be shot. "*Ich mache das leicht, ohne schmerzen*" ["I do it easily, without pain"], they would make a joke of the unfortunate ones.

Two young Tarnow girls, Rozenberg and Wajsberg, fell as victims of such wild sadism. These gentle, dear Jewish children had to listen to the mocking words of the Gestapo murderer before their death: "You are too beautiful to live as Jewish children".

The Gestapo bandit Jek once caught a group of Jews praying. The murderer asked how many Jews were lacking for a minyan [10 men needed for prayer] and, as it was seen that there were more Jews than were necessary for a minyan, he led out several Jews and shot them on the spot.

The Gestapo member Jek came from a village near Mielec (where a German colony had existed). He was raised in a Jewish environment and, therefore, Jewish religious customs were familiar to him, which was useful to him in searching for Jews at the periphery of the city or in surrounding villages.

Once, he entered a Jewish residence that looked completely empty. Jek quickly put on a *talis* [prayer shawl] and *tefillin* [phylacteries] and ostensibly began to pray. When the Jews, who were hidden in various hiding places in the residence, heard this, they began to crawl out of the holes. The murderer, Jek, shot them all on the spot.

[Page 176]

– 14 –

The Jewish residents in the ghetto now lived with one thought: how to save themselves, how to hide before another deportation, which everyone was convinced would come. Tarnow Jews already knew what [was happening] at Belzec. They heard about the cruelties and about the hell in the death camp, from which no one had yet returned.

Therefore, we no longer waited with folded arms for a further deportation. Everyone tried to do something in order to have the possibility of hiding at a decisive hour. There were Jews who took off their armbands and left Tarnow looking for a hiding place with Polish acquaintances in other areas or in neighboring forests. There were those who began to prepare bunkers or at least were comforted by giving their children to their Aryan acquaintances.

However, on the "Aryan" side, Jews with Aryan papers also were not secure in their lives. That is how the Germans caught the wives of Dr. Salit and Dr. Menderer, who did not wear armbands. Both women were taken to the cemetery in Tarnow by the hangman Grunoff and they were shot there.

Henek Wajs and his wife (family name Brand) and child also were caught. Grunoff also shot them at the Tarnow cemetery.

Only one hope now filled the hearts of a large majority of the Tarnow Jews: the work card. A labor office was active at the Judenrat, whose office was located in the building of the autobus station at Wolność Platz. The chief care of the labor office since its opening was to provide the demanded contingents of Jewish workhands for the Germans. No one rushed to work for the Germans during the first months of occupation, but now everyone wanted to give away everything to receive work for the Germans and to become the possessor of a work card, which ostensibly protected one from anything bad. Now work was a privilege, not accessible to everyone.

[Page 177]

The work also was important because those who had a work location that was located on the Aryan side also had the opportunity to go outside the ghetto gates every day and at that opportunity could also obtain food products, although this involved great danger, and still more. Such an "outsider" more easily had opportunities and chances to secure Aryan papers or to find a hiding place outside the ghetto.

The majority of Jews in the Tarnow ghetto still believed that the work card was the best means of security, that by giving their health and their strength to the Germans allowed them to save their lives, theirs and [the lives of] their families. Tarnow Jews still lived with the hope of the immediate end of the war. The front was not far away. And the German defeat on the front was no longer a secret to anyone. In addition, we had only one purpose…to endure…to work with more than our strength because whoever survived, we believed, would wait impatiently for the defeat of Hitler, may his name be erased.

It is no wonder that each of us dreamed about receiving a workplace and, in connection with it, a work card.

At this time, German enterprises arose in Tarnow that operated both outside the ghetto and on the site of the Tarnow ghetto itself.

Tailor, linen, knitwear, harness–maker workshops, among others, were active and, in addition, the so–called "black" workplaces such as the Ostban, Monatn, Hoch und Tifebau. The "Bershten Central" and the workshops of the Madritsch firm also employed many Jewish workers.

The role and the significance of the tailoring workshop of the Madritsch firm must particularly be emphasized in connection with the importance of these workshops for the Jews in the Tarnow ghetto. Madritsch[b], a genteel German, ran a tailoring workshop in Tarnow in which were employed several hundred Tarnow Jews (women and men), with whom Madritsch was humane and friendly. All of the Jewish workers who worked in the Madritsch workshop survived the Nazi hell, thanks only to the fact that they were employed in this undertaking in Tarnow and later in Plaszow. During the liquidation of the Tarnow ghetto, [Julius] Madritsch transferred the entire enterprise with all of the Jewish workers employed there to the labor camp in Plaszow, while all other work places in the Tarnow ghetto were liquidated and the workers employed there were deported to Belzec and Auschwitz.

[Page 178]

A close co–worker of Madritsch was [Raymond] Tisch, also a German, who came from Vienna. Madritsch and Tisch – two rare [people] of that era, well–mannered figures, men with a deep in–born humanity. They often, in mortal danger, had to use much effort and daring to prevent permit the deportation of their Jewish workers to the death camps.

There were other German industrialists active in the Tarnow ghetto who worked for the needs of the German rulers and hangmen. Jews worked in various tailoring and shoemaking workshops for a wage that was absolutely insufficient for stilling the hunger of the worker and his family.

The Gestapo had supervision over all the workplaces. The assembly point for all workers was on Magdeburger Platz (the so–called Pig Platz), from which they went to work in groups, under a convoy of members of the ordnungsdienst, which accompanied them to the workplaces outside the ghetto.

Work discipline was very strenuously watched. The entire work brigade would be punished for the smallest mistake, even on the part of one worker. In addition, the punishments became more severe every day. It is enough to provide the case of 12 young Jews who were shot at the roll–call Platz because they missed one day of work.

With our last strength we showed up for work in the belief that with it we would stay alive and also save our wives and children.

– 15 –

The Jewish Hospital now was located in the building of the previous old age home, outside the ghetto. The doctors and nurses created a separate labor brigade that went to work accompanied by a German militiamen guard. Active at the hospital also was a disinfection division. Every day during the morning hours, all of the sick people in the ghetto were taken out to the hospital.

[Page 179]

At first the Jews could make use of the baths in the building of the former mikvah [ritual bath], to which there were two entrances: one from the Aryan side – and the second from the ghetto side. Jews and Christians would meet at the baths and it was possible to communicate with the outside world. However, as soon as the Gestapo learned of this, Jews were forbidden to make use of the bathhouses.

Jewish old people and invalids from various hiding places were smuggled into the ghetto daily. Understand, this was done very secretly and the Gestapo could not learn of this. Therefore, the Judenrat arranged a separate support area for this group, a sort of asylum in the previous egg warehouse of the Witstum firm at Szpitalna Street 6, where daily approximately 70 such older and sick Jews were assisted. Later, when the Gestapo learned of this, they attacked this asylum and murdered all of the Jews who were found there.

With the creation of the ghetto in Tarnow, it was very difficult to provide food for the Jewish population. The efforts of the social service divisions of the Judenrat to relieve the food needs that seized so many Jewish homes were of no help. Old and dedicated communal workers, such as Meir Rozenbaum, Hirsh Eder, Pinkhas Trinczer, Chaim Tram, belonged to these social divisions. In addition, also active in the ghetto were other community workers who spared no effort and sacrifice to help their needy brothers. Four communal kitchens in the Tarnow ghetto, which gave out several thousand lunches every day, were supported with great effort and exertion.

They helped with buying food products on the black market, risking their lives. Those who went to work outside the ghetto walls received food products from the Christians through barter, which they brought back, to the ghetto in secret. Often the German and Ukrainian militiamen carried out searches of the Jews returning to the ghetto from the workplaces, and the punishment was carried out on the spot when they found the least bit of food on them…beatings and often the death penalty.

[Page 180]

Jews lived in the Tarnow ghetto under such conditions, with hunger, pain and illness. Individuals succeeded in leaving the ghetto with purchased Aryan papers. There also were those who escaped to other areas to hide with Christian acquaintances.

However, the majority of Jews imprisoned in the ghetto lived in uncertainty, in fear, not knowing what the next morning would bring.

In addition, the news reached us like thunder that an announcement of the 9th of September 1942 had been placed on the houses outside the ghetto about the deportation of Jews from the Tarnow ghetto, which was designated for the 10th of September 1942 and that the German county chief in Tarnow had threatened the death penalty for every Pole who hid or helped a Jew.

The notice of the Tarnow County Chief about the deportation of Jews from the Tarnow ghetto on the 10th of September 1942

[Page 181]

We also learned that in this notice the county chief ordered all of the Poles to report about Jewish possessions that were in their hands and forbid the Poles from appearing in the streets of Tarnow that led to the train station when the "deported" Jews were being led there.

On the 10th of September 1942 at dawn, the Gestapo and German gendarmerie surrounded the entire Tarnow ghetto. All of the ghetto residents, including those with work cards had to leave their residences and assemble at the roll–call Platz (Wolność Platz). Afterwards, when all of the Jews stood there according to their workplace, a selection began. Worker groups that the Germans still considered necessary for the German military machine left for work belatedly. On the other hand, others remained on the spot and then the actual selection took place, which was carried out by the German headquarters of Gestapo and gendarmerie officers in the presence of the ghetto commandant and members of the *Judenrat*.

This selection was frightful and cruel. Men were torn from their wives, children from their mothers.

Old people and women with children were concentrated in one place and young people in another place.

The moans were heartrending; the cries and laments. The children screamed, "Mama." And mothers called, "I want to be with you." Voices could be heard from fathers, "Do not leave me [here]."

There were parents who were desperate to give away their children to save them. But there also were parents who lamented and screamed, "Give me back my child. You can kill me with my child."

There also were parents who resisted the gendarmerie and did not want to give up their children. There also were those who threw themselves at the Gestapo bandits, who mercilessly beat them with whips.

[Page 182]

There were several heroes among the parents who during the selections showered the German murderers with curses, not being concerned with being obedient.

In the course of a day we had to kneel thus under the open sky while the sun burned us and we were dying of hunger and thirst.

When the sun set they opened the gates of the ghetto and the entire transport of parents with children and children without parents was led out of the ghetto.

My wife and I and our two children were in this group. Our older daughter, Halina, went with me. My wife led the younger one, Edit, by the hand. We were determined to not be separated from our children and to share their fate.

Before we began to march, a member of the *Judenrat*, who was standing near me, whispered that at the moment I was near the spot where the Gestapo headquarters was located, I should shout, "I am a medical professional!" I did so, but after my words I received a blow over my back with a thick whip and I heard the words, "*Ein schwein bist du*" [You are a pig].

We walked standing four people in a row. We were accompanied on both sides by German *S.S.* members and *Granatowa* militiamen. They beat us murderously with the butts of their rifles, whenever someone could not keep up with our marching, fell, could not bear the heavy blows. Thus we went through the streets, Koszarowa, Mickewicza, Seminarska, until we arrived at the military firing range that was located outside the Sports Platz of the Jewish gymnastic union, Shimshon. Old wooden barracks stood there, which the Germans now were using as horse stalls. We were driven into these barracks. It was almost completely dark. A little air entered from outside through a small window, covered with boards. A terrible odor of filthy straw battered us.

Tired and weary, we fell on the *gnojówka* [liquid manure]. In the darkness we did not see who lay nearby. We only heard the crying and lamenting of people who literally were suffocating on the stinking straw from the lack of a little air.

[Page 183]

The next day, first thing in the morning, the *Judenrat* provided us with bread and a warm drink. We received such provisions twice a day from the *Judenrat*. From time to time, a member of the Gestapo would appear who according to a list called out several people and led them from the barracks. The majority were shoemakers and tailors who worked for the Gestapo in the ghetto, and other Jews would take their place.

An acquaintance, Mrs. Leibel, the wife of the cabinetmaker Leibel, who had left a daughter in the ghetto who tried to extract her mother from the transport, was with us in the barracks. I asked this woman for mercy, that she not forget us when she left the barracks and was again in the ghetto. They promised to help us.

The next day Mrs. Leibel actually was led out of the barracks. I now had a spark of hope of being saved. But would Mrs. Leibel keep her word? Or would her efforts help me in some way?

On the third day, a Gestapo member appeared at our barracks and called my name, as well as my wife's and my two children. We quickly left the barracks, holding the *meldkart* [registration card] in our hands and the identity document from the *gesundheitsamt* [health department].

At the same time, the German *S.S.* members led the entire group from the barracks. Groups were formed to march. A number of the sick and those incapable of marching were shot on the spot. Only a small number of the sick were placed in wagons.

My wife, children and I walked in great haste in the direction of the gate that was farthest from the barracks. On the way we had trouble with the Gestapo, who checked us and, only by a miracle, did we succeed in approaching the exit gate and leave the military firing range.

We again walked along the same streets and alleys through which we had been led to the shooting spot. The Gestapo man, who led us out of the barracks, now led us into the ghetto through a back part and gave us to the *Judenrat*.

My first task was to find Mrs. Leibel; thanks to her we had been saved. She told me that she had given the Gestapo member who led us from the barracks everything that had been found in my residence. Alas, the refined Mrs. Leibel perished during the third deportation.

[Page 184]

The entire transport of Jews from the horse barracks near Shimshon Platz was deported to Belzec. Approximately 8,000 Jews perished during the second deportation action in the Tarnow ghetto.

– 16 –

Several days passed after the terrible slaughter. Jews began to crawl out of the bunkers, from the cellars, attics and other hiding places. Their appearance was frightful…starving…exhausted, they searched for those closest to them.

The area of the ghetto again grew smaller. Several workplaces were liquidated or made smaller. Life in the ghetto was as if [we were] deceased. The mood of the surviving Tarnow Jews consisted of only one thought: preparing a hiding place, building a bunker or escaping at any price because no one doubted any longer that the Tarnow ghetto was on the eve of liquidation. Individuals succeeded in sneaking out of the ghetto and hiding with Polish acquaintances, particularly with Polish workers, who in several cases did not refuse to help and permitted Jews escaping from the ghetto to hide in well–prepared hiding places. They dug out an entrance to a cellar in ground floor residences, under the bottom of a sideboard. Or they would dig out a simple, deep pit in the kitchen, which would be covered, and thus accommodate six to seven people, pressed together one near the other. Double walls would be built in bathrooms.

Larger bunkers also were built for around 100 people in particularly inaccessible areas. Such a bunker was located in the Tarnow ghetto in an attic of a house at Lwowska Street 4. This bunker was built by a member of the Tarnow *ordnungsdienst*, a certain Plocki (he did not come from Tarnow), who had to be well paid for a place in the bunker.

[Page 185]

A similar bunker was located at Nowa Street, under the ruin of the new synagogue, where special underground activities were carried out. Bunkers were also built in Grabowska and in other places in the city.

My greatest care now was to hide my two children. I would take my two children with me every morning when I left for work in the hospital. In addition, my wife, who was employed in the dispensary establishment, also went to work. I would leave the children not far from this establishment. When the Gestapo members appeared in the hospital building, my wife would hide the children in the delousing facility because the German perpetrators never would open the door there and, therefore, this was the best hiding place for the children.

– 17 –

Three months had barely gone by after the last murder action. The wounds had still not healed after the last slaughter and already on the 15th of November 1942, at eight o'clock in the morning, divisions of the Gestapo and *S.S.* surrounded the entire area of the Tarnow ghetto, only letting out the individual labor brigades. All of the Jews who remained in the ghetto had to appear at Magdeburger Platz.

My wife focused herself immediately on what the threat was and in the blink of an eye she and the children entered a bunker, while I left for the hospital with my work group. We were completely cut off from the ghetto area and we had absolutely no news from there.

A Jewish militiaman came to the hospital in the afternoon and brought me the news that my wife and both children had survived through miracles. When I returned from work in the evening, they already were waiting for me at home.

Later, when we had calmed ourselves after the most recent events, my older daughter began to describe the wonderful way in which all three had survived. She said that in the bunker in which they were bricked in, 50 more people had been hidden, the majority women and old men, without any contact with the outside world. Several hours had barely passed and the bunker was opened. They heard the barking of the dogs and the voices of the Germans who shouted that we should leave the bunkers quickly.

[Page 186]

One by one – one after the other, everyone crawled out of the bunker. My wife and the children were the last. Halina, the older one, went first. When she came to the exit of the bunker, the militiaman from the *ordnungsdienst*, who stood there, asked her name and when she said her name he asked about her mother who had arrived with the younger Edit in her arms at just that moment. The man lightning–fast hid all three – my wife and two daughters – in the boxes that stood nearby and reported to the Germans that all of the people in the bunker had already gone to the roll–call Platz. The brave man, a certain Cymet, knew my wife from Jasło, from which he himself came.

Approximately 3,000 young Jews capable of working perished during the last deportation action in the Tarnow ghetto. All of the bunkers and hiding places were found in the ghetto with the help of dogs and denouncers. Whoever was caught was shot on the spot.

After this murder action, the area of the ghetto again was made smaller. We went to work earlier, in groups. Our older daughter, Halina, worked as a helper on the Aryan side in a tailoring workshop.

Now there only remained the security of our younger daughter, Edit, and we decided to arrange for her to be with an Aryan family.

I became acquainted with a Pole at the hospital, about whom rumors went around that he had taken many Jews to Warsaw. I searched for this Pole and entrusted him with the fact that I was looking for a hiding place on the Aryan side for my Edit. He immediately sent a Christian woman to me, who was ready to hide my little daughter Edit with her. She lived not far from the Lipie forest, about two kilometers [a little over a mile] from Tarnow and, after discussing the conditions, she came the next day in the morning to take our Edit. Although our child still was very young, she already had a great deal of common sense, so she understood the conditions in which we found ourselves and that we were giving her from our home for her good. In addition she did not show any opposition and wished us much health and strength to persevere and immediately to see her after the war – she came out of the house quietly, with tears in her eyes.

[Page 187]

– 18 –

The *Judenrat* tried to calm the surviving Jews after the last deportation from the Tarnow ghetto with assurances that no more deportations would take place in the Tarnow ghetto because the remaining Jews were necessary for work for the German military.

In addition to this, rumors now spread in the Tarnow ghetto that all surviving Tarnow Jews would be deported to a labor camp in Szebnie, near Jaslo, or to Plaszow. These rumors were spread by the German murderers who tried even more to disturb the mood of the exhausted Jews in order to make it easier to torture and annihilate them. Meanwhile, they grabbed Jews who were searching for hiding places in the neighboring village. Jews, who were caught in the bunkers were taken to the cemetery and shot there.

No one was secure in their life. Hunger and need reigned in Jewish residences. The German terror grew stronger every day.

Our Christian woman from the Lipie forest now returned with our small daughter in her arms. She brought the child back to us because, as she explained to us, she could no longer keep her because of fear of her neighbors.

Thus our daughter Edit again was with us. We now had to heal her because she returned with frozen feet. As she told us, she lived with the Christian woman in terrible conditions. The Christian woman's residence consisted of two small rooms and a kitchen. Behind the oven in the second room were baskets in which our Edit sat through the entire day and where she slept at night. The room was not heated and it is no wonder that the child left there with frozen feet. She did not cry. She told us that she suffered very badly from hunger, from the cold, but still more from longing for us.

– 19 –

[Page 188]

We were very uneasy when we noticed that the Gestapo members were often guests in the office of the *Judenrat*. Their appearances in the ghetto always evoked a general panic. Therefore, as soon as they saw them they began the search to prepare hiding places. Whoever had the opportunity quickly hid in the bunkers, in cellars or in other holes.

In 1943 the commandant of the Tarnow ghetto was the *S.S.* member Hermann Blache. At the beginning he lived on the Aryan side in a house that bordered the ghetto near Lwowska Street near the "New Apothecary," from which there was only one exit into the area of the ghetto where he would stay for the entire day.

He was a cruel, true animal in human form. He was present at every roll call; he controlled the forced labor of the Jewish slaves; he stood at the distribution of the "meals." Blache did not rest in the ghetto. He raged, shot, pillaged whatever he could take from the Jews.

Rommelmann, the chief of the Jewish division in the Gestapo, and his bandit–like aides Grunoff, [Josef] Kastura, Iklerf, Jek, Oppermann and others did not remain behind the times and came to the ghetto almost every day and under various pretexts, murdered, ransacked Jewish possessions.

In August 1943 a division of *wachdienst* [security guards] composed of Ukrainians, with the German gendarme, [Johann] Kessler at the head, came to the ghetto. One section of this division surrounded the entire ghetto area on the third side and manned the entrance gates and the other [section] searched for Jews in every corner of the ghetto itself.

We had no doubt that we were on the eve of a new murder action. My daughter Halina, who was then 12 and a half years old, decided to hide on the Aryan side. She was tall and had an Aryan appearance. Our difficult experiences up to then had strengthened her character. She tried to convince us that without a doubt if we were together, we would all perish. When each of us was hidden in a different place, there was a possibility that she and all of us could be saved.

[Page 189]

The decision to separate from Halina was difficult, but we understood that there was no other way out. In addition to a few *zlotes*, she had a certificate, which we had prepared earlier, and a notebook with the addresses of relatives who lived abroad. We agreed that after the war – God willing – if we survived – we would meet in Tarnow.

In the morning of another day our Halina went with her group to work on the Aryan side. Now our greatest worry was to find a hiding place for our Edit.

– 20 –

On the 2nd of September 1943, the fourth deportation action began in the Tarnow ghetto. This was supposed to be the last expulsion of Tarnow Jews. After the action, Tarnow was supposed to be *Juden–rein* [free of Jews].

This bloody murder action was carried out by Amon Göth, the camp commandant from Plaszow, whom the Germans had specially sent to Tarnow with the task of finishing the slaughter in the Tarnow ghetto, to thoroughly destroy the rest of Tarnow Jewry, so that there would not remain any trace of a Jewish community in Tarnow.

The brutal murderer appeared in the Tarnow ghetto accompanied by higher *S.S.* officers and Gestapo divisions and immediately announced that the Tarnow ghetto was being liquidated and all of the residents would be deported to the labor camp in Plaszow.

It is difficult to describe the confusion and turmoil that arose in the ghetto when the news spread about the new expulsion. Now there was a race on all sides to prepare bunkers and hiding places.

On the same day, at dawn, the entire ghetto area was surrounded by the Gestapo and *S.S.* divisions. By order of Amon Göth, all of the Jews had to assemble at Wolność Platz (roll–call Platz) and arrange themselves in groups according to their particular workplace.

The roll–call Platz immediately became full of the working groups. An identification board stood in front of each group, which gave the name of the work spot, as, for example, the *Ostban*, Madritsch, tailoring workshop and so on. A number of Jewish militiamen stood with each group. Göth went to each group with his accompaniers, asked questions and pulled out individual people from the groups, whom the militia immediately took away to Staro– Dombrowska Street, where men and women were placed separately.

[Page 190]

Everyone awaited their fate with a trembling heart. The murderer Göth decided everything about a person. When a woman approached him and asked that she be assigned to the group in which her groom was located, he drew out his revolver and shot the poor woman on the spot without answering.

When the group of men at Staro Dombrowska Street reached the number 200 and the group of women 100, both groups were taken to two separate wooden barracks that belonged to the "Zege Factory" Zinger firm. Both barracks were now guarded by an *S.S.* division and completely sealed off. I was assigned to the group of men and my wife to the group of women and she succeeded in hiding our daughter Edit. I had the ability to see everything that later took place there through the small window of our barracks, which looked out to roll–call Platz, such as Göth and Blache shooting at children and women. The terrible details of this last slaughter in the Tarnow ghetto have already been described in the first volume of the memorial book, Tarne [Tarnow].

I was assigned to the group whose task was to clean Wolność Platz of the corpses, the victims of the last slaughter. We took them to the cemetery and buried them in a shared, mass grave. Among the corpses then, I recognized Mrs. Klapholc (Khizkal's wife) and her children, Mrs. Messinger and Mrs. Getsler.

One transport of Jews, which was designated for deportation during the selection on the first day of the fourth deportation action – around 5,000 Jews – left for Auschwitz and the second transport with trade workers – approximately 3,000 Jews – left for Plaszow. Just as during the previous actions, all the severely sick and people incapable of being transported were shot.

Göth even had liquidated the temporary, small hospital. He shot the eight sick people he found there. And thus the bestial murderer Amon Göth finished the liquidation of the Tarnow ghetto.

After the war, the bloody hangman Amon Göth was sentenced to death by the highest Polish national tribunal on the 5th of September 1946.

[Page 191]

This murderer had the audacity to turn to the President of Poland with a request for clemency. It was not given and on the 13th of September 1946, the mass murderer Amon Göth went to the gallows.

– 21 –

Our group (200 men and 100 women) were designated with the name *Säuberung–Commando* [cleaning commando] and had the task of cleaning up the ghetto of signs of the last murder action. [*S.S. Oberscharführer* – senior squad leader – Hermann] Blache locked us in two houses at Wolność Platz numbers 10 and 12. We left for work at seven o'clock in the morning and the gates from the two houses were closed immediately after we returned at night, at six in the evening. We were guarded by Ukrainian guards for the entire night.

Our work in the ghetto emptied of Jews was difficult.

We first cleaned the bloodied streets and at the storehouses located at the Szacki School, we gathered the things remaining in Jewish residences, the so–called *Judenguts* [Jewish possessions], and there we sorted everything and packed and prepared them to be sent to Germany. In all of the ghetto residences, in all attics and cellars we had to search through all corners and clean and erase the signs of the German crimes.

One day they brought to me at the Szacki School the registration card of my brother Chaim, which had been found in his jacket. A postcard addressed to me was attached to the registration card, on which my brother, of blessed memory, had given me the news that he was located in the Szacki School and that our parents were somewhere else.

The murderer Blache made use of various criminal means to entice the few Jews who were still in hiding, from their various hiding places. For this purpose he published a call to the Jews who were hiding, that they should return to work and, when this did not help, he ordered the water system to be shut off in all the houses and the electrical current to be cut off. The exhausted, sick Jews now had to leave their hiding places and came out into the daylight. In the second half of September 1943 an entire transport of approximately 700 such illegal, ghetto residents were deported to Szebnie. The entire transport did not perish in this camp. On the way, around 600 people were shot and their bodies burned in the forest near Tarnow. Around 100 people arrived in Szebnie from this transport.

[Page 192]

A transport of Jews being led to be shot in the forest near Tarnow
(Buczyna forest)

Blache himself ran around like a wild animal in the emptied ghetto and searched. Perhaps there was still a victim hidden somewhere? Thus, he shot the young Sztum when he suddenly came out of his hiding place wanting to jump over the wall of the ghetto.

Blache's son excelled in shooting Jews – the young 15–year–old murderer. Blache would brag to his Gestapo comrades that his son had quickly learned the trade of shooting Jews.

Blache would imprison every Jew who was pulled from a hiding place, in a dark cellar in Koch's house at Wolność Platz and when 100 Jew had been assembled there, they were all driven out to the so–called "garbage heap" at Stara Dombrowska Street and there they were shot. Those executed had to take off everything.

[Page 193]

Tarnow Jews being led to their execution at the cemetery in Tarnow

They ripped out the gold teeth from the corpses and poured kerosene and benzene over the bodies and burned them. In a short time, around 500 Jews were annihilated there. *ARTZ* Dr. Lustik and the nurse Chaya Argand also perished there because they were taking care of an older Jew who lay in a bunker and became sick there. When Blache learned of this, he immediately ran there with his helpers and the entire group was led out of the bunker to the "garbage heap" and brutally shot there.

Meanwhile, our group from the "cleaning commando" worked hard at sorting and packing the remaining possessions of the murdered and deported Jews. Everything had a value to the German murderer – bedding, linen, clothing, shoes. We sorted everything separately and separately packed it and sent it away to the freight train, by which approximately 10 freight cars with such goods left for Germany every day.

[Page 194]

From time to time at the morning roll call Blache would remind us that we should give the gold items, such as money or jewelry to the guard room at Wolność Platz. At the delivery of these things we stood in rows…men and women separately. We went up to the room one by one with small steps, where Blache, the commandant of the guard division, Kessler, and a guard sat. And the bundle of gathered "treasures" was given to them. Then Blache himself would carry out a body search.

During such a search, Blache shot the young Goldberg, a son of the owner of the soap factory at Lwowska Street, because he ostensibly found a dollar on him.

Meanwhile, there was less to do in the storehouse. We trembled at the simple thought that we would soon be without work and what would become of us then?

My wife and I had no doubt that our fate was sealed. However, we wanted at any cost to save our daughter Edit, who we had only kept alive until then by a miracle.

Our former servant, Dasha, who remained devoted to us, lived on the Aryan side and would help us in any way she could. We communicated with her with great difficulty and she was ready to help us by hiding our Edit. On a designated day, Edit hid in a wagon that would leave the ghetto to bring food products. Our servant Basha waited on the Aryan side and took our Edit from the wagon.

The work of cleaning the ghetto and taking away the stolen Jewish possessions was almost finished. Suddenly on the 3rd of November 1943, several trucks arrived in the ghetto from Szebnie with S.S. members led by the camp commandant, [Josef] Grzimek, and took 150 people from our liquidation group. The entire transport left for Szebnie.

The Gestapo now ill–treated the handful of surviving Tarnow Jews, looking for new tortures for the city. They tormented us daily with long–lasting investigations under the suspicion that we were in contact with Aryans and were preparing to escape. During a roll call, they would pull individual people from the row, take them to the "garbage heap" and shoot them there.

At the end of 1943, when the liquidating work already had ended, the Gestapo murderers annihilated the members of the *Judenrat* who still remained in the ghetto in a savage way.

[Page 195]

We, the 115 Jews from the "cleaning group," under guard by the Gestapo, left the Tarnow ghetto for Plaszow. Tarnow was *Juden–rein* [free of Jews].

In May 1945 I was liberated from the terrible Mauthausen camp by a victorious American Army division. In August 1945 I returned to Tarnow in the hope of finding someone from my family. Then I learned that my little daughter Edit, who had been hiding with a Christian woman, had died. Rumor went around that she had been poisoned.

After long searching, I learned that my dear wife, Rywka, of blessed memory, was deported from the labor camp to Auschwitz and from there to Bergen–Belsen, where she perished on the 15th of April 1945 – right on the day when Bergen–Belsen was liberated by the American Army.

After the slaughter in the Tarnow ghetto

Several months later, my older daughter, Halina, returned from forced labor in Germany. She is now 15 years old and already has gone through the seven circles of hell.

Original footnotes:

a. Detailed report from the proceedings against Rommelmann is given in another place. Ed.
b. There is a detailed article about this personality in another part of this book (Ed.)

[Page 196]

The Trial of Wilhelm Heinrich Rommelmann,
may his name be erased
The Murderer of Tarnow Jewry

Translated by Gloria Berkenstat Freund

The trial of the murderer of Tarnow Jewry, Wilhelm Heinreich Rommelmann, may his name be erased, who was sentenced to death, took place at the district court, during the days from the 17th until the 19th of March 1948.

We have a copy of this verdict, which gives us the opportunity to learn in detail about the horrible brutality and criminal deeds of the Gestapo in the Tarnow ghetto.

We are publishing almost the entire verdict without abridgement in Yiddish translation. We provide in the original Polish language only a part of the sentence from the verdict up to paragraph I. We repeat the same section in the Yiddish translation and quote it to the end in Yiddish.

[Page 197]

District Court VI Penalty Division
Tribune of the 25th of March 1948
No. 8 1025/47 K.

The Sentence for the Verdict

In the name of the Polish Republic!
The 25th of March 1948

The District Court in Tarnow, Sixth Penalty Division of the following composition: President: County Court Judge Dr. St. Krol; Concessors [jurors]: Wladyslaw Lorenc, Lieber Gottlob; Recorder: Apl. Dr. Piechowicz.

Considering in the presence of the prosecutor of the District Court, *Magister* [academic degree given in Poland equivalent to a master's degree] St. Szatki, on the days of the 17th, 18th and 19th of March 1948 of the trial of:

Wilhelm Heinrich Rommelmann, born on the 1st of February 1907 in Bremen (Germany), son of Wilhelm and Wilhelmina, née Shene, Evangelical, German citizen, of German nationality, middle school education, married, without possessions, last residence in Bremen, detained by the British occupation organs of power on the 3rd of June 1946, arrested on the 28 of February 1948, now located in the prison in Tarnow, accused of this, that:

I. During the German occupation, he was in Polish territory, namely: in Krakow and Tarnow, secretary of the State Secret Police Gestapo and took part in a criminal organization created by the organs of power of the German state that had as its purpose the crimes against humanity.

II. During the years 1942 and 1943, as a member of the Gestapo criminal organization to accommodate the regime of the German state in certain areas, took part in carrying out murders of the civilian population in the manner that:

A) During the time from May 1942 to autumn 1943, in the Tarnow district as well as in the Brigel and Dąbrowa districts, fulfilling the supervisory functions in the isolation areas for Jews (ghettos) as consultant on Jewish matters, he took part in mass and individual murders of people of Jewish origin, shooting these people or exterminating

[Page 198]
them in another manner, and personally or through his subordinate organs ordering that they be shot and annihilated, thus he would torture his victims in this manner so that before being shot, they were held in a closed room for a number of days without food; they were forced to undress until naked and to lie with their faces to the ground when being shot and gave the order to burn the shot and still living victims in a pyre.

B) In June and July 1943, he took part in the so-called pacification actions against the Poles in Otfinówo, Karsy, Nieciecza, Gręboszów, as well as in other areas of the Dąbrowa district and in neighboring districts, during which he shot a number of people, among others: Stanislav Borduch from Przysławice, N. Lir from Wielople, Jozef Bochenek from Karzy, N. Piontek from the former Polish military, with the pseudonym, Adrowoncz from Gręboszów and Janina Wozniak from Borislaw; in addition, he tortured the latter by taking her to the [non-Jewish] cemetery; he had her undress completely and he wounded her in her hand with his first shot from his revolver and then he murdered her with the second shot to her head.

C) In August 1943, in Brigel (Brzesko), he took part in the shooting of Irena Pyrkowa of Zakliczyn, a pregnant woman in the 6th month, as part of a repressive arrest for hiding her husband Franciszek Pyrek, for whom the Gestapo was searching as a suspect in activities destructive to the German state; before the shooting he took revenge against Irena Pyrkowa, beating her and beating her in a terrible manner.

D) In July 1943, he took part in the mass murder of people of Roma origin in Żabno, personally shooting them with the help of subordinate German gendarmes and this was in the number of about 70 people, men, women and children; in addition, he tortured his victims, ordering them to completely undress and to lie with their faces to the ground.

III. In 1942 and 1943, as a member of the Gestapo criminal organization, he served the regime of the German state, developed activity to the detriment of people who were sought and persecuted by the regime for national, racial reasons, in such a manner that:

A) In 1942 in Tarnow, in the Tarnow district as well as in the Brigel

[Page 199]
and Dąbrowa district, took part in organizing and creating places of isolation, ghettos, for people of Jewish origin with the purpose of having control over these people and to exterminate them through excessive gathering of a large number of people in a small area, through systematic starvation and coercing them to do extraordinarily hard labor, creating conditions that caused the loss of health and life among the people there.

B) At the time from June 1942 to autumn 1943, in Tarnow and in the districts of Tarnow, Brigel (Brzesko) and Dąbrowa, he himself with the help of subordinates in the organs [of power] carried out mass selections of the people imprisoned in the ghettos and deported them to places of extermination in various concentration camps.

C) During the years 1942 and 1943, in Tarnow and in the districts of Tarnow, Brigel and Dąbrowa, he took part in mass and individual arrests of civilians, for secret and detrimental activities against the German State and that he caused the confining of the arrestees in prisons and concentration camps where they, in the majority, perished and, in addition, he ridiculed these victims, beating and kicking them.

IV. During the time from May 1942 to autumn 1943, in Tarnow and in the districts of Tarnow, Brigel and Dąbrowa, as a member of the Gestapo criminal organization and as a consultant on Jewish matters, as a member of the German State organs of power, he took part in the mass looting of possessions, particularly of clothing, shoes, work tools, furniture, appliances, money and other items of value taken from people of Jewish origin, and with these items strengthened the power of the German Reich and its citizens.

V. During the time from June 1943 to autumn 1943, in Tarnow and in the districts of Tarnow, Brigel and Dąbrowa, using the conditions created by the war, such as the plight of the Jews, doomed by the German rulers, as well his position as a member of the Gestapo – he forced people of Jewish origin to provide ransoms and hard currency and cash under the threat of deporting all of the Jews from the given area.

The above-described actions constitute: under I the crime of article 4, paragraph 3, point C – under II. A/B/C/D crimes of article 1, point 1 – under III. A/B/C crimes of article 2 – under IV. Crimes of article 2 – under V crimes of article 3 of the degree of 31.VIII.1944.

[Page 200]

The Court Decided

Concerning the accused Wilhelm Rommelmann for responsibility in the crimes of article 1, point 1 and 2 in connection with article 4, paragraph 1, in connection with article 2/A and 3/C of the decree of 31.VIII.1944, item 46/377 Legal Gazette of the Polish Republic –that during the German occupation in Tarnow and in the area of the counties of Tarnow, Brigel and Dąbrowa from spring 1942 until the winter 1943, he supported the regime of the German state, as a Gestapo official, belonging to a criminal organization, created by the government organs of the German state, whose purpose was crimes against humanity – and personally taking part in carrying out the mass-murders of people from among the civilian population in paragraph II A-D of this accusation closely described – and that he had as Gestapo official and consultant on Jewish matters at the Tarnow Gestapo through his taking part in organizing the ghetto and catching people from the Polish and Jewish population and confining them in the prison and in the ghetto, with collaborating in the selection of people from the Jewish population, designator to various work or to deportation to extermination camps, as well as collaborating in the liquidation of the ghetto in Tarnow and in Zakliczyn and through taking part in the theft of their possessions – proceeded to harm this population, demanding and persecuting them through the German regime organs for political, national and racial motives.

And Sentenced

This Wilhelm Rommelmann on the basis of article 1 of the above decree

To the Death Penalty

And on the basis of article 7 A/B of this decree and article 52 paragraph 2 and article 47, paragraph A/1 of the punishment decree to lose forever the public and honorary citizen rights and the confiscation of all of his possessions.

[Page 201]

Despite the civilian demands of the Jewish district committee in Tarnow, the committee itself will carry the cost of the trial.

Against Exempting

The accused Wilhelm Rommelmann of other points of the accusation and charging the state treasury with part of the trial costs, which have a connection to this point of the accusation and on the basis of article C/581 of the penalty procedures.

Motivation

The accused Wilhelm Rommelmann declared during the trial that he, as a citizen of the German Reich, in 1927 entered service in the German security police after finishing middle school and, in that role, he became active in the city of Bremen until the year 1937, finally in the rank of a security guard (supervisor) of an older district.

In 1937, he transferred to service with the criminal police (*Kripo*). At the end of 1938, he transferred to the police school in Berlin, where he remained until the outbreak of the German-Polish War in September 1939.

Spring 1940, he was sent from Germany to the occupied Polish territory and assigned to service in the German criminal police in Krakow, at Pomorska Street.

Summer 1942, he was taken from Krakow to Tarnow, being assigned to the German criminal police and, simultaneously, he was given the supervision of the possessions of the Jews deported from Tarnow and its surroundings; he remained in this post until autumn 1943 and then he was sent back to Germany.

Clarifying the course of his service in such a manner, the accused denied that he belonged to the Gestapo organization and that he carried out the criminal actions of which he was accused in the act of prosecution.

[Page 202]

The court based on the results of the testimony presented established that the accused was an official of the Gestapo – German State Secret Police – during his service in Tarnow, where he carried out the persecution of Jewish matters and, finally, from the second half of 1943 until leaving Tarnow, he also was involved in matters that had a connection to the Polish population.

The court supported these decisions on the sworn, steadfast, unquestionable witness statements of a number of witnesses and particularly of: Engineer Jozef Kowalik, Jerzy Kostura, Lean Lezer, Eizik Izrael, Josef Kornilo, Dr. Jerzy Iwanski, Dr. Henrik Wachtal, Dr. Henrik Faber, Wilhelm Lerner.

The witnesses just mentioned, particularly the former official in the Tarnow ghetto, Jerzy Kostura, knew the accused very well; they observed his activity in the area of the Tarnow ghetto and also, on this basis, they confirmed in an authoritative manner – and the court accepted this as proof – that the accused was a very important member of the Gestapo.

Also, the witnesses: the priest, Jozef Kloch, Zigmunt Wczotek, *Magister* Roman Krzisztopowicz, Eugenia Fyrek – confirmed that the accused during his actions in Otfinówo, Żabno, Brigel, appeared as a member of the Gestapo and, in general, he was known in the role.

In light of these factual statements, the assertions of the accused that he was an official of *Kripo* and not of the Gestapo are considered completely untruthful.

It is clear that the accused, a routine, professional police functionary, had an exact understanding of the liability made by the connection of his membership in the Gestapo organization and its criminal activity and consequently made an effort – although helpless and in contradiction of the clear facts and evidence – to distance himself from this organization and its activities.

The connection of the activity of the accused during his presence in Tarnow and his service in the Tarnow Gestapo is shown in the first plan, with his taking part in the liquidation of the ghetto in Tarnow and Zakliczyn, then in the mass murder of the Jewish population as well as the annihilation of a group of Roma in Żabno.

[Page 203]

On the basis of the sworn declaration of the witnesses – Engineer Jozef Kowalik, Dr. Jerzy Iwanski, Josef Kornilo, Wilhelm Lerner, Jerzy Kostura, Leon Lezer, Asher Blajwajs, Dr. Henrik Wachtal, Maria Ziskind – the court in reference to the participation of the Tarnow Gestapo in general and the accused (Rommelmann) in particular in the organizing and the liquidation of the Jewish ghetto in Tarnow, asserted as follows:

The first of the routine, planned actions against the Jews, whose purpose it was to concentrate all Jews who lived in Tarnow and its vicinity in an enclosed living quarter, a so-called ghetto, began in the area of Tarnow on the 10th of June 1942. This action was carried out by a special group of *S.S.* men from Krakow ([*S.S.*] *Sonderkommando* – special units of men from various *S.S.* offices) with the participation of the Tarnow Gestapo and the German gendarmerie.

During this action, which lasted several days, 8,000 to 10,000 Jews, the majority old people, the sick, children and those incapable of physical labor, were murdered in their residences, on the streets, at the Jewish cemetery and on the Zbylitowska Mountain. In addition to this, several thousand people of both sexes, were loaded into prepared train wagons at the train station and deported to extermination camps, from which none of the deported returned.

The remainder of the Jewish population, survivors of the above actions numbering about 20,000 people, were placed in the ghetto, which was divided into a ghetto A for those incapable of working and a ghetto B for those capable of working. Rommelmann, the accused, took an active part in this action; at that time he had just come to Tarnow from Krakow and as Gestapo consultant for Jewish matters was at the organization of the ghetto and transferred the Jewish population there.

As seen from the further course of events, the action which began on the 10th of June 1942 was only the first step of the plan to murder and annihilate the entire Jewish population. This plan was realized in a cruel manner. In September 1942, they began to make the ghetto smaller by liquidating ghetto A, by deporting several thousand people from there who were incapable of working to the death camp and a number of the incapable workers were shot on the spot.

[Page 204]

In November 1942, around 5,000 people were deported from the ghetto to the extermination camps, and another group of the ghetto residents were shot on the spot and their bodies were burned on a pyre.

At the end of 1943, the rest of the Jewish population was deported from the Tarnow ghetto – except for a group of around 300 people who were for a certain time to work in the ghetto and [they were] finally deported to the concentration camp in Płaszów and to Szebnie, from which only a small number survived. The Tarnow ghetto was thus liquidated.

As a result of this action, around 40,000 people from the Jewish population were murdered both on the spot in Tarnow and its vicinity and in the death camps.

In addition to taking part in this mass murder and in the general actions of the annihilation of the Jewish population, individual Gestapo members would appear almost daily in the territory of the Tarnow ghetto during its existence and under the smallest pretexts they murdered both individuals and groups of several people and also ill-treated those murdered with beating, kicking and imprisoning them in bunkers.

The Gestapo members Grunow and Rommelmann particularly excelled in such individual murders. On the basis of the statements of the witnesses Leon Lezer, Asher Blajwajs, *Magister* Franciszko Krisztal, Maria Ziskind, Dr. Jerzy Iwanski, Jozef Kornilo – the court ascertained that the accused, Rommelmann, was a terror to the ghetto and he carried out the murders with much sadism, coldly. This was demonstrated by the accused in the territory of the ghetto – and he was an almost daily guest there – that he threw a deadly fear on everyone he encountered.

On the basis of the reading of the statement of the leader of the so-called "employment exchange" in Tarnow, the Viennese German, Emil Utzinger, the court ascertained that the accused had a reputation as a sadist even among his collaborators, as diligent in murdering Jews, ascertained what was characteristic for the evaluation of the person as a criminal type and of his brutal activities.

[Page 205]

It was impossible to ascertain the exact number of victims shot by the accused – only because they were murdered in various places; the families of the victims are not alive and also because almost the entire population of the Tarnow ghetto was murdered and there are no longer witnesses to the murders.

However, on the basis of the facts about the shooting at the Jewish population by the accused ascertained from the testimony of survivors, it must be accepted that the accused was one of the bloodiest Gestapo-hangmen.

The court particularly ascertained on the basis of statements from the witnesses: Engineer Jozef Kowalik, Asher Blajwajs, Dr. Jerzy Iwanski, that the accused himself shot eight men in October 1942 on the territory of the Tarnow ghetto, at the then so-called Magdeburger Platz, because they were not at work. In addition to this, on the basis of the statements of the witness, Engineer Jozek Kowalik, ascertained the fact of the shooting of six women of Jewish origin by the accused in September 1942 on the territory of the ghetto.

On the basis of the statement of the witness, Leon Lezer, the court confirmed the fact of the shooting of eight Jews by the accused in the courtyard of the *Judenrat* [Jewish council] in August 1942 and on the basis of the statement of the witness, Asher Blajwajs, the fact of the shooting in this courtyard in a close, unspecified time, of five Jewish workers because they were incapable of working.

On the basis of the statement by the witness, Lola Gimpel, the court ascertained that on the 4th of December 1942, the accused shot two Jewish women from among four he employed in the firm, Madritsch.

The witness, Josek Mansdorf, confirmed the fact of the shooting by the accused in October 1942 of the sisters of the witness and the witness, Dr. Henrik Wachtel confirmed the fact of the shooting on Starowolski Street by the accused of two Jews, Miller and Folksman, who he encountered outside the ghetto and three Jews and two Jewish women at Magdeburger Platz. In addition to this, the witness confirmed the fact of the shooting by the accused of 10 Jewish boys in the area of the ghetto and a Polish woman near Ochranka Street because she entered the ghetto.

[Page 206]

The witness, Hersh Buch, corroborated the fact of the shooting by the accused at an unascertained time, of two Poles because they entered the ghetto.

The statements of witness Wilhelm Lerner, who was a Jewish militiaman in the Tarnow ghetto and, therefore, had the opportunity to observe the activity of the accused, established for the court the following facts about the shooting by the accused of people from among the Jewish population: several days after the first action, the accused shot 12 people incapable of working and at about the same time he shot a Jewish militiaman who was standing guard at the gate of the ghetto wall because he let a woman enter the ghetto.

In June 1942, he shot six men, two women and a child who had been brought from the city; in addition to this, he shot Dr. Lustig and his two sisters and a certain Jew who had asked him to be left in the ghetto because he could and would work.

The witness Norbert Manheimer confirmed the fact of the shooting of a certain woman, Mrs. Beller, by the accused in October 1943, and that he himself had been tortured by the accused and imprisoned in a cellar.

On the basis of signed statements given under oath by the witnesses Rucza Finder, Mina Laub, Dr. Jerzy Iwanski – the court ascertained that on the 21st of December the accused liquidated the ghetto in Zakliczyn, where approximately 50 people were murdered and the rest were taken to the ghetto in Brigel (Brzesko). There, on the day of their arrival from Zakliczyn, they were shot at the cemetery, except for three young Jewish girls who were taken to the Tarnow ghetto, where, except for Rucza Finder, who managed to escape, they were shot.

In addition to the above ascertained murders, the accused also took part in murdering a group of Roma at the cemetery in Żabno. In particular, the court, on the basis of the statements sworn to under oath by Roman Krzisztopowicz, ascertained that the accused during his stay in the area of Żabno during the second half of 1942, two young Romas were shot near the mill, one aged 16 and the other 17.

[Page 207]

On the basis of the statement of the above witness and of witnesses Stanislaw Przybitek, Stanislaw Sztreng, as well as on the basis of the written statement of the witness Stanislaw Paionk, the court established that not long after shooting the Romas, in around the beginning of July 1943, the accused organized the detention and transfer to the Jewish cemetery in Żabno, in groups of several people, a group of Romas and the women and children – in the number of about 60 people. All were led to the Jewish cemetery by the accused with the assistance of the German gendarme Gustek, shot, ordering them to completely undress and to lay with their faces to the ground. In such a manner, he shot all of the Romas, who were staying in Żabno at that time.

At the same time, the accused also was active in the area of the community of Otfinówo, where he lived for several weeks beginning in June 1943 at the parsonage of the priest, Jozef Kloch.

What did the accused intend in Otfinówo? This is impossible to ascertain, but the accused indicated that he had had the task of observing the airplanes flying by. However, it is a fact that the accused marked his sojourn there by shooting the following people: Boduch, Lira, Bochenek, Piontek, as well as Janina Wozniak; he stood near her, ridiculed her before her death and after undressing her completely, he first lightly wounded her and, then a second later, he murdered her.

These facts of the murders in the area of Otfinówo were confirmed and ascertained on the basis of the statements of the witnesses: the priest, Jozef Kloch, Anna Slowik, Zygmunt Wczostek, Jan Lipinski and Zofia Bochenek.

On the basis of statements given under oath by the witnesses Eugenia Fyrek, Franciszek Fyrek, Leopold Fyrek, the court ascertained that the accused arrested Irena Fyrek, the wife of Franciszek, during the month of August 1943 and took her to Brzesko and the residence of Eugenia Fyrek and there demanded that she indicate the place in which her husband was hiding. He beat her, kicked her – although she asked him for mercy, saying that she was in the sixth month of her pregnancy. After he tortured her for several hours, he led her outside of the house and shot her near the toilet.

[Page 208]

The witness, Eugenia Fyrek, recognized the accused during the interrogation and confirmed that he had shot Irena Fyrek.

On the basis of statements given under oath by the witnesses Helena Fuzio, Wladyslawa Labendz, Stefania Ramzowa, the court ascertained that the accused jointly with the member of the Gestapo, Libor, in October 1943 arrested Maria Fuzio, a resident of Tarnow, under the suspicion that she was trading in gold and foreign currency and during her interrogation at the Gestapo, he beat her so badly that she actually died.

On the basis of the statements given under oath by the witnesses, Karol Lit, Maria Lit, Jan Woszczina – the court ascertained and confirmed that the accused had carried out an investigation concerning the matter of the socialist activist, well known in Tarnow Eugeniuz Szit, pseudonym, Sroka – who hid from the Gestapo and in connection with this, in March 1943 the accused arrested Jan Woszczina, Karol Szit and caused their confinement at the Auschwitz concentration camp.

During the interrogation of Maria Szit, the accused undressed her completely and then beat her until she lost consciousness.

The accused did not confess to any of the ascertained deeds and confronted by a particular witness – he in general did not speak in reference to their statements maintaining that they were in error, that they did not pertain to him and they were erroneous in ascribing deeds to him, which he did not carry out.

The court did not believe the answers of the accused, seeing in his denials of the confirmations made by the witnesses' facts, an expression of fear of his responsibility for the cruel crimes that he carried out during his service in the Gestapo in Tarnow.

Analyzing the activity of the accused in light of the above assertions – the court accepted as proof, first of all, that the accused did take part in the organizing of the Gestapo – that was recognized as a criminal organization on the basis of the verdict of the International Tribunal in Nuremberg and on the basis of article 4, paragraph 2, letter C of the decree of the 31.8.1944, item 377/46, Legal Gazette of the Polish Republic. No closer explanation of the criminal character of the Gestapo was needed on the basis of the above assertions – which cannot be questioned. And as it was shown that the accused was a member of the Gestapo, it is superfluous to further consider accusing him of taking part in a crime through the organs of power of the German state-created organization.

[Page 209]

What subjective relevance there is concerning the responsibility for taking part in this organization, the court's procedures show:

    A.   that the accused voluntarily undertook service in the Gestapo.
    B.   that he knew the purposes and work methods of the Gestapo.
    C.   that beyond every discussion by the court, that the Gestapo had for its purpose to carry out crimes against humanity and that this purpose – concerning the activity of the Gestapo in Tarnow – he consistently understood.

In connection with the assertion under A) – the accused – although he was and is a German citizen and without doubt had the right to voluntarily become a member of the Gestapo, the organization created by the state organs – yet as a member of this organization recognized as a criminal organization by the International Tribune – he was just responsible for taking part in it.

Item B) The accused – possessing a middle school education, knowing of the 25 points of the *N.S.D.A.P.*[1] knew and was well aware of what the Gestapo – the implementation organ of this party – had as its purpose –relative to the Jewish population and also gave an account of it that the Gestapo in carrying out this program relative to the Jewish population made use of brutal and savage annihilation methods.

Item C) The carrying out of these purposes on the territory of the Tarnow ghetto had such a clear expression that there can be no doubt about the purpose and the means of realizing his crimes against humanity. The accused not only belonged to the organization whose purpose and methods he knew – but he – as was ascertained – took an active part in realizing this purpose and made use of its criminal methods.

[Page 210]

In particular, he took part in the actions of the Tarnow Gestapo – as its member, connected to the shared purpose of the entire collective – in liquidating the Jewish population, in murdering them and deporting them to death camps because of racial, religious and national origin.

Contemplating at the starting point the individual activity of the accused – namely the actual murder of people from among the civilian population, as well as choosing them for racial, national reasons – while these actual murders essentially comprise crimes, they must be accepted as an expression of the consequences of membership in the Gestapo, an organization with shared purposes and methods of activity on the part of all its members. The accused as a member of the Gestapo on the territory of Tarnow, or the Zakliczyn ghetto or outside the ghetto, shot at individual people in the Jewish population, he shot Roma in Żabno and Poles on the territory of the community of Otfinówo and he shot Irena Fyrek in Brzesko. – In all of the cases, he carried out the crimes of murdering these people in connection collectively on behalf of all of the members of the Gestapo, because to realize the principles and purposes of the Gestapo organization – that is, to annihilate Jews as well as Roma, they were persecuted because of their racial affiliation and the Poles for political and national motives.

Everything carried out by the accused and the crimes established above rise to a crime against humanity as a result of the participation of the accused in such a criminal organization as the Gestapo.

The criminal activity of the accused that was proven during the trial to have been done by him includes all of the judicial facts in the case, which was foreseen in article 1, item 1, 2 and in article 4 and paragraph 1 of the decree of the 31st of August 1944. Item 377/46 of the Legal Gazette of the Polish Republic.

[Page 211]

The connection, in particular, to these crimes of article 4, paragraph 1 and of article 1, paragraph 1 and 2 of the earlier decree – according to the above conduct and with the directives of article 36 of the penalty decree, everything was considered as one criminal action that approves both directives of this decree and that corresponds to the qualifications of article 1, point 2/1 – as a directive that contains more severe punitive sanctions, simultaneously the court accepted that the criminal conduct of the accused during his sojourn and activity in the Gestapo carries the character of one continuing crime, which had as its purpose to support the organs of power of the German state and to harm the people of the civilian population, indifferent to whether they were Jews, Poles or Roma. With these particular deeds of the accused being only an external expression carried out in such a manner and with such a purpose of criminal actions, the accused must therefore be held responsible for the entire scope of his activity as a sum of his criminal deeds.

For these reasons, the court recognized the accused Wilhelm Rommelmann as guilty in crimes only from article 1, item 1/2 and connected with article 4, paragraph 1 of the decree of the 31st of August 1944 item 377/46 Legal Gazette of the Polish Republic, which encompasses the total of his criminal activities. In calculating the penalty, the court took into consideration the enormity of the crimes carried out by the accused, each one of which justifies the sentencing exclusively to the death penalty.

In light of the factual evidence brought out, the accused is an extraordinary criminal and dangerous type, so, it is absolutely necessary to eliminate him from a society with a sense of legality.

The accused cannot answer with the assertion that as a citizen of the German state, he must support it because of the feeling of patriotism, that the duty of loyalty and devotion to his own land are fundamental and understandable motives of the activity of every citizen that must be taken into consideration. [These assertions] cannot in any way defend the carrying out of such unnatural crimes against humanity that were exhibited by the accused and were applied in the sentence of the court. These crimes upset the basic order of international rights such as the principles of equal rights of all human creatures and their right to develop and exist without distinction as to their racial or national origins.

[Page 212]

Whereas these crimes were carried out by the accused within the area of the Polish State and with regard to its citizens and Poland is one of the signatories of the London Agreement of the 8th of August 1945 concerning the prosecution and punishment of the main war criminals and accordingly with the promulgating of international law, it implemented the decree of 31.8.1944 and the decree of 10.12.1944 item 377 Legal Gazette of the Polish Republic – the article 4 concerning the responsibility for taking part in a crime, through the organs of power of the German state-created organization – it has the right to persecute war criminals, to which must be included the accused, on the basis of the above London Agreement as well as on the basis of article 3 of the penalty decree.

The determination concerning the loss of public and citizenship rights, as well as concerning the confiscation of his possessions, is compulsory in regard to the death sentence article 7 A/B) from the decree and article 52, paragraph 2 of the penalty code cited above. Because the accused has no possessions, the court frees him from the trial costs and court charges.

The further part of the verdict deals with the clause of the accusation in regard to the accused taking part in organizing and liquidating the ghettos in Dąbrowa and Brzesko – which were not exhibited, and therefore, we have not considered it.

At the end are the following signatures. the president: Dr. St. Krol and the Concessors [jurors]: Lieber Gottlob and Wladyslaw Lorenc.

Editor's note:

1. National Socialistishe Deutschish Arbeter Parti [National Socialist German Workers Party.

[Page 213]

A Mother's Prayer
(A chapter from the memorial book "The Jews of Tarnow")

Dedication: to the memory of my dear parents Menachem and Yocheved Ginzberg and my sisters, Batia and Malka who died as martyrs in Belzec on Rosh Hashana 5703 (1943)

by Nathan-Ari Ginzberg, Bene-Brak, Israel

Translated by Daniel Kochavi

Nathan-Ari Ginzberg

The year of 5702 (1942) is almost over, a bloody year when hundreds of Jewish communities were wiped out and millions of Jews died martyred in all manners of death.

The Tarnow ghetto too suffered sacrifices. During the first days of the "action" thousands from various surrounding locations were cruelly murdered in cemeteries by the cursed Nazis. Jewish blood was spilled like water and thousands of ghetto residents were transported in cattle cars under horrible conditions. They died in the gas chambers of the Belzec extermination camp.

But that was only the beginning of the execution of the Satanic plan known shamefully as "the Final Solution".

Life in the ghetto was one of fear, hunger and hard labor for those condemned to die. "Those who work will live" was the deceptive slogan of the Nazis to delude the Jews. Their ugly aim was to preserve Jewish manpower as long as possible.

Early in the morning, groups exited the ghetto gates to work at hard labor. We worked for 12 hours and returned to the ghetto tired, dirty, hungry, in pain. In spite of this, every man and woman continue to work to survive. Exploited Jews carry out hard and dangerous work. This hard labor and poor nourishment weaken people day by day. This was our life, constantly fearful during work and upon returning to the ghetto, where we suffered from diseases, overcrowding and depression. As the saying goes: " with fear in your heart you ask in the morning who will see the evening and, in the evening, you ask who will see the morning".

[Page 214]

At the same time, Job-like news about the slaughters of Jews taking place all over occupied Poland begin to reach us. We become aware that the entire civilized world has forgotten us and no one will rescue us from our horrible situation. The Gentile neighbors are against us. We become aware of Jews who hid in surrounding villages and, after their money and meager properties were taken from them, were denounced to the abominable Gestapo, tortured and killed.

We start desperately to look for hiding places in basements, attics and warehouses. Young people who look "Aryan" obtain phony Polish IDs and escape from the ghetto. Then, two days before Rosh Hashana, sleep eludes Jews in the ghetto. A bitter rumor spreads like a storm, started by the Jews who live at the edge of the ghetto, that heavy guards from the police force and the SS armed with light and heavy weapons are stationed around the ghetto to prevent any escape. No one sleeps in the ghetto. A terrible panic spreads among the unfortunate Jews.

The Judenrat (Jewish council) officials announce that every worker must surrender his work ID to be stamped by the Gestapo. Workers who receive a special stamp will remain alive because they are considered essential to the war effort. A large crowd gathers near the Judenrat to obtain the special stamp on their worker permit. However only a few workers get their permits right away. After several hours a riot breaks out when thousands of workers, including myself, are left without permits since they are never returned. Some forged stamps are used but, unfortunately, I am left without a permit after it is taken by the Judenrat police.

Later that night I return home. On the way I encounter families with children and bundles - running away terrified, like animals caught in a trap, in order to hide in bunkers prepared earlier. Here and there the hiding places are further improved, well-hidden and stocked with some food and water to wait out the storm. Everybody looks for ways to save their life and their family.

When I arrive home, all are ready to hide in the bunker. Each has a bundle and they also have prepared some food and warm clothes for me. I join my family and we all struggle to enter the small storeroom that is already crowded with 15 people including small children. It is terribly hot and suffocating, making it hard to breathe. Any light sound that can be heard outside causes great fear of discovery. We especially must strictly keep the young children quiet.

The children are asleep early in the morning. But the adults started to recite Slichot prayers. I am standing next to my dear mother who is reciting her Slichot prayers (note: special prayers before Rosh Hashana) with heartbreaking sobbing. Her tears are flowing on her prayer book. Standing so close to her, I can make out parts of her prayers recited with sublime devotion.

Her eyes are closed and her lips recite a silent prayer. She pleads for mercy: Our God who is in heaven...I know that we are in great danger...who knows what our fate will be....if it is so decreed I am ready to die a martyr's death...I plead that a remnant of my family be spared and children survive. That at least a small memory of ours remains...

[Page 215]

Her holy and pure lips murmur the last prayer that I heard from her and will never forget it, "a mother's prayer" said simply and with utter belief that the last hour has arrived and the end is near.

In the east dawn has broken. The men wrap themselves in the Tallit and put on the Tefillin. Who knows--this may be their last prayer? They recite it with great devotion. I also join the prayer. Afterwards I come out of the bunker to escape the suffocating air inside and breathe some fresh fall air. Other people are afraid to come out, but I gather my courage after listening to my mother's prayer that instilled in me the belief that I would be saved.

That morning, Jews who returned from the assembly ground tell me that the Nazis have started to round up and deport ghetto Jews who did not have "stamps". I also found out that young people's work IDs are stamped.

I return to the bunker to consult with my parents about risking a return to the assembly ground. This would be extremely dangerous, practically submitting to the jaws of the Nazi lion not knowing if I would survive. My parents advise me to go, kiss me and hope that I will return alive.

Approaching the square, I see from afar young men returning holding work certificates stamped by the Gestapo. I finally decide to enter the square and am initially seized with fear when I see a large number of Germans running around the square. Work permits are stacked in a corner. I quickly find mine and stand in line for the table where a Gestapo man with a murderous face is sitting. He asks my age and my work place. After looking me over from top to bottom he finally stamps my ID card thus keeping me alive. I quickly leave the area. Nearby I see Jews on their knees with their heads to the ground, unfortunate Jews caught by the Nazis to be sent to the extermination camp in Belzec. Germans armed with weapons and sticks surround and guard them. Anyone trying to raise his head is beaten to a pulp.

To this day I cannot understand how I survived. A real miracle since, after several hours, I found out that I was among the last people to obtain the stamp. People arriving after me in the square were caught and deported.

The Germans, knowing that Jews were hiding in bunkers and were hard to find, realized that when they found out about the stamps on work permits people would come out on their own. Hundreds of Jews were thus caught and sent to Belzec.

I return to my family and to tell them about my stamped ID. My dear father encourages me and tells me to remain strong when facing hardships. My dear mother tells me that her prayers the previous night helped bring this about. My parents give me a blessing that no evil will happen to me and that I will be saved from the evil hands of the vicious Nazis.

[Page 216]

This is the last night of the year. I give up my place in the hideout to ease the crowding since I am "privileged," having received the stamp on my work card. Most young people live in the apartments since they were certified by the Nazis as laborers worth saving. Their parents and small children hide in the basements, the attics and closets.

In the morning I return to the bunker to check on my family and to bring them and other people food and water. I find very tired and sleepy people. The small children sleep a sweet sleep, not knowing of the terrible danger they are in.

In the morning I leave my precious family with wishes that we meet again in the evening. I close the bunker tightly and use a cabinet to hide the entrance. I then step outside to see what's happening.

Almost immediately I hear savage voices of Germans approaching with terrifying sniffing dogs yelling "Raus"! They order every person to come out to the yard and from there transport us under heavy guard to the deportation square. Other Germans with dogs stay behind and carry out a thorough search.

In the square there is terrible uproar dominated by yells of the Nazis who are gathering Jews from every corner of the ghetto. Men, women and children, old women and old men crouch in the center of the square. Poor Jews arrive continuously desperate, terrified and beaten as they are subjected to shoving and horrible shouts from the murderers. They are transported in groups of hundreds to a central place located in a school outside the ghetto. The sick, elderly and disabled who cannot walk are immediately murdered by hundreds of Nazis scouring the deportation square. Those who are able to work and allowed to remain in the ghetto are moved to the edge of the square. We remain there for hours in the burning heat without water and unable to move anywhere. Not far from us the selected Jews crouch. Seeing these poor Jews is heartbreaking as we are powerless to help.

At 3 PM the last transport leaves the ghetto to the assembly station outside. The action is about to stop until the cursed Nazis realize that the count of Jews to be sent to Belzec does not meet the target of their Satanic plan. They decide to choose the missing quota of hundreds more from those remaining in the camp.

A fat German, one of the Gestapo officers, is standing in the center of the square holding a stick. All the Jews who obtained the stamp by various means and believed they were safe, have to go in front of this German who decides in a blink of an eye "who shall live-and who shall perish". The first victims are the elderly and anyone holding a child by the hand. Parents, realizing this, cut an opening in the fence and smuggle the small children through that opening. The children escape and hide in the yards and the houses near the square. By now the German murderers realize what's happening and start chasing the escaping children. A shocking and nightmarish sight ensues. Like wild beasts the Germans catch up with the poor small children and kill them in cold blood. Very few children are able to escape and save themselves. A hair-raising spectacle occurs in the center of the square. A father does not want to be separated from his young son and both are murdered right there by a Nazi.

[Page 217]

It gets dark outside. The "action" nears the end. The remaining Jews, families with children and all those with stamps chosen nevertheless for deportation leave the ghetto. The Nazis have completed their criminal tasks and let us return home.

5702 (1942) ends, a bloody year of martyrs, including Tarnow martyrs. A new year, 5703, is about to begin. Those remaining in the departure square, mostly the youths who left their families in their hiding places and bunkers before going out, run quickly to find out what happened to their loved ones. I, among them, quickly reach our house where our bunker is located. The silence in the house is a bad omen. My heart tells me that a terrible disaster has happened. The bunker is completely empty. I only find some pieces of clothing and holy books strewn on the floor. I run like a mad man to our apartment to see if my loved ones are home. But, sadly, I find no one in the apartment. I burst into heartbreaking tears as do hundreds and thousands in the ghetto who today lost their dear ones. All walk around out of their mind, shocked and numbed by the immense pain.

That night we observe the beginning of the New Year (Rosh Hashana). But in the ghetto, it feels like "Tisha B'Av" (day of mourning to mark the destruction of the Jerusalem temples), loss, destruction, mourning and tears caused by the enormous disaster. Who could have imagined this? Only that morning I talked with and left my loved ones hoping to see them again after the storm. But the separation was forever. I am sentenced to never see them again and I walked mindlessly all night wondering and asking why? Why are we condemned to lose our parents and families and become orphans in a single day?

I then recall Rosh Hashana evenings before the war. Prayers in our synagogues full of people, the festive and elated spirits of the congregation. The streets crowded with Jews returning from synagogues and greeting each other with "Shana Tova" blessings. The house full of light and joy. A white tablecloth on the table, candlesticks lit up and festive foods with the entire family around the table.

The next day (in the ghetto) is the first day of Rosh Hashana. Here and there small groups of Jews gather for holiday prayers. In basements and well-hidden closets with a lookout posted to warn the worshipers should the Nazis approach.

[Page 218]

The "Eicha" melody [translator note: the melody that is used on the holiday of Tisha B'Av to read the book of Eicha] is sung for the Rosh Hashana prayers. All the worshipers weep bitterly over the loss of their loved ones who were taken so cruelly from us. The "Unetanah Tokef [Note: a major prayer recited on Rosh Hashana and Yom Kippur] has a special meaning for us as we, the condemned to death by the cursed Nazis, recite the verses " who shall live and who shall die, who by water and who by fire, who by strangling and who by stoning". In dread we recite the prayer quietly and our hearts weep. Who knows whether at this very moment our martyred beloved are being strangled and burned and what our fate will be? Who knows what bitter fate awaits us? We picture thousands of holy and pure Jews being led to the altars of extermination in Belzec. Thousands of Jews who in life and death are never parted.

In those hard moments I suddenly remember my dear mother's prayer and the last words of my wise father who told me to be brave and strong and to struggle courageously to stay alive.

I continue my prayers and pleas and my heart is filled with faith and certainty that, in the next world, I will be rescued from the killing hell and that my mother's prayer will come true.

Monument to the memory of the victim of the Nazi regime in Tarnow who were murdered in 1942-1943

[Page 219]

Tarnow Rabbis Who Perished *oyf Kiddush Hashem*[a][1]

by Menashe Unger

Translated by Gloria Berkenstat Freund

The Grodzisker Rebbe, Reb Eliezer Horowicz (Horowitz)

The Grodzisker Rebbe, Reb Eliezer Horowicz, who lived in Tarnow, was one of the first rabbis in the city who perished *oyf Kiddush haShem*. His cry of *Shema Yisroel* [Hear, o Israel – the central prayer of Jewish worship] before the Germans shot him made the entire Jewish community tremble.

The Grodzisker Rebbe, Reb Eliezer Horowicz, was a son of Rebbe, Reb Avraham-Chaim Horowicz from Plontsch [Polaniec], who lived in *Radomyšl*, (western Galicia) and in Rzeszow after the First World War.

Reb Eliezer was born in 5461 (1881). He was the son-in-law of Rebbe, Reb Meir Yehuda Szpira of Bukowsko.

The Plontscher Rebbe, Reb Avraham-Chaim, was a son of the Rozwadówer Rebbe, Reb Moshe Horowicz, may the memory of the righteous man be blessed. He was born in 5610 (1850). He knew his paternal grandfather, the Rebbe, Reb Naftali Zwi Horowicz, but he did not know his maternal grandfather, the Sigheter Rebbe, Reb Yekutial-Yehuda Teitelbaum of Sighet, the author of *Yetev Lev* [Hasidic Torah commentary], although he spoke of him.

The Plontscher Rebbe, Reb Avraham-Chaim, was a son-in-law of Reb Betsalel Pilzner, a rich Jew. He got married at age 13. His father-in-law provided financial support in Rozwadów as long as his father-in-law, who was the Rozwadówer Rebbe, may the memory of the righteous man be blessed, was alive. The Rozwadówer Rebbe, Reb Moshe, may the memory of the righteous man be blessed, died on the of Sivan 5654 (1894) and Reb Avraham-Chaim became Rabbi in Plontsch, Congress Poland. He then moved to Radomysl. He had a great knowledge of Jewish law and he studied many Talmudic texts with his brother-in-law, the Zabner Rebbe, Reb Sholem-Dovid Unger, may the memory of the righteous man be blessed, Rebbe Avraham-Chaim continued to be supported financially by the Rozwadówer Rebbe.

The Plontscher Rebbe was an honest man and full-hearted. He had a mellifluous voice and on Friday nights he would sing *Shabbos* [Sabbath] songs at the table.

[Page 220]

His singing of *Ma Yedidut* [How Beloved is Your Rest] and *Me'ein Olam Haba* [A Taste of the World to Come] would evoke a great moral resurgence among the Hasidim.

Friday night, at the Shabbat table, before sharing learning, he would quietly hum a melody. His face would light up and when he began to share his learning, he would stumble over his words, so that it was difficult to understand his teaching. A devoted Hasid of his, Reb Chaim Fefer, could grasp the sounds and the half words of the Plontscher Rebbe and he then repeated the teaching to the assembled Hasidim.

During the First World War the Plontscher Rebbe fled with his household to Budapest, Hungary and after the war, he settled in Rzeszow and established his rabbinical court there.

The Plontscher Rebbe died on the eve of Rosh Hashanah, Cheshvan 5679 [24th of September, 1919].

The Plontscher Rebbe had three sons: Reb Dovid, Pshezlaver, who was then the Rebbe in Rzeszow (he perished *oyf Kiddush haShem*), Reb Shlomo, who was a son-in-law of the Rebbe Yehiel, the Pakshivnitzer Rebbe (he died when he was young) and Reb Eliezer, who was the rabbi in Grodzisk and after the First World War lived in Tarnow and had three daughters. One son-in-law was the Satmar Rebbe, Reb Yoelish Teitelbaum (his wife and children perished at the hands of the Germans).

The Grodzisker Rebbe, Reb Eliezer married when he was 16-years-old. His father-in-law provided financial support and was the esteemed Bukowsker Rebbe.

In 5669 (1909), when the Bukowsker Rebbe died, Reb Eliezer became the rabbi in Grodzisk, a *shtetl* [town] in western Galicia, near Tarnow.

The new Grodzisker Rebbe, Reb Eliezer, lived in Tarnow in the *Grabówka district* [on Lwowska Street], a distance from the center of the city and there functioned in the position of Hasidic rebbe.

In addition to having three daughters, the Grodzisker Rebbe had two sons: Reb Moshe, who was a son-in-law of Reb Yosef Horowicz from Kras (he died as a young man), and Reb Dovid, who was a son-in-law of Reb Mordekhai-Zev Halbershtam, Rabbi in Grybow. His daughter, Hene, married Reb Moshe Teitelbaum of Krakow; his daughter, Alte-Chaya was the *rebbitzen (wife)* of the Rozwadówer Rabbi, Reb Moshe Horowicz (they and their household perished *oyf Kiddush haShem*); and his daughter Rywka, was the wife of the Rabbi, Reb Dovid-Ber Fersztman, the editor of *Dos Yiddish Wort* [*The Daily* Word] in Zamość-Warsaw.

[Page 221]

* * *

When the Germans entered Tarnow, they issued edicts against the Jews, one more severe than the next, to imbitter the life of the Jews.

At that terrible time, the Germans looked to destroy the spiritual leaders of the Jews – the rebbes; then it would be easier for them [the Germans] to send all of the Jews from Tarnow to the gas chambers at Auschwitz.

The rebbes searched for a place to hide.

The Grodzisker Rebbe lay hidden in a bunker at Lwowska Street number 10, where his cousin, the Żabner Rebbe, Reb Eliezer Unger, may God avenge his blood, lived.

"The Germans burst into the courtyard and discovered the bunker. They threw a gas bomb into the bunker and the Grodzisker Rebbe had to come out of the bunker." – says a letter from Mordekhai Ebersztark, one of the survivors from Tarnow, who lives in Antwerp, Belgium. According to this letter, this occurred on Rosh Hashanah; he makes an error in the date, because this was the 7th of Kislev 5703 (1943).

Mordekhai Ebersztark writes further in this letter:

"The Grodzisker Rebbe came out of the bunker. He still had his beard and *peyes*, although the Germans had issued an order that all Jews had to cut off their beards and *peyes* [uncut sideburns worn by religious men].

"The Germans placed the Grodzisker Rebbe against the wall and told him that he would be shot in 10 minutes; if he had a wish, he should say so.

"The Grodzisker Rebbe asked them to bring the robe that he had inherited from his father, the Plontscher Rebbe and his *talis* [prayer shawl]. The Grodzisker Rebbe put on his father's robe and the *talis* and when he saw the Germans aiming their revolvers at him, he shouted *Shema Yisroel*, which echoed in all of the surrounding houses and in all of the bunkers in which Jews were hiding.

"That day the Germans shot 3,500 Jews in their houses, in the courtyards and on the staircases.

[Page 222]

"When taking the corpses to the cemetery, one Hasid took the holy body of the martyr, the Grodzisker Rebbe, and gave him a Jewish burial.

"At that moment, with the passionate shout, *Shema Yisroel*, the Grodzisker Rebbe perished *oyf Kiddush haShem*, may God avenge his blood."

The Dzikówer Rebbe, Reb Alter Horowicz - Perished *oyf Kiddush haShem*

The Rebbe, Reb Alter Horowicz of Dzików was the last rabbi of the Dzikówer-Ropshitzer dynasty.

The Dzikówer Rebbe lived in Tarnow after the First World War, but he was still called the Dzikówer Rebbe. The Dzikówer Rebbe perished *oyf Kiddush haShem* at the hands of the Germans in Krakow.

Dzików (Tarnobrzeg, also called Dzików) was a *shtetl* [town] in western Galicia that lay at the border with Congress Poland on the right side of the Vistula [River].

The Jewish community in Dzików was over 500 years old. Dzików was well known in the Hasidic world. After the Ropshitzer Rebbe, Reb Naftali Hersh Horowicz, died (11th of Iyar 5587 – [8th of May] 1827), his son Reb Eliezer became the rebbe in Dzików. From then on Dzików became the continuation of Ropshitzer Hasidic dynasty and four generations were rabbis there until the coming of the savage blow of the German murderers, cut the Ropshitzer-Dzikówer tree – and the Dzikówer rabbinical dynasty disappeared.

The Rebbe, Reb Eliezer did not want a large group of Hasidim. He distanced himself from the Hasidim and did not permit stories to be told about his miracles.

Once the Rebbe, Reb Eliezer, in his teaching, translated: *Zakeinu l'Kabel Shabatot* [And may we merit to receive Shabbos]... *Mitokh miut avanut – miut avanut* [and in the midst of a few sins – few sins] to mean one should have few Hasidim because the Hasidim delude themselves that they are full of sin – if one has few Hasidim, one has fewer sins...

The Rebbe, Reb Eliezer did not want his teachings to be published in a book.[2] Rzeszow, Reb Eliezer, gave a reason in a jest:

[Page 223]

"I do not want a Jew to eat his fill Friday night at the feast and convince himself that he was a Hasid and then he would take my book to bed before sleeping, look at it. I do not want to sleep with such a Jew in his bed…"

And although the Rebbe, Reb Eliezer did not believe in miracles and said that since the death of the *seer* of Lublin, the appearance of miracles and prophetic inspiration had declined, his Hasidim told a story that was a kind of prophetic inspiration.

The Rebbe, Reb Eliezer had a custom that on Rosh Hashanah, when he was called to the Torah, he would recite the *Mi Shebeyrekh* [the one who is blessed – prayer said for a person or group] for all of the Hasidic rebbes. On the eve of Rosh Hashanah, he would write a list on a piece of paper of the rebbes and he would always place the Rzeszower Rebbe first on the list. The *shamas* [synagogue beadle] would always call out the names when the Dzikówer Rebbe was called up to the Torah.

In 5611 (1850), the Dzikówer Rebbe asked that the name of the Sanzer Rebbe, Reb Chaim *ben* [son of] Miriam be placed at the beginning of the list and that the name Reb Yisroel *ben* Chana, the name of the Rzeszower Rebbe, not be place at the beginning of the list.

And on Rosh Hashanah, at being called to the Torah, he did not ask for the saying of the *Mi Shebeyrekh* for the Rzeszower Rebbe. The Hasidim did not understand the reason and the same year, on the 3rd of Cheshvan [9th of October 1850], the Rzeszower Rebbe died.

The Hasidim said that the Rebbe, Reb Eliezer had recognized the spirit of inspiration that the Rzeszower Rebbe would not live to the end of the next year.

The story of the Rebbe, Reb Eliezer, about when he swore in 5620 (1860) in the *sukkah* [temporary structure in which one has meals and may sleep during the holiday of *Sukkot* – Feast of Tabernacles] that *Moshiekh* [messiah] would not come that year, also was well known.

There was faith among Jews that *Moshiekh* would come in 5620. Allusion to this had been found in the *Zohar*. The Rebbe, Reb Eliezer, on a *Sukkos* night at the table during a teaching, said with great ardor: "*Rabbeinu shel olam* [God the Creator], we ask You: You, Merciful Creator, favor us to be worthy of sitting in the skin of the Leviathan and then I swear that *Moshiekh* [redeemer] will not come this year!'

[Page 224]

After *Sukkot*, the Rebbe, Reb Eliezer, questioned his son as to why he [Eliezer] had sworn that *Moshiekh* [redeemer] would not come in that year:

"I am afraid that the faith that *Moshiekh* will come this year has spread so strongly among the multitudes that if, God forbid, he does not come, atheism will be strengthened. I have sworn that *Moshiekh* will not come. If he does not come, they will know about my oath; if he does actually come this year, so, let him come and, if need be, I will remain a liar…"

The Rebbe, Reb Eliezer died on the 3rd of Cheshvan 5621 (19th October 1861). However, he left four sons, two of whom founded their own dynasties that had thousands of Hasidim. They were: the Rebbe, Reb Meirl, may the memory of the righteous man be blessed, the first-born son, who became the rebbe in Dzików, and his second son, the Rebbe, Reb Moshe Horowicz, may the memory of the righteous man be blessed, of Rozwadów, died the 10th of Sivan 5654 ([14th of June] 1894).[3]

The Rebbe, Reb Meirl Dzikówer followed in the path of his father and grandfather. He combined piety and brilliance. His book of responsa, *Imrei Noam* [*Words of Pleasantness*] was known in the scholarly world.[4]

Reb Meirl also published the book *Imrei Noam* on the teachings. The teachings are full of gematria, according to the path of the covenant of priesthood.

Whereas, the Rebbe, Reb Meirl did permit his works to be printed, he diverged from the custom of his father and grandfather who said that their interpretations should not be printed.

The author of *Imre Noam* had a custom that every night of Chanukah he would play with the *dreidel* [top] with his children and in the year in which he died – the Hasidim say – the Rebbe, Reb Meirl also played with the *dreidel* with his children, but during the game, the *dreidel* constantly fell on the [Hebrew letter] *nun*. The Rebbe, Reb Meirl spun the *dreidel* three times and it fell on the *nun* all three times. The author of *Imre Noam* sadly immediately stopped playing. The Hasidim did not know the reason. During the same year, on the 5th of Tammuz 5638 (1878), the Rebbe, Reb Meirl, died in Carlsbad (the *mun* was supposed to be an allusion to *nifter* [the Yiddish word to die]).

[Page 225]

The author of *Imre Noam* was brought to Dzików from Carlsbad and he was buried in the *Ohel* [structure over a grave] of his father, the Rebbe, Reb Eliezer.

* * *

After the death of *Imre Noam* [Reb Meirl was known by the name of his book], his son, Reb Yehoshale became his successor.

The Rebbe, Reb Yehoshale, was widely known in the world for his brilliance and insight. He also was known by the name of his book, *Ateret Yehoshua* [*The Crown of Yehoshua*]. He also was the author of the book, *Emek Halakha* [Talmudic responsa] and other books.

The author of *Ateret Yehoshua* did not think highly of the Austrian state that was pieced together from various nations: from the Hungarians, Czechs, Poles, Bosnians and other nations. He compared the Austrian-Hungarian state to Reb Zaynvl Ropshitzer's *tefillin* [phylacteries] bag.

Reb Zaynvl Ropshitzer was the spokesperson in the Ropshitzer Rebbe's court. Once Reb Zaynvl lost his *talis* and *tefillin* bag.

The Ropshitzer Rebbe said to him: "Zaynvl, why are you so troubled? You have not lost more than the *tefillin* bag, while you will yourself admit that the *talis* was a Turkish one; the *tefillin* were only one pair – Rashi's *tefillin* and the second pair, Rebbenu Tam's *tefillin*; the *tefillin* bag was your own…"[5]

The Austrian-Hungarian state is also the same, the Dzikówer Rebbe concluded, of the entire state, not more will be left than the *tefillin* bag – Vienna and the small Austrian provinces.

Thus, before the First World War, the Dzikówer Rebbe foresaw that the Austrian-Hungarian Empire would fall like a house of cards and only Vienna and its Austrian provinces would remain of the large state.

[Page 226]

The Dzikówer Rebbe, Reb. Yehoshale, the author of *Ateret Yehoshua* [*The Crown of Yehoshua*], died on the 11th of Tevet 5672 (1912) and after his death, his son, Reb Alter became rebbe.

* * *

The Rebbe, Reb Alter was born in 5639 (1879). He was an only son and weak, with many illnesses, but over time he overcame his illnesses

The Dzikówer Rebbe, Reb Alter when young married the daughter of his uncle, the Rebbe, Reb Yizroeltshe Hager from Wisnicz, who had the reputation of a lover of the Jewish people.

Reb Alter's father-in-law provided financial support in Wisnicz and then he returned to Dzików and was hired as the younger rabbi.

The Rebbe, Reb Alter Dzikówer was very much beloved by the Hasidim because by nature he was a kind-hearted person. He hosted his Hasidim at the *Shabbat* meal on Friday nights, according to the way of the Dzikówer-Ropshitzer, they stayed until morning and although he himself was not a talented singer, there always were a group of Hasidic musicians who sang Ropshitzer- Dzikówer Hasidic melodies.

After the First World War, the Ropshitzer Rebbe lived in Tarnow at *Holtz Platz* [Wood Square]. Hundreds and hundreds of Hasidim from Galicia and rich Hasidic men from Antwerp and London would come for Rosh Hashanah.

When the German oppressors entered Galicia, the Dzikówer Rebbe escaped to Krakow. He thought that he could hide there. He was in the ghetto there until the German murderers caught him. The Dzikówer Rebbe perished *oyf Kiddush haShem* at the hands of the Germans on the 5th of Adar 5703 ([12th of March] 1943), with his *rebbitzen* [wife], the Wisznicer Rebbe's daughter.

His son, Reb Mendele, who was the rabbi in Dzików, also was in a concentration camp in Plaszow near Krakow, for a time. He then was taken to a second camp at Mauthausen and he died there on *Simchas Torah* in 5704 ([the 10th of October] 1944).

His wife, the young *rebbitzen*, was taken to Danzig and she was drowned in a river by the Germans along with hundreds of other women. The Dzikówer Rebbe's two other sons, Reb Meirl and Yekele, were murdered by the Germans.

[Page 227]

The Dzikówer Rebbe's daughter, Dwoyrale Abramovicz-Arnun[6] and the Dzikówer Rebbe's son, Reb Yehudale, who lives in Jerusalem, survived. He could have continued the Dzikówer rabbinical dynasty. However, he does not want to be a rebbe.

The Żabner Rebbe, Reb Eliezer Unger - Perished *oyf Kiddush haShem* [for sanctification of God's Name]

The Żabner Rebbe, Reb Eliezer Unger, was a son of Rebbe Sholem-Dovid Unger, may the memory of the righteous man be blessed.

The Żabner rabbinical dynasty extends to Rebbe, Reb Mordekhai-Dovid Unger, may the memory of the righteous man be blessed, of Dąbrowa (western Galicia), who was a student of the Rebbe, Reb Yakov Yitzhak Horowitz, called the *khozeh* [seer] of Lublin.

The Żabner rabbinical line had many founders of Hasidism in its branches in Poland and Galicia. The Żabner Rebbe was a descendent of the Rebbe, Reb Elimelekh of Lizhensk, from Rebbe, Reb Yisroel – the *Kaczenicer Magid* [preacher], of the Ropshitzer [Ropczyce] Rebbe, Reb Naftali Zvi Horowicz and the Żabner Rebbe, Reb Yakov Yitzhak, may the memory of the righteous man be blessed, and was the son-in-law of Rebbe, Reb Meirl Horowicz of Dzików [Tarnobrzeg], who was one of the great Jewish personalities.

The Dzikówer Rebbe, Reb Meirl, may the memory of the righteous man be blessed, authored the books, *Imrei Noam* [*Words of Pleasantness*] on the Torah and responsa.

The Żabner Rebbe, Reb Sholem-Dovid, may the memory of the righteous man be blessed, lived in Tarnow before the First World War. His son, the next Żabner Rebbe, Reb Eliezer Unger, who perished *oyf Kiddush haShem*, also lived there.

* * *

As soon as the Germans took power in Tarnow, they began to liquidate the Jews from the surrounding *shtetlekh* [towns]. They deported the Jews from Dąbrowa, Stutszyn, Żabno, Brigel and other *shtetlekh*; the Germans murdered a large number of Jews on the spot and pushed the others into the ghetto that the Germans created in Tarnow.

[Page 228]

And the *aktions* in Tarnow itself began immediately.

On the 9th of September 1939, the Germans, in honor of the memorial day of the *Putsch* they had carried out, celebrated their black holiday by burning all of the synagogues, houses of prayer and small synagogues in Tarnow.

On this day, the Germans burned the "Old Synagogue," which had been built in 1581,[7] the house of prayer near the synagogue, the Tempel Synagogue, Devora Menkes' Synagogue, the synagogue at Strusine Street, the New Synagogue, the various Hasidic prayer houses, the synagogue at Lwowska Street, the Porter's Synagogue in the Grabowka district and all of the synagogues in the Jewish neighborhoods as well as the Torah scrolls and thousands and thousands of religious books.

When the Germans issued an order that the Jews had to leave their residences and enter the ghetto, the rabbinate in Tarnow issued a proclamation that every Jew should fast and those who could not fast, should donate atonement money to support the poor Jews.

The first frightening, savage act of the Germans, which made all of the Jews in the city tremble, was taking out 10,000 Jews and placing them at the marketplace. They all had to kneel and then they were shot. Blood ran in the gutters. The German murderer, the leader of the mass-slaughter, brought his two children to see how Jews were being shot…

At night, as the 10,000 martyrs lay shot, the German commander asked for a cup of water and clean towel. He washed his hands of Jewish blood and drove away with his children to a concert…

At that terrible time, the rebbes searched for a place to hide. The rebbes knew that their names were the first on the Gestapo's list of those to be annihilated. Hasidim went to the Żabner Rebbe and asked him to leave Tarnow. They asked him to go to Żabno, where a secure bunker had been prepared. It had been prepared so that he and his entire family could live there until the fury passed… But the Żabner Rebbe did not want to leave his community of Jews in Tarnow.

[Page 229]

And every day new edicts were issued against the Jews. The Germans constantly gave new orders to the Jews, everything in order to belittle them and to denigrate them so that it would then be easier to send them to the death camps.

Thus an order was issued that Jews must wear arm bands; another time, that Jews must cut their beards and *peyes* [side curls].

Until then, the Żabner Rebbe, Reb Eliezer still had a beard and *peyes*. He often walked in the street with his face wrapped, so it would be thought that he had a toothache. However, when an order was issued by the Germans that the beard and *peyes* had to be cut off, the Hasidim went to the Rebbe and asked him to spare his life and to let his beard and *peyes* be cut off.

The Żabner Rebbe had a devoted Hasid, Reb Shimeon-Yakov Fridman, in Tarnow. The Rebbe asked Reb Shimeon-Yakov to cut of his [the Rebbe's] beard and *peyes*, but the Hasid could not do it.

The Żabner Rebbe asked his *gabbai* [sexton], Itshe Einhorn, to cut off his beard and *peyes*…

The *gabbai*, Reb Itshe, had been the *gabbai* for the previous Żabner Rebbe, Reb Sholem-Dovid Unger, may the memory of the righteous man be blessed. He came from Rozwadów and his father, Reb Yosef was one of the *gabbaim* for the old Rozwadówer Rebbe, Reb Moshe Horowitz, may the memory of the righteous man be blessed.

The Rozwadówer Rebbe's son-in-law, Reb Sholem-Dovid may the memory of the righteous man be blessed, still received financial support from his father-in-law. His father-in-law, the Rozwadówer Rebbe asked the young man, Itshe, to be his son-in-law's sexton.

By the time that he finished receiving support from his father-in-law in Rozwadów, the Żabner Rebbe already had two children, his first-born son, Reb Eliezer, and his daughter Perl.[8] The Żabner Rebbe moved to Żabno and became the rabbi and rebbe there in place of his father, Reb Yakov-Yitzhak Unger, may the memory of the righteous man be blessed. And his father-in-law, the Rozwadówer Rebbe, gave him the *shamas* [synagogue beadle], Reb Itshe as his *gabbai*.

Reb Itshe got married in Żabno and became the personal assistant at the Żabner [rabbinical] court. He was the chief *gabbai* for the Żabner Rebbe for all his years.

[Page 230]

At the beginning of the First World War, when the Żabner Rebbe, Reb Sholem-Dovid, and his entire household escaped from the Russians to Vienna, where he had many Hasidim and his own small synagogue, he took Reb Itshe his *gabbai* with him.

Reb Itshe as the *gabbai* was thus bound to the Żabner Rebbe, Reb Sholem-Dovid.

After the First World War, the Żabner Rebbe, Reb Sholem-Dovid, may the memory of the righteous man be blessed, settled in Tarnow.

* * *

The Żabner Rebbe, Reb Sholem-Dovid, may the memory of the righteous man be blessed, was famous as a brilliant man. At age 35, he wrote commentaries anonymously on his grandfather's book of responsa, *Imrei Noam* [*Words of Pleasantness*], part 1 by the Rebbe, Reb Meir Horowicz, may the memory of the blessed man be blessed, of Dzhikov.

In 1911, the Żabner Rebbe also published his book of responsa, *Yad Shalom* [*Hand of Peace*] without his name.[9]

The old Żabner Rebbe, may the memory of the righteous man be blessed, died in Vienna on the 2nd of Elul 5683 ([14 August] 1923). The coffin was brought to Żabno on a special train and he was placed in the *Ohel* of his father.

The Hasidim crowned his oldest son, Reb Eliezer as rebbe[10] and the *gabbai*, Reb Itshe remained the *gabbai* with Reb Eliezer in Tarnow.

* * *

It was the old Reb Itshe *gabbai* who needed to cut the beard and *peyes* of the Żabner Rebbe, Reb Eliezer, when the Germans issued the order that all Jews must cut their beards and *peyes*.

The *gabbai*, Reb Itshe, closed himself and the Rebbe in a separate room and the *gabbai* began to cut the Żabner Rebbe's beard and *peyes*. While cutting, the *gabbai* fainted and the Hasidim had to revive him.

At first, the Żabner Rebbe hosted his Hasidim at the *Shabbos* meal every *Shabbos* in secret.

[Page 231]

* * *

When the Nazis began the war against the Soviet Union, their fury against the Jews no longer had any limit. Every day they caught Jews for work and they strongly beat them at work, so that many of the Jews never returned…

And once, German soldiers entered the Żabner Rebbe's house and grabbed the rebbe to accompany them to go to work.

In the house was Reb Itshe the *gabbai*, who was then an old Jew. He did not want the rebbe to go alone; he wanted to go with the rebbe to ease the work for the rebbe.

Reb Itshe the *gabbai* ran to the German soldiers and requested:

"Take me, too!"
The German soldiers did not understand his intention and looked at each other in astonishment;
"The first time that a dirty Jew is asking that we take him to work… You must be his father, therefore you will definitely not go with him – they laughed out loud – *du wirst krepier* [you will die] on the spot and not at work!" – No, I am only the *gabbai*! – he fell to the feet of the rebbe and cried out loudly – A *gabbai* cannot live without a rebbe. I want to go with the rebbe!
And the German murderers had "pity" for Reb Itshe the *gabbai* and also took him to work…

The German killers murderously battered the Rebbe and the old Reb Itshe the *gabbai* as they worked, so both became very sick from the blows.

* * *

There was an old man in Tarnow – Reb Yehiel-Meirl, who prayed with Rebbe, Reb Yisroel-Yosele Unger, may the memory of the righteous man be blessed. He also took upon himself the religious obligation to bury the dead. A murderous typhus epidemic raged in the city; many Jews died. The Gestapo also shot Jews in the courtyards in which they lived and they would call out members of the *Chevra Kadisha* [burial society] to bury the dead. The members of the *Chevra Kadisha* were afraid to come into the courtyard. However, the old man, Reb Yehiel-Mierl, was no longer afraid of anything. When the Gestapo murderers, Rommelman, Molutki and Grunow came into the ghetto for fresh victims, the old man, Yehiel-Meirl was not afraid to run to the kitchen for the poor, to bring home a spoon of cooked food for his sick neighbor…

[Page 232]

Several days later, after the *gabbai*, Reb Itshe, voluntarily went to work with his rebbe, he died and the old man, Reb Yehiel-Meirl, carried out the burial rite.

* * *

A Tarnow Jew, M. Ebersztark, who survived in Antwerp, Belgium, describes the death of the Żabner Rebbe, Reb Eliezer, may God avenge his blood, *oyf Kiddush haShem*.

M. Ebersztark's father was a Żabner Hasid. He writes: "In November 1939, the Germans caught your brother, the Żabner Rebbe, for work. They took him through Krakowska Street. They made a *Purim-shpeil* [a Purim play] out of him and murderously beat him. I also remember how one brother, Reb Eliezer, went on foot to the train station with 10,000 more Jews to be deported. The Germans pushed the Jews into the goods wagons [boxcar], 160 people in one goods wagon. On the way, the Żabner Rebbe's hat fell off. He wanted to pick it up, but the Germans beastly beat him and did not let him pick up his hat.

The Żabner Rebbe walked with both hands covering his head. He did not want to go bare-headed and blood ran from his head and face…

The Germans filled the goods wagons with 40 centimeters of lime; thus, when the train with the goods wagons arrived in Bochnia, everyone had already breathed out their holy souls. Only three small children remained alive…"

The Żabner Rebbe, Reb Eliezer Unger, may God avenge his blood, perished *oyf Kiddush haShem*, in such a cruel manner, with his *rebbitzen* Adele, who was the daughter of the Krasner Rebbe, Reb Ahrele Twerski, and their daughter Leah'tshe and his 11-year-old son, Motele (Mordekhai-Dovid), may God avenge their blood.

Only his daughter, Gitel, who was saved from the death camp at Auschwitz, and his oldest daughter, Malka'le (from his first wife), who left for *Eretz-Yisroel* after the Second World War, survived.

Original Footnotes:

1. Reprinted from the author's *Sefer Kdoyshim* [*Book of Martyrs*] – Rebbes who died as martyrs – which was published in New York, 1967, by Schulsinger Brothers Publishers.
2. The Ropshitzer [Ropczyce] Rebbe did not allow his [work] to be published. After the death of the Ropshitzer Rebbe, his student, the Sanzer Rebbe, the brilliant man, Reb Chaim Halberstam, decided that they should print the book, *Sera Kodesh* [*Sacred Seed*], of the Ropshitzer Rebbe.
3. The other two were the Rebbe, Reb Ruvin of Dembic and Reb Yisroel of Baranow.
4. My father, the Żabner, Rebbe, Reb Sholem-Dovid, may the memory of the righteous man be blessed, a grandson of Reb Meirl and son-in-law of Rebbe, Reb Moshe of Rozwadów, published annotations on the first part of the responsa, *Imre Noam*, at the age of 30-plus years and my uncle, the Tokolower Rebbe, Reb Yehuda, may the memory of the righteous be blessed, published the second part of *Imre Noam* with his annotations.
5. Hasidim carried *talisim* [prayer shawls] made in Turkey and they were called "Turkish *talisim*."
6. In a series of articles in the newspaper, *Tog* [*Day*], New York, she described in detail how she saved herself and her child.
7. During my visit to Tarnow in 1960, I found only the *Bima* [synagogue lectern] from the "Old Synagogue" that was made of twisted iron, as a monument, surrounded by a small garden that the city managing committee in Tarnow had erected.
8. She was the *rebbitzen* of the present Bloczewer Rebbe, Reb Yisroeltshe Szpira of Brooklyn, New York. She perished *oyf Kiddish haShem* in the gas chamber of Belzec on the 7th of Cheshvan [5703] [the 18th of October] 1942.
9. Printed in Tolczva, Hungary, 5671 (1911). *Yad* is much the same as *Dovid*, so that the name of the book is his name. The book, *Yad Shalom*, is now published in New York.
10. The Żabner Rebbe's second son, Reb Yisroelke, may the memory of the righteous man be blessed, was rabbi and rebbe in Żabno. He died in New York on *Rosh Chodesh* [the new month] Kislev, 1936. His *rebbitzen*, Chaya'tshe, the daughter of the Sanzer Rabbi, Reb Arya-Leib Halberstam, perished with the members of his household at the hands of the Germans.

Translator's Footnotes:

a. for sanctification of God's name
b. there is an error in the text in converting the Hebrew year to the Gregorian year

[Page 233, Volume 2]

The ADMOR [Hasidic rabbi] of Grudzisk

Translated by Daniel Kochavi

This is the image of your teacher: A picture of the wise and holy Rabbi our teacher Eliezer Horowitz Admor from Grudzisk, The Admor from Klantesh:
He was born in the year 5636 (1875) passed away in purity on 6 Kislev 5703 in Tarnow – may his memory protect us and God avenge his blood.

When the ADMOR from Grudzisk and thousands of Jews, men, women and children were taken to the gas chambers in the German death camps, the Rabbi asked permission to say a few words to the assembled Jews. The Rabbi spoke as follows: Brothers and Sisters! A Talmud Sage said "yeti vlo achminia" (Aramaic) meaning the Messiah will come but I will not see it. This wise man did not want to see the great future suffering of the Israelites before the coming of the Messiah. Only he could make that request because, in his time, salvation (i.e. the coming of the Messiah) was far away in time. Today, however, when we are standing at the threshold of salvation, at this hour when we are bleeding and purifying with our blood the way for our savior, at this hour when our ashes, like the ashes of the Red Heifer, purify the people of Israel so that they will be ready to greet our holy Messiah – we must not say the opposite. On the contrary we must be grateful that it falls on us to pave the way for the coming of our redeemer and accept with love our sacrifice and our martyrdom to the faith (Kiddush Hashem). So, Jews join together and declare with joy "Shema Israel, come let us sing Ani Maamin" … and this is what happened. All sang "Ani Maamin" with holy enthusiasm and singing they approached and entered the gas chamber……

(told by **Rabbi A.I. Halevi Herzog**, the Chief Rabbi of Israel after visiting the survivors in Italy. Published in" Olam"). (from "The Shoah and the Rebellion" - Anthology on the destruction of the European Jewry from 5700-5705 (1940-1945) published by the office of Education and Culture)

[Pages 234]

About the Heroic Role of the Jewish Children During Nazi Rule

by Ahron Szporn (Montreal)

Translated by Gloria Berkenstat Freund

The savage persecutions of the Jews began during the first months after the triumphant entry of the German troops into Poland. The capture of adult women and men for forced labor was a dark, nightmarish plague. The adults were locked in their homes and did not appear in the streets because of the persecutions. The burden of providing income and functioning as providers of food for the family was taken on by the youngest children who were not obligated to wear the sign of disgrace, the [yellow Star of David] armband, and they were not threatened with the danger of being captured for forced labor.

The intrepid Jewish children filled an original, rebellious, function with a rare heroism that was expressed in several forms, such as:

a. home providers
b. street bargaining and smuggling
c. begging

Home providers

It was necessary to stand the entire night in lines in order to receive the distribution of a small portion of bread – and when the sun began to rise, the danger of being captured for forced labor arose… It happened often that they stood in the line the entire night and at the end left with nothing because there was a sudden search and then there was no bread. Therefore, the youngest children were sent to stand in line and meanwhile they [the adults] lived in fear… when would the child return with the small amount of bread?

Street bargaining

After the war I met in Tarnow a young girl named Winer, who had lived in the Tarnow ghetto and survived through a miracle.

In a conversation with her, she told me: Everyone was involved with trade, so I also became involved… Did I have a choice?… We did not have anything to eat and I had to be the provider… I would walk with my friend around and bargain… She was then 13 and I was 11…

[Page 235]

Jewish children in the Tarnow ghetto

Smuggling

Life became unbearable after the publication of the ordinances according to which there was the threat of death for leaving the ghetto. It was now almost impossible to smuggle food items into the ghetto and hunger threatened to entirely depress those Jews already physically and spiritually weakened. With such a hopeless situation, Jewish children began to smuggle food from the Aryan side into the imprisoned ghetto. What moral exaltation… What courage and boldness these children, the only providers of food for their homes, possessed … Unafraid, they risked their lives and many of these young heroes perished here.

[Page 236]

Child on the way to the ghetto with food items

    This self–sacrifice by the Jewish children and their role as providers of nourishment for their parents, for their brothers and sisters was confirmed by Jonas Turkow,[1] who confirmed that the youngest children, who would sneak out to the Aryan side and from there smuggle bread, flour and potatoes into ghetto, particularly excelled in smuggling food items into the ghetto.

    It is easy to say… leave the ghetto for the Aryan side… Yet the walls around the ghettos were guarded from the inside by the Jewish militia and from the outside by the Polish and German police. Often such a Jewish child had to wait for many hours until they could go unnoticed through to the Aryan side past three such guards. Hundreds of Jewish children were caught during this work and killed from the bullets of the guards.

[Page 237]

Dr. Hillel Zajdman[2] writes about the heroic role of the Jewish children as providers of food and nutrition for Jewish homes in the ghetto, commenting that the most interesting and equally the saddest chapter of the Jewish children's martyrdom was the smuggling that was carried out by the children, small children from five to eight years old, with small emaciated little bodies who would push themselves through narrow openings in the ghetto walls, through holes for the drainage of water, and go to the Aryan side. There they bought a little food for tens of *zlotes*, mostly potatoes and bread and then with these "goods" hidden underneath their clothing they would wait in a crouch near one of the ghetto gates until it was possible to sneak back into the ghetto. Woe to the child when they and their "goods" fell into German or Polish hands.

These small children, merchants, smugglers, writes Dr. Hillel Zajdman,[3] "were very clever… They were raised in difficult times and did the most dangerous work; they sharpened their minds with complicated transactions of the ghetto businesses. Many fell during this difficult struggle, fell as heroes, in devotion to their closest ones and in love of the family and many helped other Jews with a piece of bread…"

Beggars

Begging was not a successful occupation. Thus evolved a new level of "takers" who would above all take food and immediately eat it on the spot. In the Warsaw ghetto, taking was a daily phenomenon. The ghetto police carried on an unsuccessful, embittered struggle against these takers. Instead of giving the hungry children something to eat and fight the taking in an educational manner, the ghetto police applied a system of beatings with rubber sticks… However, this did not satisfy the hunger of the child takers. The beatings had the opposite effect. The takers became accustomed to the lashes and blows as the price for quieting their hunger for several hours.

[Page 238]

Bernard Goldsztajn[4] describes the following as an eyewitness: "A stampede, voices, shouting: 'Catch him!' a barefoot boy in rags, his pitch–black dirty feet trudge in mud, get entangled in a laying corpse, falls down, holding a loaf of bread in his hand and he gnaws it with his last strength…

The owner of the loaf of bread struggles with him, wants to get the bread which was so difficult for him to obtain and which is now gnawed, dirty with spit from the "taker," perhaps it is infected with typhus…

"'Takers' were a special category," writes Bernard Goldsztajn. "Those, who in their desperation and anxiety about hunger still possessed a little strength and boldness to break the sacred law for property rights for a piece of bread. They would be beaten murderously, by both the ones who had been robbed and the police… However, it was impossible to eradicate the 'takers,' just as it was to eradicate the hunger…"

Memorial tablet in the Buczyna Forest near Tarnow in memory of the 800 children murdered in 1942

[Page 239]

The Tragedy of the Children During the Deportations

Consistent with their systematic savagery, during the first half of 1942 the German hangmen began to speed up the murder *aktions* [deportations], the so–called "deportation actions," and the rope tightened around the necks of the exhausted Jewish population sentenced to death in the Polish cities and *shtetlekh* [towns].

The first victims during these murder *aktions* were the Jewish children. The Germans murderers slaughtered hundreds of them on the spot during a deportation and still more were sent to the concentration and death camps.

Rywka Kwiatkowska[5]. provides such a sad and horribly cruel picture of the tragic fate of the Jewish children during one of the deportations to the Lodz ghetto, a picture that was repeated in all of the ghettos in Poland during the entire era of extermination:

"[They stood] near their parents, lost and afraid, the confused hidden children saved by a miracle; quiet and afraid, they followed their parents, in dirty suits of clothes, washed, with hair combed, with small wooden shoes on their small feet, small tags with addresses and family names hung attached on the shuddering, depressed–by–fear childish chests."

From these heroic Jewish children, only individuals survived. Here and there, individual Jewish children hid on the Aryan side and survived all seven levels of hell in their Aryan hiding places.

Footnotes:

1. Jonas Turkow – *Azoy is Es Geveyn* [*This is How it Was*]… p. 127.
2. Dr. Hilel Zajdman – *Togbukh fun Warszawer Gheto* [*Diary from the Warsaw Ghetto*] – pp. 157–158
3. See above
4. Bernard Goldsztajn – *5 Yor in Warszawer Gheto* [*Five Years in the Warsaw Ghetto*], pp. 253–254.
5. Rywka Kwiatkowska – *Fun Lager in Lager* [*From Camp to Camp*].

[Pages 240]

Children Accuse

Translated by Gloria Berkenstat Freund

A book was published in 1947 in Poland under this name, edited by Maria Hochberg Marianska and Noakh Grim, about the martyrdom of children during the Hitlerist occupation. The testimony of the child, Josek Mansdorf[1] (born on the 21st of December 1931 in Tarnow), submitted by the Historical Commission in Tarnow, also is published in this collection. The testimony (no. 14) is found on pages 100-108 and carries the title, "Tarnow – the defeat of the family. Trading through the fence. In the village. The farmers, bad and good people."

Testimony (Translated from Polish)

Once, when the Germans were in Tarnow, a car stopped in front of our house on Widok Street. Three *S.S.* men got out of it and came into our residence with a question – who lives here? When my father said that Jews live here, they beat him and ordered everyone to go out of the apartment to the courtyard. They took away all of the best things from our rooms.

Another time, when we already were wearing armbands, I walked on Lemberger (Lwowska) Street carrying several boxes of candy to sell in a shop. A German policeman grabbed me by my armband and wanted to take the candies. Because I was crying hard, he led me to the *starostwe* [district office] and, there, after they asked where I had gotten [the candies] and where I was taking them, they permitted me to go home. I then was afraid and no long carried any candies.

Four days before the first deportation, I heard the neighbors talking about a resettlement. My oldest brother was in Wola Lubecka near Jaslo. My mother and father told me to travel to my brother to tell him to come to Tarnow. There were various disturbances and we could not return immediately. Therefore, we sent a Pole to Tarnow to learn what was happening in the city. He brought us a note saying we should not come home. There was a deportation. He went again and learned and brought the news that my mother, brother and my six-year old sister had been taken for deportation. My oldest sister, 19-years old, had been shot in her bed where she lay sick. My brother had been standing near her: "We do not need any *Yidishkes* [Jewish women]" – and there was laughter and a shot echoed. My brother was taken to the marketplace where he stood an entire day. He later received a stamp and he was permitted to go home. I was told that my brother traveled to me and my father had escaped to a village during the deportation.

[Page 241]

I returned to Tarnow and my two brothers both arrived, but my father did not return to Tarnow. He remained in the village. Later the labor office sent one brother to the airplane factory in Mielec as a metal worker. My other brother was shot by Rommelmann, a member of the Gestapo. My brother was 20 years old. I remained alone. I still had one sister; but I did not know what had happened to her during the deportation because she then was supposed to go to Krakow. I reported to the labor office, received a work card and I was ordered to report twice a week.

When the ghetto was created, the tinsmith Wajzer and his family of six people lived with us. I asked him to try to have the labor office allocate me to him for work. We left to see the director of the labor office, Miller, and asked him about this. He refused. I was too young. Wajzer told me to go to work without the allocation. I did this for three months. He told me to remove my armband and to buy butter, eggs and lard outside the ghetto and I returned to the ghetto in the evening with everything. When the workers would return to the ghetto I would put on the armband and come in with them. This lasted three months. Then I reported personally to the work office twice a week. Once I was taken away to work for a week in the *mieszczanke* [village]. Meanwhile, Wajzer looked for another boy for work. Unexpectedly, my sister returned to the ghetto. During the entire time she had been sick. She had never reported. Thus we lived together until the second deportation.

[Page 242].

With Wajzer we prepared a hiding place under the room. The entrance was through the balcony. One part was open; we sat in the second part. During the second deportation the Gestapo men ripped up the boards of the first part of the hiding place where a great deal of wood was piled. They moved several beams, but did not see anyone because the hiding place was dark. Then one of them did see me. He then stuck his head and his hand, holding a revolver, into the hiding place and then removed his head and said to the other one: "There is a great deal of wood, but there is no one there."

We left the hiding place two days after the deportation. Our residence had been completely looted. There was nothing on which to live. I thought about what to do. I borrowed 500 *zlotys* from an acquaintance, left for the Polish area, bought cigarettes and sold them at night in the ghetto. I dealt in cigarettes until the third deportation. A Polish police secret agent once noticed me when I was standing with the cigarettes. I escaped. I scattered the cigarettes. He shot after me three times but I entered another house where there was an exit to another street. Then I came home without cigarettes and very frightened. I stopped dealing with cigarettes.

I was 12-years old. I went to the ghetto fence. There I became acquainted with Poles who began to bring me butter and eggs. I bought underwear and goods in the ghetto and I exchanged the things with [the Polish acquaintances]. Thus it was until the third deportation. We again hid in the same hiding place, but there was no deportation. We waited [in the hiding place] for a whole week. Sunday I heated the oven, began to cook coffee, while my sister had to wash clothes and clean the floor. A minute later a neighbor came running [with the news] that the deportation was occurring and they already were in the hidden room. My sister woke up quickly and we barely succeeded in hiding ourselves. We barely had been able to arrange the wood in the hiding place and the Gestapo were in our residence. We had not taken anything to eat. We sat hidden for five days and had nothing to eat. We came out after five days. The Wajzers had been taken because they had not succeeded in hiding. I went out to the street and saw no one. I went into our residence, took bread and butter and returned to the hiding place. We were there for many more days until we went back into our room.

[Page 243]

My sister wanted me to leave for the Polish area without an armband and to travel to Jaslo to learn if our father was alive. When I went out I met an acquaintance from that area. I learned from him that our father was alive. I returned to the ghetto and told my sister everything.

She told me to go out of the ghetto again in order to find someone who would take us to our father for a good reward. I did not meet anyone and I returned. My sister left for the Polish quarter, but she did not return because there was a guard at the wall. I contemplated everything over two days; how to leave the ghetto. I finally decided that when the workers went to work I would put on torn village clothing and go with the group. I changed my clothes, placed my hand in a hand towel, ostensibly as if it were hurting me, so that it would be easier for me to take off the armband. The Poles as well as Polish and German police were standing on the sidewalk when we arrived at the factory. I took off the armband and hid it in my fist. In one step I moved out of the ranks [of workers], turned and then with my face to the group, loudly asked if anyone had anything to sell. The Jews entered the factory and I left with a small package in my hand. Poles ran up to me and asked if I had something to sell. I said no.

I left for Jaslo through nearby villages and arrived [in Jaslo] and went to Polish acquaintances and asked them about my father and sister. They answered that they did not know about anyone and let me stay overnight. In the morning I left for Wola Lubecka. I went to a peasant and suddenly saw through the window… my sister was walking. I went out to her and we walked together. We did not know where we were going. Night fell. I told my sister that I would go to Tarnow, buy various trifles there, such as needles, thread, combs and stay with another Pole. She agreed and was supposed to wait for me in the woods.

I left, bought everything and returned to her.

[Page 244]

This lasted for four days. I went without interruption, without rest, day and night. When I returned I said that I would go to the Poles and if I found a good person I would confess who I was and ask if he would let me stay with him for a good reward. I could not find such a person. One asked if I knew something about a servant. I answered that I knew about a resettled woman who was working for a person, but she was not being paid. Her clothes were becoming torn and she could not buy any other [clothing]. She would want to be a servant in order to buy something. He ordered me to bring her and promised to give me 100 *zlotys*. I went to my sister and we went to the peasant. She pleased him and remained there. I went further in the direction of the city of Jaslo. There I met a very good peasant. I confessed to him who I was. He said he would take me. I was with him for a month. I told him about my sister, that she had various valuable objects and asked him if he would take her in. This was not true, but I wanted to go to Tarnow in order to buy something and therefore I told him this. He agreed because he was cunning and wanted me to give him something. I told my sister everything and she praised me for finding such a peasant, because she could no longer remain [where she was]… They had discovered that she was a Jew.

By night I was in Tarnow, crawled through the fence in the ghetto and bought goods for all the money I had. Acquaintances gave me things and money to help us. The same night I left the ghetto and went to my sister and we went to the peasant together. I hid a few things in the stable, I left a little and we gave the remainder to the peasant with the pretext that every week or two I would bring him something. He agreed and we remained. Two weeks passed and I said that I was going to bring something. I went to the stable at night, took out a few things. Every two weeks I gave him something and thus we were hidden for a year. I had nothing left but 50 *zlotys*. I asked the peasant to lend me 250 *zlotys* so I could go to Tarnow and during that time he would keep my sister until I returned and I would bring him many things. In Tarnow I bought a small box of blotting paper, went through the villages with it, sold each paper individually and earned twice what I had paid. Then I bought butter and eggs and returned with them to the ghetto. I sold everything in the ghetto and I earned 500 *zlotys*. With the money I bought underwear, left for another village and sold everything. I bought butter and lard; again, I brought it into the ghetto through a fence, sold it and again bought underwear for 1,800 *zlotys*. And again I went to the village, sold it and again bought food. This was repeated eight times. After two months I had 5,000 *zlotes*. A blanket then cost 100-120 *zlotes*. I went to my sister to find what the situation was. My sister said that she wanted to leave the village because people knew [that she was a Jew]. Without the peasant's knowledge she left for another village. I searched for a spot with another peasant, again bargained and I paid for her. I took lard, but no longer into the ghetto, but to a tailoring factory where Jews were working. There I again sold food and bought various things.

[Page 245]

Meanwhile, I met a Jew with whom I went to the woods where we built a bunker. During the day I went to the city, at night I went to the woods. It already was autumn. Thus passed three months. I only thought about how to provide myself with papers so that I could go to work in an unfamiliar village. I had an acquaintance, a 15-year old Polish boy. I went to him. I asked him what his name was, when he was born, what were the names of his family. He told me everything. The next day I went to the priest, told him the name of the boy and asked him to give me a *metryka* [birth record] because I wanted to receive a *kenkarte* [identity card issued in areas occupied by Germany]. He gave me the document. I paid five *zlotes*. The next day I went to the community of Ryglice, gave them the *metryka*. They asked me to have a photograph taken and gave me a *kenkarte*. When I returned, I learned that one peasant was looking for a boy to help with his work. I reported and he took me in. He asked for my papers. I showed them to him. He left with me for the *slotis* [village magistrate], registered me as his farm hand. I was with him for a year and tended the cows. I got up early, cleaned up. The peasant was very satisfied with me. My father once came to see me in the stall unexpectedly when I was asleep. I did not know anything about [where] my father [was], but he learned about me from people. We talked the entire night. At around three [in the morning] I asked him to leave so that the peasant would not see him.

[Page 246]

He left, but my boss saw and recognized him. He guessed who I was, but said nothing. Then the entire village learned about me. But the peasant did not drive me away and people did not denounce me [to the Germans]. In the month of July when the Germans withdrew, the Gestapo moved into the convent in the village. They were quartered there. One of the members of the Gestapo once was walking by and saw a person in the distance who did not stop at his demand and he [the Gestapo member] shot three times. The "someone" escaped. The member of the Gestapo did not notice in the dark that this was a girl who entered our house and asked about a 12-year old boy. I was then in the attic and heard everything. In the evening I made a hole and hid myself. I fell asleep and slept until morning. When I went down, my boss asked me to finish eating and to leave because the Gestapo was looking for me. I went to my sister. The military also was housed there and she worked in the military kitchen. A boy was needed to carry water for the kitchen. I worked in this German kitchen for two weeks. Then the Germans left. I returned to the peasant for whom I had worked. There they already knew that it was not me who they [the Gestapo] had meant [were searching for] and although I was afraid, they asked me to remain. I again tended the cows. On Sunday I would tend the cows and go to church. I was there until September 1944. Then when they began to deport the Poles in the village of Czarna, [the Poles] came to our village. Whoever had room took them in. There was no room with us because there were many people and the peasant did not take anyone in. The deported Poles learned that he was housing a Jew; they came to him and argued that so many people were without a roof over their heads and he was housing a Jew instead of someone else. He insisted to them that this was not true and took no one in and continued to house me.

In the autumn we had to go to dig trenches. The boys in the village told the Germans that I spoke German. He was looking for such a person and summoned me and asked how I knew German. I answered that I had learned from a dictionary while I was tending the cows. He designated me as his translator. I was with him constantly and things were good for me. Someone told him that I was a Jew. One boy warned me that I should no longer go to dig because the German knew that I was a Jew. I thanked him and did not go anymore.

The peasant asked me why I was no longer going; I answered him that a translator was no longer needed. I continued to live and to work there. I put on different clothes so that I would not be recognized because they were searching for me. One day one of those who were searching for me came and asked for such a boy. The peasant said that there had been such a boy but he was no longer here.

[Page 247]

I began to be afraid and asked that he [the peasant] keep me in hiding for a certain time. I gave him an overcoat [in exchange]. I asked him to take in a deported peasant, one more-or-less like me so that in case he was asked he would have someone to show. He took in a deported family and hid me in a hiding place and no one knew what had happened to me. People asked about me, but he said that he did not know. I sat in a cellar. The cellar was fenced off with a board. There were potatoes on one side; I sat on the other side. Thus I sat until the arrival of the Russians. Then he [the peasant] told me to leave. I went out and left for Tarnow.

Footnote:

1. Today in Israel (Ramat-Gan).

[Page 248]

A Collection of Memories of the Hitlerist Hell

by Ruchl Goldberg-Klimek

Translated by Gloria Berkenstat Freund

Ruchl Goldberg-Klimek

In moments when I strive to extract myself from the abyss of forgetting my experiences – memories of the most difficult and darkest era in my life – I feel with astonishment and even with an easy embarrassment that it is difficult for me, very difficult, to wrote this down on paper.

Before I begin to tell about myself, I hold it as my duty to honor the holy memory of my dear father, Shlomo (Salomon) Goldberg, the dear man who dedicated his entire life to community activities, often neglecting his private interests and occupation. Much has already been written in the first volume of our yizkor book, *Tarne* [*Tarnow*], about the Zionist and general activities of my father. Here, I will only add a little explanation of the pain and hardships that my father had to endure from the Hitlerist murderers until he breathed out his soul in the Gestapo prison.

After the outbreak of the war, when the divisions of the *Sonderkommandos* [Jewish prisoners forced to work in Nazi annihilation camps] and the German barbarians began to destroy and burn synagogues and other institutions and Jews were ruled by panic and fear, my father, with his poise, calm and courage, set an example for all those who had fallen in spirit.

At that time, in the difficult conditions of the brutal occupation, he helped organize Jewish life in Tarnow, served everyone with advice and deeds. When the Germans applied repression and force and demanded active help and cooperation from the Jewish communal workers, my father energetically resisted. The results of this came quickly. One evening armed Gestapo members burst into the house at Walowa 18, where we had lived for many years and with the butts of the rifles knocked out the heavy gate and took our father with them, after carrying out a precise search and stealing things of value.

[Page 249]

Ruchl GoldbergKlimek

The first on the right: Dr. Shlomo Goldberg, may his memory be blessed (Ruchl's father)
The second: Yosef Goldberg and the third: M. Safir

They accused my father, among other things, of writing anti German articles in *Tygodnik Zydowski* [*Yidishe Vokhnshrift* – *Jewish Weekly*], whose editor he was for a time. My mother, Elza, may she rest in peace, made superhuman efforts to free my father – and she succeeded in this. Good friends advised him to escape from Tarnow and hide among the Poles, but my father was not prepared to do this, and remained in the city.

However, he did not remain free for long because several months later, the Gestapo again knocked at our residence. When I answered the door, a dread befell me because, among the hangmen, I recognized two well-known murderers of Tarnow Jews: the degenerate [Paul] Von Malotky and the *volks-Deitch* [ethnic German] Novak from Silesia – both well-known sadists.

I invited them into the room and went to call my father. When I told him who was waiting for him, he calmly finished a small glass of whiskey and, erect with pride, he went into the hangmen. I quickly prepared a blanket, food, cigarettes. When they left with my father, I was shaken with an inhuman lament, because I had calculated that I would never see his dear face, I would never feel his goodness, his closeness, his wisdom.

[Page 250]

The Gestapo rampaged in the city every day. They arrested several people from the Tarnow spiritual elite – Poles and Jews, among them also Dr. Schenkel, Dr. Wider and others.

From a prison cell, my father was brought to the Gestapo for a hearing. He had to run after the bicycle of the member of the Gestapo who took him. He was tortured, wooden needles were stuck under his nails, [he was] beaten over the course of several hours. Thanks to her contact with Polish prison guards who knew my father as a lawyer from before the war, my mother succeeded, for a large payment it should be understood, to send him a little food and cigarettes. As the guards had great fear of the Germans, they took even less food for my father. Thanks to them, we also knew about my father's health, his attitude and mood.

He lay in the prison hospital for two months, healing from his wounds and pains as a result of the interrogation by the Gestapo. Despite his superhuman suffering and the hopeless condition in which my father found himself, he remained an optimist and let us know that he believed that we would again be together.

After being in the Tarnow prison for a year, he was sent to Auschwitz with other arrestees. Alas, I cannot provide the exact dates because, escaping from the ghetto, I destroyed all documents and papers. My father was taken to Auschwitz before they had created the enclosed ghetto in Tarnow and before instituting the repressions and physical murder of the Jewish population. My mother was brought to the Gestapo several months later and told that her husband had died in the camp, but for technical reasons, the camp regime was not able to [give her] the urn with his ashes. (A year after the end of the war, I heard from a former Auschwitz internee that my father was still alive for another year after his ostensible death, but this is uncorroborated information and I want to believe that he was not tortured for that long.)

[Page 251]

* * *

The outbreak of the war found me in Tarnow during the summer vacation from the Warsaw University, where I was studying English literature and language. Although a great deal had been written in the press about the forthcoming war and the explosion at the Tarnow train station took place before the war's operations – the majority of the population was not mentally prepared and for them even the events of the 1st of September came unexpectedly.

The German occupiers carried out their previously developed plan from the first moment, which had as its purpose to break us first morally and then physically annihilate us. It started with small harassments, with stepping on human honor – to even more severe sanctions, setting fires, blowing up synagogues, putting on the yellow patch, not permitting movement. Later, they created the ghetto and drove all of the Jews there from other streets and neighborhoods. The individual acts of murder in time were transformed into the more massive extermination.

During the first period of the occupation, I belonged to a group of young people who had decided to fight the despair and apathy with our means. Belonging to this group were: Lusha Maszler, Sonja Roskes, Erik and Fritz Szpiler, Maks Szpindler, as well as several girls and boys from Bielsk, among them – my future husband.

We decided to carry on a more normal life, as if there was no war and no Hitleristic occupation. Mostly, we came together at the Szpiler's [house], listened to music from records, arranged gatherings in the evenings, danced; in addition to this, we cleaned a piece of land and organized a place to play volleyball. Despite the hopelessness of our situation, we tried to live normally as young people. Not having the ability to study, we learned languages: English and French.

However, we were not permitted to act this way for very long. We were taken for forced labor for the German war industries. Because of increasing terror, we lost a great deal of our ardor and optimism. Particularly after our removal from our own residences and being squeezed into the crowded ghetto.

The persecutions became stronger; they began to shoot Jews in the street; there even were cases of murdered female peasants who had brought products to sell in the Jewish quarter. Despair, helplessness, loneliness reigned in the Jewish neighborhood. On a certain day, the Germans gathered all of the old people and shot them at the cemetery. That is how my grandmother perished.

[Page 252]

After an Execution

During the first *aktion* [deportation], thousands of people were murdered, their bodies taken away in trucks and buried in mass graves that were dug by our young people. Many recognized the dead bodies of the people closest to them My cousin, Milek Primerman, buried his own father…

A number of our group were taken to the camps during the first and second *aktions*; others again, straight to the crematoria of Auschwitz. This happened to Erik Szpiler and Lusha Maszler. Others perished in horrible conditions in various camps. Fritz Szpiler lived until the liberation of the camp, then died of malnourishment and hunger in the arms of his father. Sonja Roskes, whose father was abroad on the day of the outbreak of the war and managed to arrange passports and entry visas to a South American country, survived the war in a camp for interned foreigners and arrived in Canada with her mother and sister.

[Page 253]

I worked for the transport company, Bronikowski, which, during the war years, was transformed into a German construction company.

* * *

Before the second *aktion*, the Germans stamped the work cards of the employed Jews and only those who worked for the war industries received the stamp. This signified life, because not having the stamp was a death sentence. The firm in which I worked was not recognized by the Gestapo as "dedicated to important war [activity]." Therefore, I was psychologically prepared for death when the murderers began dragging everyone who did not receive the "lucky" stamp, from their houses. When the Germans came to our house, what happened can be recorded as a miracle. After a short conversation with me in the German language, they let me stay in my home. I do not know if they felt ashamed because I was a young woman or the good German that I spoke pleased them – the fact was that I was saved; those closest to me were besides themselves with the luck. However, the joy did not last long.

The Gestapo suspected that simple German soldiers might show pity for the unlucky Jews, so they sent Jewish policemen into the ghetto, who had to drive the entire Jewish population to the autobus square. Although my mother asked the policemen (among whom were, incidentally, good acquaintances from before the war) to leave me, nothing helped. They drove us to the square, where those with the stamps were sorted from those without them. Those without the stamp were ordered to kneel in the middle of the square, near the building that served as the waiting room for the autobuses and during the occupation as the office of the German labor office. As I did not have the stamp, they took my mother, my husband and me and with a blow from a rifle butt forced us to kneel on the stones (*ketsishe kep* [cat heads], with which the autobus square was paved). I was completely indifferent, felt no fear, no hope, waited resigned and passive for death.

[Page 254]

In the meantime, my husband, risking his life, entered the labor office and began to ask the manager to help me. He knew my husband, who had worked for him in his residence, well and promised to take me out of the transport. The manager came to me and told me to go to the table where the Gestapo was sitting and to say that my husband works at an important undertaking for the Germans and I was asking to stay with him. With our hearts palpitating, my husband and I went to the table that in my eyes looked like a plank bed for a body. My voice shaking, I asked to stay in the ghetto. One member of the Gestapo took my card and after reading it, said: "You have a different name than your husband." I told him that our wedding had taken place not long ago and I had not had the possibility of changing my family name. Then I took out the marriage certificate. The German said ironically: "The certificate was prepared today." At this, Folkman, the chairman of the *Judenrat* [Jewish council], who was standing behind the German said: "I signed this. It is a correct certificate." Now, a tense stillness reigned – live or not live… Suddenly, one of the Jewish policemen gave me a brotherly tap on my back and said: "I was at your wedding" – and at that moment the member of the Gestapo placed a stamp on my work card… Thus my life was extended, thanks to several words from the policeman, who I did not know, it should be understood, and was not at my wedding, a very sad wedding in war conditions.

When, surprised and confused, I finally found my mother and husband, I was a witness to the events that surpass in every way our concepts about Dante's hell. The Germans ordered everyone who possessed a stamped card to stand in rows of six and march around the square with cards raised high. Then they pulled out of the rows fathers and mothers carrying small children as well as the old and the stout. This selection was completely secondary. The square was surrounded on all sides by gendarmes and *S.S.* divisions, which held machine guns aimed at the victims.

[Page 255]

Despondent parents tried to hide their small children with all of their strength; others tried to get outside through the high fence or pushed the children through the openings in the fencing. The murderers immediately opened fire on these Jews and the stones were dyed with their blood. When we were driven back into the ghetto through a small passageway, the desperate fathers or mothers, who had just lost their children banged their heads on a wall, tore the hair from their head, screamed from pain and wildness. Now I began to comprehend what *gehinim* [hell] means…

That day, we decided to escape from the ghetto with Aryan papers.

* * *

We succeeded in receiving a correct certificate from a Polish woman who was living abroad and created a precise plan for escaping. It was decided that at first, I would leave alone to prepare everything for my husband and my mother. I received a letter of recommendation from a friendly Polish family to Halina Lisowska, a young Polish woman in Warsaw, the daughter of a former Tarnow village elder. Her father was in London then and her mother had been arrested and sent to Auschwitz.

At the end of July, I joined a group that marched out of the ghetto to work. On the way I made use of the inattention of the German gendarme and escaped through a nearby gate, taking off my armband with the *Mogen-Dovid* [Shield of David, also called the Star of David], threw away my work uniform and went to the office of the Bronikowski firm, where I had previously worked. Kaczik, the chauffeur employed there, an honest and good Christian, offered me his help and together we went to the train station. This was an extremely dangerous undertaking because I was known in Tarnow. Particularly after my aunt, Mrs. Primerman, was shot on the street by a Polish policeman when she wanted to save herself and escape from the ghetto.

However, I succeeded in reaching Warsaw and thanks to Halina Lisowska, who helped me rent a room, I settled there. It should not be forgotten that the most difficult problem of that time in Warsaw was actually the question of a residence because the Poles did not want to take unfamiliar people into their apartments.

[Page 256]

I made all of the necessary preparations for my husband and my mother to come to Warsaw. With the help of Mr. Kczak, Szpiler's partner, whose factory of valises were located not far from the ghetto; I succeeded in telling my closest ones my Warsaw address. My husband arrived quickly, then we brought my mother. At the beginning, we lived in very difficult conditions, in hunger and cold, during a difficult winter, in a room without windowpanes, which had fallen out during the bombing of Warsaw in 1939. Thanks to advertisements in the newspaper, we found work. My husband worked in the Filipswerke factory on the Wolye, I, in a small, private German firm that was located – the irony of fate – opposite the journalist school in which I so strongly wanted to study before the war, but they did not accept me because of my origins. Now the uniform warehouse of the *S.S.* was located in the school.

I rented a room for my mother because safety was wished for, and not too many people should live in one room. Sadly, my mother had been kept in the Tarnow ghetto and led the kitchen there and knew how to wrestle with all the difficulties of that time – but now she broke completely because of the frequent blackmail by the Polish scoundrels, the so-called *shmaltsownikes* [blackmailers who would demand money from the Jews on threat of denouncing them to the Germans], who often dragged her through a gate and threatened her with being turned over to the Germans if she did not "pay a ransom" of money or jewelry to them. They would take her few *zlotes* and say that she should be happy that they were not turning her in to the Gestapo, which would "transform her into soap." Because of the constant blackmailing, she often had to change her apartment. Finally, she was lodged with a family of train workers at Muranowska Street, which bordered the ghetto. When the uprising began in the ghetto on the 19th of April, the owners proposed that she watch how "they are murdering the young people…" It was an interesting spectacle for the train workers, and my mother in order not to evoke any suspicion had to watch everything with all her strength hiding the despair that befell her. She had suffered with gall stones for many years, but had been healed of this. Now depressed by the terrible fury and the burning of the ghetto residences, her illness reappeared in a sharp form. She suffered from terrible pains and died in the hospital, on the operating table. She was buried at the Brudner cemetery. In addition to me, *Magister* [holder of an advanced university degree] Felek Perlberg, who also hid with Aryan papers and tragically perished after the war accompanied her to her eternal rest.

[Page 257]

A year later, the Polish uprising broke out under the leadership of General [Tadeusz] Bór-Komorowski. Over the course of three months, we found ourselves in Żoliborz, bombed by the Germans from the air and from the ground. The Tarnow doctor, Zigmunt Szjanfeld, who now lives in Warsaw, worked as a surgeon in the hospital for those taking part in the uprising in Żoliborz. During the uprising, Yanka and Maks Szpindler perished. After the Germans took Żoliborz, we were transferred to one of the transition camps in Pruszkow, then to the *shtetl* Konskie, where a half year later we were free, because of the end of the war.

[Page 257, Volume 2]

Memories of the Uprising in the Tarnow Ghetto

by Hela Bornsztajn-Ross

Translated by Gloria Berkenstat Freund

We lived on Folwarczna Street in Tarnow, not far from the large synagogue – a giant, massive one with a large cupola. For half a century, they had made an effort to rebuild it. And therefore it was not so easy for the Hitlerist destroyers to demolish it quickly. The drunk Germans tried for 24 hours by exploding the synagogue with dynamite, until the cupola fell in the middle of the ruins with such a rush and noise, as if the world was being destroyed. The Germans, drunk with victory over the demise of the house of prayer, shot into the windows of Jewish houses on their way home. We sat huddled together, afraid of what would happen, not knowing that what would happen later would be more terrible.

We quickly were driven into a ghetto that in the beginning encompassed the entire Jewish quarter. There played out a true hell: seizures, selections, *umshlog platz* [place where Jews were assembled forcibly for deportations] and liquidations, leading to the crematoria. The Jewish population was annihilated lightning fast, shrunk and in terms of to its size, the ghetto constantly became smaller. In general, I will not repeat the known facts of the spiritual and physical annihilation, which the brown [shirt] bandits carried out against the unprotected Jewish population. However, I will never forget the image that played out in our neighborhood. This took place in the *Pod Dębem* [under the oak tree] ghetto during the first liquidation. Wild German soldiers entered an apartment that had long ago lost its appearance of a human residence. Lisha Unger lived there with his family. The Germans began to shoot blindly, killing his entire family. Lisha, seeing this, lay down near the dead body of his wife, asking the murderers to shoot him, too. The Germans mocked the Jew who was lying down, kicked him and beat him until they shot him. My father, Gedalia Barnsztajn, of blessed memory, saw this tragic event.

[Page 258]

There were frequent cases of open rebellion on the part of the persecuted Jews in Tarnow. Facher, the furrier, from whom the Germans wanted to take his child, did not allow them to do so and he beat, scratched and kicked the members of the Gestapo. Finally, they lay him on the ground, shot at him and his child and also murdered him with rifle butts in a beastly manner.

The 18-year old Alban also defended himself with dignity in the face of death. He did not want to kneel at the *umshlog-platz* and received a blow from the *S.S.* man who stood near him. The Germans tore him [while he was still alive] to pieces.

It is worth underlining the heroic conduct of some 40 Jews who hid in Rotenberg's bunker. When they were discovered, they shot at the Germans, killing several of them. They fought heroically until their deaths.

The resistance movement here [in Tarnow] especially was embraced by the young who began to organize themselves. In time, contact was established with the resistance movement of the young people in Krakow and with the Polish underground organization. It should be understood that because of the danger lying in wait and persecutions, liquidations and torture, the contact was loose and often interrupted. However, our young people organized a defense with superhuman strength. The son of the *shochet* [ritual slaughterer] (alas, I do not remember his name) went over to the Aryan side from the ghetto to maintain steady contact with the Krakow Jewish young people and the Polish underground. The Germans discovered him and arrested him. However, he successfully extracted himself from their hands and escaped, shooting at his persecutors. He arrived in the ghetto and the murderers, not being able to catch him, threatened the ghetto with the murder of 1,000 Jews if the *shochet's* son was not handed over The young man handed himself over to the Germans to prevent such a mass murder.

[Page 259]

There also were sporadic and organized cases of revolt and self-defense by other courageous young people, but alas, the notes about them were lost during my escape from the Tarnow ghetto. Therefore, I only provide facts that have been etched in my memory.

Despite the fact that another group or individuals in the rebellions would fall into the hands of the Gestapo, a group of young people from *Hashomer HaTzair* [socialist-Zionist – The Youth Guard] had an effect in the area of the Tarnow ghetto. It organized the crossing to the other side of the border – to Hungary and Czechoslovakia. The last liquidation of the ghetto was unexpected by this group and they did not succeed in making contact with the agents who led the underground movement. The Rebhon brothers, Szisler, both Szisler sisters, Mrs. Bridre (née Gras), Sztraus and the well-liked guard, known by the pseudonym, "Kubczu" and his younger brother belonged to this group. The ghetto walls were heavily surrounded then with armed soldiers. An armed German or Ukrainian stood every 10 steps. However, this did not completely frighten the *Shomrim* [Jewish guards] from carrying out their intended plan. They escaped at night with weapons in their hands, shooting, succeeding in reaching outside the ghetto walls and went to the southern part of the city in the direction of the Tuchawer forest. Here they reached an *S.S.* group. [The *S.S.*] surrounded and murdered them. Only "Kubczu," wounded in his hand, and his brother survived. They had no other option. They returned to the ghetto to try their luck for the second time, which also was successful for them. According the available rumors, both brothers are alive.

It should be understood that this was not an isolated plan. Many other young people defended Jewish honor with weapons in their hands.

The Jews driven together to the Tarnow ghetto from the surrounding *shtetlekh* [towns] also showed various forms of revolt. I must mention here the 65-year old Mrs. Ester Flejszer from Dabrowa near Tarnow. She escaped twice from transports, that were going to crematoria. She tried to make contact with the partisans in the surrounding forests. Alas, before she reached them, she was caught during the last liquidation of the ghetto. She committed suicide, swallowing luminol, which had previously been readied so that she would not fall into the hands of the Hitlerists.

[Page 260]

Seeing that the Hilterist devils were systematically murdering the Jewish population, I, locked in the ghetto, decided to escape to save myself and my parents. On the eve of the third deportation, on a Sunday evening when the Gestapo members would get drunk, I exited the ghetto through a break in the fencing. This was a moment of superhuman effort and toil because the Ukrainian scoundrels who guarded the ghetto were as diligent as the Germans themselves in persecuting the Jews. Yet I was successful in getting out from the closed quarter and ran in the direction of the water pipes near the village of Krzyż and where, guided by instinct, I went to a peasant who once had worked for my parents. He had a bunker where the Szmukler family (five people) already was hiding. The peasant gave me a roof over my head and I was able to convince him to make contact with my parents to take them out of the ghetto. Fortunately, he just then had work in the area of the ghetto, taking certain materials in his wagon. Using an extraordinary trick, he successfully brought my parents out of the ghetto. Then we were eight people in a narrow bunker where we hid for 27 months. The bunker was built in such a way that we could not stand, but we lay or sat. The hiding place was in an attic; it was dark, wet and extraordinarily cold. After 12 hours, bread would become completely moldy. During rain or a storm, we could permit ourselves to speak a word and this quietly. The throat, after many weeks of silence, would begin to hurt badly when we opened our mouths to say something. We lived in fear because this area would be searched often and the specter of death would always be before our eyes. The moment was terrible when one of our co-inhabitants, a young man, left the bunker on a dark night and never returned. Every day that we remained in the bunker we were like crazy people. We were sure that the captured young man would reveal our hiding place. Finally I decided to leave the bunker, having Aryan papers in my possession. While digging ditches I was recognized by a Polish school friend. I lived through minutes of deadly fear; who knew if he would turn me in? This did not happen. I succeeded in returning to the bunker, where I was hidden until the liberation.

[Page 261]

We were the first Jews who appeared in the streets of liberated Tarnow. The Poles looked at us as if at something of a wondrous. We, ourselves, were intoxicated and surprised by the daylight and we did not yet believe in our ability to move freely, that we were alive, that we were free, that we were no longer persecuted dogs. For a long time we could not throw off the most otherworldly experiences and nightmares of the not too distant past.

How Miriam Korn Heroically Died

by Lili Wider–Rozenberg, Israel by Ya'akov Kenner[a]

Translated by Nancy Bassel, Leonard Blank, Barbara Blaustein, Philip Frost & Natanya Nobel

In one of my reports I described the event in which a 28-year-old Kalisz woman, Chana Aronovich-Rockman, who was raised in a political environment, in the prewar Polish "Hashomer Hatzair," had, during the Nazi occupation of Poland, openly slapped a German officer. As a result, she was shot at once, killed together with her child.

Chana Aronovich-Rockman from Kalisz was not the only Jewish woman who had acted so bravely. There were more Jewish women in Poland who rose to a level of true heroism, even sacrificing their young lives in order to save the honor of their people. One of these quiet heroines, an active comrade of the leftist 'Poale Zion,' is described in this report — which is not (G-d forbid) a made-up story, but a true story based on a factual account.

[Page 262]

The story was recounted to me by an eyewitness who currently resides in the United States, in North America. In order to verify the story, I asked the brother of this heroine who now lives in Sweden. In his written answer, which is based on detailed research, the whole story fits 100% with the description of the aforementioned eyewitness—so much so that there is no doubt that we are dealing with a true story. And the person who will be further described is entitled to a "place of honor" amongst the gallery of unsung heroes—who bravely and boldly performed heroic deeds.

This is the story of comrade Miriam Korn from Tarnow, the wife of David Lengovich, the Poale-Zion representative on Tarnow City Council. She was murdered by the Germans in 1943 in Rave-Ruska in central Galicia. Miriam, or as she was called in the Party circles of western Galicia, comrade Mania—had her political-social upbringing in the Poale Zion Youth Organization of Nowy Sacz where she was born and raised in a respectable Chasidic family. But Miriam was, at an early age, drawn to the educational circles of the Poale-Zion Youth and under the influence of the then youth leader Emanuel Ringleblum—who later became a legendary personality in the Warsaw Ghetto. Mania Korn, in her own right, became one of the most active leaders first in the Youth groups and later in the main Poale-Zion organization in Nowy-Sacz.

Later she attached herself to comrade David Lenkavich from Tarnow and soon became the darling of Tarnow's Jewish working class. She was praised for both her tireless organizing of workers in the local professional organizations and in the cultural education among the youth.

In the first days of Hitler's occupation in September 1939, comrade Miriam's husband, the banished comrade David Lenkovich, was able to smuggle himself to Eastern Galicia, where Soviet authorities had already established themselves. After he left, comrade Miriam remained in Tarnow with their only child. She decided that she would use all her strength to care for and raise the child until the Germans would be driven out of Poland and her husband would return.

Miriam Korn-Lenkovich suffered under German rule in the Tarnow ghetto until the end of 1943. The Germans had allowed this ghetto to exist longer than in other cities because a large number of Jews were considered "work capable" and were slaves in the factories of the Bakelite industry.

[Page 263]

At the end of 1943 when the Germans returned to liquidate the Tarnow ghetto, Miriam Korn obtained an Aryan document and on a dark evening when a group of Jewish workers were returning to the ghetto, she took the opportunity to exit the ghetto gate with her child.

Exiting the ghetto with her child was successful but she was noticed by a scoundrel who was a member of the Jewish ghetto police. That despicable man immediately snitched on her to a German officer. The Nazi officer chased after her and before she could hide in a small side street, he grabbed her. The officer first figured out who she was, and asserting that she was from the skilled work force, he decided that she could return to the ghetto without punishment but she had to leave the child, even though children were of no use to the German army.

Miriam Korn did not, however wish to give up her child to the German murderers, as she was also well aware, in any case, that sooner or later her fate was death if she returned to the ghetto. She therefore decided the in no way would she turn the child over to the officer.

When the officer insisted and tried to pull the child from her with force Miriam Korn, (in the presence of the group of Jewish laborers who were delayed at the ghetto gate) first spat in the face of the Jewish stool pigeon policeman who had exposed her. She then spat on the officer who had ripped the child from her hands and openly slapped him.

The German officer grabbed his revolver and shot comrade Miriam on the spot. She had enough time to curse the officer before her murder, thus uplifting her heroic soul. The frenzied German officer then grabbed the child and with wild anger smashed the child's head against the nearby wall until, in this beastly manner, he murdered the child.

So as not to witness the death of her innocent child, Miriam paid the price of her own life.

[Page 264]

In this manner did comrade Miriam Korn-Lenkovich from Tarnow die. She will always be remembered by those who knew her and for those who did not know her personally, a memento and an example of courage and heroism.

Original footnote:

a. A meritorious leader in Poale Zion, one of the founders of the Poale Zion organization in Galicia, who passed away in Israel in 1951

[Page 264, Volume 2]

Memories of Those Terrible Times

by Lili Wider–Rozenberg Israel

Translated by Gloria Berkenstat Freund

Lily Wider-Rozenberg

September 1939 was the end of a happy and carefree childhood for me and the beginning of a hell with the occupation of the Hitlerist murderers. The persecutions against the Jews – police curfews, obligatory wearing of the armband with a *Mogen–Dovid* [Shield of David – the Jewish Star], the closure of schools for Jewish children – began immediately that month when the *Wehrmacht* [German armed forces] and S.S. divisions occupied Tarnow. Rutka Wajs, her cousin and I studied in private with the [female] teacher, Mila Tirkel. In addition, I also studied English.

On the 3rd of May 1940 the Gestapo arrested my father, Dr. Emil Wider, of blessed memory, and in December 1940, we received a telegram from Auschwitz that my father had died there. In order to increase our suffering, the Gestapo summoned my mother ostensibly to give her details of her husband's death. In truth, they wanted to make fun of her despair and thus did not spare her any blows. The Germans did not forget from time to time to send us my father's things: his suit, postage stamps, money. And finally – a can of the ashes of my father, of blessed memory, whom we buried at the cemetery in Tarnow.

[Page 265]

In time it became dangerous and risky for a Jew to appear on a Tarnow street. The Germans beat, tortured, grabbed [Jews] for work, cut off beards. The children were sad. They met in residences; they tried more and more not to be in the street.

The first shootings of people began in 1941. First, those who had returned from the eastern areas occupied by the Russians. Among others who perished during those shootings were Dr. Janek Ritter, Otto Wajs, Dr. Wilek Holender. To my great despair, going to my lessons I saw Jews who had been shot lying on the street. However, the worst came in June 1942 – the first deportations. We did not yet know that deportation meant death. Therefore, everyone tried to appear at the marketplace where the collection point was located. From our apartment at Targowa 3, we saw the Germans, who shouted, cursed, shot and beat while driving the old people and children into the trucks. We constantly heard shooting from the *Rynek* [marketplace]. My mother and I made it safely through the aktions [deportation] because we had a paper from the security police furnished with a stamp.

Several weeks after the first deportation, everyone was confined to the ghetto. We also learned about the death camps. The children reacted in different ways. Several believed that they would not survive the war; others, including myself, believed that we would save ourselves.

I received work in the Czacki School in the ghetto, sorting and disinfecting the clothing of the deported Jews. My mother worked at Riszen and I was never certain that we would see each other when we returned work. And meanwhile, the Germans shot at Jews in the ghetto without any reason, without any selection. My mother and I decided to make false documents and to escape from the ghetto. We postponed this from day to day. After we succeeded in avoiding the second deportation, we left the ghetto in September 1942. We spent the first night in the Rzedziner forest; then we left on foot for Czarna and from there to Lemberg by train. I wanted to believe that it would be easier to hide in a larger city. Moreover, we lived with the hope that Lemberg shortly would be liberated by the Russians. We spent the night in a private inn that later seemed to be a trap for Jews. As soon as we lay down, the Gestapo and the Ukrainian policemen came. They began to examine our documents. My mother quietly said: "Pretend that you are sleeping; only show your face." This time, my "Aryan appearance" saved me.

[Page 266]

The next morning we were lucky to find a room on Sapieha Street. I made up a pretext for the owner that I was hiding from being caught and sent to work in Germany. Therefore there was no reason for him to report us. We hid in the apartment for only three days a week. On the other days we traveled in the villages and bought dairy products and sold them in the city – and we survived on this. We tried to travel at night because the trains were relatively safer. In November 1942 we brought our two cousins, Gizsha and Tosha Waserlauf, of blessed memory, (from Krakow) from the Tarnow ghetto. We wanted to save them. I remained with them in Lemberg while my mother continued to travel around the villages. Several weeks later, while my mother was not with us, denouncers, who passed themselves off as "criminal investigating" functionaries entered our apartment. We bribed them with our watches, which we took off our wrists.

In the morning we left for Przemysl, leaving my mother a note that we were traveling to the well–known genteel Polish woman, Jozefina Lumbe. She welcomed us with tears in her eyes and hid us for three full weeks, At the same, time my mother had jumped from a train on the route from Lemberg to Przemysl because of fear of the Germans. She was brought to the hospital in Przemysl in an unconscious state.

My two cousins had to leave the apartment of the good Christian woman and return to the ghetto, where they perished. Mrs. Lumbe allowed me to stay with her as long as my mother lay in the hospital. But this lasted for weeks because the doctors asserted that because of her unfortunate jump, the patient had gotten tuberculosis in her bones and who knew if she would ever walk again. I took my mother to Lemberg, to a well–known specialist, Professor Gruca, who took her to his clinic and began to heal her and put on casts.

In Lemberg I rented a residence on Kurkowe Street. In 1942, during a police raid on the street, I was caught and sent to Germany on forced labor. I was despondent because my mother could not walk and I also was afraid that a more thorough inspection of my false papers would lead to the discovery that I was a Jewish child. Then it became apparent that my being sent to Germany had saved my life. My mother, on the contrary, had remained completely alone in her casts; she had walked in order to earn a livelihood.

[Page 267]

I experienced many and varied things in Germany. In the hall in a transit camp I became acquainted with Janina Ruczicka, also a Jewish girl. We became good friends, but never mentioned our origins. We were separated after several weeks. She was sent to Salzwedel and I, thanks to the help of an unknown German, was sent to the weapons factory – Stock et Kampf, in Stalberg–Tirathal, as a translator from German to Russian and French. When it immediately became apparent that I did not know any of the languages, thanks to the help of a German translator I succeeded in receiving work in the bookkeeping bureau. Later, they suggested that I register as a Volksdeutsche [ethnic German], which would permit me to continue to work at my posts. I refused and therefore I was taken to work in a train restaurant and later to a farmer. I was freed by the American Army in April 1945.

[Page 268, Volume 2]

Belzec, the Place of Death of the Tarnow Jews

by Jerzy Bergman

Translated by Gloria Berkenstat Freund

The Hitlerist death camps are one of the darkest and most shameful pages in the history of humankind. In order to give an impression of this orgy of bestiality and all of its effects, the Nuremberg Tribunal, which judged the war criminals, had to enrich human language with only one word, which contains in it the terror, pain and rage: genocide!

The following description is dedicated to only one such place, a single place on the dense and large death map – the map of the mass murder of innocent people. This small place is the mass grave of 600,000 human creatures, the cemetery of 600,000 dead Jews from Poland, Russia and Czechoslovakia.

Here, in Belzec, also was the place of death for thousands of Tarnow Jews.

This small *shtetl* [town] on the southeastern edge of Lublin Province, eight kilometers [about five miles] from Tomaszow-Lubelski, was sadly well-known during the years of the Hitlerist occupation, when at the beginning of 1942, one of the largest death camps was erected, which had only one task: to kill Jews.

The first transports began to arrive on a special side train line in March of that year. One hundred and fifty people were pushed into each train wagon. The camp was completely fenced in and guarded so that no one outside could see into it or could enter.

A barracks stood near the train line where the victims had to undress. An inscription hung over the one small window in the barracks: *kosztowności* (*kostbarkeiten* [treasures] or jewelry). A room with 100 seats was also located in the barracks and an inscription: "hairdressers."

[Page 269]

After undressing, the victims were driven into a characteristic corridor – a passageway, fenced in with barbed wire on both sides, 50 meters [164 feet] long, which led to the *laznia i inhalatorium* (bathhouse and disinfection room), as the inscriptions on the fencing informed them. They approached a building whose outward appearance reminded one of a bathhouse. Flowers and various bushes grew on both sides. There was a sign with a painted *Mogen Dovid* [Shield of David – a Jewish star] on the roof with the inscription: *Fundatsia Hokenholta* (Hackenholt's Foundation). [Lorenz] Hackenholt, the *Unterscharführer* [junior squad leader] of the *S.S.*, made use of the diesel motors, which produced the gas to kill the Jews in the rooms. The inscription was only a cynical irony for the victims.

On the 11th of June 1942 at a late night hour, or at the dawn of the 12th of June, the transport of 8,000 Tarnow Jews arrived at that actual spot, at the large factory of death, which consisted of several modest buildings.

And thus, as with all other transports, we can imagine that last road:

After a ride of long duration in train wagons designated for transporting cattle, the transport, guarded by Germans and *Granatene* [Blue Police – Polish police in German-occupied Poland] (Polish) policemen, arrived at the Belzec train station. Here they were taken over by the Ukrainian bandit guards, who, without a doubt, had sworn to protect the secret of the camp, although the smoke and smell that was carried from it revealed the terrible secret.

Several train wagons were detached from the transport, which were taken through the side train line. Two hundred Ukrainians stood around the train wagons and began to drive out the unfortunate Jews with blows and wild shouting. Orders were heard through a loudspeaker: "Everyone take off everything, even glasses and prostheses. Money and jewelry should be given at a small window with the inscription *kosztowności* [jewelry]. Women and children go to the hairdressers where hair is shaved!"

The naked men, women and children then were sent to the gas chamber, through the heavily fenced passageway. The *S.S.* man who stood at the entrance spoke mildly: "Nothing will happen to you; all you have to do is breathe deeply…"

[Page 270]

Quietly, but pushing one another forward, the victims went up the wooden steps into the building in which the gas chamber was located. Many recited a prayer. Seven to eight hundred men were pushed into an area of 93 square meters [about 1,000 square feet]. Then the door was sealed shut and the motors, which dispersed the death gas, started immediately.

…Twenty-five minutes passed. Through the small window one could see (the gas chamber was illuminated inside) that many victims already were dead. Thirty-two minutes after bolting the door – everyone was dead. Jewish prisoners from the other side of the barracks waited for an order to open the wooden door – and a terrible picture was revealed before their eyes: the gassed Jews stood as if in stone columns, unmoving because the crowdedness and narrowness was without limit there. One could recognize families by the hands and arms they wrapped around each other in saying goodbye…

More than 20 camp inmates then were involved with checking the teeth of those who had perished. They opened the clamped, closed mouths with iron hatchets. Those with gold teeth, to the left, those without gold in their mouths, to the right. Others looked in the hidden parts of the bodies, looking there for money, gold, diamonds.

After this check, the gassed bodies were thrown into a large pit (approximately 100 by 12 meters [approximately 328 by 39 feet]) that was located near the gas chamber in the eastern part of the camp. After several days, the mass of bodies swelled and rose up – a sign that the gas had begun to leave… Then the bodies were laid on giant furnace grates, doused with kerosene and set on fire. The ashes were spread in the surrounding fields or buried deep in the earth.

Such gruesome scenes played out here almost every day over the course of the entire time of the camp's existence. The death "production" in the Belzec camp reached up to 15,000 victims a day. The liquidation of the Belzec camp began in December 1942. There was no longer any trace of the Belzec camp at the beginning of 1943. The camp chief, Christian Wirth, a major in the *S.S.*, took care of this. Pine trees were planted on the smoothed out terrain and all traces of the death factory were erased.

[Page 271]

However, now, 24 years after the liquidation, Belzec is not erased in human memories. It is true no documents remain, but the thousands of individual bones from the human skeletons give evidence of the German crimes at that spot. And a monument was erected at the very center of the former camp, for which a handful of surviving Tarnow Jews, who came to honor the martyrs, assembled for the 24th anniversary of the first deportation in Tarnow. Candles were lit at the monument; prayers were said and quiet sobbing was heard.

The German murderers did not succeed in completely erasing the traces of their terrible crimes in Belzec. The bones that are found forever tell of the great tragedy that occurred there.

*

The descriptions about the ways of killing the victims are taken from the statements of the *S.S.* Colonel Dr. Kurt Gerstein, an anti-fascist, who told the French military regime about the Belzec extermination camp several days before the end of the war. His statements do not necessarily relate to the transport of the Tarnow Jews, but there is no other living witness to the hell – and we may assume that our Tarnow Jews perished the same way.

Gerstein's description is the only one about the Belzec camp.

[Page 272, Volume 2]

The Belzer Rebbe Gave Me His Blessing

by Dr. Yeshayahu Hendler (Tel-Aviv)

Translated by David Schonberg

Dr. Yeshayahu Hendler

I had already left Tarnow in 1924 and I only came back home to Tarnow to my parents and siblings in 1940 when it was under the Nazi overlords and the criminal acts of the Gestapo and their accomplices had embittered the lives of the Jewish population.

Till the first 'Resettlement' *aksia* [action] I was able to work as a private doctor and I treated patients in the residence of my friend, the otolaryngologist, Dr. Ruben (he is still active in Tarnow as a doctor). From 1942 I started working also in the Jewish Hospital.

The Extermination action against the Jewish population were carried out by the Nazi murderers systematically- brutally and mercilessly. First they deported and drove the Jewish inhabitants from smaller to larger localities, where they created the nightmarish constricted ghettos.. those weary and tormented/ oppressed ghetto residents who remained alive for a while were finally deported to the death camps, meeting their final demise.

Only a few were able to extract themselves from the Nazi hell. Jews tried to hide in bunkers, be hidden by Christians, lived on Aryan papers or for large sums of money tried to smuggle themselves abroad.

[Page 273]

Such a place, from where there was smuggling of Jews to Hungary- was in Bochnia, a *shtetl* [small town] between Krakow and Tarnow. It need be understood that this smuggling was extremely dangerous and often such an attempt to save oneself from *Gehinnom* [*Gehenna*- hell] had a tragic end.

* * *

In 1942 - when there took place in Tarnow with great brutality the first mass murders of the Jewish population- the so-called first 'resettlement' action — when approximately 20,000 Jews during this murderous action were annihilated, either in Tarnow itself or by deportation to the gas chambers of Auschwitz or Belzec - it fell upon me by destiny to assist to save the Belzer *Rebbe*, whose *Hassidim* [*his devoted followers*] in the last moment took him out of Belz and really, in the last moment, extracted him from the claws of the Nazis.

As I was only later to find out, this was the Belzer *Rebbe*, R' Ahrele Rokeach , zs'l [may the memory of the righteous be a blessing] who had then fled from Belz to Sokal and from there he fled further with all his family and a number of his Hassidim to Przemyślany [a town in the Ukraine]. But there too, the *Rebbe* found no rest as the German murderers had burnt down the small town and almost its entire Jewish population found their demise in the fire.

Due to the efforts of several Belzer Hassidim, the *Rebbe* was rescued. They found a Polish taxi-owner who for a large sum of money agreed to take the Belzer *Rebbe* to Vishnitz near Bochnia, from where he was to be further smuggled over to Hungary. Travelling together with the Rebbe were his brother, the Bilgoray Rebbe and another two Belzer Hassidim- the Rebbe's attendants [*gabaim*]. The journey went smoothly till the village Rzędzin not far from Tarnow, where the taxi with the people suddenly overturned into a ditch, and the *Rebbe* and those accompanying him were seriously injured.

That night, when the accident occurred – there came running to me a Tarnow Jew, a certain Goldfarb who was extremely upset and he begged me that I [travel] come with him immediately to the Belzer Rebbe who was lying severely injured at a non-Jew's place in Rzędzin near Tarnow and he quickly related to me about the rescuing of the Belzer Rebbe from the burning *shtetl*, his journey with the taxi which on the way had overturned and that the Rebbe and those accompanying him were severely injured.

[Page 274]

Notwithstanding that to leave the ghetto without a permission was punishable by death, I quickly prepared the necessary medicines and several instruments and we began my way to the injured *Rebbe* and his attendants. At the exit of the ghetto there was waiting for us a Polish Christian with horses and wagon and thanks to the fact that the night was pitch-dark, no one came upon us. After about an hour we came to the village and approached a small house, situated aside, where the injured were. We went inside the house where the Rebbe was lying on a bench.. his face wrapped in a red cloth (kerchief), as if he was suffering from a tooth-ache. he needed to hide the shame.. how terribly he had suffered, having had to let his beard and *payot* [side-curls] be cut off.. His whole head… his hands and clothes were stained with blood.

On a second bench lay another injured Jew, also with his beard and *payos* cut off and his hands and clothes were covered in blood.

I instructed them to get more light in the dark room and after cleaning the *Rebbe*'s face from blood, I determined [established] that he had a deep wound in his forehead and on his arm. Similarly, in regard to the second injured person.

After cleaning and sewing the open wounds and later after making the necessary prophylactic injections, the *Rebbe* asked me as to what he should pay.. my answer was that I don't required any payment [not a groshen] as I had only carried out my human duty and that I was really happy that everything went well through all right and that I had the honor to help the *Rebbe* and those accompanying him in a time of trouble.

Then the Rebbe blessed me and my whole family and also gave me a 20-zloty coin, together with blessings and told me that that I should hold onto it as to an amulet… We heartily took our leave and with the same non-Jew who brought us to the Rebbe, I returned together with Goldfarb to Tarnow.

Immediately at the outset of our journey Goldfarb asked [begged] me to 'sell' him the amulet from the Rebbe.

[Page 275]

"Doctor- he argued- you are not religious.. for what do you need the amulet…?"

He started with 2,000 zlotys.. and then already wanted to offer 20,000 zlotys and then finally, any sum that I would ask.. My answer was only this- the coin that the *Rebbe* gave me was given to me personally, as a charm- amulet for blessing for me and my family. We didn't speak more of the amulet and the amulet remained with me.

Later, when we were deported from the Tarnow ghetto to Plaszow and there it had come to the stage of liquidating the work-camp, I buried the amulet and other important documents in the earth next to the hut where I had stayed.

After the war, my first journey took me to Plaszow, to the hut where I had stayed. Nothing remained of it and only after much searching I found the place where the hut stood. I dug for some time till I came upon the tin [metal] box- and there inside was the amulet and so it is that I have it, till today.

Not once have I thought.. that I came out alive from the Nazi Gehenna [hell] due to the merit of the blessings that the Belzer *Rebbe* blessed me in giving me the 20 zloty coin.

* * *

It is such thoughts that arise/ awaken in my mind, when deep in my memories it seems incredible the miracle, that despite going through the 7 sectors of hell, despite the difficult wanderings and the suffering that I went through, that I stayed alive and unconsciously bound up in my rescue [survival/ being saved] is the amulet and blessings of the Belzer *Rebbe*.

In 1940 I left Krakow and went to Tarnow because I was convinced that in my hometown it would be easier to save my family. Unfortunately, from my whole family only me and my younger sister Leah (Lutke) remained alive (we both were lucky and worked in the military clothing factory- at first in Tarnow and later in Plaszow). My older brother Josef was drafted at the outbreak of the war to the Polish army and remained in Lemberg [Lvov], When the city found itself in Russian hands and later, when the German divisions

[Page 276]

occupied Eastern Galicia, including Lemberg, he was the director of the Jewish hospital in Drohobycz and worked there as a surgeon and gynecologist.

In one of the resettlement actions in 1943 he died together with his son, Artek.

My younger brother Moshe, also a doctor, was killed in Turobin, where he was sent to fight a typhus epidemic that broke out in the Lublin area. During the liquidation of the Jewish population he died together with all the Jews there.

I was unsuccessful in my attempts to save my family, who lived in the Tarnow ghetto. There died my parents a'h, there died my sister Rivke Braun with her children, my brother Hirsh Zvi and my sister-in-law with her child.

And the Belzer *Rebbe*, who I last seen in Rzędzin next to Tarnow after I bandaged his wounds, had escaped. Already in Israel the Belzer Hassidim gave out a booklet describing the whole episode of the Belzer *Rebbe*, R' Ahrele's zs'l [of blessed memory] rescue and that of his brother, the *Rebbe* from Bigoray, who was with him in the taxi that overturned, and relating fully the help of the doctor, that I have told, that was given to the seriously injured Belzer *Rebbe* and those who accompanied him.

As told in the booklet, the Belzer *Rebbe* soon after my visit was able to travel safely to Vishnitz (next to Bochnia) and from there to Hungary. From Hungary he travelled to America. He came to live in Israel only in 1954, and there he died in 1957.

[Page 277, Volume 2]

The Social Aid in Jewish Tarnow During the German Occupation

by Dr. Avraham Chomet (Khumit), Ramat–Gan

Translated by Gloria Berkenstat Freund

The Hitlerist organs of power, the Gestapo and S.S. divisions, began to make concrete their criminal plan for the total annihilation and destruction of Polish Jewry during the first days of the German occupation of Poland.

The initial phases of this plan were outlined in detail in secret *telefonograms* [telegrams sent by telephone], the so called *schnell–brief* [express–letter], which the chief of the security police [Reinhard] Heydrich sent to the leaders of the Einsatzgruppen [S.S. and police units in charge of security in occupied areas], which were active in the occupied Polish areas on the 21st of September 1939.

A great deal of organization was displayed in the first phase of this plan, which was to undermine and destroy the economic base of the Jewish population – first through pushing the Jews out of their economic positions.

In addition to a flood of anti–Jewish edicts, which were designed to legalize the daily murder and robbery activities on the part of the Hitlerist holders of power, in addition to the bloody terror in the cities and *shtetlekh* [towns] in regard to the unprotected Jewish population, in addition to the terrifying annihilation actions with exploding and burning synagogues and houses of prayer, in addition to the confiscation of Jewish possessions, the Jews were pushed out of various industrial enterprises, from commerce and trade. The Jewish intelligentsia were removed from their workplaces; Jewish doctors, lawyers, teachers and scientists lost their income.

The right to pensions, annuities and other social insurance was stolen from the Jews and as a result Jewish retirees and war invalids met with great misfortune.

[Page 278]

Greatly contributing to the difficult economic situation of the Jewish population in occupied Poland was the German order of the 18th of September 1939, which was published at the end of October, according to which Jews were strongly forbidden to possess more than 2,000 *zlotes* and the rest of their money had to be deposited in a bank in a blocked bank account, from which the bank could pay out [to the depositor] at most 250 *zlotes* a week.

This edict was later strengthened on the 20th of November 1938 with a decree according to which only 500 *zlotes* a month were permitted to be paid out from such a savings account. It should be understood that under such conditions every Jewish enterprise, not having the ability to make use of its blocked money, had to cease its activity.

The fate of the Jewish artisans was sad. They were forbidden to move from one workshop to another without the permission of the German officials who held the power and they were also forbidden to sell their work tools.

According to the decrees of the 16th of December 1939 and of the 9th of November 1940, the Jews could not benefit from the support for the unemployed.

According to the decree of the 7th of March 1940, the Jewish population of the entire General Government had no right to benefit from the medical aid from the sick fund, although they had to pay monthly sick fund dues.

From March 1940, the activity of the Jewish credit cooperative was forbidden. Later, when the Jewish Social Self–Help (*YISA*) began its activity, the distribution of interest–free loans was one of the tasks of the *Tsekabe* [Central No–Interest Loan Office] Society, which presented *YISA* a paper about "interest–free loan funds."[1].

The results of this German extermination action in relation to the Jewish population in occupied Poland did not take long to arrive… During the first half of 1940 hunger and need reigned in Jewish homes.

– 2 –

The Jewish community in Tarnow was not an exception. Here, too, there were clear signs of a state of shock in Jewish economic life during the first months of the German occupation.

[Page 279]

It did not take long before almost the entire population of Tarnow found itself in a state of economic impoverishment as hunger, cold and illnesses reigned in the Jewish neighborhood. Also, the fact must be considered that the number of Jews in Tarnow rose immediately during the first months of the occupation of the city by the Germans because since the month of December 1939 deported Jews came to Tarnow from neighboring and distant areas.

Twenty–five thousand six hundred Jews lived in Tarnow in September 1930[2]. Despite persecutions, shootings and deportations, the number of Jews in Tarnow in the month of March 1942 reached 28,000 souls.[3]

There still were communal workers from before the occupation in Tarnow, who made efforts to help their needy brothers. They endeavored to help in a reciprocal, unorganized way. In place of the *kehile* [organized Jewish community], the Germans created a *Judentrat* [Jewish council] whose task, among other things, was to lead the social aid activity on behalf of the Jewish population in the city. A separate aid commission was created at the *Judentrat* that led the so–called *wohlfarht* [welfare].

However, the new, horrible conditions in which the Tarnow Jews now had to live – pressed together in more limited areas than before… robbed of stable sources of income – provided very important tasks for the members of the social division of the *Judentrat* in Tarnow.

According to an order from the Tarnow county chief of the 16th of September 1940, the *Judentrat* was authorized to demand a *kehile* tax of the Jewish residents of the city, the previous so–called domestic tax that they had paid before the occupation. In addition, these payments now were designated for the expense of social aid. The *Judentrat* also received the right to make use of force against every Jewish resident in Tarnow who did not pay this tax and even to arrest them with the assistance of the police.

[Page 280]

The orders of the 14th of October 1941

Only in a minimal way could the *Judentrat* make use of the income from this tax payment for social aid activities. The contributions, the various forced payments and expensive gifts for the Nazi regime organs depleted the limited financial means of the *Judentrat*.

An important contribution to the social activities on behalf of the Jewish population under the General Government was foreign help.

[Page 281]

The limited minimal aid for the impoverished Jewish masses in occupied Poland was possible in great measure thanks to the American transports that arrived in Poland beginning during the first month of 1940. They mainly came from three organizations: 1) from the American Red Cross, which sent aid for the entire civilian population – except the Germans, 2) from the American Hoover Commission (political relief) and 3) from the Joint [Distribution Committee], only for Jews.

Later, when the Jewish Social Self–Help – *YISA* – participated in the first two funds of 17 percent, it also was decided that *YISA* had to receive 17 percent of the cash grants the *NRA* [*Narodowa Rada Opiekuńcza* – National Guardianship Council] was supposed to receive from the taxes that the occupying regime organs collected from the population for social aid. This part was later – starting in May 1942 – decreased to 16 percent.

However, in the month of July 1942 this grant for *YISA* ceased.

[Among the main help given in] Tarnow was a *folks–kikh* [public kitchen], where inexpensive lunches were given out. However, this was like a drop of water. Hunger and sickness, robbery and murderous actions were daily events.

A clear expression of the tragic situation of the Jewish population in Tarnow is found in the assessment for the month of May 1940, which the county chief of Tarnow delivered to the German occupying regime with regard to the forced labor of the Jewish population in Tarnow.

He wrote in the report, "The question arose of what would happen to the Jews in the future as a result of my withdrawing from the agreement with the new system in the area of economic and nutritional organization [under which the Jews must provide] more and more from their earnings. Forced labor for the Jews creates the opportunity of employment and some limited nourishment for only a portion of the men, but not for women and children. The solution of the Jewish problem with the increasing reduction of their ability to earn is even more urgent."[4].

[Page 282]

– 3 –

During this melancholy era of despair and complete helplessness there were individuals in the Jewish social fabric who decided to break through the wall of hopelessness and resignation that ruled the mood of the tortured Jewish masses in occupied Poland. *Yidishe Sotsiale Aleynhilf* [Jewish Social Self Help] – abbreviated as *YISA* – was created at the end of May 1940, a society that was legalized by the German administration as a voluntary aid institution (*Żydówska Samopomoc Społeczna* [Jewish Social Self–Help]), with the task of leading all of the public and private social aid activities, to unify all the organizations for voluntary aid, to create the necessary means, distribute the monetary and material gifts, organize, maintain and support all establishments and institutions for social aid and to work with all foreign aid organizations through the intervention of the German Red Cross.

The first administration of *YISA* lay in the hands of a presidium of seven founders and together with a chairman and vice chairman they constituted the executive, which was to be reelected each year. According to the statutes and regulations, a Jewish social aid county committee was created in the county seat of every German city and county chief, which consisted of five members and wherever Jews lived this presidium had to right to delegates in *YISA*.[5]

In addition to member dues, *YISA* could make use of state and communal grants, dispensing cash and items, money collections, lotteries and other gifts.[6]

Four members from Warsaw and three from Krakow joined the presidium of *YISA*. Dr. Wajchert stood at the head of *YISA* during its entire existence.

However, the new aid organization in the Jewish neighborhood had a difficult problem of collecting the necessary monetary means to succeed in its great task. The *Judentrats* were obligated to subsidize the activity of the *YISA* divisions in the cities and *shtetlekh* [towns] in the occupied area.

[Page 283]

Yet the *Judentrats* were the only Jewish administrative bodies during the German occupation that were authorized to demand taxes and various payments from the Jewish population.

In connection with this, the presidium of *YISA* immediately at the beginning of its activity demanded that the *Judentrat* designate a significant grant for the *YISA* committee in its budgets. Alas, this appeal did not result in a response from the local *Judentrat*.

For a time, the *YISA* received substantial help from the Joint [Distribution Committee], which immediately placed its funds and reserves in the possession of the Jewish Aid Organization. However, in December 1941, the Joint in Poland was closed and the presidium of the *YISA* had to seek other sources of income.

In addition to income from members payments and money collections, for which the aid committees were authorized according to the statues of the *YISA* – as was previously mentioned – its presidium obtained a portion from various taxes and payments that the occupiers charged the Jewish population in the area of the General Government.

In addition to this, the "immigration tax," a kind of head tax on all adult Jews over the age of 18 in the shtetl, was implemented in by the order of the 17th of June 1940. Thus the income from this tax was designated firstly for social aid.[7]

This income actually made it possible for the Tarnow *Judentrat* to bring help en masse to the Tarnow Jews who had been taken for forced labor. As Dr. Wajchert describes in his *Memoirs*[8]: in 1940 the *Judentrat* distributed over 150,000 *zlotes* in aid for those Tarnow Jews employed in the camps and work–battalions.

It is worthwhile to relate that for the camps in Pustków, where at first 750 Jews from Dębica, Mielec, Sędziszów, Ropczyce, Wielopole and Tarnow were imprisoned, the *Judentrat* of these localities had to arrange for a kitchen, provide food for them, provide work tools, dishes and blankets for the imprisoned Jews in addition to support for their families.

A general resident's tax existed in the occupied areas.

[Page 284]

However, as Dr. Wajchert, the chairman of the *YISA*, explained in his mentioned memoirs[9], the constant resettlements of the Jewish population resulted in the fact that many Jews did not pay this tax. Thanks to the efforts of the *YISA* presidium, the division of income as a basis for the Jewish portion of this tax was based on the number of Jews who lived or were staying in an area on the 1st of April 1940 (starting with the date the tax became valid and not on the number of Jews who had paid the tax or not).

It was decided that a communal tax that would fall on a portion of the Jews would be paid to the local *YISA* committee through the county or city chief with the calculation of the 1st of April 1940[10].

On the basis of this regulation the Jewish county aid committee in Tarnow among other cities received a larger grant from this tax[11].

Later the General Governor Frank annulled these designations on the 19th of October 1941 and with the order of the 6th of December 1941 he published a uniform text for the payment of this tax, not mentioning that its income was designated to cover the expenses of the social aid activity – on behalf of the Poles as well as on behalf of the Jewish population, although this tax clearly was created for this purpose.

– 4 –

At the start, the leadership of the Jewish Social County Committee in Tarnow was placed in the hands of Dr. Szpajzer and, later, after the Gestapo had murdered him in a beastly manner, the chairman of the Tarnow *YISA* county committee became Artur Falkman, who simultaneously was chairman of the *Judentrat* in Tarnow. Still belonging to the committee were Y. Lerhauft,

[Page 285]

Yehosha Grinewize and Paul Rajs, who also led the social aid committee at the *Judentrat*.

At first, as long as Dr. Szpajzer was alive, there was close contact and useful joint work between the *YISA* county committee and the *Judentrat*. Later, the *YISA* divisions in the neighboring localities, which belonged to the Tarnow Social County Committee, such as in Brigl [Brzesko], Bochnia, etc. suffered when the same person stood at the head of both administrative bodies.

As we read in a written report,[12] which the member of the *YISA* presidium, Dr. Elihu Tisz (a child of Tarnow, active over the course of many years in the Zionist movement in Tarnow, until 1939, lawyer, Zionist and communal activist in Novy Sacz, leader of the cultural and press division of the Jewish World Congress in Stockholm after the war, emigrated to Israel in 1951 and died in Jerusalem in 1953) reported in connection with his appearance in Tarnow in October 1951, "No one in Tarnow knew about a Jewish Social Self–Help [organization]. They only knew the *Judentrat*, which is not a surprise, because Mr. Rajs served in the reception room of the social county committee in the name of the *Judentrat* and the division of the *Judentrat* that gave out various forms of permission, and also was found in the office of the county committee…"

In this report it is also stressed that the Tarnow Social County Committee was no more than a showcase for the Tarnow *Judentrat* and had very loose contact with the provinces.

In the account written by the presidium of the *YISA* in Krakow on the 20th of November 1941,[13] we read that Dr. Jakov Gans, the chairman of the *YISA* delegation in Gumniska, near Tarnow, along with the vice chairman of the *Judentrat* there provided a certain clarification with regard to the relation between the Tarnow *Judentrat* and the Tarnow *YISA* county committee. He [Yakov Gans] and Meir Bazler, the chairman of the *Judentrat* there, both complained that since the death of Dr. Szpajzer, of blessed memory, the Jewish Social Country Committee existed only on paper because Mr. Rajs, who is a good worker at the *Judentrat* is so busy there that he has no time for the Social County Committee. The same – lamented the delegates – concerns the chairman, Folkman, and the entire county committee is asleep… And although two officials, the doctors Maszler and Pfefer, are there, it is not possible to take care of things with them because they cannot make a decision on any matter. The delegates have asked them to place at least one person on the Tarnow Social County Committee who would be active only in matters of social self–help in Tarnow County.

[Page 286]

The *Judentrat* was dependent in all its dealings on the German regime organs whose orders had to be carried out. Because of the necessity of satisfying the transforming desires of the German rulers and providing the illusion that by submitting to the German bandits it would be possible to moderate and weaken the German brutality and because of the difficult economic situation, the Tarnow *Judentrat* was not capable of allotting a significant grant to the *YISA* county committee. It is enough to cite the written order, which the Tarnow county chief sent to the *YISA* county committee on the 3rd of October 1941, in which the latter was ordered to prepare beds and food for 1,000 Jews who were to arrive in Tarnow from Hamburg that day; this assignment was sent with the observation that the stay of the deported Hamburg Jews in Tarnow was expected to last approximately a week, until they received a regular place to stay.[14]

The order of the 3rd of October 1941

[Page 287]

It should be understood that providing 1,000 Jews a place to sleep and with food over the course of even one day was not an easy thing and that there would be large expenses. Burdened with such a task, both the *Judentrat* and the *YISA* county committee did not have the opportunity to develop widespread aid activities on behalf of the Jewish population in the already crowded Jewish quarter in Tarnow… Meanwhile, the number of hungry, sick and weary Jews who were robbed of their possessions grew every day. Devoid of sources of income, the great majority were degraded into habitual beggars who were now dependent upon the help of the only aid institution in the Jewish neighborhood, the Jewish Social Self Help Committee, which was identical to the social committee at the *Judentrat*.

– 5 –

Previously we have mentioned the order of the 16th of September 1940, according to which the *Judentrat* was entitled to take the pre–war community tax (local tax) from the Jewish population in Tarnow to cover the expenses of the social committee.

The right to receive this "local tax" was given exclusively to the Tarnow county committee of the Jewish Social Self–Help (*YISA*) in a new order of the 14th of October 1941 – as the only Jewish aid committee recognized by the German government and as expressed by the county chief in the cited order – "Make use of the Jewish Social Self–Help in Tarnow in the carrying out of this authorization with the help of its delegates and of the local *Judentrat*."

[Page 288]

The order of the 2nd of October 1941

This order also gave instructions as to how to act in relation to the Jews who did not pay the required communal tax sum. In such a case, the *YISA* committee in Tarnow or its delegates in a particular locality that belonged to the Tarnow county had the duty to demand the payment of the demanded sum over the course of two weeks and if this period elapsed and such a tax obligation proved fruitless that the city or the county commandant of the Polish police had to be informed of this with the request "to help" collect the tax owed and if this was not possible even to arrest the person obliged to pay.[15]

[Page 289]

However, the German holders of power made this even smaller aid opportunity in the Jewish neighborhood dependent upon safeguards so that their purpose was a means to limit and shrink the aid activity of the Tarnow *YISA* county committee.

On the 14th of October 1941 the *YISA* division in Tarnow received a copy of the order of the 2nd of October 1941 from the Tarnow county chief in which the Jewish Social Self–Help Committee in Tarnow was asked to assure that it alone as well as the Tarnow *Judentrat* required an acknowledgement that it had fulfilled its obligations on behalf of the labor office from every Jew who needed to receive support from the mentioned aid institutions. The *YISA* committee or the *Judentrat* had the duty to order from each male, aged 12 to 60, who received support, that every two weeks he obtain a registry card from the labor office[16], and with it each Tarnow Jew who wanted to make use of the drops of support that the *YISA* committee or the *Judentrat* was able to distribute, had to show that they had given their last strength to the German war machine.

The *YISA* presidium also searched for income from other sources. The German government organs placed trustees not only in the Jewish trades and industrial enterprises. The Jewish houses and locations that were outside the Jewish quarter in Tarnow were placed in the hands of German managers.

Thanks to the efforts of the *YISA* its local division could make use of the taxation on Jewish houses and places and the trustees gave a portion of this tax for Jewish social aid. This in 1941 the local *YISA* county committee in Tarnow paid the sum of 16,200 *zlotes* from this tax.[17]

According to a report from the *YISA* presidium in Krakow, the Jewish hospital in Tarnow received an allocation of medications and bandage material from the first foreign medical transport through the intervention of the Polish Red Cross.[18]

[Page 290]

Despite the difficult conditions in which it happened to unfold, at the end of 1941 this Jewish Social County Aid Committee still could show important achievements in the area of social aid work for the impoverished and already physically and spiritually weakened Jewish population in Tarnow.

As we read in a report[19], from the delegate from the *YISA* presidium in Krakow, Dr. Elihu Tisz (a child of Tarnow and dedicated Zionist activist in Tarnow since before the First World War) – who lived in Tarnow during the days from the 10th to the 18th of October 1942 and learned about the aid activities of the local county aid committee – three people's kitchens were active during this period in Tarnow from which very good meals were given out, in addition to the preparation for the opening of a fourth kitchen. According to this report, the old age and orphans home, the Jewish hospital and the out–patient clinic were found in to be in good condition.

It should be understood that despite the useful activity of the Jewish Social County Committee with the help of the social division of the Tarnow *Judentrat*, need increased with every day in the Jewish homes in Tarnow… Hunger and illness spread in a terrible manner in the Jewish neighborhood.

The situation of the Jewish orphans and homeless children was very tragic.

"The literally superhuman efforts by the local activists" – wrote Dr. Wajchert, the recently deceased chairman of the *YISA*, in his memoirs[20]. – "could not extract the tens and hundreds of thousand children from the abyss into which the occupier had hurled them. If the life of the children – whose parents had no income and were exposed to robberies, being caught [for forced labor], arrests, deportations, shootings – was difficult during the first months after the entry of the Germans, it became unbearable after the creation of the ghettos and it reached its highest tragedy after the order that threatened a punishment of death for leaving the ghetto.

The tragedy of this situation became still clearer when, according to the order of the 23rd of July 1940, all Jewish communal organizations, establishments and institutions were closed, the only possibility now to develop social–communal activities was in the framework of the Jewish Social Self–Help [*YISA*].

[Page 291]

This closed the gate for the children at all of the schools and there was need and hunger in the Jewish homes – all of this forced the leaders of the Tarnow Jewish Social County Committee to carry out concrete aid work on behalf of the neglected Jewish children in the city.

Thanks to these efforts it was possible during a given time to support the Jewish Orphans Home for Jewish orphans and to feed and clothe a large number of poor Jewish children until the first deportation in Tarnow in June 1942[21].

We learn about the manner and extent of this aid activity on behalf of the Jewish children in Tarnow during this period from a written account, which the Jewish Social County Committee in Tarnow sent to the presidium of the *YISA* on the 8th of October 1941[22]. As emphasized in this report, the activity in Tarnow was based on the situation on the 1st of August 1941:

a) The Jewish orphan home, which had been in existence since 1919 and on the mentioned day the following were supported there:

10 children aged 3 to 7
47 children aged 7 to 14
13 children aged 14 to 18

That is a total of 70 children.

b) From March 1941, a feeding station for Jewish children was active in Tarnow and as a result of the conditions on the 1st of August, supplementary nutrition was provided there twice a day for

33 children aged 3 to 7
689 children aged 7 to 14

[Page 292]

The social division at the *Judentrat* in Tarnow was busy gathering clothing and underwear for the children.

As we learn from this report, during this already difficult time for Tarnow Jewry, there were Jewish families in Tarnow who shared the little bit of food they had with hungry Jewish children.

As we learn from the previously mentioned report, much was done in the area of sanitary–medical aid activity. A sanitary commission was active at the *Judentrat*, which took care of medical aid and distributed medications without cost, controlled the health conditions of the children and supervised the hygienic conditions of the apartments.

In general, as the report quoted above states, during this period approximately 2,000 adult Jews received food at the public kitchen every day.

As we see, during the second half of 1941, the social aid activities in Jewish Tarnow stood at a certain level. The destructive process in Jewish economic life in all localities that belonged to the Tarnow Social County Committee already had led to a situation of complete impoverishment of the Jewish population, who already wrestled with the terrible nightmares of hunger, cold and illnesses.

In a letter from the Jewish Social County Committee in Tarnow of the 29th of October 1941[23]. to the presidium of *YISA* in Krakow, the tragic economic conditions of the Jewish population in all areas of Tarnow are described by the Jewish Social Aid Committee. And as we read there, "the absorption of the 'community tax' for social aid can be surmised because of the general impoverishment of the local Jewish population and its even greater difficulties." It is shown in this letter that in August 1941, all three public people's kitchens that were active then in Jewish Tarnow provided 145,333 mid–day meals.

[Page 293]

But thanks to the systematic aid on the part of the central [office] of the *YISA* in Krakow, the Jewish Social County Committee in Tarnow fulfilled its task in a limited way and it was able to support several institutions in Tarnow that brought a minimal [amount] of help for the local Jewish population and in a very limited measure also in several localities that belonged to the Tarnow Social County Committee.

Thus, for example, the Jewish Social County Committee in Tarnow, in a letter of the 20th of November 1941 to the *YISA* presidium in Krakow[24]. certified the receipt of the sum of 5,100 *zlotes* to distribute, 4,000 *zlotes* for the feeding activities, 1,000 *zlotes* for help for the Jewish children and 100 for the sanitary aid in Ryglice. As is emphasized [in the letter], the Joint provided 2,550 *zlotes* of this sum.

In general, we can establish on the basis of the remaining minutes of the meeting of the Jewish Social County Committee in Tarnow, which are in the archive of the Jewish Historical Commission in Warsaw, that until the end of 1941 the members of this committee, despite the great difficulties, showed an active nimbleness in the area of distributing aid for the still existing Jewish social institutions in Tarnow.

As we learn in the minutes[25]. of a meeting of the Jewish Social Aid Committee in Tarnow of the 31st of October 1941, the latter paid out in October 1941:

1,000 *zlotes* for the Jewish old age home in Tarnow
1,000 *zlotes* for the Jewish orphans' home in Tarnow.

From a second set of minutes[26]. from a meeting of the same committee on the 30th of November 1941, we again learn that in November 1941 was paid:

2,000 *zlotes* for the division of infectious diseases at the Jewish hospital,
1,000 *zlotes* for the out–patient clinic at the Jewish hospital to buy medicine.
1,500 *zlotes* for renovating the ovens at the Jewish old age home.

The Jewish Social County Committee also received grants from the Polish Main Social Services Council (*Rada Główna Opiekuńcza*) in Krakow.

[Page 294]

This we know from a letter from the Jewish Social County Committee in Tarnow to the above–mentioned Main Council in Krakow of the 21st of October 1941[27]: that the Tarnow committee received 100 pairs of wooden shoes with shoelaces and immediately the next month, the 18th of November 1941,[28] the Jewish Social County Committee in Tarnow was designated the recipient from the Polish Main Council:

170 kilos "bacon" (pig meat)
100 blankets
100 liters fish oil

The members of the Jewish Social County Committee in Tarnow placed great weight on the question of nutrition because the majority of the Jewish population in Jewish Tarnow during the second half of 1941 already was dependent upon the people's kitchens as the only source of nutrition. The Jewish Social County Committee in Tarnow actually went in that direction, and as we learn from written information from this committee of the 11th of December 1941[29] to the presidium of *YISA* in Krakow, the fourth people's kitchen was opened on the 14th of December 1941 at Lwowska Street 7, which was mainly designated for working artisans.

During this period the active members of the Jewish Social County Committee in Tarnow made additional attempts to create new work opportunities for Jewish working people, particularly for the adult Jewish young people.

We learn this from a letter of the 17th of December 1941 from the presidium of the *YISA* in Krakow to the Jewish Social County Committee in Tarnow that the latter made attempts to organize trade courses in Tarnow.

As Dr. Wajchert related in his memoirs,[30] the Jewish Social County Committee in Tarnow planned to found a farm on the Goldman family's farm (the so called Goldmanuwke), but as this estate was confiscated by the Germans on behalf of the Ukrainians, the *YISA* presidium in Krakow attempted to free this area from confiscation. However, at the end of 1941 this devilish game by the German hangmen ended; the true intentions of the German murderers in regard to Polish Jewry began to be revealed.

[Page 295]

After the outbreak of the German–Soviet War, the Germans began to implement the long–planned extermination activities in regard to the Jewish population in the Polish cities and *shtetlekh* [towns].

During the second half of 1941 the German preparations for a systematic action to physically annihilate the already spiritually and economically weakened Tarnow Jewry began to be more apparent in Tarnow.

Actually, at the time when the process to eliminate the Polish Jews from economic life had ended and the number of Jews grew larger who had been robbed of their workshops and who remained without income and without the ability to feed their wives and children, as we described previously in another place, the Joint, whose funds in the greatest measure made possible the aid activity of the *YISA*, was closed.

Consequently, the situation of this aid institution was now very serious. At the end of March 1942, the *BVF*[31] issued an order that the *YISA* presidium was authorized to carry on the activity of the Joint and was entitled to take over the foreign transports that arrived at its address.[32]

– 8 –

During the first month of 1942 a suspicion awoke in the hearts of the Tarnow Jews that the German murderers also were preparing a slaughter in Tarnow, in addition to the "deportations" of the Jewish population. Stories spread that the first to be deported would be the poor Jews who received support from the *Wohlfahrt* [welfare] at the *Judentrat*. Jews in massive numbers refused support from the *Judentrat* and even tried to have their names erased from the list of those receiving charity.

[Page 296]

When the tumult of the work cards with the various stamps began in Tarnow, Tarnow Jews were forced to enroll at a workplace at any cost, believing that work would free them from deportation, about which they already heard frightful reports. Artisans' communities arose in the city – work enterprises – created by artisans of various trades who worked for the German military.

As we learn from material of the 25th of March from the *YISA* presidium[33] the Jewish Artisans Union in Tarnow created such worker communities for tailors, laundresses, locksmiths, shoemakers, gaiter makers, harness makers, saddle makers, hat makers, upholsterers. German firms also appeared in Tarnow that allocated positions for Jewish artisan communities[34].

Eskate, Ostbahn, Latsina, Krakauer–Confectionary–Julius Madritsch Okon, *Zentrale für Handwerklieferungen* [Central Agency for Handicrafts] were such German enterprises in Tarnow.

At first Jews employed in the handworker unions and work communities or in the German enterprises were protected from expulsion. A stamped pass or employment from a German firm to which the Jewish workshop had supplied their production or at which they worked often saved [them] from deportation to a death camp.

Tarnow Jews worked at various German workplaces outside the city. Approximately 400 Tarnow Jews were imprisoned in the Pustków labor camp, outside Dembitz [Dębica], and more than 1,000 Tarnow Jews were employed by the German *Wehrmacht* [unified armed forces] in various localities.

There was a lasting struggle in connection with making use of the Jewish work force for the German war machine between the S.S. and the military industry around the question of whether this Jewish work force should be kept alive.

Several Christians stood out in this struggle on behalf of the Jews such as Julius Madritsch, the owner of the large textile factory, Robert Wagner, the director of the Central Agency for Handicrafts, and Oskar Schindler, the owner of the enamelware factory. A number of Jewish workers were employed in these enterprises and thanks to this a handful of Jews were saved from certain death.

[Page 297]

As Dr. Wajchert related in his Memoirs (third volume, p. 287), at a meeting of the representatives of the police and administrative organs, which took place in Krakow on the 19th of June 1942, in order to give a report about the anti–Jewish murder action which had taken place, the S.S. and police leader Scherner provided information about the security situation in the Krakow district, emphasizing that among others there were in Tarnow among the residents there 32,000 Jews – 8,000 employed at various work.

It is worthwhile at this opportunity to mention that in the first half of 1942 the number of Jews in Tarnow grew because of the transports of deported Jews [who arrived in Tarnow] from the surrounding *shtetlekh* [towns], where a number of ghettos were liquidated at that time.

The wage for the Jewish workers in these enterprises was minimal; Jews often paid so that they would be employed because the work was supposed to save them from deportation to Belzec, to Auschwitz or to another death camp.

– 9 –

The terrible material situation of the Tarnow Jews did not end by giving their strength to the German military machine. The hunger wore out the old and young. With the greatest effort, the Social Self–Help Committee and the Wohlfart at the *Judentrat* kept at its activity of supporting the four people's kitchens in Tarnow and in such conditions it was difficult to guard the city from epidemics. During the first months of 1942 typhus broke out in Tarnow. From the already mentioned material, which the presidium of the *YISA* in Krakow sent to the Central Agency for Handicrafts on the 25th of March 1942, we learn that the health conditions of the Jewish population in Tarnow, thanks to the energetic mass prevention means, was satisfactory and that from the 1th of January 1942 to the 2nd of March 1942 there they noted that 45 local and 64 – mainly from the camp in Pustków – fell from typhus[35].

[Page 298]

– 10 –

The first deportation in Tarnow was carried out in June 1942, during which approximately 10,000 Jews were murdered in Tarnow itself and the second 10,000 Jews were deported to Belzec. The ghetto in Tarnow was created after this murder action. The *YISA* division in Tarnow in the new conditions now organized its aid activity and they tried to obtain certain concessions for the tired Jewish population from the local German government agents.

However, right after the first horrible wave of bloody barbarism in the Tarnow ghetto, the German government organs communicated to the chairman of the Jewish Social Self–Help, Dr. Wajchert, on the 29th of July 1942 that the *YISA* must be dissolved – and its role in [distributing] general grants in the amount of 17 percent were taken from it.

After the second bloody deportation in the Tarnow ghetto, in August 1942, after long interventions and negotiations with the managing committee, on the 20th of October 1942 the presidium of the *YISA* continued its social activity. The name of the organization was changed and now it was called *Yiddishe Untershtitsungs Zentrale* [Jewish Support Central] (*YUS*). The presidium as well as the local division could engage in its aid activity as before. Thus, the *YUS* division in Tarnow was authorized to bring help to the Tarnow Jews who were imprisoned in the camps, particularly to supply medicine and bandage materials for them.

Of important significance was the decision that the money for the fulfillment of the social tasks of *YUS* finally had to be extracted from the Jewish population itself[36].

[Page 299]

With the ban [on distributing funds] and with again immediately permitting the activity of the Jewish Social Self–Help, even under a changed name, the German hangmen intended to fool the Jewish population and to throw a veil over their very devilish preparations for further Jewish slaughters. In order to create the impression that after the last murder action in June and August 1942 in the cities and *shtetlekh* under the General *Gubernia* the surviving Jews had the opportunity to work on behalf of the German enterprises and thus save their lives, an order was published on the 10th of November 1942 in the area of the Krakow district according to which all Jews who had been hidden in the villages and *shtetlekh* could return and settle without punishment in one of the listed five cities – that is, Krakow, Bochnia, Tarnow, Rzeszow and Przemysl and be organized in these so called "remnant ghettos." Thousands of Jews let themselves be fooled and fell victims in the murder actions immediately carried out by the Germans in these cities. And to draw the rope tighter around the necks of the surviving Jews, the German police and security organs in the General *Gubernia*, who were involved in the matters of social activity, in an order of the 18th of November 1942, annulled the previous decisions with regard to the founding of the Jewish Support Central (*YUS*). In the explanatory statement of this order it was emphasized that as the *S.S. Reichsführer* [commander of the *S.S.*] had conflicting official duties, the need to increase the deportation of the Jews while at the same time provide work–capable Jewish men and women to support the military economy and the armaments industry . The workers would be under the supervision of the *S.S.* and of the police and the activity of the Jewish support activity would no longer be necessary. During this time, all the Jews – with the exception of the above who were recorded as capable of work and confined in the labor camps – would disappear, so that basically all further social measures on behalf of the remaining Jews would lie in the hands of the *S.S.* and the police[37]

On the 1st of January 1942 Dr, Wajchert communicated about the dissolving of the Jewish Support Central for the General *Gubernia* and all of the money and material property was confiscated in order to secure its existing obligations.

[Page 300]

– 11 –

During the first half of 1943 those Jews still alive in the Tarnow ghetto no longer had any illusions that they had [not] been sentenced to death, and understood they were in a hopeless situation. In the month of March 1943, Dr. Wajchert even succeeded in persuading the occupying regime organs that the activity of the Jewish support central [committee] should be permitted to start again. But in August – barely five months after renewing the *YISA* activity – the Tarnow ghetto was finely liquidated. Several thousand Jews were deported to Auschwitz and around 2,000 young Jews were sent to Płaszów and Treblinka, to the labor camps there. Almost all of the bunkers in the city were torn open and hundreds of Jews were discovered and shot. Then the occupiers again – for the third time – forbade the aid. The remainder of the Jewish population in Tarnow, the 300 Jews of the clean–up command, starved and worked at hard labor on behalf of the German hangmen. And in February 1944, when even this small group of exhausted Jews was deported, some to Szebnie and some to Płaszów, Tarnow was *Judenrein* [free of Jews].

Original footnotes:

1. Mikhal Wajchert – *Zikhroynes* [*Memories*] – Third volume, page 300.
2. According to official statistical sources.
3. Mikhal Wajchert – *Zikhroynes* [*Memories*]– third volume, page 257.
4. *Eksterminacja Żydów na ziemiach Polskich w okresie okupacji hitlerowskiej* [*Extermination of Jews, in the Polish Lands during the Nazi Occupation*], Warsaw, 1957. Page 210.
5. Dr. Wajchert – *Memoirs* – volume 3, page 25.
6. Dr. Wajchert – *Memoirs*– volume 3, page 16.
7. Dr. Wajchert, *Memoirs*– volume 3, p. 141.
8. Ibid, p. 83.
9. Ibid, p. 142.
10. Wajchert *Memoirs*, third volume, p. 142.
11. Wajchert *Memoirs*, third volume, p. 142.
12. According to the photocopy of the original that is located in the archive of the Central Jewish Historical Commission in Warsaw.
13. Ibid.
14. See the photocopy of the order of the 3rd of October 1941.
15. See the photocopy of the order of the 14th of October 1941, p. 280.
16. See 15.
17. Dr. Wajchert – *Memoirs* volume 3, p. 118.
18. Dr. Wajchert – *Memoirs*– volume 3, p. 158.
19. According to a photocopy of the original, which is located in the archive of the Central Jewish Historical Commission in Warsaw.
20. Wajchert – *Memoirs*– volume 3, p. 314.
21. Dr. Wajchert – *Memoirs*– third volume, p. 313.
22. According to a photocopy of an original that is located in the archive of the Central Jewish Historical Commission in Warsaw.
23. According to the microfilm of the original that is located in the archive of the Central Jewish Historical Commission in Warsaw.
24. ibid
25. According to a photocopy of the original that is located in the archive of the Historical Commission in Warsaw.
26. ibid
27. See 25.
28. See 25.
29. According to a photocopy from the original that is located in the archives of the Jewish Historical Commission in Warsaw.
30. Wajchert – *Memoirs*– third volume.
31. *Befelkerungs–vezn und Firzorge* [Population Organization and Welfare] – this division of the managing committee of the General *Gubernia* [Province] – was concerned with all social matters in the General *Gubernia*.
32. Wajchert – *Memoirs*– volume 3, p. 275.
33. Dr. Wajchert – *Memoirs*– volume 3, p. 275.

34. Dr. Wajchert – *Memoirs*– volume 3, p. 268.
35. Dr. Wajchert – *Memoirs*– volume 3, p. 275.
36. Dr. Wajchert – *Memoirs*– volume 3, p. 318.
37. Dr. Wajchert – *Memoirs*– volume 3, p. 319.

[Page 301, Volume 2]

Christians Who Saved Tarnow Jews

by Dr. Avraham Chomet, Josef Kornilo

Translated by Gloria Berkenstat Freund

The anti–Semitic policies of the Hitlerist occupation regime had as their purpose the brutal and barbaric annihilation of the Jewish population and for this purpose the Nazi murderers used every possible criminal means. In order to annihilate the Jewish population systematically and methodically, the Nazi hangmen drove the weary Jews into a ghetto during the deportation actions, into the surrounded by locked and guarded gates. The Nazis made any contact with the outside world impossible and cut off the possibility of Jews escaping from this hell as well as contact with relatives and friends who could provide help, because there was the threat of death for leaving the ghetto… And every Christian who hid a Jew or tried to help with a piece of bread would receive the punishment of death…

*

The Tarnow Jews also found themselves in such a situation… A ghetto was created in Tarnow immediately after the second deportation, after the mass murder of over 20,000 Jews. The Jews imprisoned in the Tarnow ghetto now felt entirely surrounded, besieged… Hunger and illness now raged in the overcrowded Jewish residences. The true intentions of the Nazi murderers were now clear… Therefore, the Jews began to search for ways to save themselves… They began to build bunkers and other hiding places.

There were cases of people escaping from the ghetto and furnishing themselves with Aryan papers… There were individual cases where Poles showed full feeling and compassion and brought help to the Jews imprisoned in the ghetto, mainly by creating hiding places on the Aryan side.

There were cases where peasants hid several people, Jewish families, escapees from the ghetto for a reward. It is described in the first volume of the Tarnow Yizkor book, that thanks to this help, several souls from the Postrong, Landman, Mitler and Betribnis families survived…

[Page 302]

There were very few courageous Christians who ignored the dangers that lay in wait at every step of the way; placing their own lives [in danger] and standing face to face with death, they struck out their hands to the persecuted Jews and many were saved from a sure death.

We call them "the Righteous Among the Nations," for which Yad Vashem in Jerusalem has arranged a separate "Garden of the Righteous" on the Mount of Remembrance, and each of these Christians who, with superhuman courage, saved Jews during the Shoah era, are recognized with the honor of inclusion as "the Righteous Among the Nations" and with the planting of a tree in this garden.

We collected the details about a handful of Christians who, during the time of cruel, murderous actions in the Tarnow ghetto, in their deep human nobility showed superhuman courage and self…sacrifice and spared no strength or effort to save Jewish lives from the Nazi hell.

Julius Madritsch

Ramund Titsch

[Page 303]

The place of honor in the pantheon of the Righteous Among the Nations is occupied by the noble, Viennese Christian, Julius Madritsch, and his co–worker, Raimund Titsch[a]

Jews rushed to work for the German war industry, during the era when the Nazi occupation under the Galicianer General Government living with the illusion that the work would protect them from death.

Madritsch had already opened a tailoring workshop in the Krakow ghetto in 1941, in which he employed hundreds of Jewish workers, provided them with the necessary food and applied much effort and exertion – often risking his own life – to protect the workers from selections and deportations.

Madritsch opened a branch of his Krakow tailoring enterprise in Płaszów and later in Tarnow where a large number of clothing workers had lived since before the war.[1]

Raimund Titsch, also a German Christian from Vienna, was helpful in the leadership of the clothing workshop in Tarnow. He often placed his own life in danger giving his workers news from the warfront. The number of Jewish workers was up to 500 and those who survived the Nazi hell cannot praise enough the humane and auspicious conditions in which they were able to work in this enterprise.

In the forward to the German memoir that Madritsch wrote and published after the war in 1962, under the title *Menschen in Not!* [*People in Distress!*], Dr. David Shlang, the general–secretary of the Zionist Federation in Austria, wrote: In order that we can give the appropriate honor to the author of the book, we would have had to live in the ghetto, we would have had to see the rows of people who worked in Julius Madritsch's workshops and were led through the small gate in the ghetto wall every day… The people who had the good fortune to be assigned to Madritsch's work–commando [group of forced laborers] felt as if they were the "chosen ones" of the ghetto and later, the same way at the concentration camp in Płaszów–Krakow… The unfortunate Jewish population that was locked out of human rights, found in the person of the author a true supporter – he often was called the Angel of Płaszów.

[Page 304]

During the entire time, all of his workers received meals from the factory kitchen; thus Madritsch received permission to reward every worker with two loaves of bread a week from his own pocket. Thanks to his efforts, all of his approximately 500 Jewish workers at the Tarnow clothing enterprises were moved to Płaszów in the month of September 1943 during the liquidation of the Tarnow ghetto and in Płaszów received employment in the Madritsch clothing factory there.

In the most difficult conditions, when it appeared as if everything was lost, both, Madritsch and Titsch did not give up and with extraordinary energy and stubbornness, they searched for means and ways to save their Jewish workers from certain death.

Even at the end of the Nazi anti–Jewish annihilation action, when the Nazi hangmen decided to liquidate the Płaszów camp, the two genteel Christians did not forget their unfortunate Jews sentenced to death. They succeeded, with great difficulties and efforts in saving 100 of their Jewish workers, creating work for them in the enterprises of Oskar Schindler in Czechoslovakia where they awaited their liberation by the Allied army.

The Jews saved in such a manner, who emigrated to Israel, did not forget the heroic self–sacrificing good deeds of these two genteel Christians. Both, Julius Madritsch and Raimund Titsch, in an expression of thankfulness and in recognition of their heroic actions in the area of saving Jews persecuted by the Nazis rulers, were given the honor of entering the pantheon of the Righteous Among the Nations.

In April 1965, Madritsch and Titsch, who were invited as guests by the saved "Madritscher" [those who were saved by Madritsch] to a solemn welcome reception on the Mount of Remembrance in the Avenue of the Righteous Among the Nations. Madritsch and Titsch each planted a tree there and the leaders of *Yad Vashem* gave each one a special Certificate of Honor with the dedication: **"He who keeps one soul alive, it is as if he had kept the entire world alive."**

[Page 305]

Maria Dyrdałowa Kiełbasa

In a letter that Julius Madritsch wrote in March 1966 to Josef Kornilo, he expresses the wish to come to Israel immediately to meet again with the surviving Jews and to see how the tree he had planted had grown…

Superhuman heroism and moral elevation during the Nazi occupation of Tarnow was shown by the Tarnow Christian, Maria Dyrdałowa who knew no fear and overcame the most difficult obstacles when it was a question of saving a Jewish child from certain death. Herself a poor woman who worked hard for a piece of bread, a servant in Jewish homes for many years, she possessed a genteel heart full of understanding and compassion for human suffering. With full knowledge of the boldness of her deeds, she often risked her life to save unfortunate Jews.

"Maria Dyrdałowa is among the most beautiful personalities among the Righteous Among the Nations (we read in a treatise that was published in the local newspaper, *Letste Neies* [*Last News*] of the 4th of November 1964, in which the details about her self–sacrificing deeds), "which so rarely brightened those cruel days when it was shown that the image of God was eternally erased from the earth and only the animal remained…"

[Page 306]

Honor Award Certificate from *Yad Vashem* for Julius Madritsch

And when one learns of the courageous and purely humane action of Maria Dyrdałowa one must admire the unsophisticated, poor and modest woman who radiated goodness and showed such courage and strength in opposing the angry devils of that dark time.

[Page 307]

Honor Award Certificate from *Yad Vashem* for Raimund Titsch

After the imprisonment of the Tarnow Jews in the ghetto, when Maria Dyrdałowa began to trade and would travel with her "goods'" from city to city, she arrived in Bochnia and there in the house of one of her customers heard the cry of a child… According to the statement of the woman with whom the child was found, this was a Jewish child of seven months whose parents had been shot by the Nazi murderers and now there was no one to pay for raising and hiding the child. Maria Dyrdałowa did not hesitate for long, she gave all of her goods to the Christian woman and took the crying Jewish child…

[Page 308]

Honor Award Certificate from *Yad Vashem* for Dyrdałowa

Maria Dyrdałowa's life now was difficult and filled with danger… Death hovered in every corner… Tearing herself from the talons of the Gestapo because of suspicion that she was hiding a Jewish child, she had to wander from one city to another… And even after the war, she had to wrestle with all kinds of difficulties…

[Page 309]

When the girl she saved from Bochnia was 15 years old Maria turned her over to the Jewish Youth House in Tarnow from where she emigrated to Israel in 1957. Elisheva, this was now the name of the girl who had been saved – spent several years in Neve Eitan [a kibbutz – collective community], and from there she moved to Tel Aviv and a little later she married Avraham Patt, a young man from Bnei Brak. Elisheva remained in heartfelt contact with Maria Dyrdałowa and considered her as a "mother."

On the page of the magnificent, heroic actions of Maria Dyrdałowa are the additional records of the history of the two children of a Tarnow Jew, a certain Moshe Lewinowski… When he became very sick and he felt that he was going to die, he summoned the woman he was friendly with, Maria Dyrdałowa, and asked her to take and raise his two children, and principally, that she should make sure that they remained Jewish children and would go to Israel.

Maria Dyrdałowa did not refuse and undertook the fulfillment of Moshe Lewinowski's testament… A difficult road of effort and exertion began again, until she and the two children arrived in Israel and she carried out the promise she had given to Lewinowski.

For her courageous deeds, for her humane conduct, for her self–sacrifice in saving Jewish children from death during the Nazi rule, *Yad Vashem* bestowed on her the honor of belonging to the Righteous Among the Nations and as such she planted a tree in the Garden of the Righteous on the Mount of Remembrance.

*

Another Polish Christian from Tarnow, Bronislawa Gawelczyk, planted a tree in the Garden of the Righteous Among the Nations in Jerusalem.

It was close to the end of the liquidation of the Tarnow ghetto when the murderous extermination action against the remnant of the Jewish population in Tarnow reached its highest point of cruel slaughter. In their despair, the Jewish mothers searched at the very least for a way to save their youngest children who were the first victims of Nazi brutality. Mrs. Ela Hofmajster, the mother of a daughter, Sura, who was not yet two years old, made such an effort.

[Page 310]

Jozef Banek and his daughter Irma Banek

And when the Nazi hangmen threw themselves like wild animals on the Jewish children during the last resettlement actions in the Tarnow ghetto in September 1942, Mrs. Hofmajster turned to the Christian woman, Bronislawa Gawelczyk, known to her as a client acquaintance from business, with the request that she take the child who had been in a bunker for several months… The Christian woman agreed immediately and took the small Surala, not asking for any payment. There also was no lack of hardships and dangers from bad neighbors, informers and blackmailers. Mrs. Bronislawa went through the most difficult trials with extraordinary heroic firmness and hid the small Surala for four months, despite the Nazi threat to shoot every Christian who dared to provide help to the Jews.

Surala's parents, her mother and father, perished in a Nazi death camp… After the war, in 1947, Sura emigrated to Israel with the Youth Aliyah, where she graduated from a Hebrew middle school and the Judicial

[Page 311]

Kazimierz Jarmula

Law School at Hebrew University in Jerusalem… She then married and remembered her rescuer, Bronislawa Gawelczyk…. And to express this sincere feeling of thankfulness of this genteel Christian woman, Surala and her relatives who had survived the Nazi hell invited her to Israel.

Mrs. Gawelczyk also was given the distinction of entering the pantheon of the Righteous Among the Nations for her heroic deeds during the Shoah era and was given the honor of planting a tree in the Garden of the Righteous Among the Nations.

*

To the number of Tarnow Christians who in the most difficult conditions and with mortal danger during the Nazi occupation of Tarnow saved Jews, should be added Josef Banek and his daughter; Irma. They hid several Jews for three years in their residence and thus saved them from certain death. The deeds of Josef Banek and his daughter Irma, who lived in Tarnow on Czelona Street, were confirmed by the district committee in Tarnow in its writing of the 10th of August 1947. These two Polish Christians hid and cared for, without payment, the Tarnow Jews: Chaim, Dora and Inge Betrubniss as well as Shmuel Rapaport, Sabina Lichtinger and her family members. These two Christians also will soon be recognized as Righteous Among the Nations.

[Page 312]

Among the limited number of Christians who overcame fear and were active in the Polish underground movement, Kazimierz Jarmula, who lived in Tarnow on Paderewski Street, helped Jews a great deal during the Nazi rule in Tarnow.

He was arrested in August 1940 by the Gestapo for "harming German interests" and he was deported to Auschwitz several days later and, from there, to other concentration camps until he was freed by the Allied Armies in 1945. This heroic Christian soon also will be given the distinction of becoming one of the Righteous Among the Nations.

The monument to the memory of the Tarnow residents annihilated by the Nazi murderers in the years 1940–1945

Footnote.

a. He died on the 9th of March 1968 in Vienna.

Translator's footnote:

1. The article refers to confectionary workers. They had worked in confectionary workshops, but the workshops began to produce textiles when Madritsch saw that he could earn more money doing so.

[Page 315, Volume 2]

After the Holocaust

What Remained of Our Jewish Tarnow

by Yosef Kornilo

Translated by Gloria Berkenstat Freund

On the 18th of January of this year [1968], it is twenty–three years since the Soviet Army liberated Tarnow and ousted the Nazi occupiers. During the first year after the liberation, a handful of Tarnow Jews who survived in the bunkers, with Christians, in the camps and forests or those repatriated from Soviet Russia made efforts to rebuild foundations for a new Jewish life that would be a continuation of the previous Jewish existence and way of life in Tarnow.

Details about the difficult and conscientious activity by the Jewish communal workers in Tarnow in all social, communal and cultural areas on behalf of the impoverished survivors of Tarnow Jewry were provided in the first volume, as well as here in the second volume, of the *Tarnow* Yizkor Book.

Our task is to provide a picture of life today in Tarnow and to answer the question of what remains today of the former Jewish Tarnow…

* * *

As is clear, the attempts to build a new Jewish life at a cemetery did not succeed…because nothing of our magnificent Jewish community in Tarnow remained…

The terrible destruction… the deserted, dead, empty streets brought dread with their emptiness…

How bloodied our hearts were when we saw non–Jewish faces looking out of the windows of the houses on the Zydowska (Jewish) Street. They were undisturbed by the circumstances that found them living in this quater, entirely Jewish for hundreds of years and once full of *Yiddishkeit* [Jewishness, connoting an emotional connection to Judaism and/or to the Jewish people and their history, beliefs and customs].

Therefore, it is no wonder that the few Jews who returned to Tarnow – first took a look at the graves of those closest to them at the cemetery.

[Page 316]

They remained standing by the desecrated graves with tossed and broken headstones. The first task for the Tarnow Jews who returned to Tarnow after years of suffering and wandering was to clean the area of the pile of garbage… Gather the headstones from the sidewalk at the Tarnow streets and return their honor to them.

A group of survivors of Tarnow Jewry at the first Jewish committee in Tarnow after the Holocaust – which was active with collecting and re-erecting the scattered headstones at the cemetery in Tarnow

Standing from the left: Adler, Blajwajs, Aszer, *Magister*[1] Birken-Krisztal, Betribnis, Szifer, *Magister* Tirkel-Klapholc, Kornilo, Yosef, (–) Klapholc
Kneeling from the left: Miss Zughaft, Lauber Sz. (–)

There was no longer a place for creating new means of existence, for rebuilding economic standing, workshops or branches of trade.

Tarnow Jews began to wander; a large group first went to Lower Silesia, in the former German territory that was taken over by Poland after the war. Simultaneously, Tarnow Jews began to seek ways to join the then strong flow of illegal emigration to *Eretz-Yisroel*.

In 1947, there still were about 700 Jews in Tarnow, but by 1948 barely 360 Jews lived there. In 1965, 35 Jews lived in Tarnow the majority lived in neighboring villages. Of the 25,000 Jews who lived in Tarnow in 1939 before the Holocaust, today, in 1968, only a few families remain.

[Page 317]

A group of *halutizm* [pioneers] from the *Ihud* [unity] organization in Tarnow on their way to *Eretz–Yisroel* with the illegal emigration in Austria in 1946

1947 on Cyprus

[Page 318]

The destruction in Tarnow during the German occupation was mainly in the Jewish part of the city, where the Jews lived – particularly where the ghetto was located.

New modern apartment houses have been built in the area of the ghetto. On the spot where the monumental, large New Synagogue stood, huge, many–storied housing blocks were erected, also in the entire area of the square where the houses of the Jewish *kehile* [organized Jewish community] and Devora Menkes synagogue stood… Only the beautiful building of the *mikvah* [ritual bathhouse] neighboring these new houses remained untouched during the German annihilation action; it is now used as a municipal public bath institution.

In Tarnow, the buildings of Szancer's mill, of Szwanenfeld's liqueur factory, of the modern shoemaker–cobbler's lasts factory, which belonged to Jewish owners, were not disturbed. The buildings of the confectionary [clothing] factories, such as Kac, Wurcel and Daar, the Braun brothers and other Jewish owners of large confectionaries [clothing] and linen workshops, in which hundreds of Jewish and non–Jewish workers were once employed, remained untouched. All production institutions, which were built and developed by Tarnow Jews over the course of generations and in which Tarnow Jewish community took pride remained.

There are no longer any Jewish owners of these now purely "Aryan" factories and enterprises.

* * *

The buildings in Tarnow of the *Safa–Berura* [clear language] school, the *Yavne* [religious Zionist] school, of the merchant's school, the *Talmud–Torah* [free religious primary school for poor boys] buildings, the Jewish Orphans' home, the Jewish Hospital and old age home, as well as the house of the Bundist Workers' Home named after M.[2] Michalewicz remained undamaged.

How much toll and superhuman effort and sacrificial work went into the building of the Hebrew *folks-shul* [public school] and *Safa Berura gymnasia* [secondary school], which was the true treasure of the Jewish school system in Galicia. Today, a dormitory for Polish students at the technical mechanic school is located in this building, the fruit of long years of effort by the best Zionist social workers in pre–war Tarnow.

And how difficult it was to accumulate the necessary sum of money, to buy the magnificent building of the former Baron Hirsch school at Topolowa Street in Tarnow for the *Mizrachi* [religious Zionists] school, *Yavne*.

[Page 319]

The building of the *Talmud–Torah*

Today there is a municipal technical school for plastic…

Years passed until the *Talmud–Torah* building was built and with it was created a solid foundation for the existence of a spacious institution, which filled the important tasks in the area of religious education; today a state school for nurses is located in the building of the Tarnow *Talmud–Torah*.

And the exemplarily led *Agudah Beis–Yakov* [religious schools for girls]… Or trade school of Henrik Rausz, the professional head of the accounting courses for many years… And even Professor Bau's music school… All well-equipped buildings that are today occupied by non–Jewish institutions.

No trace remains of the large people's library, *sefaria amamis*, with its over 10,000 books… The same fate also was met by Jewish *Folks–Bibliotek* of *Poalei–Zion* [Marxist Zionists] with several thousand books… As well as the libraries of *HaShomer Hatzair* [socialist Zionists] and many other Jewish youth organizations.

[Page 320]

The building of the Workers' Home named for B. Michalewicz

What wonderful developments were made in Jewish sport and the gymnastic unions none of which rested until their own stadium was erected with all kinds of gymnastic facilities.

After the war, residences were erected on the wide "Shimshon" playing field and the area of the Bundist organization, the *Jutrzenko* [dawn] playing field was arranged as gardens for the Christian residents of the city… Today there are various storehouses and warehouses on all of the other Jewish playing fields.

[Page 321]

The building of the Jewish orphans' home

The first Froebel school for surviving Jewish children in liberated Tarnow in 1946

Members of the managing committee:
Standing from the left: Edward Klapholc, Betribnis and Josef Kornilo
Sitting from the left: *Magister* Birken–Kirsztmal, *Magister* Tirkel, Szifer

[Page 322]

The building of the Jewish home for the aged

The dedicated activity of the Bundist workers in Tarnow was so extraordinary that they reached their goal and built their own Workers' Home. They named their building after B. Michalewicz and it was situated on Lwowska Street in the center of Jewish working–class Tarnow, where all Bundist institutions in Tarnow were concentrated… Today, too, there is a municipal institution there.

* * *

On a higher level stood the social–communal activities in the Jewish neighborhood such as charitable unions, the Jewish hospital, the pavilion for lung diseases, the old age home, the orphans' home and nursery, the various Froebel schools – all institutions on behalf of the Jewish poor in Tarnow… What has remained of all of these very useful institutions?…

Plagued, wrestled by all kinds of difficulties and obstacles until untiring Jewish social workers secured the existence of these institutions…

Today, everything is in non–Jewish hands… Because Tarnow Jewry has been exterminated, annihilated…

[Page 323]

During the reading of the *parsha* [weekly Torah portion] of the week in the small synagogue in Tarnow in 1968

From the left: Yakov Taubeles and Michal Gutter–Bergstein

Members of the Bund in Tarnow after the Holocaust in 1948

[Page 324]

Only one trace of the former effervescent Jewish life in Tarnow remains.

The small handful of Tarnow Jews who today remain in Tarnow have received one divided room in the building of the former Hotel Soldinger on Goldhammer Street, in which is concentrated all of Jewish "life" in Tarnow today.

The bima [synagogue platform from which the Torah is read] of the Old Synagogue

[Page 325]

In addition to the Jewish Committee, a small synagogue is located in this room, in which a small light of former Tarnow *Yiddishkeit* glows. Among the honest, observant Jews who still live in Tarnow today is Reb Gutter Bergstein – known as Mekhl, who took upon himself the task of caring for the religious needs of the few Tarnow Jews who live in Tarnow today – he stands out with his particular devotion, and he does not let the light go out.

And for this last trace of Jewish Tarnow, the memory of the horrible martyrdom of annihilated Tarnow Jewry is sacred.

At every anniversary of the terrible Nazi slaughter in the Tarnow ghetto, memorial services are held at the memorials that were erected by the Jewish Committee in Tarnow and which symbolize the solitary epitaph of pain and death of Tarnow Jewry – in the Tarnow cemetery at the monuments that stand at the mass grave of 20,000 martyrs and in the nearby town of Zbylitowska, in the Buczyna forest, at the grave of over 800 Jewish children.

A rare Jewish monument is also present in Tarnow… The *Bima* with its four columns remains at the location of the Old Synagogue on Zydowska Street… It is gated in and surrounded by a small garden… This *Bima*, a sort of monument for the annihilated Jewish community in Tarnow, is also on the list of memorials in Tarnow, which is cared for by the Tarnow city managing committee.

Translator's Footnotes:

1. A magister is an academic degree given in Poland equivalent to a Master's Decree received after five years of attendance at a university.
2. On the next page, the person for whom the Bundist Workers' Home was named is given as B. Michalewicz. That is the correct name. His given name was Beinish.

[Page 326]

The "Bund" and its Activity in the Jewish Committee in Tarnow after the Holocaust

Aharon Szporn, Montreal - Canada

Translated by Mark Alsher

About the rise of the "Bund" in Tarnow, about its political, professional and social-cultural activity, about its leaders and the active builders of this very important Jewish workers movement and about its significant influence on the Jewish street in Tarnow, this writer has already written in detail in the first Yizkor book from "Tarnow" which appeared in Israel in the year 1954.

And when, in the period of the Nazi extermination actions, Tarnow Jewry was cruelly destroyed, and the glorious Jewish settlement in Tarnow was totally erased, physically and spiritually – there also remained no memory of the local so very colorful Jewish political life, with all of its political movements, with all of the cultural and social-communal institutions.

But soon after Tarnow was liberated from the Hitleristic savage claws the need to call the former political movements to life on the ruins of the Jewish settlement in Tarnow was immediately awakened among the small group of Tarnow Jews who came out of the forests and various other hiding places.

A lively activity with the goal of creating the basis for a new Bund organization in Tarnow was displayed by a group of survivors of Bund activists from before the war. The first consultation for that purpose took place in the home of Comrade Asher Bleiweiss (today in New York) with the participation of this writer and several other comrades among whom I recall only the names of Leyzer Roich, Yonah Celler, Yaakov Garnreich and my son, Zalek Szporn.

First of all the necessity of becoming more closely familiar with the activity of the "Jewish Committee" which was created with the help of the Central Jewish Committee in Warsaw immediately after the liberation was emphasized.

Unfortunately, the economic situation of the Tarnow Committee at that time was met with sharp criticism from the Jewish public.

[Page 327]

Thanks to the agreement between the "Bund" and the Zionist "Ichud," at that time the second largest Jewish organization in the city, a harmonious cooperation in the area of social activity for the Holocaust survivors of the annihilated Tarnow Jewry was possible.

The following then belonged to the reorganized inter-party Jewish Committee: Mgr. Kohn[1] and this writer as chairman, Roich as secretary, Blond as treasurer and the members: Asher Bleiweiss, Yonah Celler, Yaakov Garnreich, Lichtbloy, H. L. Shedlisker, David Weiser and Dr. Ignatz Goldfinger. The first accomplishment of the committee was the opening of a public kitchen, where any Jew who was registered in the Tarnow Jewish Committee could receive a lunch at no cost. The meeting place of the committee was in the house located at 1 Goldhammer Street.

The municipal housing office had given the entire building over to the authority of the Jewish Committee and it was therefore possible to open an infirmary there under the direction of two doctors: for adults Mrs. Dr. Bloch[2] and for children Dr. Dintenfass.

A children's home for Jewish children ages three to 15 was also set up in this same house and two teachers were appointed for these several children, one for the Yiddish and the second for the Polish language.

The budget for the Committee consisted of special funds from the Central Jewish Committee in Warsaw. Of great importance was providing housing for every Jew who returned to Tarnow hidden in the forests and bunkers or from Soviet Russia. This writer was especially employed in this work, who, having been a member of the Tarnow town council even before the war, now also represented the Tarnow Jews there and as such he was able to maintain successful contact with the municipal housing office.

As to providing all of the institutions of the Jewish Committee with the required food and other necessities, much was done in that area by the very active member Asher Bleiweiss who also represented us in the Central Jewish Committee in Warsaw.

[Page 328]

The activity of the Jewish Committee in post war Tarnow was not easy. The Tarnow Jews who came out alive from the Nazi hell or who returned from Soviet Russia with the repatriation no longer found their old homes … the sight of these Tarnow Jews was terrible … in rags and tatters … without even a place to stay for the first night. The first and only help they received was from the Jewish Committee.

* * *

When I now write memories of the recent past, when the sad state of the few survivors of Tarnow Jewry has demanded great efforts and tireless activity from the various communal workers in the Jewish Committee in Tarnow, I consider it necessary to emphasize the loyal and responsible behavior of the Zionist community leaders who, with complete devotion and seriousness, took on the tasks and work in the Jewish Committee in Tarnow. They always put the interests of the public above their own party interests as had been done in the pre-war Jewish community in Tarnow by the Zionist activists under the leadership of the recently deceased in Israel, the meritorious and universally respected community head Dr. Shmuel Szpan of blessed memory and by the last community head in Tarnow before the Holocaust, may he live long, Dr. Avraham Chomet.

It was only thanks to the harmonious cooperation which predominated in the Jewish Committee that we were able to overcome the incredible difficulties in our assistance activities. With true satisfaction I want to note here that the period of my work in the Jewish Committee in Tarnow in partnership with all of its other members belonged to the most beautiful segments of my communal activity in the Jewish street in Tarnow.

Footnotes:

1. Died in Tarnow in 1965.
2. Died in Israel in 1955.

Tarnow Jews in Israel and Abroad

10th of Tevet, General Day of Kaddish and Remembrance of the Community of Tarnow

by Tzvi Ezrachi, Tel Aviv

Translated by Hannah Hochner

Edited by Yocheved Klausner

On the 10th of Tevet, the General Day of Kaddish, a memorial ceremony was held at the Moriah public school in Tel Aviv, with the participation of Holocaust survivors. In addition, the first step at memorializing the Holy Tarnow Jewish community was carried out.

At 8:00 am, Dr. Z. Kasif, a native of Tarnow, spoke about the city of Tarnow and its Jewish community. The 6th, 7th, and 8th graders were extremely moved by Dr. Kasif's words. At 12:00 noon, Dr. Avraham Chomet, Mr. Eliezer Hadas, Mr. Yosef Kornilo, and Mr. David Schiff, representatives of the Association of Former Tarnow Residents, appeared before the children.

The 4th thru 8th grades school children gathered in the school's courtyard. The Aron Hakodesh (The Holy Ark with the Torah scrolls) was brought outside and they recited the afternoon prayer, Mincha. The children learned sections of Mishna and recited Psalms in memory of Tarnow residents who perished in the Holocaust, may God avenge their blood.

Girls from the 7th grade read a report about Tarnow Jews, that they had written following interviews with Dr. Chomet and Mr. Kornilo about the Tarnow Jewish community that was wiped out by the Nazis. Mr. Malchiel, the school principal, spoke about the importance of memorializing this special, holy community. The teacher Tzvi Ezrachi, a Tarnow native, read the Memory Scroll.

The ceremony was brought to a close with the recitation of Kaddish by Tarnow natives.

Religious articles from the destroyed synagogues in Tarnow
(from the collection of by I. Bergman in Tarnow)

[Page 331, Volume 2]

The Activity of the Tarnower *Landsmanschaft*[1] in Montreal

by Ahron Szporn (Montreal, Canada)

Translated by David Schonberg

The Tarnower *Landsmanschaft* in Montreal has behind it rich and worthy activities–accomplishments. Since its founding in 1949 it has been led by the writer of these lines.

With strict punctiliousness there has been observed the fundamental principle of the *Landsmanschaft*: to commemorate each year the Yizkor [memorial] ceremony for our Tarnow heroes and martyrs. But, at the same time, it has also placed great weight upon the full realization of our further tasks. Thus we have tried to assist fellow Tarnowians who immigrated to Israel and had to struggle with the first difficulties of organizing themselves in their new circumstances (conditions). With whole–hearted warmth (friendliness, cordiality) we have tried to keep a brotherly contact with all the various existing *landmanschaft* organizations of Tarnow Jews, in different countries. Till today we take every opportunity to participate in each event, in whatever form as may be, whose goal is to memorialize our Tarnow Jewry.

Thanks to the warm collegial (friendly) atmosphere which is manifest in our *landmanschaft*, we have been able to create a pleasant homely centre, as a symbol of our one time colourfully–rich Jewish community in Tarnow.

Of the fairly small number of Tarnow Jews who currently live in Montreal (approximately 30 families) they are almost all, with minor exceptions, members in our *landmanschaft* and there is a feeling of friendly closeness which unites us in sorrows and joy. At every opportunity, with the shared energies of our brothers and sisters belonging to the *landmanschaft*, is expressed our readiness to take part in every help–act (event) for the benefit of the survivors of Tarnow Jewry, and we respond with full devotion to every call (appeal), that comes to us and not merely from our *landsleit* (fellow townsmen) in Israel… We are always to be found in the ranks of those of the Jewish people who demonstrate by acts (actions) their warm and cordial feelings towards the State of Israel.

[Page 332, Volume 2]

In the successful activities of our *landmanschaft*, we have much to thank the circle of our wives who have taken upon themselves the concern and the yoke to create the financial means that enable us to fulfil our tasks. It is worthwhile to note, that in America and in Canada has been introduced in the social organizations that upon the women lies the duty to be concerned with the finances of the organization, and carrying this out though arranging various happenings (events) to bring in the necessary funds. In this area have the wives of the Tarnow *landmanschaft* have excelled with full devotion, in particular in arranging the traditional, already larger event–undertaking, which they carry out, yearly with great success.

Tarnow *landmanschaft* in Montreal

Seated from right, the women: Sala Geller, Regina Bleiweiss (Kaner), Mina Gelernter, Ahron Szporn [the author], Ruza Schildkraut, Klara Weizer
Standing, from the left: Abraham Goldman (Flink), Chaim Rubenstein, Moshe Birman (Nusboim), Eliezer Bienenstock z'l (passed away in 1968)– yvl'a[2] Regina Hazelberg (Roth), Ephraim Gelernter, David Weizer, Herschel Ziss, Mendel Hazelberg (Hoenig), Zalek Bleiweiss (Ziskind) and Shlomo Schildkraut

[Page 353, Volume 2]

As I have earlier pointed out, the commemoration (marking) of the memorial–day for our *kdoshim* (the holy ones) of Tarnow is at the centre of our activities. Every year, when the day of the 26th Sivan draws near, we feel a deep sadness in our hearts… A sadness that brings us back to our memories– thoughts of our Tarnow home, that was cut down– where Jewish energy, Jewish spirit, Jewish creative force could be seen in every corner of the town.

With sorrow and pain in our hearts we remember on the *Yizkor* (memorial) day our Tarnow Jews, who were put to death so brutally by the German murderers. In this *Yizkor* (memorial) day we honour the memory of our tortured fathers and mothers, brothers and sisters, children and friends.

They will always remain in our memory… Our *landmanschaft* will scrupulously observe the memorial–day for our Tarnow *kidoshim* (holy martyrs).

Tarnow *landsleit* from New York and Montreal in a [joint] gathering in Montreal in July, 1965

On the photo: Family Berger from New York, Family Tellerman from New York, Family Lebenkorn from Bridgeport, Ahron Szporn, Family Goldman, Family Bleiweiss and Family Geller

Translator's footnotes:

1. Organization of people from the same town
2. May be separated for long life

[Page 334, Volume 2]

From the *Landsmanschaft* in Toronto

by Abraham Singer (Toronto)

Translated by David Schonberg

Details as to the founding to the Tarnower *Landsmanschaft* in Toronto and its activities we already gave over in Volume 1 of the *Yizkor–bukh* (Memorial book), 'Tarnow' that was published in 1954.

In the 14 years of our existence we didn't save (conserve/ limit) any energy and efforts to fulfil our tasks, thus we held close contact with our brother–organization in Montreal, which was since its founding in 1948 led by our important, and so worthy and devoted community leader– activist, Ahron Szporn.

Ahron Szporn and his grandchild, Chaim, at his *Bar–Mitzva* celebration in Montreal in 1968

[Page 335, Volume 2]

How much he is valued (appreciated) and loved amongst all of the survivors of the Tarnow Jewry, not just by us here in Canada, was shown by the cordial greetings (wishes) and blessings that he received not long ago on the occasion of the *bar–mitzva* of his grandson, Chaim…

The bunch of survivors from our Jewish Tarnow, that managed to reach the shores of Canada, could not forget the terrible Churban (holocaust– lit. destruction) of the Jewish Tarnow that was cut down and thus we, those that found our way to Toronto, Tarnow Jews– exactly as in Montreal– we kept together in our Tarnow *Landsmanschaft* together we grieved after our annihilated (destroyed) fathers and mothers, brothers and sisters..

With reciprocal (mutual) help we tried to overcome the various difficulties of ordering ourselves in life and work conditions.

And the most important: Thanks to the *Landsmanschaft* we didn't feel alone there was something of continuation of our old Tarnow home, that was so cruelly destroyed by the Nazi murderers and their accomplices.

We didn't forget our needy *landsleit* (fellow townsmen) who by hundreds of miracles were saved and still had to wait in Tarnow for the opportunity to escape from their now–destroyed home and especially we tried to assist our Tarnower brothers and sisters, who went as *olim* (immigrants) to Israel and needed help in arranging themselves.

But the greatest efforts we always made, when it was concerning help for Israel. On every call we answered with generosity and a readiness to sacrifice. It is enough to show the fact that in the charity event after the 6–Day War our *Landsmanschaft* with its small number of members, collected 1,100 dollars– besides the sums that each of us contributed to this goal, privately and in the synagogues and several social–public organizations and professional associations.

And in the end I would also like to mention (recall) that exactly as we were active, took part and assisted in the giving out of the first volume of the *Yizkor–bukh* (Memorial book), 'Tarnow' also now we understood the importance of the work for the second volume and we have with our constricted (limited) powers added a few bricks to the holy monument to our one–time lovely Jewish Tarnow town.

[Page 336, Volume 2]

Of course, we could have done a lot more in various areas of our tasks in the *Landsmanschaft* of Tarnow Jews in Toronto. But this in a large extent is dependent upon our Tarnow *landsleit* … Let us hope, that in the future our activities will increase (grow) and there will be greater interest in our *Landsmanschaft* and thus we will be able to develop broader activities for the benefit of the *she'eris hapleita* (the remnants– the survivors) of Tarnow Jewry that has been cut–down… For the efforts to observe the memory of our past dear Jewish town of Tarnow and primarily for the benefit of our State of Israel.

[Page 337, Volume 2]

From the Tarnow *Landsmanschaft* in New–York

by L. Gottleib (New–York)

Translated by David Schonberg

Leon Gottleib

As to the *Landsmanschaft* of Tarnow Jews in New–York and its activities until approximately 1955 a great deal has been written already in the first volume of the of the *Yizkor–bukh* {Memorial book], 'Tarnow'.

Notwithstanding the good and useful help and work of Tarnow *landsleit* in New–York, which since 1945 has been organised within the framework of the 'Relief Committee of Tarnow and Outlying Areas', in favor of our brothers who came in the post–War immigration stream, and also for the Sh'erit ha–Pletah [Surviving Remnant] of Tarnow Jewry who built for themselves a new life in Israel, or those who still were in Poland – unfortunately in later years this significant work has of the Relief Committee has declined. There has been a waning of interest for the tasks of the organization which had a very lose character lacking organizational structure and in particular lacking funds to pay monthly costs. Without laboring a sad fact though, there is today in New York and surrounding area about 1000 Tarnow Jews. Unfortunately, it is not possible to bring together even ten of the *landsleit* to a gathering and when a meeting of the Relief Committee is called, to which belong 15 members, only between 3 and 7 members come to the meeting.

The result of this is that the relief finds itself in a very difficult financial situation. We cannot even allow ourselves to rent a premises for a gathering or meeting as the costs can reach between 25 to 140 dollars. In such a situation it is no wonder that not once we have found ourselves in a situation that we cannot answer to requests for help, which come even now from different directions from Tarnow *landsleit*. The main reason for this, as we have earlier mentioned, is that one pays no monthly contribution to create a fund for even a limited relief–work.

[Page 338, Volume 2]

In general, there is –amongst our Tarnow *landsleit*– a tendency to forget their former Jewish home in Tarnow… a tendency to run away from memories of the tragic past that enwraps the dreadful nightmare of hell – the life that was, at the time of the Nazi occupation… and therefore one has a pretext not to come to a Yizkor event, which we arrange each year in order to commemorate the memory of our lovely Jewish town, of which nothing has remained.

Difficult and full of responsibility is the task of the few members of our Relief Committee. Despite all the obstacles which we face in our activities we try to explain to our Tarnow *landsleit* that the bloody wounds have not yet been healed and the tears for our fathers and mothers, brothers and sisters, children and friends, have not yet dried out– they who the Nazi murderers bestially annihilated, gassed, burned or buried alive.

Therefore we call from this place all our Tarnow *landsleit* wherever they may be, not to forget the cruel *Churban* (Holocaust) of the Tarnow Jewish community… and in particular we call upon our Tarnow Jews in New–York, one time a year, to hallow the memorial day of the [mass]death of Tarnow Jewry. Let us hope that Tarnow Jews in New York and its vicinity will follow our call to come together on the *Yizkor* day to unite with the souls of Tarnow's *kaddishim*, holy ones, who were killed.

[Page 339, Volume 2]

From the Tarnower *Landsmanschaft* in Paris

by Abraham Chomet

Translated by David Schonberg

The activities of the Tarnower *landsmanschaft* in Paris have been very vibrant and valued.

Since 1948 the Tarnower *landsmanschaft* in Paris has gone under the name 'Friends of Tarnow and Its Vicinity' which put out in 1966 a modest *Memorial book* in Yiddish and French, with a preface by an active public figure in the Paris Tarnow circles, Shlomo Klapholtz. As he states in his preface to the above–mentioned *Memorial book*, whose Yiddish section has 40 pages, the Tarnower *landsmanschaft* in Paris has dual goals – material and cultural. Thus an important place in its activities, besides help for the Land of Israel, has been the matter of a cemetery, which in the particular local circumstances has been a complicated issue, since the Jewish community has not a Jewish cemetery of its own and each Jewish *landsmanschaft* need buy or lease for a long term a particular site in the general cemetery and there build (develop) a burial place for its members on their passing.

As we learn from the above–mentioned *Memorial book* the committee of the Tarnow *landsmanschaft* in Paris has developed (built) in the general cemetery a burial site for itself with a *matzevahs* that overlooks it which, at the same time, serves as a monument to the memory of the Tarnow Jewish heroes and *kiddoshim* [holy ones, martyrs].

There are also inscribed there the names of the Tarnow leaders who died as martyrs [*al kiddush haShem* – sanctifying G–d's name].

The Tarnow Jews in Paris– states Shlomo Klapholtz at the end of his preface 'try to carry out faithfully the duties that they took upon themselves at the foundation of the association in the framework of their possibilities'.

[Page 340, Volume 2]

From the Tarnower *Landsmanschaft* in Israel

by Abraham Chomet

Translated by David Schonberg

In Tel–Aviv

The Tarnower Association in Tel–Aviv has developed regular activities. Besides the annual commemorations in memory of the destroyed Tarnow Jewry which has already become a tradition, once or twice a year we have a gathering of Tarnow *landsleit*.

The charity [*gemillus chesed*] fund, handled with exemplary order, gives out non–interest loans with light payment terms–conditions.

Together with the Yad Vashem effort for Israeli schools to adopt destroyed communities, the State religious school Moriah in Tel–Aviv has adopted our destroyed community, the Jewish Tarnow of the past.

In order to move forward the decision of this school to adopt the Tarnow community much was done (brought to bear) by our Tarnower *landsman* Zvi Ezrahi (Meth), who works there as a teacher and who has expended much effort to arrange the forming of the ties between the school and our destroyed Tarnow community. He writes about this separately in another place in this *Yizkor–bukh* [note: see page 330].

Memorial of the Tarnow *k'doshim* [holy martyrs] – Tel–Aviv, Beit HeHalutzot, 1964

On the platform, seated from the right: Dr. Isler, Mrs. Deborah Abramovich–Arnon, Dr, (Mrs.) Sroka, Dr. Yeshayahu Szpira, Dr. Abraham Chomet (speaking), Attorney Yaakov Bienenshtock, Feld A., Maria Dirdalowa (guest from Tarnow– one of the *Righteous Gentiles*), Yosef Kornilo, Dr. Z. Kasif

[Page 341, Volume 2]

In order to express gratitude for the readiness of this school to memorialise our Tarnow community and to awaken and strengthen the interest of the schoolchildren in the history of the Jewish community of Tarnow the leadership of the *Tarnower association* in Tel–Aviv established two awards– one of 200 Israeli–lirot and the other of 100 Israeli lirot for the best school–work (essays) on the theme related to the life and destruction of Tarnow Jewry.

In Haifa

A painful loss was suffered by our Tarnower *landsleit* in Haifa in March 1967 with the passing of Dr. Shmuel Shpan z"l, the long–standing chairman of the Tarnower *landsmanschaft* in Haifa. He was the popular and overall cherished leader of the Tarnow Jewry of the past, the successful and veteran leader of the Zionist movement in pre–War Galicia and for many years a member of Zionist–Congress court.

On the Jubilee–celebration in Haifa in 1955 – of the 75th birthday of Dr. Shmuel Shpan, z"l

[Page 342, Volume 2]

For the *shloshim* (30 days after the burial) of the departed one the Tarnow *landsmanschaft* in Israel together with "Drit Rishonim" and the general Zionist (liberal) organisation in Haifa organised a memorial ceremony, to which came a large number of Tarnowers from Tel–Aviv and other places in Israel.

Also hard hit were our Tarnower landsleit in Haifa with the death of David Baum, z"l, the active long–standing leader of the Tarnow *landsmanschaft* in Haifa. Thanks to his dedication, the Tarnow landsmanschaft in Haifa developed very active relief–activities for needy *landsleit*. The departed (David Baum z"l) put much effort into supporting the efforts to maintain cordial brotherly contact with Tarnowers in other parts of the country and in the diaspora.

In Jerusalem

A general sadness was in the hearts of Tarnower Jews in Israel with the death of Daniel Leibl, who for many years (from before the First World War till 1919) lived in Tarnow and was there active in the Poalei Zion movement, while at the same time being active in Tarnow's Jewish public and cultural life.

Though born in Dembitz he always proudly put himself [associated himself] with Tarnow Jewry and took part in all memorials and other ceremonies of the *Tarnower association* in Tel–Aviv and Haifa.

[Pages 345-363, Volume 2]

List of Holocaust victims

Transliterated by Shalom Bronstein

א Alef	ב Bet	ג Gimmel	ד Dalet	ה Hey	ו Vav	ז Zayin	ח Chet	ט Tet	י Yod	כ Kaf
ל Lamed	מ Mem	נ Nun	ס Samech	ע Ayin	פ Peh	צ Tzadik	ק Kof	ר Resh	ש Shin	ת Tav

Family name(s)	First name(s)	Gender	Additional family	Remarks	Page

א Alef

Family name(s)	First name(s)	Gender	Additional family	Remarks	Page
ABEND	Maurycy	M	family		345
ABEND	Shlomo	M			345
ABEND	Esther	F	family		345
ABERDAM	Osziasz	M	family		345
ABERDAM	Chaim	M	family		345
ABERDAM	Shimon	M	family		345
ABERDAM	Nisan	M	family		345
OBERLENDER	Dr. Maurycy	M	family		345
ABRAHAM	Osziasz	M	family		345
ABRAMOWITZ	Shmuel	M	family		345
ABRAMOWITZ	Reuven	M	family		345
AGATSTEIN	Alfred	M		Profession Doctor	345
ADLER	Theodor	M	family		345
ADLER	Osziasz	M	family		345
ADLER	Pinkus	M	family		345
OBER	Ernest	M	family	Profession Doctor	345
ADLER	Akiva	M	family		345
OBER	Stephen	M	family		345

AVIDA	Max	M	family		345
AVIDA	Mannes	M	family		345
ULMAN	Mannes	M	family		345
ULMAN	Herman	M		married	345
ULMAN		F		Husband's name Herman	345
AUSAIBEL	Tobias	M	family		345
UNGER	Rabbi Elazar	M	family		345
UNGER	Rabbi Kalman	M	family		345
UNGER	Rabbi Leibish	F	children		345
UNGER	Rabbi Michal	M	family		345
UNGER	Rabbi Alter	M	family		345
UNGER	Rabbi Elazar	M	family		345
ACHLER	Rabbi Yechiel	M	family		345
IZAK	Rabbi Yitzhak	M	family		345
ISRAELOVITCH	Rabbi Mairal	M	family		345
ISRAELOVITCH	Rabbi Zev	M	family	Profession Doctor	345
ISRAEL	Rabbi Shlomo	M			345
ISRAEL	Rabbi Yosef	M			345
ISRAEL	Chaim	M			345
ISRAEL	Hinda	F			345
EISEN	Shmuel	M	family		345
EISEN	Moshe	M	family		345
EISEN	Mechel	M	family		345
EISEN	Baruch	M	family		345
EISENBACH	Chaim	M	family		345
EISENBACH	Max	M			345
EISENBERG	Akiva	M	family		345
EISENBACH	Rodek	M	family		345
EISENBERG	Akiva	M			345
EISENBERG	Meir	M			345
EICHHORN	Maxmilian	M	family	Profession Engineer	345
EICHHORN	Dalek	M			345
EICHENHOLTZ	Miriam	F	family	Maiden name KORN	345
EICHENWALD	Ayzik	M	family		345

EICHENHOLTZ	Ya'akov	M	family		345
EINHORN	Chanoch	M	family		345
EINHORN	Yitzhak	M	family		345
EINSPRUCH	Nahum	M	family		345
EINHORN	Moshe	M	family		345
INLENDER	Mendel	M	family		345
INGBER	Tobias	M	family		345
INGBER	Osziasz	M	family		345
INGBER	Markus	M	family		345
INSLER	Leon	M	family		345
IRAM	Naftali	M	family		345
ALBAN	Chaim	M	family		345
ALBAN	David	M	family		345
ALWEISS	Noach	M	family		345
ALWEISS	Yosef	M	family		345
ALTMAN	Menachem	M	family		345
ALTMAN	Mendel	M	family		345
AMAIZ	Avraham	M	family		345
ANISFELD	Shachna	M	family		345
ANKER	Moshe	M	family		345
OSTERWEIL	Shimon	M	family		345
OSTERWEIL	Yisrael	M	family		345
OSTERWEIL	Leon	M	family	Profession Doctor	345
OSTERWEIL	Willhelm	M	family		345
OSTERWEIL	Gavriel	M	family		345
OSTERWEIL	Herman	M	family		345
OSTERWEIL	Hersh	M	family		345
OFNER	Yosef	M		Profession Doctor. Married	346
OFNER		F		Husband's name Yosef	346
OFNER	Leon	M	family		346
OFNER	Moine	M	family		346
OFNER	Shimon	M	family		346
APPLEBOIM	Moshe	M	family		346
APPLE	Shimon	M	family		346

APSLER	Leibish	M	family		346
APPLEBOIM	Edward	M	family		346
APPLEBOIM	Bernard	M	family		346
APPLE	Moshe	M	family		346
ARAK	Rabbi Rabbi	M	family		346
ARGAND	Naftali	M	family		346
ARIMOVIC	Hersh	M	family		346
ARMIAN			whole family		346
ORSZICER	David	M	family		346
ORSZICER	Izak	M	family		346
ORSZICER	Ya'akov	M	family	Profession Engineer	346
OVSHITZER	Yishayahu	M			346
ASHKENAZI	Ignace	M			346
EIROM	Naftali Zvi	M	family		346
ISRAEL	Shmuel	M	family		346
APSLER	Baruch	M	family		346
ALWEISS	Leah	F			346
ISAAC	David	M	family		346
ISAAC	Kalman	M	family		346
ISAAC	Izak	M	family		346
UNGER	Baila	F	family	Maiden name BAGEN	346

ב Bet

BADNER			whole family		346
BODEK	Yisrael	M			346
BAU	Professor Galo	M	family		346
BAUM	Mendel	M	family		346
BAUM	Feivel	M	family		346
BAZLAR	Anselm	M		Profession Doctor	346
BAZLAR	Herman	M	family		346
BATIST	David	M	family		346
BATIST	Ya'akov	M	family		346
BALSAM	Naftali	M	family		346
BALSAM	Max	M	family		346

BALSAM	Herman	M	family	Profession Engineer	346
BALSAM	Shmuel	M	family		346
BANK	Lazar	M	family		346
BARDACH	Henrik	M			346
BARDACH	Hilek	M			346
BARON	Eliyahu	M	family		346
BARON	Berel	M			346
BARTFELD			whole family		346
BORNSTEIN	Yidel	M	family		346
BODIN	Shmuel	M	family		346
BOOKBINDER	P	M	family		346
BUCHHOLTZ	Roiza	F	family		346
BODIN	Meir	M	family		346
BORSTEIN	Avraham	M	family		346
BORNSTEIN	Esther	F			346
BURG	Leon	M	family		346
BIBERBERG	Henrik	M	family		346
BIBERBERG	David	M	family		346
BIBERSTEIN	Aharon	M	family		346
BIBERBERG	Meir	M	family		346
BIEGELEISEN	Yehezkel	M	family		346
BIEGELEISEN	Mendel	M	family		346
BEIM	Mendel	M	family		346
BAYER	Wolf	M	family		346
BAYER	Yosef	M	family		346
BILD	Henkir	M	family		346
BILOW	Wolf	M	family		346
BILFELD	Emanuel	M	family		346
BEITCHER			family		346
BINENSTOCK	Avraham	M	family		346
BINENSTOCK	Yehuda	M	family		346
BIRENBAUM	Wolf	M	family		346
BIRENBAUM	Leib	M	family		346
BIERMAN	Natan	M	family		346

BIRENSTEIN	Melech	M	family		346
BIRER	Pinkus	M	family		346
BIRKEN	Raizel	F			346
BLAUNER	Oscar	M	family		346
BLAUNER	Meir	M	family		346
BLAUNER	Leon	M	family		347
BLAUNER	Tzila	F	children		347
BLAZER	Dr. Mendel	M		Rabbi	347
BLAZER	Yisrael	M	family		347
BLOCH			whole family		347
BLOCH	Maurcian	M		Profession Doctor. Married	347
BLOCH		F		Husband's name Maurcian	347
BLAND	Karola	F			347
BLAND	Avraham	M	family		347
BLAND	Eliash	M	family		347
BLAND	Moshe	M	family		347
BLAND	S.	M	family		347
BLAND	Ya'akov	M	family		347
BLONDER	Avraham Abba	M	family		347
WEISS	Baila	F	children	Maiden name BLONDER	347
LEIBEL	Karala	F		Maiden name BLONDER	347
BLONSKY	Y.	M	family		347
BLOTNER	Moshe	M	family		347
BLOTNER	Yechiel	M	family		347
BLUMENFELD	Natan	M	family		347
BLUMENFELD	Moshe	M	family		347
BLUMENFELD	Naftali	M	family		347
BLUMENFELD	David	M	family		347
BLEIWEISS	Meir	M	family		347
BLEIWEISS	Avraham	M	family		347
BLEIWEISS	Feiga	F	family		347
BLEIWEISS	Tobias	M	family		347
BLEIWEISS	Osziasz	M	family		347

BLEIWEISS	Eliyahu	M	family		347
BLEICHER	Hersh	M	family		347
BLEICHER	Shlomo	M	family		347
BLEICHFELD		M		Profession Magister	347
BLITZ	Shmuel	M	family		347
BEDER	Reuven	M	family		347
BETAIL	Chaim	M	family		347
BEBELSKY	Yisrael	M	family		347
BETRIVNIS	Shmuel	M	family		347
BETRIVNIS	Moshe	M	family		347
BELLER	Esther	F	family		347
BECK	Ya'akov	M	family		347
BECK	Shmuel	M	family		347
BERGMAN	Yoel	M	family		347
BERGMAN	Berel	M	family		347
BERGMAN	Naftali	M	family		347
BERGMAN	Salamon	M	family		347
BERGMAN	Yosef	M	family		347
BERGER	Shabtai	M	family		347
BERGER	Yehuda	M	family		347
BERGER	David	M	family		347
BERGER	Shaul	M	family		347
BERGER	Herman	M	family		347
BERNFELD	Max	M	family		347
BERNKNOPF	Menashe	M	family		347
BERNER	Shaul	M	family		347
BEREL	Mechel	M	family		347
BERKOWITZ	Mordecai	M	family		347
BERNSTEIN			whole family		347
BERKELHAMMER	Moshe	M	family		347
BERKELHAMMER	Yishayahu	M	family		347
BERKELHAMMER	Karol	M	family		347
BERKELHAMMER	Zelig	M	family		347
BERKELHAMMER		M	family		347

BERKELHAMMER	Berel	M	family		347
BRODHEIM	Matis	M	family		347
BRODER	Yitzhak	M	family		347
BARON	Zelig	M	family		347
BARON	Shmuel	M	family		347
HENDLER	Rivka	F	family	Maiden name BARON	347
BARON	Yerucham	M	family		347
BRAUNFELD	Emil	M	family		347
BRACHFELD	David	M	family		347
BRAM	Ya'akov	M	family		347
BRAM	David	M	family		347
BRAND	Moshe Aharon	M			347
BRAND	Mechel	M	family		347
BRAND	Avraham	M	family		347
BRAND	Olek	M	family		347
BRAND	Baruch	M	family		347
BRANSTETTER	Ludwik	M	family		347
BRANSTETTER	Henrik	M	family		347
BRAUNSTEIN			whole family		347
BRUDER	Binyamin Wolf	M	family		348
BRIG	Artur	M	family		348
BRUDER	Yosef	M	family		348
BROVEH	Yitzhak	M	family		348
BRUCKNER	Ya'akov	M	family		348
BRILAND			whole family	Family of Dr. BRILAND	348
BERGMAN	Mendel	M			348
BERGMAN	Yitzhak	M			348
BERGMAN	Avraham	M			348
BERGMAN	Moshe	M			348
BERGMAN	David	M			348
BORMAN	Mindeleh				348
BINENSTOCK	Melech	M			348
BLUMENSTEIN	Hadassah	F	children		348
BLUMENSTEIN	Meir	M			348

BARON	Sima	F	children	Maiden name POTASCHMANN	348
BLEIWEISS	Yitzhak Pinchas	M			348
BLAUNER	Yehezkel	M	family		348
BLAUNER	Mendel	M	family		348
BALSAM	Izak	M	family		348
BECK	Etka	F			348
BECK	Rosa	F			348
BECK	Giza	F			348
BECK	Esther	F			348
BEEBER			whole family		348
BEEDER	Markus	M			348
BROD	Izak	M			348
BROD	Leib	M	family		348
BOGEN		M	family		348

ג Gimmel

GOLDBERG	Shlomo	M		Profession Doctor. Married	348
GOLDBERG		F		Husband's name Shlomo	348
GOLDBERG	Chaim	M	family		348
GOTLOB	Moshe	M	family		348
GOLDBERG	Melech	M	family		348
GOLDBERG	Edward	M		Profession Engineer	348
GOLWASSER	Yisrael	M	family		348
GOLWASSER	Ya'akov	M	family		348
GOLDFARB	Wolf Mendel	M	family		348
GOLDWASSER	Leon	M	family		348
GOLDFARB	Eliyahu	M	family		348
GOLDSTEIN	Herman	M	family		348
GOLDSCHMIDT	Chaim	M	family		348
GOLDSTAFF	Chaim	M	family		348
GOLDFINGER	Yishaya	M	family		348
GOLDFINGER	Chava	F			348
GOLDFINGER		F		Mother's name Chava	348
GAVRALOVITCH	Binyamin	M	family		348

GANZ	Gershon	M	family	348
GANZ	Emil	M	family	348
GANZ	Yehoshua	M	family	348
GANZ	Salo	M	family	348
GAST	Aharon	M	family	348
GASTWIRTH	Melech	M	family	348
GUTWIRTH			family	348
GUTMAN	Levi	M	family	348
GUTER	Herman	M	family	348
GUTER	Leib	M	family	348
GUTER	Ayzik	M	family	348
GUTER	Zalman	M		348
GUTER	Shlomo	M	family	348
GUTER	Yehuda	M	family	348
GORLITZER		M	family	348
GINGER	Ignace	M	family	348
GISER	Leon	M	family	348
GLASS	Osziasz	M	family	348
GLAZER	Emanuar	M	family	348
GLAZER	Yechiel	M	family	348
GLAZER	Izak	M	family	348
GLATZNER	Yisrael	M	family	348
GLATZNER	Shimon	M	family	348
GLINIK	Shimon	M	family	348
GLINIK	Chaim	M	family	348
GLICK	Pinkus	M	family	348
GLEICHER	Zvi	M	family	348
GETTINGER	Chaya Tauba	F		348
GELB	Salo	M	family	348
GELB	Janas	M	family	348
GEWIRTZ	Eliyahu	M	family	348
GEVELB	Tila	M	family	348
GELBWAX	Yisrael	M	family	348
GELERNTER	Avraham	M	family	348

GEMINDER	Herman	M	family		348
GELDTZELER	Y.	M	family		349
GETZLER	Wolf	M	family		349
GETZLER	David	M	family		349
GERTNER	Nahum	M	family		349
GERTNER	Kalman	M	family		349
GERSTEN	Gavriel	M	family		349
GERSTEN	Zvi	M	family		349
GERSTEN	Meir Max	M	family		349
GERTNER	Shlomo	M	family		349
GERTLER	Leopold	M	family		349
GRABKAVITCH	Leon	M	family		349
GRAUVER	Helena	F	child		349
GROSSMAN	Leib	M	family		349
GROSSMAN	Shmuel	M	family		349
GROSS	Shlomo	M	family		349
GROSS	Shmuel	M	family		349
GROSS	Miriam	F	children	Maiden name MANHEIMER	349
GROSS	Chaim	M		Wife's name Malka	349
GROSS	Malka	F		Husband's name Chaim	349
GROSS	Ya'akov	M			349
GROSS	Yisrael Iva	M	family		349
GROSSMAN	Eliyahu	M			349
GROSSBART	Ya'akov	M	family		349
GRUSCHOV	Ya'akov	M			349
GRUSCHOV	Ayzik	M	family		349
SCHWARTZ	Lola	F		Maiden name GRUSCHOV	349
GRUSCHOV	Willhelm	M	family		349
GARZAIMAN GRAIZMAN	Willhelm	M	family		349
GRAIZMAN	Eliyahu	M	family		349
GRALITZER	Avraham	M	family		349
GRALITZER	Leibish	M	family		349
GREEN	Hinda	F			349

GREEN	Hersh	M	family		349
GREENEVIZA			family		349
GREEM	Ezra	M	family		349
GREENBOIM	Tuvia	M			349
GREENBAUM	Yitzhak	M	family		349
GREENBAUM	Ayzik	M	family		349
GREENBERGER	Yosef	M	family		349
GREENBERG	Naftali	M	family		349
GREENBERG	Peretz	M	family		349
GREENBERG	Yisrael	M	family		349
GREENBERG		F		Maiden name APPEL	349
GREENHUT	Shmuel	M	family		349
GREENKRAUT	Ida	F	children	Maiden name ENGLANDER	349
GREENSTEIN	Mendel Leib	M	family		349
GREENSPAN	Emanuel	M	family		349
GREENSPAN	Naftali	M	family		349
GREENFELD	Shmuel	M	family		349
GREENFELD	Roman	M			349
GREENSPAN	Adzia	F	family	Maiden name WEIMISNER	349
GELERNTER	Moshe Wolf	M			349
GELERNTER	Mendel	M			349
GELERNTER	Lipa	M			349
GUTER	Ya'akov	M			349
GREENSPAN	Yitzhak	M	family		349
GOLDKLANG		M	family		349
GREENSPAN	Shimon	M	family		349
GEVIAZDA		M			349
GREEN	Chaim	M		married	349
GREEN		F	family	Husband's name Chaim	349
GLICKMAN		M	family		349
GINZBERG		M	family		349

ד Dalet

DOM	Moshe	M			349

DOMAST	Chaya	F	family		349
DORMAN	Yishayahu	M	family		349
DOR DREISIGER			family		349
DORLICH	Shimon	M	family		349
DORF	Fishel	M	family		349
DOMLER	Artur	M	family		349
DINTENPAS	Max	M	family		349
DINTENPAS	Shmuel	M	family		349
DEGEN	Moshe	M	family		349
DEGEN	Yosef	M	family		349
DICKSTEIN	M.A.				349
DENER	Ayzik	M	family		349
DRESNER	Julius	M		Profession Doctor. Married	349
DRESNER		F		Husband's name Julius	349
DRELICH	Shmuel	M	family		349
DRUCKER	Avraham	M			349
DAVID			whole family		349
DINDAS	Feivel	M	family		350
DRINGER		M	family		350
DOMINITZ	Yehoshua	M			350

ה Hey return

HABER	Avraham	M	family		350
HABER	Chaim	M	family	Profession Doctor	350
HABER	Alter	M	family		350
HABER	Shmuel	M	family		350
HABER	Ya'akov	M	family		350
HABER	Yitzhak	M	family		350
HABER	Yosef	M	family		350
HABER	Zigmund	M	family		350
HABERMAN	Julius	M	family		350
HAUSER	Aharon	M	family		350
HAUSER	Avraham	M	family		350
HAUT	Yishayahu	M	family		350

HAUT	Natan	M	family		350
HAUSNER	Ya'akov	M	family		350
HAUSMAN	Henrik	M	family		350
HOCHNER	Ayzik	M	family		350
HOCHHAJZER	Henrik	M	family		350
HOCHHAJZER	Yosef	M	family		350
HOCHBERGER			whole family		350
HOLLAND	Shalom	M	family		350
HALBERSTAM	Rabbi Leibish	M	family		350
HALBERSTAM	Kalman	M			350
HOLLANDER	Henrik	M	family		350
HOLLANDER	Zigmund	M	family		350
HOLLANDER	Yitzhak	M	family		350
HOLLANDER	Ya'akov	M	family	Profession Doctor	350
HOLLEDER HOLLANDER	Herman	M	family		350
HOLLANDER	Fela	F			350
HOLLANDER	Meir	M	family		350
HOLLANDER	Hersh Leib	M	family		350
HOLLANDER	Rabbi Michal	M	family		350
HOLLANDER	Menachem Mendel	M	family		350
HOLLANDER	Natan	M	family		350
HOLLANDER		M		Profession Doctor	350
HOLER	Shmuel	M	family		350
HOLER	Hersh	M	family		350
HOLTZER	Ayzik	M	family		350
HOLTZER	Tobias	M	family		350
HOLTZER	Ignatz	M	family	Profession Doctor	350
HOLESHITZER	Ayzik	M	family		350
HAMMER	Chaim	M	family		350
HALPERN	Yisrael	M	family		350
HAMMERSCHLAG	Shmuel	M	family		350
HONIG	Moshe	M	family		350
HONIG	Chaim	M	family		350

HONIG	Ya'akov	M	family		350
HONIG	Yoachim	M	family		350
HONIG	Petachyahu	M	family		350
HONIG	Chanoch	M	family		350
HOFFMAN	Raphael	M	family		350
HOFFMAN	Mendel	M	family		350
HOROWITZ	Rabbi Alter	M	family		350
HOROWITZ	Rabbi Elazar	M	family		350
HOROWITZ	Rabbi Yechiel	M	family		350
HOROWITZ	Rabbi Yitzhak	M	family		350
HOROWITZ		M	family		350
HAAR		F			350
HOROWITZ	Ben-Zion	M	family		350
HOFFMEISTER			family		350
HODES	Yehoshua Yasha	M	family		350
HODES	Yosef	M	family		350
HOTER	Maurycy	M	family		350
HOLES		M	family	Profession Doctor	350
HOLES	Yosef	M	family		350
HOLES	Shmuel	M	family		350
HOLES	Herman	M	family		350
HITNER	Moshe Meir	M	family		350
HITTER	Shlomo	M	family		350
HITTER	Simcha	M	family		350
HIZIGER	Zelig	M	family		350
HIZIGER	Moshe	M	family		350
HIRSCHFELD	Moshe	M	family		350
HEIBERG	Ayzik	M	family		350
HEIBERG	Ya'akov	M	family		350
HIRSCH	Markus	M	family		351
HIRSCH	Alter Chaim	M	family		351
HIRSCHFELD	Sarah	F	family		351
HEINBERG	David	M	family		351
HIRSCHHORN			family		351

HIRSCH	Ida	F	family		351
HELIN	Yitzhak	M	family		351
HELLER	Shmuel	M	family		351
HELLER	Avraham	M	family		351
HELLER	Maurcian	M			351
HENIG	David	M	family		351
HENIG	Yisrael	M	family		351
HENIG	Yehuda	M	family		351
HENENBERG	Yisrael	M	family		351
HERBST	Yosef	M	family		351
HERBST	Yishayahu	M	family		351
HERBST	Shlomo	M	family		351
HERTZBERG	Moshe	M	family		351
HERZOG	Willhelm	M	family		351
HERZIG	Herman	M	family		351
HEREL	Adolf	M	family		351
HENIG	Azriel	M	family		351
HERSHKOWITZ	Shabtai	M	family		351
HOCHBERG	Noach	M	family		351
HENDLER	Yosef	M	family	Profession Doctor	351
HENDLER	Maineh	M		Profession Doctor	351
HABER	Zisha	M	family		351
HERBSTMAN	Yosef	M	family		351
HOFFMAN	Hersh	M	family		351
HERTZMAN			family		351

ו Vav

WAZNITZER			whole family	351
WACHTEL	Yosef Meir	M	family	351
WACHTEL	Menashe	M	family	351
WACHTEL	Ya'akov	M	family	351
WACHTEL	Salek	M		351
WOLF	Ayzik	M	family	351
WOLF	Mendel	M	family	351

WOLF	Zelig	M	family		351
WOLF	Leah Latka	F			351
WOLF		M		Mother's name Leah Latkah	351
WOLFOWITZ	Mendel	M	family		351
WOLFOWITZ	Shlomo	M	family		351
WOLFOWITZ	Yisrael	M	family		351
WOLFOWITZ	Moshe	M	family		351
WALLACH	Ya'akov	M	family		351
WALLACH		F	family		351
WALLACH		F			351
VOLK	Zalman	M	family		351
VOLK	Nachman	M	family		351
WANDSTEIN	Shmuel	M	family	Profession Doctor	351
WANDSTEIN	Moshe	M	family		351
WANDSTEIN	Jan	M		Profession Magister	351
WANDSTEIN	Yosef	M	family		351
WANDSTEIN	Alexander	M		Profession Magister. Married	351
WANDSTEIN		F		Husband's name Alexander	351
WANDSTEIN	Roiza	F			351
WANDSTEIN		F		Mother's name Roiza	351
WANDER	Mendel	M	family		351
WASSERMAN	Shlomo	M	family		351
WASSERMAN	Herman	M	family		351
WASSERMAN	Manfred	M	family		351
WASSERLAUF	Herman	M	family		351
WASSERFEL			whole family		351
WASSERSTEIN	Pinkus	M			351
WASSERMAN	Frederick	M	family	Profession Doctor	351
WASERSZTROM	Shlomo	M	family		351
WAXMAN	Reuven	M	family		351
WAXMAN	Markus	M	family		351
WAXPRESS	Gutman	M	family		351
WAXPRESS	Naftali	M	family		351
WAXPRESS	Simcha	M	family		351

WAXPRESS	Meir	M	family		351
WACHS	M.	M	family		351
WAROWITZ	Avraham	M	family		351
WARENHAUFT	Shmuel	M	family		351
WURTZEL	Shlomo	M			351
WURTZEL		M		Father's name Shlomo	351
WURTZEL	Ozer	M	family		351
WEISER	Eliezer	M	family		351
WEISER ROSENGARTEN	Tuvia	M	family		351
WEISER	Aharon Lazar	M	family		351
WEIDENBERG	Chaim	M	family		351
WIDEMAN	Leibish	M	family		352
WEIDER	Emil	M		Profession Doctor	352
WEIDER	Herman	M	family		352
WILDSTEIN	Yekel	M	family		352
WEIL	Shmuel	M	family		352
VEIT	Ya'akov	M	family	Profession Doctor	352
WEINRIB	Shlomo	M	family		352
WEINRIB	Aharon	M	family		352
WEINRIB	Oscar	M	family		352
WEINTRAUB	Alter	M	family		352
WEINDLING	Chaim	M	family		352
WEINBERGER	Eliyahu	M	family		352
WEINFELD	Max	M	family		352
WEINBERG	Chaim	M	family		352
WEINSTEIN		M	family		352
WEIKSELBAUM	Moshe	M	family		352
WEISS	Chaim	M	family	Profession Doctor	352
WEISS	Shaul	M	family		352
WEISS		M	family		352
WEISS	Meir	M	family		352
WEISS	Shlomo	M	family		352
WEISS	David	M	family		352

WEISS	Lola	F		Maiden name Fenichel	352
WEISSMAN	Moshe	M	family	Profession Doctor	352
WEISSMAN	Ya'akov	M	family		352
WEISSMAN	Arnold	M	family		352
WEISSBERG	Menashe	M			352
WEISENBERG	Avraham	M	family		352
WILDSTEIN	Bernard	M	family		352
WILDSTEIN	Y.	M	family		352
WILD	Natan	M	family		352
WILF	Chaim	M	family		352
WILK	Chaim David	M	family		352
WILK	Moritz	M	family		352
WIMISNER	Herman Hesiak	M			352
WIMISNER	Meir	M	family		352
WIND	Yisrael	M	family		352
WIETSHNER		M	family		352
WEINER	Mordecai	M	family		352
WEINER	Pinkus	M	family		352
WEINER	Avigdor	M	family		352
WEISTREICH	Ya'akov	M	family		352
WEISTREICH	Yosef	M	family		352
WEITZ	Ben-Zion	M	family		352
WITZTOM			whole family		352
WISZNOWITZ	Max	M	family		352
VEG	Chaim	M	family		352
VEG	Shimon	M	family		352
VEG	Aharon	M	family		352
WELTSCH	Moshe	M	family		352
WELTSCH	Shlomo	M	family		352
WENGER	Yehuda	M	family		352
WESTRAIN	Leon	M	family		352
WESTREICH	Ya'akov	M	family		352
WEXLER	Wolf	M	family		352
WEXLER	Yisrael	M	family		352

WEXLER	Moshe	M			352
WEXLER	Meir	M			352
WERMUT			whole family		352
WERTEIMER	Yehezkel	M	family		352
WERNER	Wolf	M	family		352
WROCLAWSKI	Aharon	M	family		352
WEROBEL	Yosef	M	family		352
WEROBEL	Ayzik	M	family		352
WASSERKURTZ	Naftali	M	family		352
WASSERMAN	Manfred	M			352
VULCAN	Moritz	M	family		352
WEINSTOCK	Maria	F	children		352
WOZNICER	Sarah	F	family		352
WALD	Naftali	M	family		352
WALD	Rivka	F	family		352
WEROBEL	Baila	F			352
WASSERREICH	Moshe	M			352
WURM	Moshe	M			352

ז Zayin

ZAVERSTROM	Henrik	M	family		352
ZAMLER			whole family		352
ZALTZ	Dr. Avraham	M	family		352
ZOMER	Chaim	M	family		353
ZOMER	Simcha	M	family		353
ZOMER	Shmuel	M	family		353
ZOMER	Yitzhak	M	family	Profession Doctor	353
ZANDHOUSE			family		353
SIGMAN	Emanuel	M	family		353
ZIGLER	Leon	M	family		353
ZIGFRIED	Shlomo	M	family		353
ZEIDEN	Moshe	M	family		353
ZEIDEN	Eliyahu	M	family		353
ZEIDEN	Malka	F			353

Surname	Given Name	Sex		Profession	Page
ZEIDENWERG	Ignace	M	family	Profession Doctor	353
ZAINVELL	Shmuel	M	family		353
SILBER	David	M	family		353
SILBER	Yechiel	M	family		353
SILBER	Hilda	F	family		353
SILBIGER	Zigmund	M	family		353
SILBERMAN	M.D.	M	family		353
SILBERMAN	Yosef	M	family	Profession Doctor	353
SILBERMAN	Willhelm	M	family		353
SILBERMAN	Tuvia	M	family		353
SILBERMAN	Leibish	M	family		353
SILBERMAN	Eliezer	M	family		353
SILBERFENIG	Raizel Yenta	F			353
SILBERFENIG	Hindel Ita	F			353
SILBERFENIG	Yishayahu	M	family		353
SILBERFENIG	Netaniel	M	family		353
SILBERSTEIN	Moshe	M	family		353
SILBERSTEIN	Shmuel	M	family		353
SILBERSTEIN	Meir	M	family		353
SILBERSTEIN	Marek	M	family	Profession Magister	353
SILBERSHATZ			whole family		353
SINGER	Efraim	M	family		353
SINGER	Yechiel	M	family		353
SINGER	Ya'akov David	M	family		353
SINGER	Alter	M			353
SINGER	Chaim	M			353
SINGER	Yosef	M			353
SINGER	Yehezkel	M	family		353
SINGER	Sabina	F			353
ZISS	Yitzhak	M	family		353
ZISS	Shlomo	M	family		353
ZISS	Eliezer Lipa	M	family		353
ZIELANKA		M	family		353
ZISSER	M.	M	family		353

ZISKIND	Zlata	F			353
ZISKIND	Aharon	M	family		353
ZISKIND	Pinchas	M	family		353
ZISKIND	Natalia	F	child	Maiden name MANN	353
SELINGER	Lazar	M	family		353
SELINGER	Zigmund	M	family		353
ZEVELLE	Ya'akov	M	family		353
ZEBALD	Yisrael	M	family		353
ZARKER	Wolf	M	family		353
ZAVADER	Moshe Leib	M	family		353
ZAVADER	Leon	M	family		353
ZILMBERMAN	Mendel	M	family		353

ח Chet

CHOCZNER	Aharon	M	family		353
CHOCZNER	David	M	family		353

ט Tet

TODER	Shimon	M	family		353
TAUB	Aharon	M	family		353
TAUBER	Osziasz	M	family		353
TAUBENFELD	Wolf	M	family		353
TAUBELES	Frieda	F	family		353
TALLER	Victor	M	family		353
TALLER	Hersh	M	family		353
TORN	Avraham	M	family		353
TURNHEIM	Shlomo	M	family		353
TURNHEIM	Leon	M	family		353
TURNHEIM	Edward	M	family		353
TURNHEIM	Chuna	M	family		353
TOMM	Shlomo	M	family		353
TOCHFERDERBER			whole family		353
TOCHFERDERBER	Yehuda	M		married	353
TOCHFERDERBER		F		Husband's name Yehuda	353
TURTLETAUB	Yisrael	M	family		353

TOCHSHERER	Moshe	M	family	353
TEITELBAUM	Avraham	M	family	354
TEITELBAUM	Baruch	M		354
TEITELBAUM	Chaim	M	family	354
TEITELBAUM	Simcha	M	family	354
TEITELBAUM	Ben-Zion	M	family	354
TEITEL	Pinkus	M	family	354
TEICHLER	Hela	F		354
TISCH	Henrik	M	family	354
TISCH	Basia	F		354
TIMBERG	M.	M	family	354
TELLER	Shimon	M	family	354
TELLER	Yosef	M	family	354
TELLERMAN	Leib	M	family	354
TEMPLER	Pinkus	M	family	354
TEMPLER	Eliezer	M		354
TEMMER	Yosef Leib	M	family	354
TEMMER	Izak	M	family	354
TENNENBAUM	Shimon	M	family	354
TRATNER	Reuven	M	family	354
TROP	Naftali	M	family	354
TROM	Lipa	M	family	354
TRINTSHER	Lipa	M	family	354
CZOBAN	Jan	M	family	354
CZOBAN	Berel	M	family	354
TALLER	Ya'akov	M		354
TIFENBRON		M	family	354
TINGER		M	family	354
TALLER	Ya'akov	M		354

י **Yod**

YAKOBOWICZ	Leib	M	family	354
YAKOV	Shmuel	M	family	354
YAKOV	Kalman	M	family	354

YABLONSKI			whole family		354
YARMUSH	Shlomo	M	family		354
YEKEL	Ya'akov	M	family	Profession Doctor	354
YAKOBOWICZ	Markus	M	family		354
YAKOBOWICZ	Yosef	M	family		354
YACHNAWICZ	Leibish	M	family		354
YACHNAWICZ	Markus Victor	M			354
YECHIEL	Rabbi Mairal	M			354

כ Kaf   return

KAHANA	Chana	F	family		354
KATZ	Fishel	M	family		354
KAHANA	Wolf	M	family		354
KOMET	Yoanna	F	family	Maiden name LIEBESKIND	354

ל Lamed   return

LADNER			whole family		354
LAUB	Maurycy	M	family		354
LAUB	Shimshon	M	family		354
LAUB	Ayzik	M	family		354
LAUBER	Adolf	M	family		354
LAUB	Markus	M			354
LAUTERBACH	Ya'akov	M	family	Profession Doctor	354
LAUFER	Efraim	M	family		354
LAUFER	Asher	M	family		354
LAUFER	Bernard	M	family		354
LAUFER	Markus	M	family		354
LAUFER	Mordecai	M	family		354
LAUFER	Wolf	M	family		354
LAUFER	Tosza	F	family		354
LAUFER	Shimshon	M	family		354
LAUFER	Leib	M	family		354
LAMENSDORF			whole family		354
LANDMAN	Chaim	M	family		354
LANDMAN	Shaul	M	family		354

Surname	Given Name	Sex	Relation	Notes	Page
LANDMAN	Avraham	M	family		354
LANGER	Chaim	M	family		354
LANGER	Ya'akov	M	family		354
LANGER		M	family	Profession Engineer	354
LANGER	Baruch	M	family		354
LAST	Wolf	M	family		354
LAST	Petachia	M	family		354
SCHILDKRAUT	Chana	F		Maiden name LAST	354
LAST	Yehoshua	M	family		354
LAST	Leibish	M			355
LASHKOWITZ	Shlomo	M	family		355
LUSTGRARTEN	Izak	M	family		355
LUSTIG		M		Profession Doctor	355
LUBASH	David	M	family		355
LUSTGOLD		M	family		355
LIEBLICH	Ignace	M	family		355
LIEBER	Meir	M	family		355
LIEBERMAN	Leon	M	family		355
LIEBER	Moshe	M	family		355
LIEBER	Shimshon	M	family		355
LION	Maurycy	M	family		355
LION	Ignace	M	family		355
LEIB	Bernard	M	family		355
LEIBEL	Anselm	M	family	Profession Doctor	355
LEIBEL	Karol	M	family		355
LEIBEL	Zigmund	M	family		355
LEIBEL	Aharon	M	family		355
LEIBEL	Moshe	M	family		355
LEIBEL	David	M	family		355
LEIBEL	Akiva	M	family		355
LEISTEN	Hersh	M	family		355
LEICHTER	Moshe	M	family	Profession Engineer	355
LEINWAND	Avraham	M	family		355
LEINWAND	Yisrael	M	family		355

LEISTER	Lazar	M	family		355
LEINWAND	Golda	F			355
LICHTBLAU	Adolf	M	family		355
LICHTIK	Alter	M	family		355
LICHTINGER	Osziasz	M	family		355
LICHTIG	Mendel	M	family		355
LINHARD	Meir	M	family		355
LISS	Kalman	M	family		355
LIFSHITZ	Yosef	M	family		355
LIFSHITZ	Meir	M	family		355
LIFSHITZ	Hersh	M	family		355
LIPINER	Mechel	M	family		355
LIRER			whole family		355
LEDER	Naftali	M	family		355
LEZER	Aharon	M	family		355
LEZER	Mendel	M	family		355
LEZER	Yosef	M	family		355
LEVNIOWSKI	Yosef	M	family		355
LEVNIOWSKI	Mendel	M	family		355
LEVINGER			whole family		355
LEBENCROWN	Leib	M	family		355
LEVNIOWSKI	Henrik	M	family		355
LEMEL	B.	M	family		355
LEMBERGER	Yehezkel	M	family		355
LEMBERGER	Moshe	M	family		355
LEMBERGER	Izak	M	family		355
LEFEL	Moshe	M	family		355
LEFELHOLTZ	Shlomo	M	family		355
LERNER	Binyamin Wolf	M	family		355
LERNER	Herman	M	family		355
LERMAN	Pinkus	M	family		355
LERNER		M		Profession Doctor	355
LERFELD	David	M	family		355
LERNER	Zelig	M	family		355

LERER	Rachel	F			355
LERR	Rosa	F			355
LERFELD		M		Wife's maiden name POST	355
LERFELD		F		Maiden name POST	355
LANGER	Yosef	M	family		355
LANGER	Yehoshua	M	family		355
LICHT		M	family		355
LICHTBLAU	Eva	F			355
LICHTBLAU		F		Mother's name Eva	355
LERER	Markus	M	family		355
LICHTENGER	Esther	F	family		355

מ Mem

MAHLER	Avraham	M	family		355
MAHLER	Regina	F			355
MAHLER	Yehoshua	M	family		355
MAURER	Pinkus	M	family		355
MAURER	Hersh	M	family		355
MAURER	Shlomo	M	family		355
MOSEL	Golda	F			355
MOZES	Aharon	M	family		355
MAIBRUCH	Moshe	M	family		355
MAYER	Mendel	M	family		356
MAYERHOF			whole family		356
MALKISHER	Professor Gustav	M	family		356
MOR	Rosa	F	children	Maiden name HERTZMAN	356
MALKISHER		M	family	Profession Administrator	356
MANN	Isidor	M	family		356
MANN	Yosef	M	family		356
MANDEL	Moshe	M	family		356
MONDSCHEIN	Emilia	F	family		356
MANDELBAUM			whole family		356
MANHEIM	Avraham	M	family		356
MANHEIT	Chaim	M	family		356

MANSDORF	Tauba	F	family		356
MONDERER	Julius	M	family		356
MANGEL	Wolf Herman	M	family		356
MONDERER	Izak	M	family		356
MOSNER	Chaim	M	family		356
MARDKOVITCH	Sima	F	family		356
MARGOLIUS	Shlomo	M	family		356
MANTEL	Ya'akov	M	family		356
MARMOR			whole family		356
MARDER	Lazar	M	family		356
MORGENBESSER	Ya'akov	M	family	Profession Professor	356
MARKUS	Moshe	M	family		356
MARGOLIUS	Adam	M	family		356
MARGOLIUS	Artur	M	family		356
MARKFELD	Yosef	M	family		356
MARGOSHES		F			356
MASCHLER	Leon	M		Profession Doctor. Married	356
MASCHLER		F		Husband's name Leon	356
MASCHLER	Ignace	M	family		356
MASCHLER	Yosef	M	family		356
MOSHEL	Chaim	M	family		356
MILLER	Zigmund	M	family		356
MILLER	Yisrael	M	family		356
MILLER	Yosef	M	family		356
MINGELGREEN			whole family		356
MINTZ	Mendel	M	family		356
MINTZ	Menachem	M	family		356
MITZ	Leon	M	family	Profession Magister	356
MINTZER	Hersh	M	family		356
MIREH	Osziasz	M			356
MIREH	Shmuel	M	family		356
MITZ	Chaim	M	family		356
METT	Ya'akov	M	family		356
MEREL	Chaim	M	family		356

MELINGER	Natan	M	family		356
METZGER	Wolf	M	family		356
MEHR	Shlomo	M	family		356
MELINGER	Avraham	M	family		356
MESSINGER	Herman	M	family		356
MEREL	Izak	M	family		356
MEVES	M.	M	family		356
MENDERER	Mstislav	M	family	Profession Doctor	356
MESSINGER	Wolf	M	family		356
MESSINGER	Markus	M	family		356
MESSINGER	David	M	family		356
METZGER	Izak	M	family		356
MERTZ		F	family		356
MERTZ	Julius	M	family	Profession Doctor	356
MELACH	Rivka	F			356
MESHEL	Rosa	F		Maiden name BLOND	356
MANSDORF	Chava	F		Maiden name REIVER	356
MINGELGREEN		M	family		356
MAIS	Pinkus	M	family		356
METZENDORF		M	family		356
MAHLER	Anda	F		Maiden name ZAVADER	356

נ **Nun** return

NOVAK			whole family		356
NATT	Hersh	M	family		356
NATT	Shaul	M	family		356
NATT	Zigmund	M	family		356
NACHMAN	Wolf	M	family		356
NEIBERG	Zisha	M	family		356
NIZINSKY	Ya'akov	M	family		356
NEIGASSER	Willhelm	M	family		356
NEIGASSER	Emil	M		Profession Magister	356
NEIMAN	Shlomo	M	family		356
NEIMAN	Ben-Zion	M	family		356

NEIMAN	Herman	M	family	Profession Doctor	357
NEIMAN	Henrik	M	family		357
NEIMAN	Yehezkel	M	family		357
NISSENFELD	Karol	M			357
NEIMAN	Moshe	M	family		357
NATHAN	Salamon	M	family		357
NEIFELD		M	family		357
NATT	Sabina	F			357
NATT		F		Mother's name Sabina	357
NISSENFELD	Chana	F			357
NISSENFELD	Kalman	M			357
NAVAMIAST		M	family		357

ס Samech return

SALAMON	Ignace	M	family	Profession Pharmacist	357
SALPETER	Zelig	M	family		357
SALPETER	Shmuel	M	family		357
SOLENDER	Hersh	M	family		357
SAMBAR	Max Meir	M	family		357
SALAMON	Fruma	F	children	Maiden name GELLER	357
SAPIR	Klara	F			357
SIMCHEH	Maurycy	M	family	Profession Doctor	357
SOKMAN	Chaim	M	family		357
SOKMAN	Yosef	M	family		357
SOKMAN	Isser	M	family		357
STASZOWSKI	Hersh	M	family		357
SPODEK	David	M	family		357
SROKA	Meir	M	family		357
SROKA	Yisrael	M		Profession Doctor	357
SOKOLER	Leon	M	family		357
SALAMON	Azriel	M	family		357
SALAMON	Reuven	M			357
SACHWALD	Shimon	M	family		357

 Ayin

EVERSHTARK	Izak	M	family		357
EDER	Hersh	M	family		357
EDER	Shmuel	M	family		357
EDER	Izak	M	family		357
EDELSTEIN	Antonina	F			357
EDELSTEIN			whole family		357
ETTINGER	Avraham	M	family		357
ELIASH	Chaim	M	family		357
ELIASH	Yoel	M	family		357
ELEND	Ya'akov	M	family		357
ELEND	Markus	M	family		357
ENGELHARD	Moshe	M	family	Profession Engineer	357
ENGELHARD	Artur	M		Profession Doctor	357
ENDER	Sender	M	family		357
ENGLANDER	Gutman	M	family		357
ENGLANDER	Avraham Ya'akov	M	family		357
ENGLANDER	Chaim	M	family		357
ENGEL	David	M	family		357
ENGEL	Yechiel	M	family		357
ENGLANDER	Shmuel	M	family		357
ENGELBERG	Yitzhak	M	family		357
ENGLANDER	Yechiel	M	family		357
ENDER	Zelda	F			357
ENDER	Rivka	F			357
EKSTEIN		M	family		357
EHRLICH	Yehoshua	M	family		357
EHRLICH	Vigdor	M	family		357
EHRLICH	Chaim	M	family		357
EHRLICH	Fishel	M	family		357
EHRENFREUND	Henrik	M	family	Profession Doctor	357
EHRLICH	Moshe	M	family		357
ECKER	Shmuel	M	family		357
EHRENBERG			whole family		357

ENGLANDER	Moshe	M			357
ECKER	Mendel	M			357
ECKER	Sarah	F			357
ECKER	Yehezkel	M			357
ENGEL	Motel	M			357
ENGEL	Wolf	M			357
EHRLICH	Rivka	F		Maiden name ZAVADER	357

פ Peh

FABER	Izak	M	family		357
FABER	Binyamin	M	family		357
FABER	Natan	M	family		357
FABER	Mala	F	child	Maiden name ENGELHARD	357
FABIAN	Ya'akov	M	family		358
FOGLER	Bernard	M	family		358
FAGELFANG	Hersh Leib	M	family		358
FAGELFANG	Alter	M	family		358
FOGELHUT	Shlomo	M	family		358
PADAVER	Yosef	M	family		358
PADAVER	Naftali	M	family		358
POST	Avraham	M	family		358
POST	Naftali	M	family		358
POTASCHMANN	Berel	M	family		358
POTASCHMANN	Maita	F			358
POTASCHMACHER	Mendel	M	family		358
PACHER			whole family		358
POLANECKY	Janas	M	family		358
POLANECKY	Artur	M	family		358
PALMAN	Simcha	M	family		358
POMERANTZ	Lazar	M	family		358
POMERANTZ	Anna	F			358
FAST	Regina	F	child	Maiden name SAMBAR	358
FAST	Shimon	M	family	Profession Rabbi	358
FAST	Moshe	M	family		358

PASTERNACK	Yehezkel	M	family		358
PASTRONG	Sender	M	family		358
PASTRONG	Shlomo	M	family		358
PASTRONG	Hersh	M	family		358
FARSHTENZER	Hersh	M	family		358
FARNEM	Naftali	M	family		358
FARNEM	Yisrael	M	family		358
FARSHIRAM	Sarah	F	family		358
PODER	Yisrael	M	family		358
FOX	Shmelka	M	family		358
FOX	Shalom	M	family		358
FOX	Nisan	M	family		358
POSS	Sender	M	family		358
FINDER	Shimon	M	family		358
FINDER	Izak	M	family		358
FEIVEL	Lazar	M	family	Profession Doctor	358
FEIVEL	Ya'akov	M	family		358
FIRESTEIN	Noach	M	family		358
FAIGENABAUM	Shmuel	M	family		358
FAIGENABAUM	Yosef	M	family		358
FIREAIZEN	Moshe	M	family		358
FIER	Yisrael	M	family		358
FIER	Anshel	M	family		358
FIER	Hersh	M	family		358
PILARSDORF	Zigmund	M	family		358
FINEBERGER	Eliash	M	family		358
PINTER	Binyamin	M	family		358
FINK	Naftali	M	family		358
FINK	Wolf	M	family	Profession Judge	358
FINK	Ignace	M	family		358
FINK	Adolf	M	family		358
FINKELSTEIN	Yosef	M	family		358
FISH	Meir	M	family		358
FISH	Pinkus	M	family		358

FISH	Yehuda	M	family	Profession Professor	358
FISH	Ignace	M	family	Profession Doctor	358
FISH	Chaim	M	family		358
FISH	Mordecai	M	family		358
FISHLER	Yosef	M	family		358
FISHMAN	Moshe	M	family		358
FISHBEIN	Wolf	M	family		358
FIRESTEIN	Paul	M	family		358
FEINER	Yidel	M	family		358
FEINER	Shimon	M	family		358
FEINER	Vigdor	M	family		358
FISHELBERG	Emanuel	M	family		358
FISHLER	Shaul	M	family		358
FISHLER	Hersh	M	family	Profession Doctor	358
FLAUM			whole family		358
PLATO			whole family		358
FLAUMENHAFT	Oscar	M	family		358
FLAUMENHAFT	Ya'akov	M	family		358
PLATNER	Adolf	M	family		358
PLEMTSER	Herman	M	family		358
PLASHEN	Moshe	M	family		358
PLACHTEH	Leon	M	family	Profession Engineer	358
FLEISHER	Sofia	F			358
FLOR	Henrik	M	family		358
FLOR	Eliash	M	family		359
FLOR	Max	M			359
FLEISCHER	Shmuel	M	family		359
FLEISCHER	Eliezer	M	family		359
FLEISCHER	Zenon	M	family		359
FLEISCHER	Izak	M	family		359
FLINK	Lazar	M	family		359
FLINK	Zelig	M	family		359
FLINK	Asher	M	family		359
FLINK	Leon	M	family		359

FLECK	Leib	M	family	359
FLETSCHER	Shlomo	M	family	359
FELBER	Mechel	M	family	359
FELDBAUM	Gustav	M	family	359
FELD	Julius	M	family	359
FELD	Aniella	F	family	359
FELD	Maurycy	M	family	359
FELD	Moshe	M	family	359
FELD	Arnold	M		359
FELDMAUS	Chanina	M	family	359
FELDGREVER	Osziasz	M	family	359
FENIG	Yisrael	M	family	359
FENIK	Aharon	M	family	359
FENIK	Adolf	M	family	359
FELLER	Mendel	M	family	359
Fenichel	Reuven	M	family	359
Fenichel	Esther	F	family	359
Fenichel	Mendel	M	family	359
Fenichel	Chuna	M	family	359
Fenichel	Zigmund	M	family	359
Fenichel	Chaim	M	family	359
Fenichel	Bernard	M	family	359
FEFFER	Chanina	M	family	359
FERBER	Mechel	M	family	359
PERLBERGER	Bronislawa	F		359
PERLBERGER	Markus	M	family	359
PERLBERGER	Yosef	M	family	359
PERLMUTTER	Vigdor	M	family	359
PERLBERGER	Osziasz	M	family	359
PEARLSTEIN	H.	M	family	359
FARSHTENDIK	Max	M	family	359
FRIEDMAN	Rabbi Zev	M	family	359
FRANK	David	M	family	359
FRANK	Hadassah	F		359

PROWIZER	Henrik	M	family		359
PRIMUS		M	family	Profession Magister	359
FRIEDMAN	Chaim	M	family		359
FRIEDMAN	Menachem Mendel	M	family	Profession Hatmaker	359
FRIEDMAN	Ya'akov Shimon	M	family		359
FRIEDLER			whole family		359
FRIED	Osziasz	M	family		359
PRICE	Feivel	M	family		359
PRICE	David	M	family		359
PRICE	Leah	F			359
PRICE	Shimon	M	family		359
PRICE	Leon	M	family		359
PRICE	Moshe	M	family		359
PRICE	Ya'akov	M	family		359
PRICE	Ignace	M	family		359
FERENTZ	Chana	F	children	Maiden name PRICE	359
FREIMAN	Natan Nahum	M	family		359
FREIMAN	Markus	M	family		359
FREIREICH	Yehuda	M	family		359
FRISHTAK	Ya'akov	M	family		359
FRISH	Yosef	M	family		359
FRELICH	Meir	M	family		359
FRANKEL	Eliyahu	M	family		359
FRANKEL	Avraham	M	family		359
FRIEDLICH			whole family		359
FOGEL	Shimon	M	family		359
FOGEL	Lazar	M	family		359
FABER	Miriam	F	family	Maiden name POTASCHMANN	359
POMERANTZ	Franciska	F			359
FEDER			whole family		359
FARGASH	Fanny	F			359
FARSHIRM	Baruch	M	family		359
FELD	Professor	M	family		359

צ Tzadik

SOUDER	Izak	M	family		360
SOUDERER	David	M	family		360
ZUGHAFT	Abba	M	family		360
ZUGHAFT	Shmuel	M	family		360
ZUCKER	Shmuel	M	family		360
ZUCKER	Shlomo	M	family		360
ZWEIBEL	Chaim David	M	family		360
ZWEIBEL	Ya'akov	M	family		360
ZWEIG	Reuven	M	family		360
ZWICKELBERG	Ya'akov	M	family		360
ZWECHER	Zvi	M	family		360
CETAR	Shmelka	M	family		360
CITRONENBAUM	Bezalel Meir	M	family		360
CITRONENBAUM	Yitzhak	M	family		360
ZIGELTUCH	Dora	F	family		360
CESEAR	Shmuel	M	family		360
ZIMMERMAN	Ya'akov	M	family		360
ZIMMERMAN	Yisrael	M	family		360
ZIMETBAUM	Shmuel	M	family		360
ZEICHNER	Hela	F			360
ZEICHNER	David	M		Mother's name Tzila	360
ZEIZLER	Natan	M	family		360
ZEIZLER	Yosef	M	family		360
CHIECHODOWSKY	Aharon	M	family		360
ZINZ	Shmuel	M	family		360
ZETEL	Tzila	F	family		360
ZELNICK	Asher	M	family		360
ZELT	Shmuel	M	family		360
ZELNICK	Lazar	M	family		360
ZECH	Bernard	M	family	Profession Doctor	360
ZEIZLER	Pesach	M	family		360
ZEIZLER	Yisrael	M	family		360

ZELLER	Yosef	M		360
ZEMIR	Yosef	M	family	360
ZELT	Ya'akov	M	family	360
ZELNICK	Rosa	F		360

ק Kof

KAHLER			whole family	360
KAUFMAN	Markus	M	family	360
KAUFMAN	Ayzik	M	family	360
KAUFMAN	Chaim	M	family	360
KAUFMAN	Reuven	M	family	360
KOCH	Yisrael	M	family	360
KOCH	Moshe	M	family	360
KOCH	Menka	F	family	360
KOCH	Feivel	M	family	360
KOCH	Yehezkel	M	family	360
KOCH	Shimon	M	family	360
KOCH	Mendel	M	family	360
KOLB	Henrik	M	family	360
KALPOS	Yitzhak	M		360
KAMPF	Shmuel	M	family	360
KAMPF	Henrik	M	family	360
KAMPF	Moshe	M	family	360
KAMPF	Osziasz	M	family	360
KAMPF	Ayzik	M	family	360
KANARECK	Yehoshua	M	family	360
KANT	Henrik	M	family	360
KANER	Feiga	F	family	360
KOSE	Leib	M	family	360
KOSTMAN			whole family	360
KAPLER	Oscar	M	family	360
KAPELNER	Bernard	M	family	360
KAPELNER	Maurycy	M	family	360
KAPELNER	Izak	M	family	360

KATZ	Binyamin	M	family		360
KATZ		F		Maiden name MUSKATENBLIT	360
KORN	Chaim Hersh	M	family		360
KORN	Hershel	M			360
KORNHAUSER	Emanuel	M	family		360
KORNHAUSER	Yechiel	M	family		360
KORNBLITT	Lazar	M	family		360
KORNREICH	Hersh Meir	M	family		360
KORNREICH	Sarah	F	family		360
KORNILO	Shalom	M	family		360
KORNILO	Rivka	F			361
KORNILO		F		Mother's name Rivka	361
KORNREICH	Matityahu	M	family		361
KWADRATSTEIN	Leib	M	family		361
KWADRATSTEIN			whole family		361
COOPERMAN	Markus	M	family		361
COOPFER	Yoel	M	family		361
COOPERBLULM	Aharon	M	family		361
COOPERMAN	Moshe	M	family		361
KORTZ	Yitzhak	M	family		361
KORTZ	Ya'akov	M	family		361
KORTZ	Yechiel	M	family		361
KORTZ	Leib	M	family		361
KORTZ	Rabbi Shlomo	M	family		361
KISTEN	Avraham	M	family		361
KIPPEL	Yosef Meir	M	family		361
KIPPEL	Feivel	M	family		361
KIPPEL	Shlomo	M	family		361
KIRSCH	Adolf	M	family		361
KIRSCH	Mendel	M	family		361
KIRSCH	Herman	M	family		361
KIRSHENBAUM	Rabbi Yosef	M	family		361
KIRSHENBAUM	Izak	M	family		361

KEITELMAN	Herman	M			361
KIEL	Ya'akov	M	family		361
KIEL	Lazar	M	family		361
KIEL	Salo	M	family		361
KIEL	Avraham	M	family		361
KAITCH	Avraham	M	family		361
KAITCH	Yisrael	M	family		361
KITAY	Professor	M	family		361
KLAHR	Willhelm	M	family		361
KLAHR	Yosef	M	family		361
KLAUSNER	Moshe	M	family		361
KLAUSNER	Shmuel	M	family		361
KLAPHOLTZ	Henrik	M	family		361
KLAPHOLTZ	Yehezkel	M	family		361
KLAPHOLTZ	Izak	M	family		361
KLAPHOLTZ	M.	M	family		361
KLAPHOLTZ	Shlomo	M			361
KLUGER	Herman	M	family		361
KLEIN	Yosef	M	family		361
KLEINMAN	Chaim	M	family		361
KLEIN	Eliash	M	family		361
KLEINHENDLER	Herman	M	family		361
KLEINHENDLER	David	M			361
KLEINHENDLER	Shimon	M	family		361
KLEINMAN	Leon	M	family		361
KLEINBERGER	Ignace	M		Profession Doctor	361
KLEIN	Karolina	F			361
KLEIN	Pesach	M	family		361
KLEIN	Zelig	M	family		361
KLEINPISAL	Artur	M			361
KLEINMAN	Pinkus	M	family		361
KLEINKOPF	Shlomo	M	parents		361
KLEINBERGER	Yehuda	M	family		361
KLEIN	Shimon	M	family		361

KLEINER	Osziasz	M	family		361
KLEIN	M.	M	family		361
KLEPEL	Sh.	M			361
KNABEL	Pinkus	M	family		361
KNOBLOCH	Yosef	M	family		361
KNECHT ZEIDMAN	Yehezkel	M	family		361
KEGEL	Maurycy	M	family		361
KEGEL	Gizellah	F		Maiden name GROSS	361
GROSS		F		Mother's name Gizella	361
KELLER	Yosef	M	family		361
KELLER	Shmuel	M	family		361
KELNER	Markus	M	family		361
KENIG		M	family	Profession Doctor	361
KERNER	Zigmund	M	family		361
KROKNER	Wolf	M	family		361
KEGEL	Dora	F	family	Maiden name KRANTZ	361
KRISHER	Markus	M	family		361
KRESCH	Professor	M	family		361
KRUMHOLTZ	Zigmund	M	family		361
KREIGER	Yehezkel	M	family		361
KRIEZLER	Henrik	M	family		361
KLAUBAUF			family		361
KAMM	Leibish	M			361
KAMM	Fishel	M			361
KALPOS	Naftali	M	family		361
KOCH	Leib	M	family		362
KELLER	Gizellah	F			362
KORN	Ya'akov	M			362
KLAPHOLTZ	Berta	F		Maiden name POTASCHMANN	362
KRANZLER	Idsa	F		Maiden name Fenichel	362
KESTENBAUM		M	family		362
KRISHER	Peretz	M	family		362
KETZ	Chaim	M	family		362

KATZNER			whole family		362
KRANISH			whole family		362

ר Resh

RAAB	Bernard	M	family		362
RADWAN	Malka	F	family		362
RAUSH	Henrik	M	family		362
RAUSH	Aharon	M	family		362
ROCHVERG	Maria	F	family		362
ROCHVERG	Eliezer Lazar	M	family		362
ROVNER	Edward	M	family		362
ROSEN	Meir	M	family		362
ROSNER	Yehuda	M	family		362
ROSENBERG	Markus	M	family		362
ROSENBERG	Shalom	M	family		362
ROSENBERG	Gittel	F	family		362
ROSENBLATT	Ya'akov	M	family	Profession Engineer	362
ROSENSZTOK	Simcha	M	family		362
ROSENBLIT	Willhelm	M	family		362
ROSENBLIT	Chaim	M	family		362
ROSENBAUM	Ya'akov	M	family		362
ROSENBAUM	Meir	M	family		362
ROSENBAUM		M		Wife's maiden name DOMLER	362
ROSENBAUM		F		Maiden name DOMLER	362
ROSENTAL	Leib	M	family		362
ROSENBUSCH	Dr. Maxmilian	M			362
ROSENBLATT	Bendit	M	family		362
ROSENZWEIG	Aharon	M	family		362
ROT	Herman	M	family		362
ROT	Berel	M	family		362
ROT	Theodor	M	family		362
ROTENBERG	Binyamin	M	family		362
ROTENBERG	Salo	M	family		362
RAND	Natan	M	family		362

Surname	Given Name	Sex	Relation	Profession	Page
RAPAPORT	Ayzik	M	family		362
RAPAPORT	Wolf	M	family		362
RUBEL	Klara Chaya	F	family		362
RUBEL	Yosef	M	family		362
RUBIN	Alexander	M	family		362
RUBIN	Chaim	M	family		362
RUBIN	Stanislaw	M	family	Profession Magister	362
RUBINSTEIN	Hersh	M	family		362
RITER		M	family	Profession Doctor	362
REIVER	Yosef	M	family		362
REIN			whole family		362
REICH	Shmuel	M	family	Profession Doctor	362
REICH	Moshe	M		Profession Engineer	362
REICH	David	M	family		362
REICH	Ignace	M	family	Profession Magister	362
REICH	Chaim	M	family		362
REICH	Vaitziach	M	family		362
REICH	Yisrael	M	family		362
REICH		M	family	Profession Pharmacist	362
RIMER	Naftali	M	family		362
REICHMAN	Shlomo	M	family		362
REICHMAN	Chaim	M	family		362
REINHOLD	Melech	M	family		362
REINHOLD	Aharon	M	family		362
REINER	Tina	F	family		362
RICE	Paul	M	family		362
REIFEN	Meir	M	family		362
RINDER	Yosef	M	family		362
RINDER	Baruch	M			362
RICK	Moshe	M			362
REBHAN	Avraham	M	family		362
REBHON	Lazar	M	family		362
REDER	Yosef	M	family		362
RESSLER	Chaim	M	family		362

RESSLER	Professor	M	family		362
REMER	Rosa	F	children	Maiden name KEGEL	362
ROSEN	Shlomo Kalman	M			362
ROSEN	Zev	M	family		362
ROSEN	Avraham	M	family		363
RAPAPORT	Shabtai	M			363
ROSENSZTOK	Yisrael	M	family		363
ROSENSZTOK	Nisan	M	family		363
REICH	Ya'akov	M			363
ROSENSZTOK	Hersh	M	family		363
RUBIN	Ernestina	F			363
ROCHVERG	Shabtai	M	family		363
ROSENZWEIG	David	M			363
REINBACH	Yosef	M			363
REINBACH	Yisrael	M			363
REINBACH	Avraham Gershon	M			363
REINBACH	David	M			363
RENNERT	Nachman	M	family		363

ש Shin

SHACHNER	Leib	M	family		363
SHACHER	Ya'akov	M	family		363
SHALIT	Dr. Edward	M	family		363
SHAMROT	Moshe Hersh	M	family		363
SCHANZER	Karol	M	family	Profession Engineer	363
SHAPIRA	Sh.	M	family		363
SHORNSHTEIN	Dr. Julius	M		married	363
SHORNSHTEIN		F		Husband's name Julius	363
SHULBAUM			whole family		363
SCHWARTZKACHEL	Herman	M	family		363
SHULERER	Gedalyahu	M	family		363
SCHWARTZKICHEL	Leon	M	family		363
SCHWEITZ	Yisrael	M	family		363
SHWEIDT	Izak	M	family		363

Surname	Given Name	Sex	Family	Notes	Page
SCHWARTZ	Abush	M			363
SCHWARTZ	Ya'akov	M	family		363
SCHWARTZ	Shimon	M	family		363
SCHWINGER	Zev	M	family		363
SCHWIMMER	Shlomo	M	family		363
SCHWEBER	Moshe	M	family		363
SCHWEBER			whole family		363
STARK			whole family		363
STARKMAN	Franciska	F			363
STAMBERGER	Shlomo	M	family		363
SHTUB	Yishayahu	M	family		363
SHTURM	Ya'akov	M	family		363
SHTURM	Avraham	M	family		363
SHTEIER	Zigmund	M	family		363
SHTEIER	Eliash	M	family		363
SHIDLER	Herman	M	family		363
SHIDLER	Leon	M	family		363
SHIDLER	Edward	M	family		363
SHINAGEL	Artur	M			363
SHINAGEL	Ignace	M			363
SHINDEL	David	M	family		363
SHINDEL	Ya'akov	M	family		363
SCHIFF	Aharon	M	family		363
SCHIFF	Adolf	M	family		363
SCHIFF	David	M	family		363
SCHIFF	Chanina	M	family		363
SCHIFF	Zigmund	M	family	Profession Engineer	363
SCHIFF	Shmuel	M	family		363
SCHIFF	Shlomo	M	family		363
SCHIFF	Willhelm	M	family		363
SHIPMAN	Moshe	M	family		363
SCHEPS	Pesach	M	family		363
SCHIFFER	Yitzhak	M	family		363
SCHIFFER	Abek	M	family		363

SHTIL	Nehemia	M	family	363
SHTIL	Yona	M	family	363
STEIN	Ayzik	M	family	363
STEINHAUER	Hersh	M	family	363
STEINER	Ya'akov	M	family	363
SHTIGLITZ	Herman	M	family	363
SHTIGLITZ	Wolf	M	family	363
STEIGLER	Julius	M	family	363
STEIGLER	Maurycy	M	family	363
SZTEINBOK		M	family	363
STEIN	Yitzhak	M		363
STEIN	Chasha			363
SZTEINHORN	Binyamin	M	family	363
STRAUSS	Reuven	M	family	363
STRAUSS	Ayzik	M	family	363
STRAUSS	Henrik	M	family	363
SZTROM	Avraham	M	family	363
STRAUSS	Avraham	M	family	364
SZTROM	Dora	F	family	364
SHTRAMER	N.	M	family	364
SZTROM	Moshe	M	family	364
SZROBING	Moshe	M	family	364
SZTROM	Ya'akov Zvi	M	family	364
STERN	Natan	M	family	364
STERN	Lazar	M	family	364
STERN	Adolf	M	family	364
STERNLICHT	Izak	M	family	364
STRICKER		M	family	364
SCHLANGENKOPF		M	family	364
SCHLAFF	Yisrael	M	family	364
SHLISEL	Ya'akov	M	family	364
SHLISEL	Yisrael Chaim	M	family	364
SHLISEL	Moshe	M	family	364
SCHLESINGER	Leib	M	family	364

SCHMUKLER	Leon	M	family	364
SCHMUKLER	Chaim	M	family	364
SCHMIDT	Lipa	M	family	364
SCHMIDT	Azyik	M	family	364
SCHMIDT	Mendel	M	family	364
SCHNUR	Yitzhak	M	family	364
SCHNUR	Shaul	M	family	364
SCHNUR	Naftali	M	family	364
SCHNEIDER	David	M	family	364
SCHNEIDER	Ben-Zion	M	family	364
SCHNEIDER	Peretz	M	family	364
SCHNEIDER	Shlomo	M	family	364
SCHNEPS	Hinda	F	family	364
SCHECHTER	Feivel	M	family	364
SCHECHTER	Yisrael	M	family	364
SCHECHTER	Pinkus	M	family	364
SHENAUG	Moshe	M	family	364
SHENBERG	Shlomo	M	family	364
SHIVITZ	Avraham	M	family	364
SHILAI	Ya'akov	M	family	364
SCHILLER	Shimon	M	family	364
SCHILDKRAUT	Yisrael	M	family	364
SHEDLESKER	Aharon	M	family	364
SHEDLESKER	Necha	F	children	364
SHENBERG	Chaim	M	family	364
SHENBERG	Roman	M	family	364
SHENVETER	Willhelm	M	family	364
SHENFELD	Dr. Simcha	M	family	364
SHENKEL	Dr. Wolf	M	family	364
SHENKEL	Natan	M	family	364
SHENKEL	Nahum	M	family	364
SHENIRER	Asher Arieh	M	family	364
SHENKEL	Yisrael	M	family	364
SHENIRER	Yehuda Moshe	M		364

SHER	Shalom	M	family		364
SHER	Eliash	M	family		364
SHPATZ	Chaim	M	family		364
SHERMAN	Yehuda	M	family		364
SZPORN	Shlomo	M			364
SZPORN	Feiga	F			364
SZPORN	Hinda	F			364
SZPORN	Chaim	M			364
SZPORN	Avraham	M			364
SPANGELET	Avraham	M	family		364
SPANGELET	David	M	family		364
SPANGELET	Alter	M	family		364
SPEIGEL	B.	M			364
SPEIGEL	Dr. Leon	M	family		364
SPEISER	Henrik	M	family		364
SPEISER	Dr. Bezalel	M			364
SHPIELFOGEL	Henrik	M	family		364
SCHWARTZBARD	Herman	M			364
STEINER	Berel	M	family		364
STAREL			whole family		364
SZTROM SHPITZEN	Yisrael	M	family		364
SZTROM	Nisan	M	family		364
SHINDEL	Chaim	M	family		364
SCHIFF	Yehuda	M	family		364
SCHIFF	Ya'akov	M	family		364
SCHIFF	Yitzhak	M	family		364
SCHIFF	Rachel	F	family		364
SCHIFF	Shaul	M	family		364
SCHIFF	Yehoshua	M		Profession Engineer	364
SCHIFF	Adolf Avraham Ya'akov	M			364
STRASSBERG	Risia	F			364
SCHLENGER	Alter	M	family		364
SCHLENGER	Mendel	M	family		365

SHMOLBERG			whole family		365
SCHMUKLER	Leon	M	family		365
SCHNEIDER	Moshe	M	family		365
SCHNEPS	Avraham	M	family		365
SHENBACH			whole family		365
SHPANGELET	Sarah	F	family		365
SHER	Sheindel Tzlova	F			365
SCHECHTER	Ya'akov	M	family		365
SPERBER	Yehezkel	M	family		365
SPERLING	Avraham	M	family		365
SHPITZIN SZTROM		M	family		365
SPIELMAN	Henrik	M		Profession Magister	365
SPINROD			whole family		365
SPINROD	Dr. A.	M	family		365
SPINROD	Ludwik	M	family		365
SHPILER	Eric	M			365
SHPILER	Fritz	M			365
SHAPIRA	Yosef	M			365
SHAPIRA	Yehezkel	M	family		365
SHAPIRA	Maurycy	M	family		365
SHAPIRA	M.	M	family		365
SPENADEL	Moshe	M	family		365
SHPET	Alter Moshe	M	family		365
SHPRITZER	Eliash	M	family		365
SHPRINGER	Eliash	M	family		365
SHPRINGER	Shmuel	M	family		365
SCHREIBER	Moshe	M	family		365
SHAROV	Hersh	M	family		365
SCHREIBER	Bluma	F	family		365
SHINDEL	Tuvyahu	M	family		365
SHPANGELET	Sarah	F		Maiden name HONIG	365
SCHILING	Gittel	F	family		365
SCHILDKRAUT			whole family		365

[Page 369]

Memorial Pages

Annual anniversary [Yahrzeit] 26th Sivan
For the Martyrs of the Community of

Tarnow

and the surrounding area

This stone shall be for us a memorial and an everlasting reminder of the memory of our parents, brothers, sisters, wives and children - martyrs who were murdered and slaughtered, were cremated and buried alive following terrible torture by the cruel Nazis, Germans and their accursed accomplices, may their names be erased, in the days of annihilation and murder during the years 5699-5705. The earth shall not cover their blood and the purity of their memory shall not part from within us.

May the Lord avenge their blood. May their souls be bound in the bond of eternal life. In perpetuation, the former inhabitants of Tarnow.

Chamber of the Holocaust
Jerusalem - Mount Zion

[Page 370]

In remembrance of our lost souls

Gavriel and Berta Osterweil

Perished in the Shoah. May G–d avenge their blood.

Memorialized:
Yosef Kornilo

In Memoriam

My father **Yosef Izrael** son of **Avraham** born 1869

My mother **Fayga** daughter of **Avraham Yitzhak Bajtrag**

My son **Yosef Izrael** son of **Avraham** born 1940

My sister **Mina Brand** daughter of **Yosef** born 1896

My sister **Berta Adler** daughter of **Yosef** born 1898

My brother **Dovid Izrael** son of Yosef born 1899

All perished in the Tarnow ghetto

May their souls be bound up in the bond of everlasting life

Memorialized:
Avraham Izrael – Montreal-Canada

[Page 371]

In Eternal Memory

My father **Akiva Ajzenbach**

My mother **Rywka Ajzenbach** born: **Metzker**

My sister **Gita Rajn**

My brother-in-law **Yakov Rajn**

Their children **Henri and Regina**

And the entire **Ajzenbach** family who were annihilated during the Holocaust

Memorialized in grief:
Anshel Ajzenbach Nancy – France

In Sacred Memory

My father **Naftali Zev Irum**

My mother **Sima**

And their children:
Rywka, Dovid, Miriam and Moshe Yekl

From the left: Reb Naftali Zev Irum and Reb Alter Lewi

This picture of my father and his friend, Reb Alter Lewi was found by a German family in Germany it gives evidence of what manner the Nazi rulers ridiculed their victims.

My father, of blessed memory, who dealt with the needs of the people, and over the course of many years was *gabbai* [sexton] at the *Talmud Torah* [school for poor boys], in the Sandzer *kloyz* [one-room synagogue] and the *Chevra Kadishe* [burial society] in Tarnow.

My entire above-mentioned family was annihilated by the Nazi murderers.

May G–d avenge their blood.

Memorialized:
Elimelekh Irum, Tel Aviv

[Page 372]

In Memory

Dovid Batist

The valuable activist from the Bund in Tarnow

Memorialized:
Comrades and Friends

Dovid Batist

In Sacred Memory

My father **Nusan Birman**, died in the year 1932

My mother **Mindla Birman**

My sister **Chana Birman**

My sister **Sala Birman**

My sister **Monka** and child

My sister **Lola Birman**

Mother and sisters perished at the hands of the Nazis in 1942

May G–d avenge their blood.

Presented by:
Maurici Birman, Montreal-Canada

In Sacred Memory

Yosef Bergman and wife **Anna Bergman** born **Gelb**

Mendl Bergman and wife **Cecilia** born **Kamp** and children **Rayzl and Hirsh**

Avraham Bergman and his wife and child

Moshe Bergman and his wife and child

Dovid Bergman and wife **Cesia** born **Ickowicz** and child **Hersh**

Sura Bergman born **Lerman**

May their souls be bound up in the bond of eternal life.

Memorialized:
Yezsha Bergman, Tarnow

[Page 373]

In Eternal Memory

My father **Avraham Binensztok** perished in Auschwitz in 1942
My mother **Chaya** daughter of **Menasha** perished in the Tarnow ghetto in 1943

My sister **Dwoyra Herszkowicz** perished in the Tarnow ghetto in 1942

My brother-in-law **Shabtai Herszkowicz** perished in the Tarnow ghetto in 1942

Their children: **Sura, Ita, Perl and Menasha** perished in the Tarnow ghetto, 1942

My brother **Melekh Binensztok** and his wife **Gitl** and daughter **Rut** perished with a Christian family in Germany

My brother Mendl perished in the Melk concentration camp in 1944

May G–d Avenge Them

May their souls be bound up in the bond of eternal life.

Memorialized by:
Leizer (Eliezer) Binensztok*
Yisroel Binensztok
Moshe Binensztok
Montreal-Canada

*Alas, Eliezer Binensztok died in Montreal at the beginning of 1968. The pre-mature death of the many years active member and chairman of the auditing committee of the Tarnow *Landsmanschaft* [society of people from the same town] in Montreal – evoked deep sorry in the hearts of the Tarnow *landsleit* [people from the same town] there. The managing committee of the *landsmanschaft* in Montreal with the Friends Ahron Szparn (chairman) and F. Gelernter, M. Birman and M. Hazenberg (vice chairman) expresses in this manner to the family of the deceased, Mrs. Regina, the daughter Helen, the sons, Hershl and Shmuel and the brothers, Moshe and Yisroel, our most heartfelt sympathy in their deep sadness with the hope they will not know any more hardship.

[Page 374]

In Eternal Memory

Haber and his wife born Blauner and their son

Leon Blauner and wife **Leah** born **Ajzner**

Yehezkiel Blauner and wife **Rukhl** born **Wild** and children **Pinek** and **Ada**

Nusan (Nutek) Blauner and wife **Tsila** born **Biber** and two daughters

Fredek Haber and wife **Hania** born **Blauner** and son **Hilush**

Moshe Ajzen and wife **Hinda** born **Blauner** and daughter **Romek Blauner**

All were murdered at the hands of the Nazi murderers

May their souls be bound up in the bond of eternal life

Memorialized:
Mina Blauner-Ziskind, Berlin

[Page 375]

For an eternal memorial

Rabbi Dr. Mendel Blazer

Yisrael Blazer

My brother **Yisrael Blazer**

My brother Rabbi Dr. **Mendel Blazer**

They were killed tragically during the days of the Holocaust/Shoah

May G–d avenge their blood

May their souls be bound in the bonds of life

Commemorator in pain and suffering:
Yitzchak Blazer, Haifa

[Page 376]

In Eternal Memory

My father **Yehezkiel Blat**

My mother **Fayga Blat**

My brother **Dovid Blat**

My brother **Yakov Blat**

My sister **Khania Reich** born **Blat**

My sister **Bluma Flugajzn** born **Blat** and her daughter **Pajydzia**

All murdered by the Nazi murderers

May G–d avenge their blood

Memorialized in sadness:
Manuel Blat, Yonkers, New York

In Sacred Memory

My father **Ruwin Beder**
Died before the war

My mother **Hinda Beder**

My brother **Shmuel Beder (Telerman)**

My sister **Gitl Beder**

All murdered by the Nazi murderers

May G–d avenge their blood

Memorialized:
Yakov Telerman
Brooklyn, New York

Reuven Beder

To Eternal Memory

Fayga Blajwajs family and sons

From the Blajwajs family

My mother **Fayga Blajwajs** daughter of **Avraham**

My brother **Avraham Blajwajs** son of **Ayzyk**

My brother **Yakov Blajwajs** son of **Ayzyk**

Gitl Blajwajs daughter of **Yehiel** and son **Dovid Tzvi** son of **Zalman Blajwajs**

From the Ladner (Kaner) family

Mother **Fayga Ladner (Kaner)** daughter of **Zelig**

Brother **Zelig Ladner (Kaner)** son of **Yitzhak**

Sister **Ester Ladner (Kaner)** daughter of **Yitzhak**

All murdered by the Nazi murderers

May G–d avenge their blood

May their souls be bound up in the bond of eternal life

Memorialized in sadness;
Zalen Blajwajs and wife
Regina Blajwajs born **Ladner (Kaner)**
Montreal-Canada

[Page 378]

In Sacred Memory

Ruza Meszel with her little daughter Nina

My father **Yakov Blond**

My mother **Dina Blond**

My brother **Elihu (Oliash) Blond**

My sister **Karola Blond**

My sister **Sura Sperber** born **Blond**

My sister **Ruza Meszel** born **Blond** and her daughter **Nina**

Murdered by the Nazi murderers

May their souls be bound up in the bond of eternal life

Memorialized:
Izak Blond, Bronx, New York

[Page 379]

In eternal sadness for

My father **Chaim Bethajl** son of **Avraham**

My mother **Toba Bethajl (Birnbaum)**

My brother **Zev (Wolf) Bethajl** son of **Chaim**

My brother **Nakhum Bethajl** son of **Chaim**

My sister **Perl Bethajl** daughter of **Chaim**

My sister **Rywka Bethajl** daughter of **Chaim**

My sister **Chayala Bethajl** daughter of **Chaim**

My sister **Leah Bethajl** daughter of **Chaim**

All murdered by the Nazi murderers

May G–d avenge their blood

May their souls be bound up in the bond of eternal life

Memorialized:
Toba Rajnsztajn born **Bethajl**
Toronto-Canada

In eternal sadness for our dear parents, brothers and sisters:

Father **Yeshayhu Berkelhamer**

Mother **Fraydl Berkelhamer**

Sister **Zisl Berkelhamer**

Brother **Moshe (Moric) Berkelhamer**

Sister **Miriam Berkelhamer**

Brother **Khona Berkelhamer**

Brother **Abish Berkelhamer**

Brother **Tovya Berkelhamer** (died in Toronto in 1965)

All murdered by the Nazi murderers

May G–d avenge their blood

May their souls be bound up in the bond of eternal life

Memorialized:
Aharon and Herman Berkelhamer and family in Toronto

[Page 380]

To the Eternal Memory of
our comrade and friend

Perec Grinberg and his wife **Sura** born **Szpinrad** and their two sons

May their souls be bound up in the bond of eternal life

Memorialized:
Avraham and Yosef Zinger
Toronto-Canada

To the Eternal Memory of
my dear friend, the gentle Jew

Emanuel Grinszpan and his wife and child

Perished *al Kiddish haShem* [in the sanctification of God's name]

May G–d revenge their blood

Memorialized in deep sadness:
Avraham Zinger
Toronto-Canada

To the Eternal Memory

Gutter, Englander and Betrubniss Families

Parents **Yaakov** and wife **Hadas**

Parents **Lipa** and wife **Yehudit**

Their sons: **Moshe, Zalman and Billah**

Their sister **Breindel Englander**

Daughter **Gittel**

Wife **Bracha Gutter**

Her daughter **Bila Shprinza**

All were lost in the Shoah and destruction

May their blood be avenged

May their souls be bound in the bond of eternal life

Memorialized:
Gutter-Bergstein, Tarnow

In Eternal Memory

Chaim Gros

Malka Gros

My father **Chaim Gros**, my mother **Malka Gros** born **Szindelhajm**

My brother **Yisroel** and his wife **Ruza** born **Lew** from Drohobych

My brother **Yakov Gros**

My sister **Gizela Keler** born **Gros** and their young daughter **Hania**

My aunt **Gizela Sztil** born **Szindelhajm** and her husband **Yona Sztil** and children: **Shlomo and Fraydl**

All perished at the hands of the Nazi murderers

May G–d avenge their blood

May their souls be bound up in the bond of eternal life

Memorialized:
Shlomo Gros, Berlin

Ruza Gros   Yisroel Gros

[Page 382]

To the Eternal Memory

Chaya Tova Gutinower

Shlomo Kalman Rosen

Sara Rosen

Zev and Miriam Rosen and children

Avraham and Chaya Rosen and children

Dov Rosen and his wife

Malka Rosen

Mordechai Rosen

Naftali and Sara Wakskritz and children

All died in the days of the Holocaust and destruction

May G–d avenge their blood

May their souls be bound up in the bond of eternal life

Memorialized:
Irna (Gutinower) Easton
United States

To the Eternal Memory

My father **Avraham Akiva Gelernter**

My mother **Sura Rywka Gelernter**

My brother **Moshe Wolf Gelernter**

My brother **Mendl Yisroel Gelernter**

Perished during the Shoah years

May G–d avenge their blood

May their souls be bound up in the bond of eternal life

Memorialized:
Efroim Gelernter, Montreal-Canada

[Page 383]

In Eternal Memory of Our Dear Family

Menakhem Mendl Holender son of **Zvi**
Died in Montreal in 1953

Shayndl Holender daughter of **Menakhem Mendl**
Died in Russia in 1943

Yitzhak Salomon son of **Avraham Dovid**

Henny Salomon daughter of **Avraham Dovid**

Rayzel Salomon daughter of **Avraham Dovid**

Ruwin Salomon son of **Yitzhak**

Malka Salomon daughter of **Yitzhak**

Ester Sztajner daughter of **Zvi**

Berl Sztajner son of **Yitzhak**

Hershele Sztajner son of **Dov (Berl)**

Yitzhak Sztajner son of **Dov (Berl)**

Mendel Holender

Murdered by the Nazi murderers

May G–d avenge their blood

May their souls be bound up in the bond of eternal life

Memorialized in sadness:
Malka Holender
Hinda Holender and her husband
Moshe Kutnowski
Hershel Holender
Yehudis Holender
Toronto-Canada

[Page 384]

In Sacred Memory

Henrik Holender

Zigmund Holender and his wife

Dr. Ignaci and Luci Zajdenwerg and their son

Perished during the Shoah years

May G–d avenge their blood

Memorialized:
Yosef Salholc
New York

In Eternal Memory

Yitzhak Hollander son of **Shmuel**

Genia Hollander daughter of **Shmuel**

Meir Hollander son of **Shmuel**

Chana Hollander daughter of **Avraham**

Shmuel Hollander son of **Yitzhak**

Irina Hollander daughter of **Meir**

Perished in the Holocaust

May G–d avenge their blood

Memorialized:
Sabina Leibler from the Hollander Family
Tel Aviv

In Eternal Memory

Sister: **Chaya Sora Hirsz** daughter of **Efroim**

Brother-in-law: **Alter Chaim Hirsz** son of **Zvi**

Nephew: **Naftali Zvi Hirsz** son of **Alter Chaim**

Brother: **Yakov Korn** son of **Efroim**

Sister-in-law: **Chaya Sura Korn** daughter of **Akhtar** and three children

Murdered by the Nazi murderers

May G–d avenge their blood

Memorialized:
Dovid Wajzer
Montreal-Canada

In Eternal Memory

Our dear cousins: **Zishe Haber** and his wife **Gitel** daughter of **Chaim Tova** and son **Yitzhak** son of **Zishe** and his wife **Dvora Haber** daughter of **Chaim**

Daughter: **Bayla (Beshi) Gast** and her husband **Ahron Gast** son of **Shimeon** and their children: **Sura Gast** and **Yitzhak Gast**

Daughter: **Etl Bernfeld** daughter of Zishe Haber and her husband **Maks Bernfeld** and their children

Son: **Yosef Haber** son of **Zishe**

Daughter: **Sura Alwajs** daughter of **Zishe Haber** and her husband **Yosef Alwajz** and their children

Murdered by the Nazi murderers

May G–d avenge their blood

Memorialized:
The brothers
Avraham and Yosef Zinger
Toronto

[Page 385]

In Eternal Memory of Our Dear Relatives

Moshe Hercberg

Tsipa Hercberg

Yeshayahu Hercberg son of **Moshe**

Minya Hercberg daughter of **Moshe**

Eliezer Hercberg son of **Moshe**

All perished at the hands of the Nazi murderers

May G–d avenge their blood

May their souls be bound up in the bond of eternal life

Memorialized:
Avraham Zinger, Toronto-Canada

In Eternal Memory

Moshe Weinstein

Dr. Shmuel Weinstein son of **Moshe**

Yeshayahu Yosef Weinstein son of **Moshe**

Rosalia Weinstein daughter of **Moshe**

Dr. Alexander Weinstein son of **Moshe**

Major Jan Weinstein son of **Moshe**

All were lost in the Holocaust - May G–d avenge their blood

May their souls be bound up in the bond of eternal life

Memorialized:
Dr. Yakov Weinstein, London

[Page 386]

In memoriam

Petachia Honig son of **Shmuel**

Gitel Dvora Honig daughter of **Mechel**

Reshka Rak daughter of **Petachia**

Necha Honig daughter of **Petachia**

Ara Honig daughter of **Petachia**

Rivka Mahler daughter of **Mechel**

Frida Komlos daughter of **Petachia**

Hela Honig daughter of **Petachia**

Norbert Honig son of **Petachia**

Petachia Honig

My father, **Petachia Honig**, was a tenant farmer near Tarnow. He was an Orthodox Jew, well known in the town and its surroundings, father to a large family and while being Orthodox he gave his children an advanced education and was a Zionist. On the dark day for Tarnow Jews, March 1942, he and my mother, **Gitel Dvora**, were murdered by the Nazis. The children of the family, **Reshka, Edka, Rivka, Frida, Hela, Norbert** and their families were deported to the extermination camps after the liquidation of the Tarnow ghetto.

May their souls be bound up in the bond of eternal life

Remembered by:
Dr. Mordechai Gris-Honig
Rehovot-Israel

Necha Honig

[Page 387]

In memory of the family of Israel Weksler

R. **Israel Weksler** - one of the outstanding citizens in Tarnow, chairman of the Friends of "*Talmud Torah*", member and more of the "Students of Torah ", landowner and banker.

His wife, **Roza** daughter of R. **Zachariah Mendel Weksler** from the family of **Avraham**.

Their daughter **Rachel Bezkes** daughter of **Israel**, intelligent and philanthropic with a generous spirit

Lawyer Dr. **Yurek Bezkes** , husband of **Rachel**, a man of noble spirit and positive character

Mordechai Weksler son of **Israel**, legal expert.

All perished in the Shoah

May their memory be a blessing

Organized by
Dr. Zechariah Weksler and his family
Sydney , Australia

In Eternal Memory

Father: **Tovya Wajzer Rozengarten** son of **Ahron**

Mother: **Fayga Wajzer-Rozengarten**

Brother: **Moshe Wajzer-Rozengarten**

Sister: **Perl Wajzer-Rozengarten**

Brother: **Meir Wajzer-Rozengarten**

All perished at the hands of the Nazi murderers

May G–d avenge their blood

May their souls be bound up in the bond of eternal life

Memorialized:
Elihu (Elya) Wajzer-Rozengarten
Montreal-Canada

In Eternal Memory

Sister: **Tauba Wildsztajn** daughter of **Klunimus** and her husband **Yakov Wildsztajn** daughter of **Moshe** Their children: **Kalman and Moshe**

Brother: **Avraham Shmuel Izrael** son of **Klunimus**

Brother: **Moshe Ber Izrael** son of **Klunimus**

Brother: **Chaim Izrael** son of **Klunimus**

Sister: **Hinda Izrael** daughter of **Klunimus**

All perished at the hands of the Nazi murderers

May G–d avenge their blood

May their souls be bound up in the bond of eternal life

Memorialized:
Shayndl Hirszenhorn
Toronto-Canada
Toronto

[Page 388]

In Eternal Memory

Miriam Volken (Resler)

Moritz Volken

Ruth Volken

Miriam Volken (Resler) daughter of **Chaim Mendel**

Moritz Volken

Ruth Volken daughter of Moritz

Family of **Motel Shapiro**

Family **Leib Kook**

All perished in the days of destruction and Shoah

May their memories be of blessing

Remembered by:
Penny (Feiga) Buna family of Resler
Children Institution- Bostana 7, Ramat Hasharon

We Sanctify the Memory of Our Dear Ones

From the right: Miriam Wajnrib, Bayla Bina Izak born Wajnrub and her friend

Ester Rauch born Wajnrib

Hersh Lazar Wajnrib

Father: **Shlomo Zalman Wajnrib** son of **Elihu** – murdered by the Nazi murderers, May G–d avenge his blood

Mother: **Miriam Wajnrib** daughter of **Avraham** – murdered by the Nazi murderers, May G–d avenge her blood

Sister: **Rywka Wajcman** daughter of **Shlomo** – died in Toronto in 1955

Brother-in-law: **Leibush Wajcman** son of **Avraham** – perished in the Shoah, May G–d avenge his blood

Sister: **Bayla Bina Izak** born **Wajnrib** daughter of Shlomo – murdered by the Nazi murderers, May G–d avenge her blood

Sister: **Basha Wajnrib** daughter of **Shlomo** – murdered by the Nazi murderers, May G–d avenge her blood

Sister: **Ester Rauch** born **Wajnrib** daughter of **Shlomo** – murdered by the Nazi murderers, May G–d avenge her blood

Her child: **Tobala Rauch** daughter of **Eliezer** – perished at the hands of the Nazis

Sister: **Frimet Wajnrib** daughter of **Shlomo** – perished in Soviet Russia

Brother: **Avraham Yitzhak Wajnrib** son of **Shlomo** – killed by the Nazi murderers

Brother: **Hersh Lazar Wajnrib** son of **Shlomo** – died in Poland in 1946

May their souls be bound up in the bond of eternal life

Memorialized:
Gitl Zinger born **Wajnrib** and husband **Yosef Zinger**
Toronto-Canada

[Page 390]

In Eternal Memory

Ben Tzion Wajc son of **Yosef** and wife **Miriam** daughter of **Zvi**

Chana Fayge Wajc daughter of **Ben Tzion**

Zvi Wajc son of **Tzion**

Avraham Chaim Sztrom son of **Zvi**

Nusan Sztrom son of **Avraham**

Sora Sztrom daughter of **Avraham**

Pesha Sztrom daughter of **Avraham Chaim**

All perished at the hands of the Nazi murderers

May G–d avenge their blood

May their souls be bound up in the bond of eternal life

Memorialized
Shlomo Rauch and wife **Ester** born **Ben Tzion Wajc**
Toronto-Canada

To the Sacred Memory

Zawader, Rajnkraut and Gelernter Family

Father: **Moshe Leib Zawader** son of **Avraham** and wife

Brother: **Leml Zawader** and his wife **Anda** born **Maler** and child

Brother: **Dovid Zawader** and sister: **Rukhl Gelernter** born **Zawader** and two children

Rywka Rajnkraut born **Zawader** and **Bluma, Brukha, Tsila** and **Gitel**

Perished in the days of the Shoah

May G–d avenge their blood

May their souls be bound up in the bond of eternal life

Memorialized:
Chaim and Dovid Zawader-Mesner and wife
Tel Aviv-Israel

In memory of the family of Yeshayahu Zilberphenig

R' **Yeshayahu Chaim** son of **Abraham Aba Zilberphenig** was born in Tarnow in 1883. Grandson of R' **Zecharia Mendel** and Mrs. **Hana Mindel Abardam**; great grandson and descendant of a family that was very active in Galicia; he was president of the Jewish community of Tarnow, member of the Tarnow city council, active Zionist, a great philanthropist, industrialist and sharp businessman. He was arrested during the occupation because of his criticism of the German authorities. He perished in Auschwitz in 1941.

R' Yeshayahu Chaim Zilberphenig about 28-30 years old

Sarah (Salomea) Zilberphenig from the family Boyminger, was born in Radom in 1881. She was a cultured woman and of noble spirit and fine manners. She was highly and widely educated. She spoke 5 languages. She perished in Stanislawow in 1941.

Dr **Yakov (Hank) Zvi** son of **Yeshayahu Zilberphenig** was born in 1904 in Tarnow. He had a doctorate in social science from the University of Vienna then studied Medicine. After the German conquest he wandered "the 7 seas" and lived his last years in Miami, Florida. He died on the six of Elul (18.8.61).

Mrs. **Golda** daughter of **Abraham Aba Mozel** family **Zilberphenig**. Born in Tarnow Around 1880. She was a strong and energetic woman who was active in the community (Jewish Hospital in Tarnow). She perished in Tarnow in the summer of 1942.

Memorialized:
Prof Dr **Helen Silbing (Henda Zilberphenig)** and her husband
Puerto-Rico
Dr **Yehudit Zilberphenig -Kestenberg** and family
New-York

[Page 392]

In memory of the family of Benyamin Ze'ev (Wolf) Zilberfenig

Mr. **Benyamin Ze'ev** (Wolf) the son of Mr. **Avraham Aba Zilberfenig** was born in 1881. He labored a lot during his short life. He united the learning of Torah with good manners. He knew languages. He was among the first of the Zionist movement and of the founders of the Mizrachi movement in Tarnow.

He died on Shemini Azeret (next to last day of the holiday of Sukkot) 1907/5668

Mrs. **Raizel Yenta** the daughter of **Shneur Zalman** (may his memory be for a blessing) **Barfenig**, nee Hodorov. She was born in Berdichev (Russia) in 1883. She was a modest Jewish woman and fervent in keeping the mitzvot/commandments. She was brave and righteous. She was widowed at the age of 24 and dedicated her entire life to the education of her children. She was murdered in Tarnow during the Holocaust (The Great Slaughter) in Sivan 5702 (June 1942)

Mrs. Raizel Zilberfenig, mother of Dr. Z. Kasif

Mrs. **Hendel Ita** the daughter of Mr. **Benyamin Ze'ev Zilberfenig**. She was born in Tarnow in 1906. She was a college graduate in the fields of German and English. She taught these subjects in the Gymnasium of the Safa Berura in Tarnow.

She was murdered during the Holocaust in Tarnow in Sivan 5702 (June 1942).

May their souls be bound in the bonds of life.

Those memorializing:
Dr. Zacharia Kasif (Zilberfenig) and his family,
Tel Aviv

[Page 393]

To the Eternal Memory

Yisrael Tzvi Zaiden son of **Yaakov** (deceased)

Yehuda Arye Zaiden son of **Yisrael Tzvi**

Malka Zaiden daughter of **Shmuel**

Hinda Schnepps daughter of **Yisrael Tzvi**

Avraham Schnepps

Channah Schnepps

Moshe Zaiden son of **Yisrael Tzvi**

Rivka Zaiden

Devorah Zaiden daughter of **Moshe**

Matilda Zaiden daughter of **Moshe**

Lulek Zaiden son of **Moshe**

Eliyahu Zaiden son of **Yisrael Tzvi**

Hinda Zaiden

Matilda Zaiden daughter of **Eliyahu**

Avraham Zaiden son of **Eliyahu**

Yaakov Zaiden son of **Eliyahu**

Yehuda Arye Zaiden and his wife Malka Zaiden

Killed tragically during the Holocaust/Shoah

May G–d avenge their blood

May their souls be bound in the bonds of life

Memorialized:
Yaakov Tzidon (Zaiden)
Petach Tikvah

[Page 394]

To the Eternal Memory

Zilberman-Hirschfeld Geula
and Yetka Zilberman and her two children

Zilberman-Hirschfeld Geula

Manfred Weisserich
and his wife Blumka from
the family Zilberman-Hirschfeld

Yetka Zilberman and her children
Michalina and Wilhem

All perished at the hands of the Nazi murderers

May G–d avenge their blood

May their memory be for a blessing

Memorialized
Shlome (Solomon) Zilberman
Brooklyn-New York

[Page 395]

We Sanctify the Memory of Our Dearest Ones

Avraham Ziskind

Zlata Ziskind born Grosbard

Yakova Ziskind

Natalia Ziskind born Man

Teofila Ziskind

Perished in the years of the Shoah

May their souls be bound up in the bond of eternal life

Memorialized in sorrow:
Ziskind family
Berlin

[Page 396]

In Constant Sadness and in Sacred Memory of Our Dear Parents and Sisters and Their Husbands and Children

Father: **Yakov Dovid Zinger** son of **Yeshayahu**
A modest, honest Jew; although he worked hard for his income, he led a respected house and provided a Jewish education for his children

Mother: **Ester Chana Zinger** daughter of **Yakov**
A dear soul of a Jewish mother. Always toiling, devoted with her body and life to her husband and children

Sister: **Bluma Sura Zinger** daughter of **Yakov**

Sister: **Yentil Tauba Zinger** daughter of **Yakov**

Sister: **Leah Grosman** born **Zinger** daughter of **Yakov**

Brother-in-law: **Shmuel Grosman** son of **Zvi** and their children: **Yosef and Maytl**

All perished at the hands of the Nazi murderers

May G–d avenge their blood

May their souls be bound up in the bond of eternal life

Memorialized in sadness:
The brothers **Abraham and Yosef Zinger**
Toronto-Canada

[Page 397]

To the Eternal Memory

Tenenbaum Family

Sitting from the right: Shmuel Tenenbaum and his wife Chaya
Standing from the right: Oskar Gros, may he be distinguished for a long life
Standing from the left: Zvi Tenenbaum, may he be distinguished for a long life

Father: **Tenenbaum Zvi** son of **Yakov**

Mother: **Tenenbaum Chaya** daughter of **Yisroel**

Brother: **Leon (Leib) Tenenbaum** son of **Shmuel**

Sister: **Khanka Tenenbaum** daughter of **Shmuel**

Sister: **Tonka Tenenbaum** daughter of **Shmuel**

All perished at the hands of the Nazi murderers

May G–d avenge their blood

May their souls be bound up in the bond of eternal life

Memorialized:
Zvi Tenenbaum
Netanya-Israel
Mina Gerlernter born Tenenbaum
Montreal-Canada

[Page 398]

In Sacred Memory

Sura Hena Honig

Meir Taler

Yakov Taler

Father: **Hershel Taler** son of **Meir**

Mother: **Chana Taler** daughter of **Yakov**

Sister: **Dvora Sztraus** born **Taler** daughter of **Hershl**

Brother: **Yakov Taler** son of **Hershel**

Brother: **Meir Taler** son of **Hershel**

Cousins: **Shlomo, Yakov, Mindl Sztraus**

Brother-in-law: **Henek Sztraus** son of **Shlomo**

Aunt: **Sura Hena Honig** daughter of **Shlomo**

Sister-in-law: **Yocheved Zilberman**

All perished at the hands of the Nazi murderers

May G–d avenge their blood

May their souls be bound up in the bond of eternal life

Memorialized: **Berl and Mendl Taler**
Montreal-Canada

[Page 399]

In Sacred Memory

Ida Jakubowicz

Markus Jakubowicz

Father: **Markus Viktor Jakubowicz** son of **Zvi**

Mother: **Ida Jakubowicz** daughter of **Mikhl**

Brother: **Moshe Jakubowicz** son of **Markus Viktor**

All perished at the hands of the Nazis

May G–d avenge their blood

May their souls be bound up in the bond of eternal life

Memorialized:
Mala Opfelbaum, Yakov Jakubowicz
Halina Sztrasberg, Genya Lajbgorn
Leon Jakubowicz

[Page 400]

To the Eternal Memory

Our father: **Shlomo David Katz**

Our mother: **Sarah Katz** born **Rimler**

Perished at the hands of the Nazi murderers in Auschwitz

May G–d avenge their blood

May their souls be bound up in the bond of eternal life

Memorialized:
Nechemia and Avraham Rimler
Israel

To the Eternal Memory

Father: **Leibish Jochnowicz** son of **Yisroel**

Mother: **Brayndil Jochnowicz** daughter of **Moshe**

Sister: **Regina Jochnowicz** son of **Leibish**

Brother: **Moshe Jochnowicz** son of **Leibish**

Sister: **Hinda Jochnowicz** daughter of **Leibish**

Brother: Yehiel Jochnowicz son of Leibish

Brother: **Avigdor Jochnowicz** son of **Leibish**

Sister: **Tsila Jochnowicz** son of **Leibish**

Sister: **Fayga Jochnowicz** daughter of **Leibish**

Sister: **Golda Jochnowicz** daughter of **Leibish**

All perished at the hands of the Nazis

May G–d avenge their blood

May their souls be bound up in the bond of eternal life

Memorialized:
Meir Jochnowicz and wife **Regina Jochnowicz**
Montreal-Canada

[Page 401]

To the Eternal Memory of
Our Dear Parents, Sisters, Brothers and Children

Father: **Efroim Laufer** son of Asher

Mother: **Rayzel Laufer** daughter of **Moshe Dovid**

Sister: **Sura Szer** born **Laufer** daughter of **Efroim**

Her husband: **Sholem Szer** son of **Moshe**

Their children:
Yosef Szer son of **Sholem**

Yehiel Szer son of **Sholem**

Avraham Szer son of **Sholem**

Brother: **Asher Laufer** son of **Efroim**

His wife: **Hela Laufer** daughter of **Avraham**

Their children:
Moshe Dovid Laufer son of **Asher**

Chana Laufer daughter of **Asher**

Sister: **Brucha Rapaport** born **Laufer** daughter of **Efroim**

Her husband: **Shabtai Rapaport** son of **Sholem**

And their three children daughter of
Mother-in-law: **Leah Langer** daughter of **Motl**

Father-in-law: **Yosef Langer** son of **Yehoshua**

Their sons:
Yehoshua Meir Langer son of **Yehoshua** son of **Yosef**

With wife **Rywka Langer** daughter of **Avraham**

Zisman Langer son of **Yosef**

Chana Langer son of **Yosef**

All perished at the hands of the Nazi murderers

May G–d avenge their blood

May their souls be bound up in the bond of eternal life

Memorialized:
Pesach and Tsipora Tajtelbaum
Toronto-Canada

[Page 402]

In Sacred Memory

Tishatkas from the Komet (Comet) family

Standing from right: Mordechai Loeb, Yaacov Kornreich and his wife Leah from the Loeb Family
Sitting: Esther Loeb from the Komet (Comet) family

Esther Loeb from the **Komet (Comet)** family daughter of **Shlomo**

Her husband: **Mordechai Loeb** son of **Wolf**

Their daughter: **Leah Kornreich** from the **Loeb** family daughter of **Mordechai**

With her husband: **Yaacov Kornreich**

And their child: **Rivka**

Hinda Tishatkas from the **Komet (Comet)** family daughter of **Shlomo**
With her husband and daughter

All were lost in the time of the Holocaust

May G–d avenge their blood

May their souls be bound up in the bond of eternal life

Memorialized:
Bilah (Berta) Bardoff from the **Loeb** family
United States
Dr. Avraham Chomet (Comet), Israel

[Page 403]

In eternal memory

My father **Avraham Lenonid** son of Eli, murdered by the Nazis, may G–d avenge his blood

My mother **Channah/Hannah Lenonid**, died in 1942 in Russia

My aunt **Helena Weintraub**, daughter of Eli, murdered by the Nazis, may G–d avenge her blood

My cousin from Ger. Adv. **Marek Zilberstein**, murdered by the Nazis, may G–d avenge his blood

My grandmother **Golda Lenonid**, murdered by the Nazis

May their memory be blessed!

Sitting from the right:
Avraham Lenonid and his mother Golda
In the middle is their daughter (may she live and be well) Mina at age 4.
Today her last name is Engelman and she lives in Ramat Gan

Standing from the right:
May she live and be well, Mina Wagschel, born Lenonid, who lives in Haifa
Adv. Mark Zilberstein, Helena Weintraub, born Lenonid and Channah Lenonid

Avraham Lenonid, may his memory be for a blessing, was a certified accountant in Tarnow, a court translator, and a graphologist for the district court. He was involved with the bornds of the community.

Commemorating:
Mina Engelman born **Lenonid** the daughter of **Avraham**
Ramat Gan

For an eternal memorial

Naftali Leder son of Aharon **Regina Leder (Rand)** daughter of **Yosef**

Anna Leder daughter of Naftali **Yosef Leder** son of **Naftali**

Herman Leder son of **Naftali**

All of them were murdered by the hateful Nazis

May G–d avenge their blood

May their souls be bound in the bonds of life

Memorialized:
Adolf Leder, Beer Sheva

[Page 404]

To the Eternal Memory

Leib Lebenkorn son of **Herman**

Nekhemia Lebenkorn daughter of **Izak**

Arfad Lebenkorn son of **Leib**

Shmuel Cizer-Tifenbruch son of **Efroim**

Yisroel Cizer-Tifenbruch son of **Shmuel**

Sabina Cizer-Tifenbruch daughter of **Shmuel**

Sida Cizer-Tiferbruch daughter of **Shmuel**

All perished at the hands of the Nazi murderers

May G–d avenge their blood

May their souls be bound up in the bond of eternal life

Memorialized:
Louis Lebenkorn, U.S.A.

**To the Memory of My Dear Friend,
Perished at the Hands of the Nazis**

May G–d Avenge His Blood

Mesinger Herman and wife **Bela**

Mesinger Markus and wife **Mina**

Miler Zigmunt and wife **Bunya**

Kapelner Bernard and wife **Wajc-Blonder Baylka**

From the right: **Mina Mesinger**, (__), Mesinger Markus, Regina Kornilo born Ler)

May their souls be bound in the bonds of life

Memorialized:
Yosef Kornilo, Israel

[Page 405]

In Sacred Memory

My mother **Sima Mordkowicz (Wajzer)**

My sister: **Royze-Rukhl Kenigberg**

My sister: **Lola Graz**

My brother: **Ahron Sznur (Wajzer)**

My uncle: **Shaul Sznur (Wajzer)**

My aunt: **Matl** and daughter **Chana Sznur**

All perished in the years of the Holocaust

May G–d avenge their blood

May their souls be bound up in the bond of eternal life

Memorialized:
Regina Binensztok (Mordkowicz)
Montreal-Canada

In Eternal Memory

My father: **Shmuel Mira** son of **Efroim**

My mother: **Pesl Mira** daughter of **Urish**

My sister: **Blima Mira** daughter of **Shmuel**

My sister: **Zeftl Mira** daughter of **Shmuel**

My brother: **Berl Mira** son of **Shmuel**

My sister-in-law: **Tauba Mira**

My brother: **Urish Mira** son of **Shmuel**

All perished in the years of the Holocaust

May G–d avenge their blood

May their souls be bound up in the bond of eternal life

Memorialized:
Merl Mira,
Montreal-Canada

**We Sanctify the Memory of our Dear Parents,
Sisters and Relatives**

Yitzhak (Izak) Merl murdered by the Nazi murderers.
May G–d avenge his blood

And his wife **Tauba Merl** born **Brandstatter** died

Lena Sztrum born **Brandstatter** murdered by the Nazi murderers.
May G–d avenge her blood

Rut Brandstatter murdered by the Nazi murderers.
May G–d avenge her blood

Hersh Fajer died

Rywka Fajer died

Yisroel Fajer and his wife **Lola** born **Korn** died

Helen Berman born **Fajer**

Brother-in-law **Zalek Bergman** and their child

Murdered by the Nazi murderers

May G–d avenge their blood

Memorialized:
Mala Einem- Brandstatter
Giza Fajer- Brandstatter
Yeshayahu Fajer
Toronto-Canada

[Page 40/]

To the Eternal Memory

This tombstone is erected on the grave of the wife
of R. Isaac Sapir in the cemetery in Tarnow.

My mother: **Klara Sapir**, wife of **Isaac**, passed away in Tarnow on April 15, 1942.

My sister: **Yola Weinberger Sapir**, perished in the Shoah. May her memory be a blessing

Dedicated in sorrow by:
Lawyer **Shimon Sapir**, Berlin

To the Eternal Memory

Father: **Chaim Sukman** son of **Avraham**

Mother: **Shaydl Sukman** daughter of **Rywka**

Brother: **Yehoshua Sukman** son of **Chaim**

Brother: **Avraham Sukman** son of **Chaim**

Sister: **Rukhl Sukman** daughter of **Chaim**

Brother: **Nisen Sukman** son of **Chaim**

Sukman Family

All perished in the years of the Holocaust

May G–d avenge their blood

May their souls be bound up in the bond of eternal life

Memorialized:
Sala Rot born Sukman
Hela Najhaus born **Sukman**
Montreal-Canada

To the Eternal Memory

Father: **Avraham Yakov Englender**
Perished at the hands of the Nazis

Mother: **Chana Englender** daughter of **Eliezer Frajlich** –
perished at the hands of the Nazis

May G–d avenge her blood

Brother: **Mendl Englender** son of **Avraham Yakov Frajlich** –
perished at the hands of the Nazis

May G–d avenge his blood

Brother: Shmuel Englender son of Avraham Yakov Frajlich –
perished at the hands of the Nazis

May G–d avenge his blood

My wife: **Pesil Frajlich** daughter of **Naftali Hercl Blumensztin**
Died in Toronto in 1963

My father-in-law: **Naftali Hercl Blumensztin** died in Tarnow

My mother-in-law: **Idis Blumensztin** perished at the hands of the Nazis

My brother-in-law: **Meir Blumensztin** son of **Naftali Hercl** perished at the hands of the Nazis

My sister-in-law: **Ester** daughter of **Naftali Hercl** – perished at the hands of the Nazis

May G–d avenge her blood

May their souls be bound up in the bond of eternal life

Memorialized:
Eliezer (Leon) Frajlich
Toronto-Canada

Pesil Frajlich

To the Eternal Memory

Engineer **Maurici Engelhardt**   **Yona Pomerantz**

Doctor **Arthur Engelhardt**   **Franziska Pomerantz**

Malvina Engelhardt-Faber

All perished in the years of the Holocaust

May G–d avenge their blood

May their souls be bound up in the bond of eternal life

Memorialized
Adolf and Blanka Pomerantz
Givatayim

[Page 109]

My father **Eliezer-Leon Fleischer**

My mother **Taoca Fleischer**

My brother **Leopold Fleischer**

They perished in the Shoah

May their memory be a blessing

Memorialized:
Yaacov Fleischer
Kibbutz Merhavia

In Eternal Memory

Father: **Chaim Fisz** son of **Eli**

Mother: **Rayzel Fisz (Grossbard)** daughter of **Kalman**

My brothers: **Eli Fisz** son of **Chaim**
Dovid Fisz son of **Chaim**

My sisters: **Chana Fisz** daughter of **Chaim**
Bayla Fisz daughter of **Chaim**

Perished in the years of the Holocaust

May G–d avenge their blood

May their souls be bound up in the bond of eternal life

Memorialized:
Hinda Fisz (Unger)
Montreal-Canada

In Eternal Memory

Pris Ferenc Khanka and children

Ferenc Marila

Ferenc Emil

Perished in the years of the Holocaust

May G–d avenge their blood

May their souls be bound up in the bond of eternal life

Memorialized:
Salomon Zilberman
Brooklyn (New York)

[Page 410]

In Eternal Memory

Haim Fenichel

Sara Fenichel

Baila Fenichel

Era Fenichel Kornslauer

Fenichel Family

Perished in the years of the Holocaust

May G–d avenge their blood

May their souls be bound up in the bond of eternal life

Memorialized:
Isaac Fenichel
Haifa

To the Eternal Memory

Yisroel Fuder son of **Zvi Eliezer**

Rivka Taub daughter of **Yitzhak**

Arya Taub son of **Yisroel**

Hersh Lazar Taub son of **Arya**

Moshe Taub son of **Arya**

Bayla Taub son of **Arya**

Yitzhak Grinszpan son of **Avraham**

Wolf Werner son of **Menakhem Yehuda**

All perished at the hands of the Nazi murderers

May G–d avenge their blood

May their souls be bound up in the bond of eternal life

Memorialized:
Chana Laub
Kurdani-Israel

[Page 411]

To the Eternal Memory

My father **Tsettel Shmuel** son of **Meir** – died in Toronto in 1965

My mother **Tsettel Cila** daughter of **Yissakhar Dov** – perished at the hands of the Nazi murderers

My brother **Tsettel Zev** son of **Shmuel** – perished at the hands of the Nazi murderers

My sister **Tsettel Sura** daughter of **Shmuel** – perished at the hands of the Nazi murderers

And the **Nizinsky** family – perished at the hands of the Nazi murderers

May G–d avenge their blood

May their souls be bound up in the bond of eternal life

Memorialized:
Yosef Tsettel,
Toronto-Canada
Haifa

To the Eternal Memory

My father: **Nachum Freeman**

My mother: **Uma Freeman**

My sister:
Rosia (Rachel) Solnik from the **Freeman** family

My sister:
Giza (Tova) Freeman

Freeman Family

All perished at the hands of the Nazi murderers

May G–d avenge their blood

May their memory be for a blessing

Memorialized
Yosef Freeman,
Ramat Gan

[Page 412]

We Sanctify the Memory of our Dearest

Father: **Yitzhak Zist** son of **Mordechai**

Mother: **Miriam Zist** daughter of **Yeshaya**

Brother: **Shmuel** son of **Yitzhak**

Sister: **Tauba Biberberg** born **Zist** daughter of **Yitzhak**
Her husband: **Meir Biberberg**
And their children: **Yosef, Yeshaya, Mordechai** and **Gavriel**

Brother: **Shakar Zist** son of **Yitzhak**

Sister: **Shasha Fridman** born **Zist** daughter of **Yitzhak**
Her husband: **Menakhem Mendl Fridman** son of **Chaim**
And their children: **Avraham** and **Frumet**

Perished at the hands of the Nazi murderers

May G–d avenge their blood

May their souls be bound up in the bond of eternal life

Memorialized:
Hershel Mordechai Zist
Sura Zist (Goldman)
Montreal-Canada

To the Eternal Memory

My brother: **Asher Flink** son of **Leibish**

His wife: **Sura Flink**

And their children: **Yosef** and **Regina**

All perished at the hands of the Nazi murderers

May G–d avenge their blood

May their souls be bound up in the bond of eternal life

Memorialized:
Avraham Goldman-Flink
Montreal-Canada

[Page 413]

To the Eternal Memory

My father: **Shmuel Fajgenbaum** son of **Arya**

My mother: **Mindl Fajgenbaum** daughter of **Shlomo Zalman**

My brother: **Eliezer Fajgenbaum** son of **Shmuel**

My brother: **Avraham Fajgenbaum** son of **Shmuel**

My sister: **Adela Fajgenbaum** daughter of **Shmuel**

My brother: **Shayek (Yeshaya) Fajgenbaum** son of **Shmuel**

My sister: **Sala Fajgenbaum** son of **Shmuel**

All perished in the years of the Holocaust

May G–d avenge their blood

May their souls be bound up in the bond of eternal life

Memorialized:
Maks Fajgenbaum Kalman
Toronto-Canada

To the Eternal Memory
of the young annihilated lives

Of my dear
Father **Yosef Knobloch** son of **Elihu**

Of my dear
Mother **Yocheved Knobloch** born **Klajn** daughter of **Yosef**

Who perished in the years of the Holocaust

May G–d avenge their blood

May their souls be bound up in the bond of eternal life

Memorialized:
Khanka Nauman born **Klajn**
Toronto-Canada

[Page 414]

To The Eternal Memory

Rozalia Brownfeld from the Potashman family

My mother: Meita Potashman

Sima Braun from the Potashman family

Miriam Faber from the Postashman family

Berel Potashman

Berta Klapholz from the Potashman family

All killed in the Holocaust by the Nazis- May G–d avenge their blood

May their souls be bound up in the bond of eternal life

Memorialized
Regina Kornilo (Potashman)
Israel

[Page 415]

To the eternal memory

Edit Kornilo

Of my dear mother
Regina Kornilo
and my little sister
Edit

Regina Kornilo born Lery

Perished at the hands of the Nazi murderers

May G–d avenge their blood

May their souls be bound up in the bond of eternal life

Memorialized:
Halina Fajngold born **Kornilo**
Paris

To the Eternal Memory

Serke Knecht and daughter Sala

Father **Yehezkiel Knecht (Zidman)**
Mother **Serka Knecht (Zidman)**
Sister **Sala Knecht (Zidman)** daughter of **Yehezkiel**
Brother **Leibish Knecht (Zidman)** son of **Yehezkiel**

Leibish Knecht

All perished at the hands of the Nazi murderers

May G–d avenge their blood

May their souls be bound up in the bond of eternal life

Memorialized:
Avraham Dovid and **Liba Knecht (Zidman)**
Montreal-Canada

[Page 416]

To the eternal memory

My sister Mila Katzenberg
Daughter of Israel

My mother Rachel Appelman Katz   My father Israel Katz son of Yeshayahu

All perished at the hands of the Nazi murderers

May their memory be for a blessing

Memorialized
Yitzhak Katz
and **Edla Katz Krauser**
Kibbutz Ein HaMifratz

To the Eternal Memory

Father: **Yitzhak Korc** son of **Yeshmael**

Mother: **Dwoyra Korc** daughter of **Nusan**

Brother: **Moshe Wolf Korc** son of **Yitzhak** [and his wife]
Tispora Korc daughter of **Avraham** and their children: **Leibish** and **Sura**

Brother: **Shmuel Arya Korc** son of **Yitzhak**

Sister: **Chana Rywka Korc** daughter of **Yitzhak**

Brother: **Yitzhak Pinkhas Blajwajs** son of **Eliezer**

All perished at the hands of the Nazi murderers

May G–d avenge their blood

May their souls be bound up in the bond of eternal life

Memorialized:
Khayke Sztajnfeld born **Korc**
Toronto-Canada

[Page 417]

To The Eternal Memory

My father:
Shalom Kornilo

My mother:
Sarina Kornilo

My sister:
Frimet (Freida) Kornilo

My brother: **Chaim Kornilo** son of **Shalom**

All perished at the hands of the Nazi murderers

May their memory be a blessing

Memorialized:
Yosef Kornilo   Gershon Kornilo
Yitzhak Kornilo   Aharon Kornilo
All in Israel

[Page 418]

To the Eternal Memory

My father **Aleksander Rubin**

My mother **Ernestina Rubin**

My brother *Magister* [1] **Stanislaw Rubin**

My sister *Magister* **Albina Rubin-Rozenblat**

All perished at the hands of the Nazi murderers

May G–d avenge their blood

May their souls be bound up in the bond of eternal life

Memorialized:
Dr. Bronislaw Rubin
Tarnow

To the Eternal Memory

Miriam Rauchwajg daughter of **Shlomo Margulis**

Lazar Rauchwajg son of **Eli Rauchwajg**

Rut Rauchwajg daughter of **Lazar Rauchwajg**

Leon Rauchwajg son of **Lazar Rauchwajg**

Salomon Margulis son of **Nakhum Margolis**

Rebeka Margulis daughter of **Yokhanan Grossbard**

All perished at the hands of the Nazi murderers

May G–d avenge their blood

Memorialized:
Leon Margulis
Montreal

Of my precious mother: **Gitel Rozenberg** daughter of **Avigdor**

Of my dear sisters:

Miriam Rozenberg daughter of **Moshe**

Sura Rozenberg daughter of **Moshe**

And my dear brother: **Kalman Rozenberg** son of **Moshe**

All perished at the hands of the Nazi murderers

May G–d avenge their blood

May their souls be bound up in the bond of eternal life

Memorialized:
Yisroel Rozenberg
Toronto-Canada

[Page 419]

To the Eternal Memory

Of the holy ones

Who were destroyed by the Nazi murderers

Benedit [Benedict] Rosenblatt 5705/1945

Miriam Rosenblatt 5702/1942

Yitzchak Rosenblatt 5703/1943

Tsila Rosenblatt 5703/1943

Golda Rosenblatt 5703/1943

May there memory be blessed!

And the soul of **Avraham Rosenblatt**
Who died tragically, 19 Kislev 5727/1967 in Detroit, United States

Memorialized:
Wolf Rosenblatt and family
Toronto, Canada

To the Eternal Memory

Of my dear brothers

Yosef Rajnbach

Yisroel Rajnbach

Avraham Gershon Rajnbach

Dovid Rajnback

All perished at the hands of the Nazi murderers

May God avenge their blood

May their souls be bound up in the bond of eternal life

Memorialized:
Maks Rajnbach
Cincinnati-Ohio

[Page 420]

To The Eternal Memory

Rot Family: Berl Rot and wife Chana and children: Leah, Yakov, Tsiri, Fayga, Chaya

Fayga Honig

Moshe and Chava Hena Honig

Of Our Dear Families:

And **Hazelberg (Honig)**:	**Rot**:
Father: **Moshe Honig**	Father: **Berl Rot**
Mother: **Chaya Hena Honig**	Mother: **Tsirl Rot**
Sister: **Fayga Honig**	Sister: **Chana Rot** daughter of **Berl**
Brother: **Manek Honig**	Sister: **Fayga Rot** daughter of **Berl**
Brother: **Simkha Honig**	Sister: **Leah Rot** daughter of **Berl**
	Brother: **Yakov Rot** son of **Berl**

All perished at the hands of the Nazi murderers

May God avenge their blood

May their souls be bound up in the bond of eternal life

Memorialized:
Mendl Hazelberg (Honig)
and **Regina Hazelberg (Rot)**
Montreal-Canada

[Page 121]

In Eternal Memory

Brother in law: **Shalom Rosenberg**

Sister: **Golda Rosenberg**

Niece: **Sarah Rosenberg**

Nephew: **Natan Rosenberg**

Sister: **Rachel Lehrer**

The Rosenberg Family

All of them were killed tragically during the Holocaust

May their memory be a blessing

Memorialized:
Vishia Fingerman-Freiman
Ramat Gan

To the Eternal Memory

Father: **Simkha Rozensztok**

Mother: **Alta Rozensztok**

Sister: **Dora Kalfus** daughter of **Simkha** and her husband and children

Sister **Chava Sachwald** daughter of **Simkha** and her husband and children

Sister: **Chana Rozensztok** daughter of **Simkha** and her husband and children

Sister: **Rukhl Rozensztok** daughter of **Simkha** and her husband and children

Brother: **Nusan Rozensztok** son of **Simkha** and his wife and children

Brother: **Avraham Rozensztok** son of **Simkha**

Brother: **Yisroel Rozensztok** son of **Simkha**

Brother: **Hersh Rozensztok** son of **Simkha** and his wife and children

Brother: **Berl Rozensztok** son of **Simkha**

All perished at the hands of the Nazi murderers

May God avenge their blood

May their souls be bound up in the bond of eternal life

Memorialized:
Dovid Rozensztok
Montreal-Canada

Translator's footnote:

1. Polish university degree equivalent to a master's degree.

[Page 422]

We Sanctify the Memory of
Our Precious Parents, Dear Sisters and Their Families

Standing from the left: **Nusan Rand, Sura and Leibish Ofsler, Rukhl and Pinkhas Ziskind**
Sitting from the left: **Mindl Rand and child, Zelda Ender, Hadasa and Yehuda Wenger**

From the left: **Borukh Ofsler, Rukhl Ofsler, Rywka Ofsler**

All perished at the hands of the Nazi murderers

May G–d avenge their blood

May their souls be bound up in the bond of eternal life

Memorialized:
Avraham and Faygel Wenger
New York

[Page 423]

To the Eternal Memory

Shlomo Rajchman son of **Moshe Tuvya**

Rukhl Rajchman daughter of **Avraham**

Son: **Chaim Rajchman** son of **Shlomo**

Daughter: **Pepa (Pesha) Rajchman** daughter of **Shlomo**

All perished in the years of the Holocaust

May G-d avenge their blood

May their souls be bound up in the bond of eternal life

Memorialized:
Avraham and Yosef Zinger
Toronto, Canada

To the Eternal Memory

Yisroel Sztrom son of **Zvi**

Fayga Sztrom Szpicen daughter of **Chaim Ahron**

Zelda Sztrom Szpicen daughter of **Yisroel**

Khanka Sztrom Szpicen

Yitzhak Haber son of **Mordekhai**

Bayla Haber daughter of **Nisen**

Mordekhai Haber son of **Yitzhak**

Moshe Haber son of **Yitzhak**

Mendl Haber son of **Yitzhak**

Hinda Brin born **Haber** daughter of **Yitzhak**

Sura Szpangelet born **Haber** daughter of **Yitzhak**

Bluma Szrajber born **Haber** daughter of **Yitzhak**

Yentil Haber daughter of **Yitzhak**

Chava Mansdorf born **Haber** daughter of **Yitzhak**

Hela Haber daughter of **Yitzhak**

All perished in the years of the Holocaust

May G-d avenge their blood

May their souls be bound up in the bond of eternal life

Memorialized:
Chaim Sztrom Szpicen and wife **Rukhl Sztrom Szpicen**
Toronto-Canada

[Page 424]

We Sanctify the Memory of Our Dear Ones

Chaim [Henek] Szporn son of Ahron – my son. Perished as a hero on the battlefield in 1945

Hinda Szporn daughter of Mordechai – my wife. Perished at the hands of the German murderers

Avraham Mordekhai (Monek) Szporn son of **Ahron** – my son, perished at the hands of the Nazi murderers

Mirl Mosner daughter of **Avraham**, my sister
Chaim Mosner son of **Yehoshua** – her husband

Tosha Sztajn born **Szporn** daughter of **Avraham**, my sister
Yitshak Sztajn – her husband

Malka Glinik daughter of **Mordekhai**, sister-in-law
Chaim Glinik, her husband – brother-in-law

Meir Blajwajs son of **Mordekhai**, my brother-in-law and his wife **Yenta Blajwajs**

Shlomo Szporn son of Avraham and his wife Fayga. My brother – perished at the hands of the Nazis

All of my sisters, sisters-in-laws and brothers-in-law perished

at the hands of the Nazi murderers

May G–d avenge their blood

May their souls be bound up in the bond of eternal life

Memorialized:
Ahron and Zalman Szporn,
Montreal

To the Eternal Memory

Father: **Chaim Mosner** son of **Yehoshua**

Mother: **Mirl Mosner** daughter of **Avraham**

Sister: **Hela Tsajchner** daughter of **Chaim** and her son **Dovid**

Sister: **Sabina Nat** daughter of **Chaim** born **Mosner** and her daughter **Helen**

Sister: **Klara Mosner** daughter of **Chaim**

Sister: **Sala Mosner** daughter of **Chaim**

All perished at the hands of the Nazi murderers

May G–d avenge their blood

May their souls be bound up in the bond of eternal life

Memorialized:
Dora Mosner born **Zis**
Khanka and Regina Zis
Montreal-Canada

To the Eternal Memory

Father **Aharon Siedlisker** z"l

Mother **Chava Siedlisker** z"l

My wife **Naama Siedlisker** z"l

My daughter **Sheindel Siedlisker** z"l

My son **Naftali Siedlisker** z"l

All perished at the hands of the Nazi murderers

May their souls be bound up in the bond of eternal life

Memorialized:
Chaim Eliezer Siedlisker
Nesher (Israel)

[Page 426]

To the Eternal Memory

Pesl Rukhl daughter of **Zvi Baruch Holender** – **Róża Schiff**

Chana Nisenfeld daughter of **Mordekhai Dovid Szif** – **Anna Nissenfeld**

Engineer **Yehoshua** son of **Mordekhai Dovid Szif** – Inź. **Zygmunt Schiff**

Avraham Yakov Szif son of **Mordekhai Dovid Szif** – **Adolf Schiff**

Kalman Nisenfeld son of **Elihu Nisenfeld** – **Karol Nissenfeld**

All perished at the hands of the Nazi murderers

May G–d avenge their blood

May their souls be bound up in the bond of eternal life

Memorialized:
Dr. **Yitzhak Szif**
Argentina

To the Eternal Memory

Father: **Hersh (Herman) Ausenberg (Szilder)**

Mother: **Rukhl Ausenberg (Szilder)**

Sister: **Lipka Ausenberg (Szilder)**

Sister: **Franka Ausenberg (Szilder)**

Sister: **Ester Ausenberg (Szilder)**

Brother: **Borukh Ausenberg (Szilder)**

Sister: **Perl Ausenberg (Szilder)**

All perished at the hands of the Nazi murderers

May G–d avenge their blood

May their souls be bound up in the bond of eternal life

Memorialized:
Yitzhak Ausenberg (Szilder)
Montreal

[Page 427]

To the Eternal Memory

Father: **Avraham Sztorm** son of **Hercka**

Mother: **Rywka Sztorm-Buchholc** daughter of **Leibish**

Sister: **Rukh (Ruzka) Buchholc** daughter of **Avraham**

Brother: **Yakov (Yanek) Buchholc** son of **Avraham**

All perished at the hands of the Nazi murderers

May G–d avenge their blood

May their souls be bound up in the bond of eternal life

Memorialized:
Monek Szturm
Montreal-Canada

To the Eternal Memory

My father: **Shlomo Sztamberger** son of **Avraham**

My mother: **Dwoyra Sztamberger**

My sister: **Leah Sztamberger** daughter of **Shlomo**

My sister: **Fayga Sztamberger** daughter of **Shlomo**

My sister: **Miriam Sztamberger** daughter of **Shlomo**

All perished at the hands of the Nazi murderers

May G–d avenge their blood

May their souls be bound up in the bond of eternal life

Memorialized:
Chana Zalcman (Sztamberger)
Montreal-Canada

[Page 428]

We Sanctify the Memory of

My father: **Alter Szpangelet** son of **Ezrial**

My mother: **Gitl Szpangelet** daughter of **Mordekhai**

My brother: **Mordekhai Szpangelet** son of **Alter**

My sister: **Zissel Szpangelet** daughter of **Alter**

My brother: **Yaruchim** son of **Alter**

All perished at the hands of the Nazi murderers

May G–d avenge their blood

May their souls be bound up in the bond of eternal life

Memorialized:
Toba Waks born **Szpangelet**
and husband **Yeshaya Waks**
Montreal-Canada

In Sacred Memory

My father: **Shlomo Sztamberger** son of **Avraham**

David Schindel son of **Schlomo**

Tuvia Schindel son of **David**

Billah Schindel daughter of **Tuvia**

Sara Schindel daughter of **David**

Henya Kahana daughter of **Tuvia**

All perished during the Holocaust

May their memory be a blessing

May their souls be bound up in the bond of eternal life

Memorialized:
Avraham Yitzhak Shindel
Bene Brak

[Page 429]

In Sacred Memory

Szildkraut Family

Father: **Yisroel Yakov Szildkraut** son of **Shlomo**

Mother: **Tila Szildkraut** daughter of **Dovid Ber**

Sister: **Luba Szildkraut (Blumenstein)** daughter of **Yisroel Yakov**

Brother-in-law: **Dovid Blumenstein** son of **Naftali Herzl**

Nephew: **Naftali Herzl Blumensztajn** son of **Dovid**

My first wife: **Chana Last Szildkraut** daughter of **Wolf**

My sister: **Drezil Szildkraut** daughter of **Yakov**

Kahana Family:

Mother: **Chana Kahana** daughter of **Nuta**

Brother: **Kalman Yosef Kahana** son of **Ahron**

Brother: **Yehezkiel Kahana** son of **Ahron**

Brother: **Nuta Kahana** son of **Ahron**

Brother: **Wolf Lib Kahana** son of **Ahron**

Brother: **Shlomo Mendl Kahana** son of **Ahron**

Sister: **Sura Kahana** daughter of **Ahron**
First husband: **Avraham Tajtlbaum** son of **Yakov**
Their son: **Ahron Tajtlbaum** son of **Avraham**

All perished at the hands of the Nazi murderers

May G–d avenge their blood

May their souls be bound up in the bond of eternal life

Memorialized,
Shlomo Szildkraut
Montreal-Canada

Memorialized:
Rayzel Szildkraut-Kahana
Montreal-Canada

[Page 430]

To the Eternal Memory

Father: **Alter Szlenger** son of **Asher**

Mother: **Malka Szlenger** daughter of **Simcha**

Sister: **Chana Nauberg** born **Szlenger** daughter of **Alter**
Her husband: **Zisha Nauberg** son of **Avraham**

My brother: **Yeshaya Moshe Szlenger** son of **Alter**
My brother: **Henek Szlenger** son of **Alter**

My brother: **Mendl Szlenger** son of **Alter**

My sister: **Eida Szlenger** daughter of **Alter**

All perished at the hands of the Nazi murderers

May G–d avenge their blood

May their souls be bound up in the bond of eternal life

Memorialized:
Oskar (Asher) Szlenger
and Family
Toronto-Canada

To the Eternal Memory

My father: **Shlomo Szperber**

My mother: **Sura Szperber**

My brother: **Izak Szperber**

My sister: **Gela Kalb** born **Szperber**

My sister: **Rayzel Rubinfeld** born **Szperber**

My brother-in-law: **Berl Rubinfeld**

All perished at the hands of the Nazi murderers

May G–d avenge their blood

May their souls be bound up in the bond of eternal life

Memorialized:
Hela Blond born **Szperber**
Bronx-New York

We Sanctify the Memory of

Elihu (Ela) Szer)

Shayndl-Sluba Szer mother of **Sura (Sala) Geler** born **Szer**

Elihu (Ela) Szer son of **Yisroel** – brother of **Sura Szer**

Fruma Salamon-Geler – mother of **Avraham Geler**

Yehezkiel Salamon-Geller son of **Mekhl** – brother of **Avraham Geler**

Lazar Salamon-Geler son of **Mekhl** – brother of **Avraham Geler**

Rayzl Salamon-Geler daughter of **Mekhl** – sister of **Avraham Geler**

All perished in the years of the Holocaust

May G–d avenge their blood

May their souls be bound up in the bond of eternal life

Memorialized:
Sura (Sala) and Avraham Geler
Montreal-Canada

[Page 432]

To the Eternal Memory

Father: **Chaim Mosner** son of **Yehoshua**

Mother: **Mirl Mosner** daughter of **Avraham**

My brother: **Yaakov Leon Schwartz**

His wife: **Ada Schwartz** from the **Herzman** family

My sister: **Rosa Rochel** from the **Schwartz** family

Her husband: **Yosef Rovel**

Her children: **Marcel, Milek, Roman Rovel**

Yaakov Leon Schwartz

All perished at the hands of the Nazi murderers

May their memory be for a blessing

Memorialized
Aharon (Schwartz) Sacher
Kibbutz Marchavia

To the Eternal Memory

My father: **Maks Szprung**

My mother: **Sala Szprung**

My brother: **Dovid Szprung**

My sister: **Basia Szprung**

My sister: **Hela Szprung**

All perished in the years of the Holocaust

May G–d avenge their blood

May their souls be bound up in the bond of eternal life

Memorialized:
Anna Blat born **Szprung**
Yonkers, New York

[Page 431]

We Sanctify the Memory of

Yosef Zohar (Klar)

fell in the call of duty on the submarine "Dakar"

Son of R' **Eliezer Zohar** (Klar), born in Tarnow, a business man who was just, respected and religious emigrated to Erez (Israel) after the Holocaust.

Yosef was born in 5706 (1946), graduated high school at the age of 17 and went to Bar-Ilan university to study Physics. After a year he decided to transfer to the Technion. Because of the difficult money situation of his parents, he began to teach elementary physics and math. He was exempt from serving in the army- because at the time he taught at the "Eztah" school.

He decided to join the army and volunteered to serve on a submarine. He completed the course with distinction and was sent to England but never returned home. He was one of the heroic victims on the "Dakar" submarine.

Honor and praise to the hero **Yosef Zohar (Klar)** !

Honor and condolences to his parents

Memorialized:
The Tarnow community in Israel

Tarnow Book Index

(Note: this is not the Necrology, which is in volume 2 of the book and was published in 1968)

A	B	C	D	E	F	G	H	I	J	K	L	M
N	O	P	Q	R	S	T	U	V	W	X	Y	Z

Abramowitz-Horowitz, Dvorah

Ackerman, Lala

Ader, Dr. Anzelem

Adler, Dr. Emil

Adler, Maurycy

Adler, Max

Adler, Y.

Afner, Dr. Yosef

Afner, Henne

Afte, Dr., Mrs.

After, Moshe

Alban, Chaim

Alban, Mendel

Alban, Shmuel

Alweis, Yonah

Amsterdam, Moshe

Anisfeld, Gisela

Anisfeld, Shachna

Anker, Moshe

Ansky, M.

Appel, Shimon

Arak, HaRav Kalman

Arak, HaRav Meir

Arantz, Moshe

Argand

Arimawitz, Hersh

Armien, Dr. Chaim

Armien, Herman

Armien, Sima

Armien, Y.

Arnold, Dr. Chaim

Arnstein, Dr. Yehuda

Arnstein, HaRav Yaakov

Arnstein, Moshe

Arshitzer, David

Arziser, Idele

Arzt, Sigmund

Asterweil, Dr.

Asterweil, Gavriel

Asterweil, M.

Asterweil, Shimon

Asterweil, Yisrael

Auerbach, Leib

Auver, Dr. Ernst

Averdam, Chaim

Averdam, Sarah

Averdam, Shimon

Averdam, Zecharia Mendel

Avida, M.

Avida, Yaakov

Avinger, Dora

Avinger, Eliezer

Avinger, HaRav Chaim Eliezer

Avinger, HaRav Shalom David

Avinger, HaRav Yisrael Yosef

Avinger, Menashe

Avinger, Ravi Meir

Avinger, Yechiel

Avinger, Yitzchak David

Avsiskin, M. M.

Baber, Dr. Herman

Badner, Benyamin

Baer, Avraham

Balzam, Max

Balzam, Mendel

Banat, Sarah

Banch, Yosef

Baran, Dr. Shalom

Baran, Eliahu

Baran, Mina

Baranowitz, HaRav

Barganicht, Dr. Leon

Barganicht, Y.

Barivitz, Michal

Batist, David

Baum, David

Bazler, Dr. Anselem

Bazler, Pinchas

Beck, Dina

Beck, S.

Becker, David

Beitch, Alter

Ben Gurion, David

Bergman, Yeshayahu

Berkelhamer, Beryl

Berkelhamer, Dr. Wilhelm

Berkelhamer, Leah

Berman, M.

Bernstein, Gedalyahu

Bernstein, Gedalyahu

Bernstein, Hersh

Bernstein, Idel

Bernstein, Yakov

Bernstein, Yekeli

Bernstein, Yisrael

Bester, Yisrael

Betrebenis, Benyamin

Betrebems, Shmuel

Bialik, C. N.

Biederman, Yisrael

Binenstock, Adam

Binenstock, Dr. Max

Binenstock, Francisca

Binenstock, L.

Binenstock, Leizer

Binenstock, Sarah

Binenstock, Yakov, M.A.

Birer, R.

Birkan, Perl

Birkan, Yosef

Birnbaum, Leon

Birnbaum, Natan

Birnbaum, Yichiel

Bistrisky, Natan

Bitner-Friedman, Golda

Bitner, Yechiel

Bitner, Yitzchak

Bland, Mrs. S.

Bland, Mrs. E.

Blazer, Dr. Mendel

Blazer, Yisrael

Blazer, Yitzchak

Bleicher, Shlomoh

Bleiweiss, Asher

Blitz, Shmuel

Bloch Mertz, Dr.

Bloch, Dr. Martshin

Bloch, Dr. Shimon

Bloch, Yaakov

Bloch, Zev

Blonder, Faivel

Bloomer, Hersh Mendel

Blumenfeld, Dr. Henrik

Blumenkrantz, Moshe

Blumenkrantz, Nachum

Blumenkrantz, Shimon

Bluner, Feige

Blutman, Chaike

Blutman, Yechezkel

Borstin, Avraham

Borstin, Pinia

Boterfas, Yitchak

Brach, Emil

Brachfeld, David

Bramberg-Vitkowsky, Dr.

Brandsteter, Devorah

Brandsteter, Michal

Brandsteter, Mordechai David

Brandsteter, Shaul

Brandsteter, Yehoshua

Brandsteter, Yizchak

Brau, Zelig

Braun, Cheninah

Braun, Naftali

Brezel

Brig, Artur

Brig, Emil

Broah, Yitzchak

Broder, Toviya

Broder, Yosef

Bronstein, Mordechai

Bruckner, Yakov

Cahane, Avraham

Cahane, Wolf

Camet, Dr. Avraham

Camet, Ester

Casher, Eva

Casher, Henia

Chiut ?, HaRav Dr. Tzvi

Cooperman, Chaim

Damast, Nataniel

Damast, Yosef

David, Dr. Elchanan

Dintenfas, Dr. Emil

Dintenfas, Max

Dintenfas, Michal, M.A.

Dintenfas, Shmuel

Doar, Mendel

Dorst, Gavriel

Drezner, Dr. Yulius

Drucker, Avraham

Drucker, Mordechai

Dzshikavs, C. (Chaim Yitzchak Korn)

Ebner, Dr. Meir

Eched, Haem

Ecksterman, Maniek

Edelstein, Antanina

Edelstein, Bernard

Eder, Hersh

Eder, Izak

Eder, Shmuel

Ehrenberg, HaRav

Ehrenberg, Yakov

Ehrenfreund, Dr. Henrik

Ehrenprise, Mordechai

Ehrlich, Chaim

Ehrlich, Henrik

Ehrlich, Yehoshua

Ehrlich, Yosef Shmuel

Eichenholz, David (Linkowitz) M.A.

Eichenholz, Dr. David

Eichenholz, Hela

Eichenholz, Yakov

Eichhorn, Shlomoh

Einhorn, David

Einhorn, Henuch

Einhorn, Maximilian, Engr.

Einspruch, Nachum

Eisen, Shmuel

Ekstein, M.

Elenberg, Dr.

Elend, Yakov

Ender, Leon

Engel, David

Engel, HaRav Wolf

Engel, HaRav Yosef

Engel, Yechiel

Engelberg, Yitzchok

Engelhart, Shmuel

Englander, Chaim

Englander, Schul-Inspector

Englander, Yechiel

Etkes, Yoel

Faber, Yitzchok

Fabian, Yakov

Fagelfang

Faner, Lipa

Farnes, Naftali

Fassel, Chanah

Fassel, Mrs.

Fast, David

Fast, Moshe

Fastring, Shlomoh

Fastring, Yechezkel

Faust, Abush

Faust, Zelig

Fedever, Yosef

Fefer, Chaim

Fefer, F.

Feig, Dr. Yehoshua

Feig, Rivka

Feigenbaum, Chaim Leib

Feines, Naftali Elimelech

Feir, Gittel

Feirstein, Nech

Feirstein, Zashka

Feitel, Yakov

Feivel, Dr. Lazar

Feivels, Mordechai Eliahu

Felber, Mechel

Feld, Marcus David

Feldbaum, Gustav

Feldbloom, Dr. Shimon

Feldgreve(r?), Chaim Itshe

Feldstein, Leon

Fenichel, Dr. Emil

Fenichel, Ruben

Fenichel, Sigmund

Fenig, Adolf

Fenig, Ezra

Fenster, Hersh

Fiereisen, Moshe

Filerstarf, Sigmund

Fink, Dean (?) Wolf

Finkelstein, Shlomoh

Finkelstein, Shoel

Finkelstein, Y.

Fish, Avigdor

Fish, Dr. Yitzchok

Fish, Yechel

Fishler, Dr. Heshel

Fishler, Shoel

Fishman, HaRav (Mimen)

Flanzer, Tolek

Flatau, Y.

Fleisher, Kuba

Fleisher, Sofia

Fleisher, Zenon

Fleisher, Zigmund

Flur, Anna

Flur, Berta

Flur, Eliahu

Flur, Henrik

Flur, Herman

Flur, Milah

Flur, Regina

Flur, Yechezkel

Fluzer, Alexander

Freeman, Yosef

Freilich, Leon

Freireich, Obediah

Frenkel, Mendel

Freund, Shalom

Friedberg, Chaim, ?

Friedlander, Antek

Friedlander, Helah

Friedlander, Mrs.

Friedman, Chaim

Friedman, HaRav Zev

Fries-Epstein, Dr.

Fries, David

Fries, Leon

Fries, Shimon

Frimes, M.A.

Frisch, Yosef

Frishman, David

Fus, Aharon

Gal-Stein, Dora

Gans, Emil

Gans, Moshe,

Garden, A. D.

Garlitzer, Markus

Garlizer, Moshe

Gastwirth, Moshe

Gelb, Ignacy

Gelb, Rivka

Gelb, Sala

Gelbwax, Baruch

Gelernter, Hanka

Gelernter, Shlomo

Gershon, Dr. Gershoni

Gersten, Gavriel

Gersten, Hersh

Gersten, Leib

Gerstner (Paris)

Gertler, Leopold

Gertner, Kalman

Gertner, Yisrael

Geshiv, Manek

Geshiv, Refaeil

Getzler, Henne

Getzler, Mrs.

Getzler, Wolf

Getzler, Yisroel

Gewelb, Avraham (?)

Gewirtz, Eliahu
Gewirtz, Yosef
Giniger, Mauricy
Glas, Yosef (?) Shmuel
Glass, Y.
Glassman
Glazer, Leopold
Glazer, M.
Glazner, Pinchas
Glazner, Yisrael
Gleicher, Dora
Gleicher, Perelka
Glik, Hersh
Glik, Pinchas
Glik, Sala
Glik, Yakov
Goldberg, Alter
Goldberg, Chaim
Goldberg, Dr. Shlomoh
Goldberg, Ilsa
Goldberg, Naftali
Goldberg, Yulius
Goldfarb, H. Engr.
Goldhamer, Dr. Eliyahu
Goldman, Alexander
Goldman, David
Goldman, Mrs. C.
Goldman, Terach
Goldstein, Leon
Goldstern, Dr. Henrik
Goldwachs, Leon
Goldwasser, Yakov
Goldwasser, Yisrael
Goldzeller, David

Goldzeller, Yosef

Gotlieb, Lieber

Grabshrift, Yonah

Gralitzer, Avraham

Grasman, Leib

Grasman, Meir

Greber, Max

Green, Anna

Green, Sarah

Greenbaum, Dr. Yitzhak

Greenbaum, Toviyah

Greenbaum, Yitzhak

Greenberg, Dr., Mrs.

Greenberg, Henrik, Dr.

Greenberg, Hersh Meir

Greenberg, Yisrael

Greenberger, Chaim

Greenberger, Yosef

Greenfeld, Bluma (Spain)

Greenfeld, Gutman

Greenfeld, Hela

Greenfeld, Wilhelm

Greenhut, Victor

Greenspan, Yitzhak

Greenstein, Dr. Yitzhak

Greenstein, Mala

Greenstein, Mendel Leib

Gruder, Mrs.

Grushow, M.

Guter, Wilhelm

Haber, Dr. Chaim

Haber, Moshe

Haber, Shlomoh Mendel

Haber, Shmuel

Haber, Sigmund

Haberman, Yulius

Halberstam, HaRav Ben Zion

Halberstam, HaRav Chaim

Halberstam, HaRav Leibish

Halberstam, HaRav Shlomoh

Halberstam, Yechezkel

Halpern, Avraham

Halpern, Yisrael

Hamer, Chaim

Hamer, Ruven

Handelsman, Rivka

Hausman, Aharon

Hausman, Herman

Haut, Natan

Hecht, Martzel

Heinberg, David

Helin, Yitzchak

Heller, Eliza

Herbst, Benyamin

Herbst, Yeshayahu

Herbst, Zissel

Hershkovitz, Asher

Hershkovitz, Ester

Hertz, Mendel

Hertz, Yitzchak Mechel

Hertzberg, Chaim

Hertzman, Chaim

Herzig, Herman

Herzl, Dr. Theodore

Herzman, Yakov

Herzog, David

Hess, Moshe

Hilfstein, Dr. Chaim

Himelfarb, Melech

Hirsh, Baron

Hirsh, Baruch

Hirsh, Yehoshua

Hirshenhorn, Dvorah

Hirshenhorn, Shmuel

Hirshfeld, RaRav Dr.

Hirshhorn, Mauricy

Hochberg, Dr.

Hochman, Moshe

Hodes, Eliezer

Hodes, Mina

Hodes, Yehoshua

Hodes, Yosef Eon (?) Fatchihu (?)

Hofert, Ludwig

Hofmeister, Aharon

Hofmeister, Yitzhak (Chetzruny) (?)

Hofsteter, Avraham

Hollander, Dr. Yakov

Hollander, HaRav Michel

Hollander, Henryk

Hollander, Hersh Leib

Hollander, Hirsh Leib

Hollander, Ignacy

Hollander, Meir

Hollander, Y.

Holtzapel, Ignacy

Holtzer, Leon

Honig, Chaim

Honig, Franka, M.A.

Honig, Yeshayahu

Honig, Yisrael

Honig, Yochanan

Horn, Yechezkel

Horowitz, HaRav Alter (Dzshikav) (?)

Horowitz, HaRav Chaim Eliezer (Gradshisk) (?)

Horowitz, HaRav Leibish

Horowitz, HaRav Meir

Horowitz, HaRav Shaul

Horowitz, HaRav Yechiel

Horowitz, HaRav Yehoshua

Horowitz, HaRav Yehuda (Dzshikav) (?)

Horowitz, HaRav Yekele

Horowitz, HaRav Yisrael

Horowitz, HaRav Yitzhak (Stustein)?

Horowitz, RaHav Menachem Mendel

Hulem, Shmuel

Hulem, Z.

Hules, Dr.

Huter, Mauricy

Huter, Max

Hyman, Avraham Yehuda

Hyman, Yosef

Isaac, Yisrael

Israelavich, Herman

Jacob, HaRav Baranaver

Jacobowitz, Baruch

Jacobowitz, Leib

Jacobowitz, Reuben

Jakimowitz, E.

Jakimowitz, Feivel

Jartner, Avraham

Jasne, A. Wolf

Jekel, Dr. Yaakov

Jekele, Reb Moshe

Jeri, Yehudah (illegible) Yehudah Jeri, Ovediya

Joris, A.S.

Kahan, Benyamin

Kahan, Dr. David
Kahan, Dr. Leon
Kahan, Yisrael
Kalb, Wolf
Kapelansky, Shimon
Katz, Benyamin
Katz, Dr. Adolf
Katz, Nechemia
Katz, Paulina
Katz, Yosef
Kaufman, Aizik
Kaufman, Reuben
Keller, Chaim
Keller, Ignatz
Keller, Mendel
Keller, Naftali
Keller, Roza
Keller, Shlomoh
Keller, Shmuel
Kellman, Meir Izak
Kellner, Dr. Leon
Kellner, Leah
Kellner, Markus
Kellner, Paula
Kellner, Rafaeil
Kellner, Viktor
Kenner, Yakov
Kerner, Sigmund
Kerner, Yashka
Kimel, Hersh
Kirshenbaum, Yosef Chaim ?
Kitsch, Y.
Klausner, Feivel
Klefel, S.

Klein, A.

Klein, Dr. Edward

Klein, Karolina

Klein, Yosef

Klein, Zelik

Kleinberger, Mrs.(Paris)

Kleinhandler, Abush

Kleinhandler, David

Kleinhandler, Herman

Kleinhandler, R.

Kligman, Chaim Leib

Klopholtz, Moshe (?)

Klopholtz, Shlomoh

Kluger, Herman

Koad-Atstein, Leib

Koch, Moshe

Kogan, Inspector

Komet (Chomet Shlomeh)

Konarek, Leibish

Konarek, Yehoshua

Konarek, Zelika

Koretz, Yehuda Leib

Korn, A.

Korn, Blimah

Korn, Chaim Leib

Korn, Marim

Korndeich, Hersh Melech

Kornhauser, Yechiel

Kornila, Y.

Kornmehl, Matel

Kornmel, Baruch

Kornreich, Aizik (Aharon Dgni) ?

Kornreich, Matityahu

Kornreich, Matityahu

Kornreich, Mendel

Korpos-Nager, Chaim

Kramer, Natan

Kramer, Yosef

Krantz, L.

Krieger, Karol

Krieger, Yechezkel

Krietzer, Dr. Yakov

Kupferwasser, K-?

Kurtz, Etshe

Kurtz, Matek

Kurtz, Shlomoh

Kurtz, Yakov, ?

Kurtz, Yechiel

Kurtz, Zalman Yosef

Ladner, Dr. H.

Ladner, Herman

Ladner, Sarah

Laker, Beler

Landau, Dr. Refaeil

Landau, Erna

Landau, L.M.

Landau, Natan Neta

Landau, Yehoshua

Landman, Avraham

Landman, Yakov

Landman, Yosef

Langer, Yakov Ber

Langsam, M. Perl

Laskowitz, Engr.

Lau, Meir

Laufban, Yitzchak

Laufer (Paris)

Laufer, Avraham

Laufer, Markus
Laufer, Mordechai
Laufer, Shmuel
Laufer, Tashke
Laufer, Zalman
Lauterbach Yosef
Lauterbach, Herman
Lauterbach, Max
Lazar, Aharon
Lazar, Alter
Lazar, David
Lazar, Dr. Henrik
Lazar, Dr. Max
Lazar, Eichel
Lazar, H.
Lazar, Leon
Lazar, M.
Lazar, Mendel
Lazar, Wolf
Lederberger, Aharon
Lefelholtz, Y.
Leffel, Moshe Leib
Leffelholtz, S.Z.
Lehman, Naftali
Lehrfeld, David
Lehrhaupt, Eliyahu
Leib, Bernard
Leibel, Aharon
Leibel, Benyamin
Leibel, Dala
Leibel, Daniel
Leibel, David
Leibel, Mordechai
Leibel, Moshe

Leibel, Shevach

Leibel, Yakov

Leiner, Shimon

Leinwand, Avraham

Leinwand, Yisrael

Lemberger, Izak

Leon, Dr. Ignatz

Leon, Mordechai

Lerner, Zelig

Levenstein, Chaim Engr

Levine, Levi

Levniavsky, Fiegeh

Lichtblau, Chaim Hersh

Lichtblau, Chaya

Lichtblau, Wilhelm

Lichter, Berl

Lichter, Moshe

Lichter, Regina

Lichtig, Chaim

Lichtig, Manik

Lichtik, Mendel

Lichtinger, A.

Lichtinger, Leib

Lichtinger, Meir

Lichtinger, Yehudah

Lieber, Rachel

Lieber, Shimshon

Lieblich, Director Yitzchok

Linkowitz, David, M.A.

Lis, Kalman

Liss, M.

Lubianiker, P.

Ludmer

Lustig, Dr.

Lustik, Leon
Madshevitsky, Chana
Mahler, Alter
Mahler, Dr. Refa'eil
Maltz, Dr. David
Mandel, Dr. Wolf
Mandelbaum, Y.
Mandsein, Amelia
Mane, Yehoshua
Mangel, Wolf
Manheimer, Dr.
Manheimer, HaRav
Mankes, Dvorah
Mann, Maurycy, M.A.
Mann, Nella
Mann, Rabbi Yehoshua
Marcus, Aharon
Marcus, M.
Marder, Eliezer
Margases, Dr. S.
Margases, Yehoshua
Margases, Yosef
Margolies, Adam
Margolies, Artur
Margolies, Dr. Yosef
Margolies, Yoel
Margolies, Yulius
Marmer, Cela
Marmer, N.
Maurer, Aharon
Maurer, Shlomoh
Mazel, Golda
Mazes, Dr. Yosef
Meher, Shlomoh

Melinger, Franya
Melinger, Hersh
Meller, Berish
Meltzer, S.
Menase, S.
Menashe, Dr. A.
Menderer, Dr. M.
Menderer, Mrs.
Menderer, Yulian
Mendlinger, Chaim Hersh
Mertz, Dr. Shlomoh
Mertz, Dr. Yulius
Mertz, Herman
Mertz, Mrs.
Mertz, Perel, Engr.
Mestel, Yechezskel
Metzger, Wolf
Meyerhoff, Hersh
Michelowitz, Beinish
Mifelev
Miller, Betzalel
Miller, Manya
Miller, Mendel
Mintz, Leibel
Mintz, Moshe
Mintz, Wolf
Mintzer, Hersh
Mitz, Dr. Herman
Mitz, Dr. Leon
Mitzenmacher, (Paris)
Mokadi
Montefiori, Moshe
Morgenstern, Moshe Baruch
Moskatenblit, Dr.

Mossler, Berish

Mossler, Chaim

Mossler, Dr. Leon

Mossler, Dr. Wilhelm

Mossler, Ignacy

Mossler, Mendel

Mossler, Yehoshua

Mossler, Yoachim

Mossler, Yosef

Nachman, Wolf

Naftali, HaRav Rafshitzer

Naiger, Chaim

Naiger, Dr. David

Naiger, Moshe Aharon

Naiger, Y.

Navatni, Moshe

Nebensal, Branislau

Neifeld, N.

Neiman, A.

Neiman, Avraham

Neiman, Henrik

Neiman, Shimon

Neiman, Yakov

Neiman, Yechezkel

Neiman, Yisrael

Neistat, Melech

Neker, Yehoshua

Nichthauser, Y.

Nogaser, Emil, M.A.

Ochler, Aharon

Omansky, David

Omansky, Yosef

Ovisibel, HaRav Yehuda—(?) Geffen, Yehuda

Pasternak, Yitzchok

Patasmacher, Mendel

Perlberger, Branislaw

Perlberger, Yosef

Perlstein, Yisrael

Pinsker, Simcha

Pinsker, Yehudah Leib

Plachte, Engr.

Pomerantz, Lazar

Preminger, Michel, HaRav

Rachmiel, Leibush

Rachmiel, Shmuel

Radek, Karol

Ragle, Yosef

Rand

Rapapart, Simcha

Rapaport, Avraham My father (?) HaCohen

Rapaport, Ben Zion

Rapaport, David

Rapaport, HaRav Yisrael

Rapaport, HaRav Yitzchok

Rapaport, Moshe

Rapaport, Shaul

Rapaport, Shimon

Rapaport, Shmuel

Rapaport, Wolf

Rappaport, Dr. Edvard

Rastel, M.A.

Rauch, Leizer

Reich, Dr. Leon

Reich, Israel

Reich, Moshe, Engr.

Reich, Shimon

Rein, Aharon

Rein, Dr. Shlomoh

Rein, Yulius

Reinhold, Abush

Reinhold, Aharon

Reinhold, Melech

Renert, Nachman

Riger, Dr. Eliezer

Ringelheim, Dr. Adolf

Ringelheim, Herman

Rokh, Yehoshua, HaRav

Rosemarin, Dr.

Rosen, Yosef

Rosenbaum, Meir

Rosenberg, Markus

Rosenblat, Bruk (?)

Rosenblat, Engr.

Rosenblit, Dr. Ruven

Rosenbush, Dr. Max

Rosenfeld, Natan

Rosenthal, Leib

Rosenzweig, Aharon

Roskes, Mrs.

Roskes, Yitzchok

Roth, R.

Roth, Teodor

Rubashav, Zalman

Rubin, Avraham

Rubin, Dr. Branislav

Rubin, Hersh

Rubin, Moshe

Rubin, Raisel

Rubin, Wilhelm

Rudnitzki, Adolf

Rumeld, Tzvi Halevi

Sachwald (Paris)

Sagan, Shachna

Saldinger, Herman

Sali, Dr. Avraham

Salpeter, Leon, M.A.

Saltz, Elimelach Yehuda

Saltz, Eva

Saltz, Moshe Yosef

Sapir-Ringel, Ida

Sapir, M.

Sapir, Shimon

Sapir, Yehoshua

Sapir, Yosef

Sauerstram, Adolf

Sauerstram, Efraim

Savader, Chaim

Schmidt, Lipa

Schneider, Benzion

Schneider, David

Schneider, Mechel

Schneider, Yonah

Schwartz, Arnold

Schwartz, Chaim

Schwartz, Dr. Naftali

Schwartz, Yosef

Schwartzbard, Dr. Yitzhak

Schwartzbard, Herman

Schwartzcahal, Eidel

Schwartzcahal, Sarah

Seiden, Adolf

Seiden, David

Seiden, Dora

Seiden, Leon

Seiden, Shimon

Seidenverg, Ignatz

Seinwel, Regina

Seinwel, Shmuel

Seis, Shlomoh

Seis, Yehoshua

Selenfreund, Dr. Z.

Selinger, Chaim

Selinger, Eliezer

Selinger, Eliyahu

Selinger, Zisha

Shabatinski, Zev

Shalit, Dr. Edvard

Shantzer, Artur

Shantzer, Henrik

Shantzer, Karol, Engr.

Shap, C.

Shapira, Moshe

Shapira, Yisrael

Shapiro, Shmuel

Sharfstein, Tzvi

Shedlisker, Avraham

Shedlisker, Chaim Eliezer

Shedlisker, Yitzhak

Sheif, Alter

Sheif, Beryl

Sheif, David

Sheif, Engr.

Sheif, Shlomoh

Sheif, Yosef

Sheifer, Bila

Sheifer, Dr. Eugeniush

Sheifer, Dr. Yitzhak

Sheifer, Yitzhok

Sheitelavsky, Dr. Chaim

Shenberg, Yosef

Shenfeld, Dr. Simcha

Shenkel, Adam

Shenkel, Dr. Wolf

Shenkel, Natan

Shenkel, Wolf Ber

Shenkel, Yakov

Shenvetter, Avraham

Shenvetter, Natan

Shenvetter, Raman

Shenvetter, Yitzhok

Shezer, Zalman

Shildkraut, Shlomoh

Shiller, Shimon

Shitzer, Dr. Leon

Shitzer, Dr. Zigmund

Shlam, Eliezer, HaRav

Shlangenkapf

Shmarak, Dr. Emil

Shmelkis, Dr. Shmuel

Shmelkis, Gedaliyahu, HaRav

Shnur, Avraham, Our Father (?), HaCohen, HaRav

Shnur, David

Shnur, Lemel

Shnur, Tedi ?

Shnur, Yoel

Shoenenfeld, Alexander

Shoenenfeld, Leon

Shoenenfeld, Mauricy

Sholdenfrai, Shoel

Sholdenfrai, Wolf

Shudmak, Shmuel

Shulerer, Gedaliahu

Shwager, Edward

Shweber, Moshe

Shweber, Yitzhak
Silbiger, Dr. Siegmund
Silbiger, Sashke
Silbiger, Yulius
Silver, Yehoshua HaRav
Silverberg, Zalman
Silverfenig, Dr. Zecharya (Chesif)?
Silverfenig, Yeshayahu
Silverman (Paris)
Silverman, Dr. Yosef
Silverman, Eliezer
Silverman, Leibish
Silverman, S.
Silverman, Shabtai
Silverman, Toviyah
Silverstein, H.
Silverstein, Meir
Sima, Pinchas
Simcha, Dr. Zushislav
Simcha, Henrik
Simcha, Perel, M.A.
Sinagel, Leopold
Sinai
Singer, Alter
Singer, Avraham
Singer, Berish
Singer, Chaim
Singer, Dr. Martzel
Singer, Efraim
Singer, Gitel
Singer, Moshe
Singer, Yechezkel
Singer, Yosef
Singer, Yosef (Canada)

Siroka, Dr. Yisrael

Siroka, Meir

Sisler, Rivek

Skowronsky, Dr. Michel

Smolenskin, Peretz

Sobelson, Zashe

Sofer, HaRav Shimon

Sofer, Moshe

Sokolov, Nachum

Solomon, Dr. Febus

Solomon, Yakov

Somerman

Somerstein, Dr. Emil

Sommer, Chaim

Sosne, Shoshan

Spadek, M.

Span, Dr. Shmuel

Spangelet, Z.

Spanoff, Shmuel

Spanoff, Yehuda

Sparn, Oren

Sparn, Shlomoh

Sparn, Yosef

Speizer, Dr. Betzalel

Spenadel, Mrs.

Spenadel, Valislav

Spiegel, Dr. Leon

Spiegel, Franke

Spiegel, Natke

Spielman, Avraham

Spielman, Henrik

Spielman, Moshe

Spiller, Hugo

Spiller, Z.

Spindler, Leon

Spira, Dr. Yeshahayu

Spira, Maurycy

Spira, Meir, HaRav

Spira, S.

Spira, Wilhelm

Spira, Yechezkel

Spira, Zecharya Mendel

Spitz, Leib

Spitzer, Chaim

Spitzer, David

Spizman

Sprai, H.

Springer, Shmuel

Spritzer, Ella

Spritzer, Gusta

Srebbel

Starkman, Yonah

Stein, Aizik

Steinbeck, E.

Steiner, Yakov

Steinhauer, Hersh

Stiglitz, Honka

Stiglitz, Yehoshua

Stockfish, David

Straim, Yosef

Stram, Roza

Strasberg, Kalman

Straus, Ruben

Suberman, HaRav Alka

Sukman, Rafaeil

Sukman, Yosef

Sussheim

Tan, HaRav Dr. Yehoshua

Taub, Ansel

Taubenshlag, Adolf

Taubenshlag, Yosef

Taubensig, Dr. Rudolf

Teder, Shimon

Teitelbaum, Avraham

Teitelbaum, Moshe

Teitelbaum, Y.

Teitelbaum, Yeruchev

Templer, Pinchas

Templer, Yitzchok

Tenenbaum, Shimon

Tenenbaum, Tzvi

Terle, Dr. Gur Arieh

Tesse, Dr. Bernard

Timberg, Manik

Tish, Dr. Eliyahu

Tish, Henoch

Toibeles, Yakov, Mgr.

Traum, Yetta

Treller, Emanuel

Trintscher, Pinchas

Truvig, Y.

Tshech, Bernard

Tshechanavsky, H.

Tuchsherer, Moshe

Wachskurtz, Abraham

Wachskurtz, Pinchas

Wachtel, Mrs.

Wald, Natan

Wald, Yehudah

Waldman-Ginter, Hendel

Walk, Nachman Leib

Walk, Zalman

Wall, Berl

Wallach, Yitzchak

Wallach, Zalman Leib

Wallafsky, Alter

Walstock, Regina

Wandstein, Dr. Shmuel

Warhaftick, Dr. Shmuel

Washitz, Dr. Efraim Fishel

Wasnitzer, Yochanan

Wasser, C.

Wasserman, Dr. Herman

Waxman, Reuben

Weg, Aharon

Weg, Shimon

Weider, Dr. Emil

Weil, Shmuel

Weinberg, Avraham

Weinberg, Prof.

Weinberger, Eliahu

Weindling, C.

Weinfeld (?), Heinrich

Weinfeld, Max

Weingarten, Lipa

Weinig, Naftali

Weinman, Ben Zion

Weinman, Hersh Tzvi

Weinreb, Berl

Weinstock, Yosef

Weintraub, Richard

Weintraub, Shmuel

Weisenberg, Avraham

Weiss-Kellner, Anna

Weiss, Chaim

Weiss, Dr., Mrs.

Weiss, Emil

Weiss, Michal

Weiss, Milek

Weiss, Shlomo

Weiss, Zala

Weissbloom, David

Weissbloom, HaRav

Weissen, Moshe Aharon

Weisser, A. L.

Weisser, Berish

Weisser, Pesachya

Weissman, Chiut Fishel

Weissman, Dvorah

Weissman, Mordechai

Weissman, Moshe

Weissman, Rabbi Chiut Mordechai

Weissman, Shmuel

Weitz, Shmuel

Weitzman, Dr. Chaim

Weitzner, Abba

Wellner, Shlomoh

Weltsh, Tuvka

Wenger, A.

Wertzel, Irma

Wertzel, Ozer

Wertzel, Shlomo

Westreich, Avraham

Westreich, Engr.

Westreich, Leon

Wexler, Devorah

Wexler, Menke

Wexler, Moshe

Wexler, Wolf

Wexler, Yisrael

Wexner, Toviya, Engr.

Wiesenfeld, Moshe

Wild, Natan

Wildstein, Miriam

Wind, Etel

Wind, Yisrael

Witte, Dr. Chaim

Witte, Reuben

Wittmeyer, Hersh

Wolf, B.

Wolf, David

Wolf, HaRav Shlomo

Wolf, Pinchas

Wolf, Y.

Wolf, Yisrael

Wolfson, David

Woolf, Yosef

Wortzel, Eliezer

Wrubel, Izak

Wrubel, Tzvi

Zangen, Ben Zion

Zanin, M.

Zei(?)er, Yaachim, M.A.

Zeisel, Y.

Zeller (Paris)

Zeller, Yosef

Zettel, Shmuel

Zichner, Yisrael

Zimand

Zimetbaum, HaRav Aharon

Zimetbaum, Pinchas

Zimetbaum, Rafeil

Zimetbaum, Shmuel

Zimmerman, Bernard, Engr.

Zimmerman, Dr. Yehuda

Zimmerman, Yakov

Zinaman, Dr.

Zins, David

Zins, Shmuel

Zins, Solomon

Zitranenbaum, Yitzchak

Zucker, Estka,

Zucker, Shmuel

Zweibel, Chaim David

Zwicker, Ella

Zwicker, Prof. Tzvi, Prof.

Tarnów Necrology Supplement

Introduction

The first necrology was published in Vol. II of the Tarnów Yizkor book as the "Alphabetical List of Names" or "זוכצעטל פון נעמען". In the years that have transpired, members of Holocaust victims' families have become active in Jewish genealogy and ancestral shtetl groups, including the Jewish Tarnow Facebook group. It became apparent that the original necrology omitted a large number of Tarnów Holocaust victims, and that an update would be desirable before the names were lost to the passage of time and memory.

In 2018, the Jewish Tarnow Facebook group solicited its members to contribute the names and information available about their family who died in the Holocaust. With over 1200 members, the contribution of names was significant. Russ Maurer, one of the group moderators, collated the supplement on behalf of the group. The supplement was added to the online Yizkor book in August 2020 and updated in July 2021. It is thus not part of the original Yizkor book and is meant as an addition to the original necrology.

The integrity of each Facebook group member's contribution has been retained in the supplement. The first surname provided by each contributor is shown in **BOLD**. These **BOLD** names appear in alphabetical order, but the overall list is not alphabetical because each member's contribution can include several different surnames. We recommend using the index to quickly locate a name in the supplement.

Jill Leibman

TARNOW NECROLOGY SUPPLEMENT

SURNAME	First Name	Notes
ABEND	Efraim (Fishu)	
AMSTER	Debora	mother of Efraim
ABEND	Shimon	father of Efraim
ABEND	Eda	sister of Efraim
ASHMAN	Sam	
FOLKMAN	Abraham	
RAUCHWERG	Maks	
RAUCHWERG	Melvina	
RAUCHWERG	Lazar	
RAUCHWERG	Ruth	
SCHWEID	Helen	
SCHWEID	Stella	
SCHWEID	Dita	
VOLKMAN	Artur	fruit store owner; lieutenant in Polish army
AUSSENBERG nee STEINER	Chaje Freude	Shot 1942, Tarnów Jewish cemetery.
BARBASCH	Joel	Died 6-Feb-1942; heirs 'resettled' (Polish wysiedleni, Nazi term for 'resettlement,' a euphemism that usually referred to transport to a death camp). Source: A. Volkman of Judenrat Tarnów, Referat Porad Prawnych L:1511/42/4 dated 21- Nov-1942.
DOMINITZ	Mozes	Died 25-Jan-1942; wife Feiga 'resettled' (Polish wysiedleni, Nazi term for 'resettlement,' a euphemism that usually referred to transport to a death camp); children Hirsch and Szyfra reside 8 Ochronek St. Tarnów. Source: A. Volkman of Judenrat Tarnów, Referat Porad Prawnych L:1511/42/4 dated 21-Nov-1942.
EISEN	Mechel	Died 8-Feb-1942; heir Natan EISEN resided 2/7 Bóźnic St., Tarnów. Information about real estate on document. Source: A. Volkman of Judenrat Tarnów, Referat Porad Prawnych L:1511/42/4 dated 21-Nov-1942.
FEDERGRÜN	Selig	Died 16-Jan-1942; heirs 'resettled' (Polish wysiedleni, Nazi term for 'resettlement,' a euphemism that usually referred to transport to a death camp). Source: A. Volkman of Judenrat Tarnów, Referat Porad Prawnych L:1511/42/4 dated 21- Nov-1942.
GOLDMAN	Izak	Died 21-Jan-1942. Born in 1853. Heirs unknown. Source: A. Volkman of Judenrat Tarnów, Referat Porad Prawnych L:1511/42/4 dated 21-Nov-1942.
HAUT	Szyja	Died 9-Jan-1942. Wife Feiga, daughters Cesia STEUER and Malka GOLDBERG were 'resettled' (Polish wysiedleni, Nazi term for 'resettlement,' a euphemism that usually referred to transport to a death camp). Daughter Ryfka TEICHNER resides at 10 Lwowska St, Tarnów. Son Adolf HAUT resides in Holland and daughter Róża BEGLEITER resides in America. Source: A. Volkman of Judenrat Tarnów, Referat Porad Prawnych L:1511/42/4 dated 21-Nov-1942.
KLEIN	Markus	Died 9-Feb-1942. Son Leon resides 3/1 Widok St. Tarnów. Source: A. Volkman of Judenrat Tarnów, Referat Porad Prawnych L:1511/42/4 dated 21-Nov-1942.
KLEINHANDLER	Chaskel	Died 28-Mar-1942; heirs unknown. Information about real estate on document. Source: A. Volkman of Judenrat Tarnów, Referat Porad Prawnych L:1511/42/4 dated 21-Nov-1942.
KOHANE	Józef	Died 18-Jan-1942. No heirs. Source: A. Volkman of Judenrat Tarnów, Referat Porad Prawnych L:1511/42/4 dated 21- Nov-1942.

LESER	Lea	Died 15-Jan-1942. Relatives Leon, ? and Abraham LESER reside at 38 Lwowska St Tarnów. Source: A. Volkman of Judenrat Tarnów, Referat Porad Prawnych L:1511/42/4 dated 21-Nov-1942.
LENKOWICZ	Chiel	Died 2-Jan-1942. Heirs 'resettled' (Polish wysiedleni, Nazi term for 'resettlement,' a euphemism that usually referred to transport to a death camp). Source: A. Volkman of Judenrat Tarnów, Referat Porad Prawnych L:1511/42/4 dated 21- Nov-1942.
LION	Izydor	Died 16-Mar-1942. Wife apparently resides in Palestine. Relative Fela LION resides at Nowa 15, Tarnów. Information about real estate on document. Source: A. Volkman of Judenrat Tarnów, Referat Porad Prawnych L:1511/42/4 dated 21-Nov-1942.
MARGULIES	Samuel	Died 10-Mar-1942. No heirs. Source: A. Volkman of Judenrat Tarnów, Referat Porad Prawnych L:1511/42/4 dated 21- Nov-1942.
MÜLLER	Pinkas	Died 15-Jan-1942. No heirs. Source: A. Volkman of Judenrat Tarnów, Referat Porad Prawnych L:1511/42/4 dated 21- Nov-1942.
PADWE	Szame	Died 26-Mar-1942. Son-in-law Gutter resides at 14a Wolności Pl. and daughter Feiga at 22/7 Lwowska. Source: A. Volkman of Judenrat Tarnów, Referat Porad Prawnych L:1511/42/4 dated 21-Nov-1942.
PICK	Leo	Died 9-Feb-1942. ' Not registered in the Office.' Source: A. Volkman of Judenrat Tarnów, Referat Porad Prawnych L:1511/42/4 dated 21-Nov-1942.
ROSENBLATT	Juda	Died 27-Jan-1942.'Not registered in the Office.' Source: A. Volkman of Judenrat Tarnów, Referat Porad Prawnych L:1511/42/4 dated 21-Nov-1942.
ROSENFELD	Jan	Died 26-Mar-1942. Heirs unknown. Source: A. Volkman of Judenrat Tarnów, Referat Porad Prawnych L:1511/42/4 dated 21-Nov-1942.
SCHMUCKLER	Samuel	Died 3-Feb-1942. Heirs unknown. Source: A. Volkman of Judenrat Tarnów, Referat Porad Prawnych L:1511/42/4 dated 21-Nov-1942.
SCHWARZ	Herman	Died 23-Jan-1942. Heirs unknown. Source: A. Volkman of Judenrat Tarnów, Referat Porad Prawnych L:1511/42/4 dated 21-Nov-1942.
SCHONWETTER	Salomon	Died 23-Mar-1942. Daughter Rozalia resides 46 b/2 Lwowska St. Tarnów Source: A. Volkman of Judenrat Tarnów, Referat Porad Prawnych L:1511/42/4 dated 21-Nov-1942.
SCHREIBER	Chaim	Died 24-Mar-1942. Heirs resettled Source: A. Volkman of Judenrat Tarnów, Referat Porad Prawnych L:1511/42/4 dated 21-Nov-1942.
SEIDEN	Hirsch	Died 27-Feb-1942. Son Zygmund resides 2 Debęn Square Tarnów. Source: A. Volkman of Judenrat Tarnów, Referat Porad Prawnych L:1511/42/4 dated 21-Nov-1942.
SPANGELET	Abraham Eliezer	Died 4-Mar-1942. Heirs Tauba Reise, Markus and Chawa reside 2/5 Zamkniętej St Tarnów. Source: A. Volkman of Judenrat Tarnów, Referat Porad Prawnych L:1511/42/4 dated 21-Nov-1942.
SPITZER	Salomea	Died 25-Jan-1942. Heirs 'resettled' (Polish wysiedleni, Nazi term for 'resettlement,' a euphemism that usually referred to transport to a death camp) Source: A. Volkman of Judenrat Tarnów, Referat Porad Prawnych L:1511/42/4 dated 21- Nov-1942.
SMIGA	Icek	Died 26-Feb-1942. Wife Sprinca resides 41/2 Starodąbrowskiej St Tarnów Source: A. Volkman of Judenrat Tarnów, Referat Porad Prawnych L:1511/42/4 dated 21-Nov-1942.
TOPPEL	Mojżesz	Died 25-Mar-1942. Heirs unknown. Source: A. Volkman of Judenrat Tarnów, Referat Porad Prawnych L:1511/42/4 dated 21-Nov-1942.
WACHSKERZ	Nicha	Died 13-Mar-1942. Heirs unknown. Source: A. Volkman of Judenrat Tarnów, Referat Porad Prawnych L:1511/42/4 dated 21-Nov-1942.
WESTREICH	Adolf	Died 21-Feb-1942. Daughter Gizela resides 34/7 Lwokska St Tarnów. Source: A. Volkman of Judenrat Tarnów, Referat Porad Prawnych L:1511/42/4 dated 21-Nov-1942.

WIKLER	Efroim	Died 9-Mar-1942. Heirs unknown. Source: A. Volkman of Judenrat Tarnów, Referat Porad Prawnych L:1511/42/4 dated 21-Nov-1942.
WITTLIN	Izak	Died 2-Feb-1942. Heirs unknown. Source: A. Volkman of Judenrat Tarnów, Referat Porad Prawnych L:1511/42/4 dated 21-Nov-1942.
ZINS	Majer Ehrlich	Died 19-Mar-1942. Wife Sprinca deceased; children abroad. Information about real estate on document. Source: A. Volkman of Judenrat Tarnów, Referat Porad Prawnych L:1511/42/4 dated 21-Nov-1942.
SÜSS	Józef	Died 5-Mar-1942. Heirs unknown. Source: A. Volkman of Judenrat Tarnów, Referat Porad Prawnych L:1511/42/4 dated 21-Nov-1942.
BARDACH	Hilek	
BARDACH	Henryk	
BARDACH nee LAUBER	Adele	Born in Tarnów, lived in Vienna, wife of Hermann BARDACH
BARDACH	Hermann	Born in Tarnów, lived in Vienna
BLONDER	Chiel Itzak	Furniture dealer
BLONDER nee LIEBE	Lea	wife of Chiel Itzak
BRANDMANN	Max (Pinchas)	Born in Tarnów
BRANDMANN nee THORSCH	Olga	Wife of Max. Born in Brno, Czechoslovakia
BRANDMANN	Egon	Son of Max and Olga. Born in Olomouc, Czechoslovakia
BRANDMANN nee ROTHSTEIN	Hanna	Wife of Egon. Born in Krakow.
BRANDST ADTER (Brandst Atter)	Extended Family	
KANAR	Extended Family	
BRANDSTATTER	Leopold	
BRANDSTATTER		Wife of Leopold.
BRANDSTATTER		Daughter of Leopold.
BRATTER	Aaron	child aged 2 or 3
KESTENBAUM		child aged ~2
BRIGG	Artur	
BRIGG-FLAUMENHAFT	Paula (Pnina, Pepi)	
BRIGG	Marta	
SOKOLER	Berta	
SOKOLER	Wilhelmina	
FLAUMENHAFT	Elik	
FLAUMENHAFT	Mojsze	
FLAUMENHAFT	Pola	
FLAUMENHAFT	Kuba	
FLAUMENHAFT	Sara	
CELNIK	Matias	Born 11 Aug 1883. Son of Asher KORNREICH and Gitel CELNIK. Husband of Anna ROSENBLUM, father of Asher, Shoshana, Helena, Sabina and William CELNIK.
CELNIK nee ROSENBLUM	Anna	Born 29 May 1888 to Leib ROSENBLUM and Ester Gluckel MARKUS. Wife of Matias CELNIK. Mother of Asher Shoshana, Helena, Sabina and William CELNIK.
ROSENBLUM	Leib	Born abt. 1866. Husband of Esther Gluckel MARKUS. Father of Anna CELNIK (nee. ROSENBLUM), Serl FROHLICH (nee ROSENBLUM), Berl ROSENBLUM and Sigmund Szaja ROSENBLUM.

FROHLICH nee ROSENBLUM	Serl	Born circa 1890 in Tarnów to Leib ROSENBLUM and Esther Gluckel MARKUS. Married Ichel FROHLICH in Tarnów in 1918. Lived in Krakow.
FROHLICH	Ichel	Born c. 1889 in Budapest to Eliasz Dawid FROHLICH and Rosa AFTERGUT. Married Serl ROSENBLUM in Tarnów in 1918. Lived in Krakow.
FROHLICH	Hans Janek	Born 17-Jan-1922 in Vienna. Son of Ichel and Serl.
FROHLICH	Emanuel	Born 28-Nov-1928 in Vienna. Son of Ichel and Serl. Died 20 Nov 1942 in Tarnów.
CELNIK	Asher	Born 1 Feb 1910 to Matias CELNIK and Anna ROSENBLUM. Married to Rozia FREIMAN. Father of Esther CELNIK.
CELNIK nee FREIMAN	Rozia	Born 21 Dec 1912 to Nachem FREIMAN and Ema Antonia LAUB. Married to Asher CELNIK. Mother of Esther CELNIK.
CELNIK	Ester	Born 1941 to Asher CELNIK and Rozia FREIMAN.
SCHACHTER nee CELNIK	Helena	Born around 1916 to Matias CELNIK and Anna ROSENBLUM. Married to Isadore Schachter.
SCHACHTER	Isadore	Married to Helena CELNIK.
CELNIK	Sabina	Sabina CELNIK born around 1919 to Matias CELNIK and Anna ROSENBLUM.
DAAR	Markus	
DAAR	Rosalia	Wife of Markus.
DAAR	Edek	Son of Markus and Rosalia.
DIAMANT	Fatel	
DIAMANT	Matla	Wife of Fatel.
FELSEN nee DIAMANT	Rachela	Daughter of Fatel and Matla, wife of Mayer.
FELSEN	Mayer	Husband of Rachela.
FELSEN	Perl	Daughter of Mayer and Rachela.
DIAMANT	Serla	Daughter of Fatel and Matla.
DIAMANT	Alta-Ethel	Daughter of Fatel and Matla.
DIAMANT	Mala	Daughter of Fatel and Matla.
DIAMANT	Avrom Yitzchok	Son of Fatel and Matla.
EISLAND	Peretz	owned "Eldorado" cosmetics factory and store
EISLAND	Rivka	wife of Peretz born in Radomysl Wielki
EISLAND	Momiek	son of Peretz and Rivka
EISLAND	Sara	daughter of Peretz and Rivka
EISLAND	Mendel	son of Peretz and Rivka - twin of Sender
EISLAND	Sender	son of Peretz and Rivka - twin of Mendel
EISLAND	Chasklel	son of Peretz and Rivka
GARN	Chaim Lev	Born in Radomysl Wielki
GARN nee FORSTENZER	Hinda	wife of Chaim Lev
HONIG nee GARN	Meshka	daughter of Chaim Lev and Hinda born in Radomysl Wielki
HONIG	Naftali	husband of Meshka born in Radomysl Wielki
HONIG		son of Naftali and Meshka born in Radomysl Wielki
Ende	Extended Family	
PLANER	Extended Family	
ENGELBURG	Izaak	Printer. Son of Salamon and Feige.
ENGELBERG nee SCHMIDT	Cyla	Wife of Izaak.
ENGELBERG	Josef	Bookbinder. Son of Izaak and Cyla. Died 18 March 1942, Auschwitz.
ENGELBERG	Zvi	Son of Izaak and Cyla.

ENGELHARDT	Dr. Artur	
ENGELHARDT	Maurycy	engineer
FABER (nee ENGELHARDT)	Malwina	
ENGELHARDT	Aleksander	
ENGELHARDT	Franciszka	
FALLMAN / FELMAN	Avram Aba	Was a merchant and very religious man
FALLMAN nee WYMISNER	Chana Leah	Wife of Avram Aba
WYMISNER / FALLMAN	Sophie	Daughter of Avram Aba and Chana Leah
WYMISNER / FALLMAN	Golda	Daughter of Avram Aba and Chana Leah
WYMISNER /FALLMAN	Malka	Daughter of Avram Aba and Chana Leah
WYMISNER /FALLMAN	Isaac	Son of Avram Aba and Chana Leah
WYMISNER /FALLMAN	Rivka	Daughter of Avram Aba and Chana Leah
FEUER	Mattias Wolf	b. Tarnów, 24 August, 1874. Died circa 1943 either in Bochnia ghetto or Belzec.
FINK nee RIEMER	Sara	Born 9/12/1879, daughter of Hirschand Rywka nee FELDMAN. Wife of Chaim FINK.
GOTLIEB nee FINK	Rozalia	Born 1903 in Tarnów. Wife of Moses.
GOTLIEB	Moses	
RACHMIL nee FINK	Beila	Wife of Aaron.
RACHMIL	Aaron	
RACHMIL	Richard (Richek)	Son of Aaron and Beila. Born 1939
ISENBERG	Helena (Helusha)	Born c.1922, daughter of Asher and Leah nee FINK.
TRAUM nee SPRUNG	T abel	Born 1875, daughter of Yehuda and Chaja/Khana. Wife of Jozef Hirsch TRAUM.
BIEDER nee TRAUM	Ida	Born 1904.
BIEDER	Stacek? (Stanisław)	Husband of Ida.
BIEDER	?	Son of Ida and Stacek.
TRAUM (maiden name)	Lucia	Born 1911
?	?	husband of Lucia.
?	?	Son of Lucia and her husband.
FISCH	Dwora	
FISCH	Efroim Fiszel	
ABEND	Gerszon	
FRISCH	Josef Wilhelm	
FRISCH nee EICHENBAUM	Dwora Keile	
GAST/ DROBNER	Zvi Herman	Son of Simon GAST and Chava DROBNER,12-Dec-1895 (Tarnów) - 17-Jul-1940 (Buchenwald)
GASTWIRT	Rifka	
GASTWIRT	David	
GASTWIRT	Extended Family	
GELB	Joseph Pinchas	Sala FABER's grandfather
FABER	Aron	
FABER	Sala	Wife of Aron.
FABER	Joseph	Son of Aron and Sala.

FABER	Noami	Daughter of Aron and Sala.
FABER	Ruth	Daughter of Aron and Sala.
GEWOLB	Extended Family	
KUDLER	Extended Family	
HONIG	Extended Family	
AFFENKRAUT	Extended Family	
GEWOLB nee AFFENKRAUT	Pesha	
GEWOLB	Freida	
GOETZ	Joseph	furrier
GOETZ	Eugenia	wife of Joseph
GOLDBERG	Kalman	on Schindler's list
GOLDBERG	Chaim	
GOLDBERG	Sarah	Wife of Chaim
GOLDBERG	Baruch (Bonek)	Son of Chaim and Sarah
GOLDBERG	Eliezer	Son of Chaim and Sarah
GOLDBERG	Josef	Son of Chaim and Sarah
GOLDBERG	Enka (Esther?)	Daughter of Chaim and Sarah
GOLDBERG	Frania	Daughter of Chaim and Sarah
GOLDBERG	Rosa	Daughter of Chaim and Sarah
GOLDMAN	Izak/Izaak	died 28 February 1942
GOLDMAN	Efroim/Efraim	Son of Izak died 1942; daughter Blanka
GOLDMAN nee TISCH	Anna	Wife of Efroim/Efraim; died 1942; daughter Blanka
FEUERSTEIN nee GOLDMAN	Emilie	Daughter of Izak died 1942. widow pre war; no children
FENICHEL	Anna	Widow of Henrych FENICHEL (who died in 1921 and is buried in Tarnów cemetery); died - thought to be in Auschwitz
GRABERs	David	
GRABER	Herman	son of David
GRABER		wife of Herman
GRABER		child of Herman
GRABER		child of Herman
GRABER	Abraham	son of David
GRABER	Maurycy	son of David
KLEIN nee GRABER	Ester Gitl	daughter of David
KLEIN	Leon	son of Ester Gitl
KLEIN	Mali	daughter of Ester Gitl
FEIGENBAUM	Samuel	
FEIGENBAUM nee HERBST	Lea Mindl	wife of Samuel
FEIGENBAUM	Eliaser	son of Samuel and Lea Mindl
FEIGENBAUM	Abraham	son of Samuel and Lea Mindl
FEIGENBAUM	Osias	son of Samuel and Lea Mindl
FEIGENBAUM	Leon	son of Samuel and Lea Mindl
FEIGENBAUM	Adela	daughter of Samuel and Lea Mindl
FEIGENBAUM	Sara Rebecca	daughter of Samuel and Lea Mindl

FEIGENBAUM	Extended Family	
GRABER	Extended Family	
GRUN	Berl	1908-1944, born in Wola Otaleska (Mielec). Owned a clothing factory.
GRUN nee DEGEN	Chaja Ruchla	1912-1942/44. Wife of Berl
ROSENBAUM nee DEGEN	Bine	1909-1943, sister of Chaja GRUN, wife of Paul ROSENBAUM. Killed at Auschwitz.
ROSENBAUM	Amalie	Daughter of Paul and Bine.
ROSENBAUM	Solomon	Son of Paul and Bine.
GRUNFELD	Sarah	trader in chickens
GRUSZOW	Hershel	shoemaker
GRUSZOW	Feige	daughter of Hershel
GRUSZOW	Alte	daughter of Hershel
GRUSZOW	Zeiftel	daughter of Hershel
GRUSZOW	Nuchem	son of Hershel
GRUSZOW nee HIRSCH	Chana	wife of Nuchem
GRUSZOW		daughter of Zeiftel, age 3
HILLER	Ruven	14-Feb-1885 in Wielopole - 22-Jun-1942 Belzec.
HILLER nee HOLLANDER	Necha	Wife of Ruven. 30-May-1885 in Piwniczna - 22-Jun-1942 Belzec.
HILLER	Yechezkel Shraga (Chaskiel)	Son of Ruven and Necha. 1910 - 12-Apr-1945. Died near Berlin with the Polish Army.
HILLER	Abraham Eliezer	Son of Ruven and Necha. 1912 - 22-Jun-1942. Belzec.
HILLER	Nuchim Hersh Zvi	Son of Ruven and Necha. 1912 - 22-Jun-1942. Belzec.
HILLER	Yeshaya	Son of Ruven and Necha. 27-Mar-1926 - 22-Jun-1942. Belzec.
HIRSCH	Avraham	
HIRSCH nee TURTELTAUB	Frimet	wife of Avraham
HIRSCH	Samuel	son of Avraham and Frimet
HIRSCH	Zelma	wife of Samuel
HIRSCH	Rueben	son of Avraham and Frimet
HIRSCH	Ryfka Laja	wife of Rueben
HIRSCH	Chaja	daughter of Rueben and Ryfka Laja
HIRSCH	Aba	son of Rueben and Ryfka Laja
HIRSCH	Szyja	son of Rueben and Ryfka Laja
HIRSCH	Max Meyer	son of Avraham and Frimet
HIRSCH	Dora Reisel	daughter of Avraham and Frimet
HIRSCH	Tauba Sarah	daughter of Avraham and Frimet
HIRSCH	Nachum	b. 1887 Son of Jakub & Gitla. Killed June 1942, Belzec.
HIRSCH nee KARTAGENER	Dura	b. 1891 Daughter of Yusef & Belia. Wife of Nachum.
HIRSCH	Smul	b. 1890 Son of Jakub & Gitla. Shot and killed outside the synagogue 1941-1942. Probably buried in mass grave at Tarnów Cemetery. Smul ran the family grain business in Skrzyszow.
HIRSCH nee TISCH	Nehla	b. 1894 in Leksandrowa. Wife of Smul. Killed June 1942, Belzec.
HIRSCH	Moses	b. 1924 Son of Smul & Nehla. Killed, Dec. 19, 1944, Natzweiler/Flossenburg concentration camp. Buried in a mass grave at Blosenberg.
HIRSCH	Jozef	b. 1894 Son of Jakob & Gitla. Killed June 1942, Belzec.
HIRSCH nee DEBEL	Regina	b. 1903 Wife of Jozef. Killed June 1942, Belzec.

HIRSCH	Henek	b. 1936 Child of Józef & Regina. Killed June 1942, Belzec.
HIRSCH	Hadassah (Helena)	b. 1895 Daughter of Jakub & Gitla.
BERGMANN nee HIRSCH	Nicha	b. 1897 Daughter of Jakub & Gitla. Killed, Tarnów ghetto.
BERGMANN	Szyia	b. 1896 From Gorlice. Husband of Nicha. Killed, Auschwitz.
BERGMANN	Jakob Salomon	b.1928 Son of Nicha & Szyia. Killed, Auschwitz.
BERGMANN	Moses	b. 1931 Son of Nicha & Szyia. Killed, Auschwitz.
HUTNER	Seri	
HUTNER	Rachel	Daughter of Seri.
HUTNER	Chana	Daughter of Rachel.
HUTNER	Hanka	Daughter of Rachel.
HUTNER	Bella	Daughter of Rachel.
ZYLBERMAN	Mayer	Son of Feiga nee HUTNER, grandson of Seri.
HUTNER	Moses Meir	Son of Seri.
HUTNER	Family Of Moses Meir	Daughter-in-law and grandchildren of Seri
FRIES	Moshe	Seri's grand-daughter's husband
FRIES	Ester	Wife of Moshe.and grand-daughter of Seri
FRIES	Deborah	Daughter of Moshe and Ester and great-granddaughter of Seri
ICKOWICZ	6 Siblings Of Artur	
INGBER	Chaim (Heinrich)	11-Feb-1877 (Nowy Sącz) to 6-Sep-1939 (Tarnów)
INGBER nee KOHANE	Adele Eiga	19-Feb-1879 (Tarnów) to 9-Feb-1941 (Tarnów). Wife of Chaim.
KAHANE	Pinchas	Brother of Adele
KAHANE	Shimon	Brother of Adele
ISLER	Isaac	son of Leib and Rachel
ISLER	Simka	daughter of Leib and Rachel
ISRAELER	Dawid	
ISRAELER nee WOLF	Bina Riwka	wife of David
ISRAELER	Miriam	
ISRAELER	Raizel	
ISRAELER	Jenta	
ISRAELER	Chaia	
ISRAELER	Zeev Dov	
FEUERSTEIN nee ISRAELER	Frania	
FEUERSTEIN	Shimon	
LANDERER nee URABIN	Jochwet	
LANDERER	Solomon	
ISRAELER	Peretz	
ISRAELER	Lola	Wife of Peretz
ISRAELER	Dawid	Son of Peretz and Lola.
ISRAELER	Gusta (Gita)	Daughter of Peretz and Lola.
GELBWACHS	Jakob	Husband of Gusta
GELBWACHS nee WOLF	Gusta	Wife of Jakob.
GELBWACHS	Salomon	Son of Jakob and Gusta.
GELBWACHS	Sucher	Son of Jakob and Gusta.
GELBWACHS	Mailech	Son of Jakob and Gusta.

GELBWACHS	Baruch	Son of Jakob and Gusta.
GOLDFARB	Markus	
GOLDFARB nee WOLF	Marjam	Wife of Markus
GOLDFARB	Elek	Son of Markus and Marjam.
KRIESER nee GOLDFARB	Zofia	Daughter of Markus and Marjam, wife of Schmiel.
KRIESER	Schmiel	Husband of Zofia.
KRIESER		Child of Schmiel and Zofia.
GOLDFARB	Moniek (Moshe)	Son of Markus and Marjam.
GOLDFARB	Sacher	Son of Markus and Marjam.
ISRAELER	Marcus (Mordechai)	brother of David ISRAELER
IZAK	Herman/Hirsch	b. 1895.
IZAK	Sabina	Wife of Herman.
IZAK	Monek	Son of Herman and Sabina.
IZAK	Lesiek	Son of Herman and Sabina.
IZAK	Irena	Daughter of Herman and Sabina.
KORNHEISER	Benjamin	
KORNHEISER nee IZAK	Frymka Frida	Wife of Benjamin. Daughter of Mendel and Rywa nee ROZENBERGER.
IZAK	Balka-Balbina	Wife of Israel IZAK
IZAK	Regina-Rifka	Daughter of Israel IZAK and Balka-Balbina. Died 1943, age 7.
IZAK	Leon	b. 1906. Son of Mendel and Rywa nee ROZENBERGER.
IZAK	Lena	Wife of Leon
IZAK	Mendel	Son of Leon
IZAK	Chaim	b. 1912. Son of Mendel and Rywa nee ROZENBERGER.
IZAK	Rozia	
IZAK	Benjamin	
IZAK	Ciotka	
ROSENBLUM nee RUDNER	Hella	
LICHTIG	Mendel	
LICHTIG nee RUDNER	Hannah	Wife of Mendel.
LICHTIG	Bronka	Daughter of Mendel and Hannah.
JAKOB	Moshe	Died Tarnów ghetto.
JAKOB nee KURTZ	Devorah	b. Vienna. Wife of Moshe.
JAKOB	Gretka (Margalit)	b. 1914. Daughter of Moshe and Devorah.
WULKAN nee JAKOB	Hela	Daughter of Moshe from a previous marriage.
HORNIK nee JAKOB	Dora	Daughter of Moshe from a previous marriage.
JAKOB	Shaul	
WULKAN	Max	
WULKAN	Aaron	
JAKUBOWICZ	Arye [Juda Lajb]	b. 1886. Son of Baruch and Zisl. Died 1942.
JAKUBOWICZ nee KORN	Debora	b. 1888. Wife of Arye. Died 1942.
KORN	Blima	Mother of Debora.
JAKUBOWICZ	Avraham	b. 1912. Son of Arye and Debora. Died 1942.
JAKUBOWICZ	Frima	Age 4. Daughter of Avraham. Died 1942.
JAKUBOWICZ	Baruch	Age 1. Son of Avraham. Died 1942.
JAKUBOWICZ	Meir Maxmillian	b. 1918. Son of Arye and Debora. Died 1943.

JAKUBOWICZ	Eliezer	b. 1921. Son of Arye and Debora. Died 1942.
JAKUBOWICZ	Malka	Age 1. Daughter of Eliezer. Died 1942.
JAKUBOWICZ	Rivka	b. 1920. Daughter of Arye and Debora. Died 1942.
JAKUBOWICZ	Regina	b. 1926. Daughter of Arye and Debora. Died 1942.
JAKUBOWICZ	Bracha Lula	b. 1930. Daughter of Arye and Debora. Died 1942.
BLUMENKRANZ	Eliasz	b. 1884
BLUMENKRANZ	Malka Amalya	
BLUMENKRANZ	Sara	
FLEISCHER nee BLUMENKRANZ	Genia	b.1911. Daughter of Eliasz and Malka. Wife of Isak FLEISCHER.
FLEISCHER	Nusia	Age 12.
KALFUS	Isaac	Born 1890 Nowy Sacz, tailor
KALFUS nee CYZER	Rachel	Born 1891 Tarnów, wife of Isaac
KALFUS	Chana	Born 1929 Tarnów, daughter of Isaac and Rachel.
KALFUS	Chune	Born 1926 Tarnów, son of Isaac and Rachel.
KALFUS	Shaya	Born 1919 Tarnów, son of Isaac and Rachel.
GELERNTER nee KALFUS	Ester	Born 1915 Tarnów, daughter of Isaac and Rachel.
GELERNTER	Lipa	Born 1915 Tarnów husband of Ester
GELERNTER	Sprinzer	Born before 1941 Tarnów, daughter of Lipa and Ester
WEISER nee CYZER	Estera	Widow of Saul WEISER
KAMPF	Extended Family	
KOENIGSBUCH	Mojzesz	Born 1903
KOENIGSBUCH nee TURTELTAUB	Beila	Born 1902, wife of Mojzesz KOENIGSBUCH
KOENIGSBUCH	Estera	Born 1930, daughter of Mojzesz and Beila
KOENIGSBUCH	Rudla	Born 1934, daughter of Mojzesz and Beila
TURTELTAUB	Mojzesz	
TURTELTAUB nee ROSNER	Beila	Born 1903, wife of Mojzesz TURTELTAUB
KORNMEHL	Mindl	b. 1885
KORNMEHL	Zillah	b. 1919. Daughter of Mindl.
WINTER nee KORNMEHL	Rosa	b. 1890. Sister of Mindl KORNMEHL.
LEDER	Baruch	b. 1868. Husband of Idessa TURTELTAUB. Died 1942.
LEDER nee TURTELTAUB	Idessa	b. 1881. Wife of Baruch LEDER. Died 1942 in Tarnów Ghetto.
LEDER	Mojsesz	b. 1903. Son of Idessa and Baruch LEDER. Died Mauthausen 11/30/1944.
LEDER nee ROSNER	Rosie	b. 1908. Wife of Mojesz LEDER. Sent from Tarnów Ghetto to Auschwitz
LEDER	Jakob	b. 1940. Son of Mosjesz LEDER. Died 1942.
LEDER	Wolf Dov	b. 1941. Son of Mosjesz LEDER. Died 1942.
ENGELHARDT nee LEDER	Feige	b. 1907. Daughter of Idessa and Baruch LEDER.
ENGELHARDT	Chaim Samuel	b. 1941. Son of Feige LEDER ENGELHARDT
RICKS nee LEDER	Esther Ryfka	b. 1911. Daughter of Idessa and Baruch LEDER.
RICKS	Chaya Rela	b. 1940. Daughter of Esther LEDER RICKS
LEDER	Naftali	b. 1913. Son of Idessa and Baruch LEDER.
WINTER	Erwen	b. 1921. Son of Rosa KORNMEHL WINTER
WINTER	Cyla	b. 1923. Daughter of Rosa KORNMEHL WINTER.

WINTER	Sami	b. 1925. Son of Rosa KORNMEHL WINTER.
WINTER	Mayer	b. 1926. Son of Rosa KORNMEHL WINTER.
WINTER	Erna	b. 1931. Daughter of Rosa KORNMEHL WINTER, twin of Bella.
WINTER	Bella	b. 1931. Daughter of Rosa KORNMEHL WINTER, twin of Erna.
WINTER	Moses	b. 1934. Son of Rosa KORNMEHL WINTER.
ALLINA nee KORNMEHL	Mina	daughter of Aron Juda KORNMEHL
KORNMEHL	Chaya	daughter of Rabbi Mordechai KORNMEHL
KORNMEHL	Mindel	daughter of Rabbi Mordechai KORNMEHL
KÜNSTLICH	Dvora	
KÜNSTLICH	Jakub	
KWADRATSTEIN (QUADRATSTEIN) nee STERNHEIM	Bruche	Born 1860. Widow of Schulem (d. 1936)
KWADRATSTEIN (QUADRATSTEIN)	Leib	Son of Schulem and Bruche.
KWADRATSTEIN (QUADRATSTEIN) nee KRISHER (KRISCHER)	Mila	Wife of Leib.
KWADRATSTEIN (QUADRATSTEIN)	Claude	Son of Leib and Mila, born 1932.
SPANGLET nee KWADRATSTEIN (QUADRATSTEIN)	Rywka	Daughter of Schulem and Bruche
SPANGLET	Jozef	Husband of Rywka
SPANGLET	Chana	Daughter of Rywka and Jozef, born 1923
BIRSTENBINDER nee KWADRATSTEIN (QUADRATSTEIN)	Rachel	Daughter of Schulem and Bruche. Lived in Brno.
BIRSTENBINDER	Izak	Husband of Rachel.
KLAUSNER nee KWADRATSTEIN (QUADRATSTEIN)	Chana (Hania)	Daughter of Schulem and Bruche.
KLAUSNER	Shmuel	Husband of Chana
KLAUSNER	Mindl	Daughter of Chana and Shmuel
KLAUSNER	Shaul	Son of Chana and Shmuel
LADNER	Rozia	b. Borek, 1895. Wife of Herman. Mother of David, Henryk and Fryderyk. Died 1942, Tarnów.
LADNER	Henryk	b. Tarnów, 1925. Son of Herman and Rozia. Brother of David and Fryderyk. Died 1942 or 1943, Tarnów.
LADNER	Fryderyk	b. Tarnów, 1930. Son of Herman and Rozia. Brother of David and Henryk. Died 1942 Tarnów.
KUPFER	Regina	Sister of Rozia LADNER. Aunt of David, Henryk and Fryderyk. Divorced. Died 1942 Tarnów.
LEDERBERGER	Leib Israel (Leon)	jewelry store owner
ROSENZWEIG-LEDERBERGER	Sarah	wife of Leib Israel (Leon)
FALLMAN	Simcha	grocery owner
LEDERBERGER-KRESCH	Rachel	

LEIBEL, nee FENICHEL	Freude	b. circa 1862; deceased in 1943. Daughter of Kalman FENICHEL and Cyrla Fenichel, born LEDERER. Married to Jakob LEIBEL. Marriage date: August 1st, 1897, Tarnów.
LEIBEL	Jakob	b. circa 1863; deceased in 1943. Son of Anszel LEIBEL and Riwka, born METEL. Police officer. Married to Freude LEIBEL, nee FENICHEL. Marriage date: August 1st, 1897, Tarnów.
LEIBEL	Zygmunt	b. circa 1894; deceased in 1943. Son of Jakob LEIBEL and Freude LEIBEL, born FENICHEL. Merchant. Married to Malwina LEIBEL, nee RAPPEL.
STURM, nee LEIBEL	Salomea (Sala)	b.circa 1897; deceased in 1943. Daughter of Jakob LEIBEL and Freude LEIBEL, nee FENICHEL. Married to Jakob STURM. Mother of Marta STURM and Monek STURM.
LEIBEL, nee LANGER	Ernestina	b. 1895; deceased in 1943. Daughter of Markus and Chaja. Married to Anzelm LEIBEL. Mother of Markus LEIBEL and Henry Leopold LEIBEL
LEIBEL	Ernestina (Estka)	b. circa 1900; deceased in 1943. Daughter of Jakob LEIBEL and Freude LEIBEL, nee FENICHEL.
LINZENBERG, nee LEIBEL	Regina	Clerk. b. circa 1910; deceased in 1943. Daughter of Jakob LEIBEL and Freude LEIBEL, nee FENICHEL. Married to Henek LINZENBERG.
LEIBEL	Dr. Henry Leopold	Medical doctor. b. May 10th, 1921; deceased in 1943. Son of Anzelm LEIBEL and Ernestina LEIBEL, nee LANGER. Brother of Markus LEIBEL.
STURM	Marta	b. 1917; deceased in 1943. Daughter of Yakov STURM and Salomea STURM, nee LEIBEL. Sister of Monek STURM.
STURM	Monek	b. 1921; deceased in 1943. Son of Yakov STURM and Salomea STURM, nee LEIBEL. Brother of Marta STURM.
LANGER, nee WESTREICH	Chaja	b. circa 1870; deceased in 1943. Married to Markus LANGER. Mother of Ernestina LEIBEL, nee LANGER.
LEIBEL	Anzelm	b. 1889; deceased in August 17th, 1943. Son of Jakob LEIBEL and Freude LEIBEL, nee FENICHEL. Physician. Married to Ernestina LEIBEL, nee LANGER. Father of MARKUS LEIBEL and Henry Leopold LEIBEL.
LEIBEL	Karol (Kalman)	Born circa 1892, deceased in 1943. Son of Jakob LEIBEL and Freude LEIBEL nee FENICHEL. Merchant. Married to Stefania.
LANGER	Mania	Born circa 1893, deceased in 1943. Daughter of Markus and Chaja LANGER nee WESTREICH. Sister of Ernestina LEIBEL nee LANGER.
UNGER	Sarah	Born 29-Nov-1920. Daughter of Izak and Dora UNGER, sister of Lya UNGER.
UNGER	Dora	Born 28-Jul-1899. Married to Izak UNGER. Mother of Sarah UNGER and Lya UNGER.
UNGER	Lya	Born 5-Feb-1924. Daughter of Izak and Dora UNGER, sister of Sarah UNGER.
LESER	Josef Nachman	son of Izaak Hersch and Lea nee SHWARTZ
LESER nee GENGER	Frida	wife of Josef Nachman
LESER	Beila	born 1929, daughter of Josef Nachman and Frida
LESER	Shlomo	born 1931, son of Josef Nachman and Frida
LESER	Benjamin Baruch	born 1933, son of Josef Nachman and Frida
LESER	Aharon	born 1935, son of Josef Nachman and Frida
LESER	Boas	son of Aharon and Pnina
LESER nee HOLLANDER	Lea	wife of Boas
LESER	Salomon-Josef	son of Boas and Lea
LESER	Reuven	son of Boas and Lea
LESER	Perla	daughter of Boas and Lea
LESER	Abraham	son of Boas and Lea
LAM/LEM nee LESER	Ester	sister of Boas, wife of Yehuda

PARNES	Naftali Mielech	Son of Mendel & Chana. Born 1875
PARNES nee SEGAL	Bascha	wife of Naftali Mielech, daughter of Izak and Gitel Cypora
PARNES	Israel	Son for Naftali Mielech and Bascha, born 1899
PARNES nee STEIN	Miriam	Wife of Israel PARNES, born 1904
PARNES	Mendel	Son of Israel and Miriam PARNES
PARNES	Abraham	Son of Israel and Miriam PARNES
PARNES	Kopel	Son for Naftali Mielech and Bascha, born 1901
PARNES nee LUFTIG	Eidel Edel	Wife of Kopel PARNES
PARNES	Henry	Son of Kopel and Eidel, born 1937
PARNES	Michael	Son of Kopel and Eidel, born 1939
PARNES	Aliza	Daughter of Kopel and Eidel born 1940
STEINHORN nee PARNES	Pola	Daughter of Naftali Mielech and Bascha
STEINHORN	Bonim	Husband of Pola nee PARNES, born 1901
STEINHORN	Haim	Son of Pola and Bonim, born 1928
PARNES	Josef	Son for Naftali Mielech and Bascha, born 1909
PARNES nee BERGLAS	Chava Eva	Wife of Josef PARNES
PARNES	Baruch	Son of Josef and Chava, born 1935
PARNES	Helena Rachel	Daughter of Josef and Chave, born 1939
EKSTEIN nee PARNES	Sara	Daughter of Naftali Mielech and Bascha born 1910
EKSTEIN	Moshe	Sara's husband born 1908
EKSTEIN	Sabina	Daughter of Sara and Moshe, born 1939
LESER nee HOROWITZ	Rachel	b. circa 1874.
LESER	Naftali Hirsch	b. 1897
LESER nee SPANGELET	Hanna	b. circa 1901
LESER	Gitel (Gitusia)	b. 1927. Daughter of Naftali Hirsch and Hanna.
LESER	Miriam (Mania)	b. 1929. Daughter of Naftali Hirsch and Hanna.
LESER	Lusia	b. 1936. Daughter of Naftali Hirsch and Hanna.
LESER	Leib Ariel	b. 1899.
LESER	Syma	b. 1899. Wife of Leib Ariel.
LESER	Stenia	b. 1936. Daughter of Leib Ariel and Syma.
LESER	Mendel	b. 1902.
LESER nee ROSENBLUTH	Rosa (Rozia)	b. 1905. Wife of Mendel.
LESER	Monek (Moshe)	b. 1927. Son of Rosa (Rozia) and Mendel.
LESER	Hanna	b. 1933. Daughter of Rosa (Rozia) and Mendel.
LESER	Joel	b. 1906.
LESER	Natti	Wife of Joel.
LESER	Moritz	b. 1936. Son of Joel and Natti.
FISCHLER nee LESER	Frieda	b. 1915. Wife of David FISCHLER, b. 1902. Husband David survived. Deported from Brno to Terezin, Dec. 1941. Died with her children, Auschwitz, Oct. 1944.
FISCHLER	Hans	b. 1937. Son of David and Frieda.
FISCHLER	Anna	b. 1939. Son of David and Frieda.
LEZER	Rachel	
SHTEUER (UBER)	Bina	
SHTEUER (HOLZER)	Franka	

LUBASCH	Dawid	Husband of Cluwe Reisel, father of Adolf, Netta, and Chane, grandfather of Daria
LUBASCH nee KLAUSNER	Cluwe Reisel	Wife of Dawid, mother of Adolf, Netta, and Chane, grandmother of Daria
LUBASCH	Adolf	Born 1919, son of Dawid and Cluwe Reisel
LUBASCH	Netta	Born 1913, daughter of Dawid and Cluwe Reisel
PLANER nee LUBASCH	Chane	Born 1909, daughter of Dawid and Cluwe Reisel, wife of Israel, mother of Daria
PLANER	Israel	Husband of Chane
PLANER	Daria	Daughter of Israel and Chane
LUST	Extended Family	
LUST	Eliahu	
LUST	Rivka	
LUST	Shlomo	
FALLEK	Extended Family	
FALLEK	Sigmund	
FALLEK	Zusya	
FALLEK	Solomon	
LUSTBADER	Berta	born 27-Apr-1909 in Tarnów, murdered 1943 in Auschwitz. Left Tarnów abt. 1918, lived in Vienna and Amsterdam
LUSTBADER nee PRESSER	Leja	mother of Berta, born 30-Jun-1885, murdered 1942 in Sobibor. Left Tarnów abt. 1918, lived in Vienna and Amsterdam Widow of Moiszes LUSTBADER (died before WWII)
MARFELD	Josef	
MARFELD	Lea	wife of Josef
MARFELD	Fritz	son of Josef and Lea
MARFELD	Martin	son of Josef and Lea
MARFELD	Simon	son of Josef and Lea
MARGULIES	Frederyka	Shot in Tarnów 15-Nov-1942 at age 10.
MARGULIES	Dorota	Shot in Tarnów 15-Nov-1942 at age 5.
GROSSBARD	Estera	Born in Zabno, shot in Tarnów 1-Sep-1943 at age 65.
GROSSBARD	Hana	Born in Husakow, shot in Tarnów 15-Jul-1942, at age 32.
GROSSBARD	Chaim	Born in Zabno, shot in Tarnów 15-Jul-1942 at age 30.
MENER	Extended Family	
EISENBACH	Extended Family	
OWIDE	Bernard Dov	
OWIDE	Jakob	Father of Bernard Dov.
OWIDE	Mindla	Mother of Bernard Dov.
OWIDE nee MIRE	Sara Lea (Leitsche)	Wife of Bernard Dov.
OWIDE	Jakow	Son of Bernard Dov and Sara Lea.
OWIDE	Mechel	Son of Bernard Dov and Sara Lea.
OWIDE	Mala (Malka)	Daughter of Bernard Dov and Sara Lea.
OWIDE	Rozia (Shoshana)	Daughter of Bernard Dov and Sara Lea.
OWIDE	Shmuel	Son of Bernard Dov and Sara Lea.
OWIDE	Shlomo	Son of Bernard Dov and Sara Lea.
MIRE nee STORM	Chaya Lieba	Mother of Sara Lea.

MIRE	Efraim Nuta (Froyim)	Brother of Sara Lea.
MIRE nee RICK	Rywka Rosa	Wife of Efraim Nuta. From Wadowice.
MIRE	Miriam	Daughter of Efraim Nuta and Rywka Rosa.
FLAUMENHAFT nee MIRE	Golda Gizela	Sister of Sara Lea.
OWIDE	Jakow	
OWIDE	Rywka	From Rzeszów, wife of Jakow.
OWIDE	Shmuel	Son of Jakow and Rywka.
OWIDE	Shalom	Son of Jakow and Rywka.
KUBIE nee WEINMANN	Rozalia	
WEINMANN	Hugo	
WEINMANN	Henryk	
WEINMANN	Manes	
WEINMANN	Chaim	
WEINMANN	Paul	Son of Henryk.
WEINMANN nee PINER	Erna	Wife of Paul.
WEINMAN	Stanisław	Son of Paul and Erna.
WEINMAN	Richard	Son of Paul and Erna.
RAICHMAN nee WEINMANN	Ilsa (Elza)	Daughter of Henryk.
RAICHMAN	Shimon	Husband of Ilsa.
RAICHMAN	Alfred	Son of Shimon and Ilsa.
WEINMANN	Julian	Son of Henryk.
PILCER	Ignacy	Son of Herman and Łucja PILCER, brother of Juliusz PILCER. Born in Tarnów, lived in Rabka.
PILCER	unknown	Wife of Ignacy PILCER
PILCEROWA (PILCER) nee FUNARSKA	Gizela Maria Irena	Widow of Juliusz PILCER (died in 1929). Last known alive in Lublin in 1943, declared dead in 1945.
FUNARSKA nee LEUCHTER	Emilia	Widow of Emil FUNARSKI (died in 1922), and mother of Gizela. Arrested and imprisoned in Nowy Sącz in 1943 and subsequently murdered.
RAND	Josef	born c. 1868-1869, son of Samuel and Riwka RAND. Grocery owner. Widower of Freude (Freida) RAND nee FRIES (died 1939). Father of survivors Dawid (David), Aron (Artur) and Rafael.
GRÜNBERG nee RAND	Dwojra	Born 1905, daughter of Josef and Freuda, wife of Jakob mother of Gizela
GRÜNBERG	Jakob	Husband of Dwojra, father of Gizela
GRÜNBERG	Gizela	Daughter of Dwojra and Jakob
LEIBEL nee RAND	Ruchel	Born 1906, daughter of Josef and Freuda, wife of Pinchas
LEIBEL	Pinchas	Husband of Ruchel
REDNER	Yaacov Yosef	Died 1942 of Typhus (Tarnów)
REDNER	Ette	
REICH	Chaim	
FRANK	Hadasa	
FRANK	Efraim	
FRANK	Chana	
RINDER	Yosef	son of Moses and Estera Malka nee FELD
RINDER	Benzion	son of Moses and Estera Malka nee FELD
ROTH	Nathan	
RUBIN	Chaim	Born 1880 in Tarnów.

RUBIN nee WEISSMAN	Chaja	Born 1881.
RUBIN	Malka	
RUBIN	Rifka	
RUBIN	Pinchas	
RUBIN	Shmuel	
RUBIN	Wolf Wilhelm	Husband of Hinde Elena.
RUBIN nee SAMET	Hinde Elena	Wife of Wolf Wilhelm.
SALAMON	Pinchas	b. 1880 Nowy Sanz, moved to Tarnów. Married to Ester Marjem EINZIGER.
SALAMON	Jacob Nathan	b. 1904. Son of Pinchas and Ester Marjem.
SALAMON	Simon	b. 1909. Son of Pinchas and Ester Marjem.
FLOR nee SALAMON	Sara	b. 1912. Daughter of Pinchas and Ester Marjem.
SALAMON nee VORSCHIM	Sabina Jenny	Married Samuel SALAMON 1942, son of Pinchas and Ester Marjem.
SCHIFF	Chaim	Born 1870 or 1876 in Brzesko, died in Auschwitz 1942. Widower of Esther nee KLAGSBALD (born 1876 in Chrzanow, died 1937 in Brzesko).
SCHIFF	Mojzesz	Born 14-Nov-1898 in Chrzanow, died Birkenau 21-Jan-1942. Came to Antwerp at the end of 1926. Husband of Rywa nee TEMPLER (born in Tarnów, married 1923, lived in Antwerp from 1928 to 1942). Father of Bajla Basia (Lunia) and Tobias (survivor).
SCHIFF nee TEMPLER	Rywa (Rivka)	Born 14-Sep-1902 in Tarnów, married in 1923, lived in Antwerp from 1928 to 1942, died in Auschwitz-Birkenau 1-Sep- 1942. Daughter of Pinkas TEMPLER (died 1928) and Beila-Belcie nee RUBIN (died 1924). Mother of Bajla Basia (Lunia) and Tobias (survivor).
SCHIFF	Bajla Basia (Lunia)	Born 18-Oct-1923 in Tarnów, died in Birkenau 15-Oct-1942. Lived in Antwerp 1928-1942. Daughter of Mojzesz and Rywa nee TEMPLER.
DYM nee TEMPLER	Sara Lea	Born 1900 in Tarnów, died ~1943 Auschwitz. Daughter of Pinkas and Beila-Belcie nee RUBIN. Wife of Benzion DYM.
TEMPLER	Isak	Born 1904 in Tarnów, died Auschwitz?. Son of Pinkas and Beila-Belcie nee RUBIN.
TEMPLER	Chaim Szaje	Born 1905 in Tarnów, died Auschwitz?. Son of Pinkas and Beila-Belcie nee RUBIN.
TEMPLER	Abram Eliezer	Born 1909 in Tarnów, died Auschwitz?. Son of Pinkas and Beila-Belcie nee RUBIN. Husband of Chaja Reizel nee SZARF.
TEMPLER	Baruch	Born 1911 in Tarnów, died Auschwitz?. Son of Pinkas and Beila-Belcie nee RUBIN. Husband of Feiga nee SPITZ.
TEMPLER	Jochwet	Born 1914 in Tarnów, died Auschwitz? Daughter of Pinkas and Beila-Belcie nee RUBIN.
TEMPLER	Nechume	Born 1916 in Tarnów, died Auschwitz? Daughter of Pinkas and Beila-Belcie nee RUBIN.
ZWIEBEL	Nussem	Son of Meilech ZWIEBEL & Chaja Sara RUBIN. Born Łancut 1882, died ~1940? Married to EHRENBERG (1887?-)?1945
ZWIEBEL	Belcie	Daughter of Meilech ZWIEBEL and Chaja Sara RUBIN. Born Łancut 1890, died 1942 Auschwitz. Married to Mozesz SCHARF.
ZWIEBEL	Leibisch	Son of Meilech ZWIEBEL and Chaja Sara RUBIN. Born Łancut 1878? 1885?, died 1943 Auschwitz. Married to Etla RUBIN.
ZWIEBEL	Jankel	Son of Meilech ZWIEBEL and Chaja Sara RUBIN. Born Łancut 1891, died 1943 Auschwitz. Married to Chaja ABRAMOWICZ.
ZWIEBEL	Riwcie	Daughter of Meilech ZWIEBEL and Chaja Sara RUBIN. Born Łancut 1894, died 1943 Auschwitz. Married to REINHOLD?
ZWIEBEL	Pinchas	Son of Meilech ZWIEBEL and Chaja Sara RUBIN. Born Łancut 1897, died 1943 Auschwitz. Married to WURM?

RUBIN	Aron	Son of Lazer RUBIN and Golde FINGERHUT. Born Tarnów 1889, died Auschwitz? Married in 1915 to Nekhe SPIRA (died Auschwitz?)
RUBIN	Maria (Myriam)	Daughter of Aron RUBIN and Nekhe SPIRA. Born Kraków 1909, died Auschwitz?
FINGERHUT	Rywka	Daughter of Lazer RUBIN and Golde FINGERHUT. Born Tarnów 1891, died Auschwitz?
FINGERHUT	Chaja	Daughter of Lazer RUBIN and Golde FINGERHUT. Born Tarnów 1892, died Auschwitz? Married in 1919 to Isak Leib BRENER (~1894 Tarnów - Auschwitz?).
FINGERHUT	Sprynca	Daughter of Lazer RUBIN and Golde FINGERHUT. Born Tarnów 1894, died Auschwitz? Married in 1919 to Josef Mayer STIEGLITZ (~1889 Tarnów - Auschwitz?).
STIEGLITZ	Hersch	Son of Josef Mayer STIEGLITZ and Sprynca FINGERHUT. Born Tarnów, died Auschwitz?
STIEGLITZ	Efraim	Son of Josef Mayer STIEGLITZ and Sprynca FINGERHUT. Born 1922 Tarnów, died Auschwitz?
STIEGLITZ	Elieser	Son of Josef Mayer STIEGLITZ and Sprynca FINGERHUT. Born 1923 Tarnów, died Auschwitz?
RUBIN	Jakob (Jankel)	Son of Lazer RUBIN and Golde FINGERHUT. Born Tarnów 1899, died Auschwitz?. Married in 1930 to Zipora GOLDMAN (1903 Dębica - Auschwitz?)
RUBIN	Esther Frimet	Daughter of Lazer RUBIN and Golde FINGERHUT. Born Tarnów 1902, died Auschwitz? Married to ?
RUBIN	Mojzesz (Moshe)	Son of Lazer RUBIN and Golde FINGERHUT. Born Tarnów 1907, died Auschwitz?. Married to ?
REINHOLD	Jacob	Son of Haim Meilech REINHOLD and Zipora RUBIN. Born Tarnów 1892, died 1943 Auschwitz. Married in 1916 to Chawa EHRENBERG.
REINHOLD	Pinchas	Son of Haim Meilech REINHOLD and Zipora RUBIN. Born Tarnów 1893, died 1943 Auschwitz.
REINHOLD	Aron	Son of Haim Meilech REINHOLD and Zipora RUBIN. Born Tarnów 1895, died 1943 Auschwitz.
RUBIN	Jankel	Son of Haim Reuven RUBIN and Chaja WEISSMANN. Born Tarnów 1905, died Auschwitz? Married to Mania ROTH (1905?-Auschwitz?)
RUBIN	David	Son of Haim Reuven RUBIN and Chaja WEISSMANN. Born Tarnów 1903?, died Auschwitz?
RUBIN	Hersch	Son of Haim Reuven RUBIN and Chaja WEISSMANN. Born Tarnów 1907, died Auschwitz?
RUBIN	Luzer	Son of Haim Reuven RUBIN and Chaja WEISSMANN. Born Tarnów 1910, died Auschwitz?
RUBIN	Avrum	Son of Haim Reuven RUBIN and Chaja WEISSMANN. Born Tarnów 1912, died Auschwitz?
RUBIN	Pinchas	Son of Haim Reuven RUBIN and Chaja WEISSMANN. Born Tarnów 1913, died Auschwitz?
RUBIN	Riwka	Daughter of Haim Reuven RUBIN and Chaja WEISSMANN. Born Tarnów 1909, died Auschwitz?
SCHLESINGER	Chaim	businessman
SCHLESINGER	Sheva	
SCHLESINGER	Henek	son of Sheva
SCHLESINGER	Yitzchak	son of Sheva
SCHLESINGER	Renia	daughter of Sheva
WIND	Jacob	

WIND	Sima	
SCHMERZ	Extended Family	
SUSSKIND	Extended Family	
ROTHKOPF	Extended Family	
SÜSSKIND nee SCHMERZ	Chana	Widow of Josef (d. 1940), mother of Chaskel, Ydel, Ratzel, and Ytzhok.
SÜSSKIND	Chaskel	Son of Josef SÜSSKIND and Chana SÜSSKIND nee SCHMERZ.
SÜSSKIND	Ydel	Son of Josef SÜSSKIND and Chana SÜSSKIND nee SCHMERZ.
	Ratzel	Daughter of Josef SÜSSKIND and Chana SÜSSKIND nee SCHMERZ.
SÜSSKIND	Ytzhok	Son of Josef SÜSSKIND and Chana SÜSSKIND nee SCHMERZ.
SCHONBERG nee KORZENNIK	Sala (Sarah-Ester)	Born 1905, Rzeszów. Wife of Abraham (Romek). Lived in Biecz. Came for a short while (without baby) to the brothers in Lvov- All planned return to Nazi-controlled Poland, but not carried out. Sala returned to parents village, Biecz, outside ghetto, hidden by Polish family. After rumours of 'illegal Jews' in area reached the Nazis, she and her baby were found & killed, as well as the Polish family that had hid them, in July 1942. Source: Testimony (of Biecz survivors) & ספר-זכרון לקדושי עיירתנו בייטש [Biecz Yizkor-bukh] (p.161).
Schönberg	Mojzesz (Moshe)	Born circa 1937-1938, presumed Biecz. ~ 5 year-old son of Sala and Abraham (Romek). Killed with mother in Biecz region, July 1942. Source: Testimony (of Biecz survivors) & ספר-זכרון לקדושי עיירתנו בייטש [Biecz Yizkor-bukh] (p. 161).
SCHONBERG Nee KLAUSNER	Freida (Franja)	Born 1882, Dąbrowa Tarnówska. Mother of of Abraham (Romek), Asher-Salo (Asher Zelig; Zygmunt)(survivor) and Natan (Natek). In Tarnów ghetto: Circumstances of death unknown.
SCHONBERG	Abraham (Romek)	Born 1904, Tarnów. Son of Freida (Franja) and Israel Hersch (Izydor). Fled Tarnów with brothers, Zygmunt (survivor) & Natek, in Sep. 1939, reaching Lvov. In Lvov ghetto, after 1941 (after German conquest). Circumstances of death unknown. Source: Yad Vashem מחוץ לחומות הגטו -1987 by Miriam Peleg- Marianska, Mordechai ben-Zvi (Ch. 5, p.67-8).
SCHONBERG	Natan (Natek)	Born 1914, Tarnów. Son of Freida (Franja) and Israel Hersch (Izydor). Fled Tarnów with brothers, Romek & Zygmunt (survivor), in Sep. 1939, reaching Lvov. In Lvov ghetto, after 1941 (after German conquest). Circumstances of death unknown. Source: Yad Vashem מחוץ לחומות הגטו -1987 by Miriam Peleg- Marianska, Mordechai ben-Zvi (Ch. 5, p.67-8).
SCHONBERG	Israel Hersch (Izydor)	Born 1880 Nowy Sącz. On marriage, came to Tarnów. Father of Abraham (Romek), Asher-Salo (Asher Zelig; Zygmunt) (survivor) and Natan (Natek). Grandfather of David (by Zygmunt). Remained at home in Tarnów, early Sep. 1939- while sons fled east and over the San river to the Russian-controlled areas, reaching Lvov. Zygmunt was arrested by Russians in Lvov & sent to Siberian labour camp; on release he joined the Polish Anders army. Israel Hersch (Izydor) was in the Tarnów ghetto. Circumstances of his death unknown.
SCHREIBER	Moses Leib	Born 1876, shot in Kraków.
SCHREIBER Nee NEUGEBOREN	Perl	Born 1878 Tarnów, wife of Moses Leib.
SCHREIBER	Bluma	Born 1898, daughter of Moses Leib and Perl.
HUTTER Nee SCHREIBER	Sara Rifka	Born 1904, daughter of Moses Leib and Perl.
HUTTER	Aron	Born 1891, husband of Sara Rifka.
SCHREIBER	Chaim Towie	Born 1907, son of Moses Leib and Perl.
SCHREIBER Nee HABER	Blima	Born 1903, wife of Chaim Towie.
SCHREIBER	Avruum	Born 1934, son of Chaim Towie and Blima, deported to Auschwitz 1942.

SCHREIBER	Chaskel	Born 1910, son of Moses Leib and Perl.
SCHREIBER Nee LEDER	Sara	Born 1905, wife of Chaskel.
SCHREIBER	Ester	Born 1912, daughter of Moses Leib and Perl.
SCHREIBER	Feiga	Born 1915, daughter of Moses Leib and Perl.
SCHREIBER	Leo	1936-1942 (Auschwitz)
SCHREIBER	Albert	1939-1942 (Auschwitz)
SCHWARTZREICH	Ginter	
SCHWARZ	Leib	Tailor, 1900 (Rozwadow) - 1942 (Tarnów)
SCHWARC Nee VIND	Etel	1920 (Tarnów) - 1942 (Tarnów)
SCHWARC Nee VIND	Yacov	Son of Leib and Regina, 1937 (Tarnów) - 1942 (Tarnów)
SCHWEIT	Josef Boaz	Son of Yitzhak
SCHWEIT Nee GROSS	Liba	Daughter of Wolf Mendel and Sarah nee SPIRA. Wife of Josef Boaz.
SCHWEIT	Rivka	Daughter of Josef Boaz and Liba.
SCHWEIT	Lea	Daughter of Josef Boaz and Liba.
SCHWEIT	Esther	Daughter of Josef Boaz and Liba.
SCHWEIT	Haia	Daughter of Josef Boaz and Liba.
SCHWEIT	Sarah	Daughter of Josef Boaz and Liba.
SCHWEITZER	Yitzchak Michael	painter
SCHWEITZER Nee TURKELTAUB	Rivkah	wife of Yitzchak Michael
SCHWEITZER	Shlomo	son of Yitzchak Michael
SCHWEITZER	Moshe	son of Yitzchak Michael
SCHWEITZER	Yosef	son of Yitzchak Michael
SCHWEITZER	Miriam	daughter of Yitzchak Michael
SCHWEITZER	Tziporah	daughter of Yitzchak Michael
SOLENDER	Sima	
SOMMER	Chaim Joseph	
SOMMER	Scheindl	
MESSINGER	Minka	
MESSINGER	Markus	
SOMMER	Yitzchak (Bulush)	
SOMMER Nee STERN	Franciska	
KLAPHOLZ	Romek	
KLAPHOLZ	Benek (Bruno)	
SOMMER	Ruth	
SOMMER	Regina (Rywka)	
MESSINGER	Zofia	
MESSINGER	Blanka	
SPANIER	Noel	Son of Nusen Lieb SPANIER and Adela nee DORNFEST. Brother of Chana Feiga SPANIER (survivor) and Mania SPANIER (survivor). Died Auschwitz.
SPANIER	Jakob	Son of Nusen Lieb SPANIER and Adela nee DORNFEST. Brother of Chana Feiga SPANIER (survivor) and Mania SPANIER (survivor). Died Auschwitz.
SPANIER	David	Son of Nusen Lieb SPANIER and Adela nee DORNFEST. Brother of Chana Feiga SPANIER (survivor) and Mania SPANIER (survivor). Died Auschwitz.
SPANIER	Benjamin	Son of Nusen Lieb SPANIER and Adela nee DORNFEST. Brother of Chana Feiga SPANIER (survivor) and Mania SPANIER (survivor).

SPIELMAN	Israel Hirsch (Henrk)	17/11/1904-16/1/1945. Son of Abraham SPIELMAN and Frida KRAUTER.
SPITZEN	Berl	b. 1884 Tarnobrzeg. Married Sara SEIDEL in Tarnów.
SPITZEN Nee SEIDEL	Sara	Wife of Berl.
SPITZEN	Edel	b. 13 Aug 1899 Tarnobrzeg.
STRUM Nee SPITZEN	Feiga	b. Tarnobrzeg. Married Israel STRUM from Tarnów.
STRUM	Israel	Husband of Feiga.
OSTERWEIL Nee SPITZEN	Zelda	b. 9 Sept 1912 Tarnów. Married Shimon OSTERWEIL.
OSTERWEIL	Shimon	Husband of Zelda.
SPITZEN	Anna (Chana)	b. 1919.
STRUM	Pearl	Died aged approx. 82 years.
SPANGELET Nee HABER	Sarah	b. 5 Feb 1899, Tarnów. Married Victor SPANGELET from Tarnów.
SPANGELET	Victor	Husband of Sarah.
SPANGELET	Mortre	Son of Sarah and Victor. Died in the ghetto, age approx. 15 years.
HABER [Or IZRAEL]	Mortre [or Markus]	b. 20 Nov 1901, Tarnów. Married Rosa (Rayzel) MANTEL.
HABER [Or IZRAEL] Nee MANTEL	Rosa (Rayzel)	b. 1907, Tarnów.
HABER [Or IZRAEL]	Leah	Approx. 11 years old. Daughter of Mortre and Rayzel.
HABER [Or IZRAEL]	Shmiel	Approx. 9 years old. Son of Mortre and Rayzel.
GREEN Nee HABER [Or IZRAEL]	Hinda	b. Tarnów. Married Shloyme GREEN in Tarnów.
GREEN	Shloyme	Husband of Hinda.
GREEN	Yankel	Approx. 10 years old. Son of Hinda and Shloyme.
GREEN	Blima	Approx. 8 years old. Daughter of Hinda and Shloyme.
GREEN	Chava	Approx. 3 years old. Daughter of Hinda and Shloyme.
HABER	Heika (Chana)	b. 1915.
IZRAEL [Or HABER]	Mendel	b. May 1910 Tarnów.
IZRAEL	Yetka (Jentel)	b. 30 Dec 1907.
MONSDORF Nee IZRAEL [Or HABER	RC]hava	b. Tarnów. Married Idel MONSDORF from Tarnów.
MONSDORF	Idel	Husband of Chava.
MONSDORF	Faygela	Approx. 2 years old. Daughter of Chava and Idel.
HABER	Yitzak	b. 1872 Tarnów.
HABER Nee IZRAEL	Beila	b. Ropczyce. Married Yitzak HABER.
IZRAEL [Or HABER]	Moshe Moses	b. 11 Dec 1905, Tarnów. Married Yetka (Jenta) SCHNOLL.
IZRAEL [Or HABER] Nee SCHNOLL	Yetta (Jenta)	b. 1913 Tarnów.
IZRAEL [Or HABER]	Mortre	Approx. 5 years old. Son of Yetka and Moshe.
STORCH	Abraham	1867-1942, son of Leib and Sara nee ELLENBOGEN, born in Kolbuszowa
STORCH Nee PLAWKER	Chane Beile	1878-1942, wife of Abraham. Daughter of Yosef SCHNUR and Yokheved PLAWKER. Born in Zawada near Dębica
STORCH		daughter of Abraham and Chane Beile
STORCH		son of Abraham and Chane Beile
STORCH		son of Abraham and Chane Beile
STURMWIND Nee SOKOLER	Doba	wife of Natan
STURMWIND	Natan	

SOKOLER	Fella	sister of Doba
STURMWIND	Israel	son of Nathan and Doba
STURMWIND	Benjamin	son of Nathan and Doba
STURMWIND	Aaron	son of Nathan and Doba
SUSSER	Tancha Lemel	seamstress
KLEIN Nee SUSSER	Genia	daughter of Tancha Lemel
SUSSER	Wolf	son of Tancha Lemel
SUSSER	Hanka	daughter of Tancha Lemel
SUSSER	Irka	daughter of Tancha Lemel
SUSSKIND	Pinkas	Born in 1883 in Przemyśl.
SUSSKIND Nee FENICHEL	Chaja Serka	Born in 1884 in Tarnów. Daughter of Ruwen Selig FENICHEL and Sheindel nee SPITZ.
GAST Nee FENICHEL	Dora	
FENICHEL Nee MANTEL	Chana	Born 1873. Daughter of Shmuel MANTEL and Golde BIER. She was married to her step-brother, Hanoch FENICHEL.
KOCH Nee BERGMAN	Tyli	
FENICHEL Nee MANTEL	Belka	
HERMELE Nee FENICHEL	Brucha	Daughter of Ruwen Selig FENICHEL and Sheindel SPITZ
FENICHEL	Chaja Sara	
FENICHEL	Haim	
FENICHEL	Huma	Seamstress
FENICHEL	Idka (Ida)	
FENICHEL	Leibisch	Clothing merchant
FENICHEL	Mendel	
FENICHEL	Shara	
KOCH Nee BERGMAN	Menakhem	
FENICHEL Nee STEUER (SZTOJER)	Sara	
WEISS	Ester	
FENICHEL	Benek (Beno)	
ALSTER	Leib	
ALSTER	Sabina	
ALSTER	Sophie	
FENICHEL	Hersch	Furrier
FENICHEL	Sender	Furrier
FENICHEL	Moshe	Merchant
FENICHEL	Rywka	
BLUMENKRANZ	Stefania	
FENICHEL	Henryk	
BOHRER Nee FENICHEL	Cecylia	
FENICHEL	Hersh	
BLUMENKRANZ Nee FENICHEL	Lotti	
FENICHEL Nee Freinkel	Rosa	
WIMISNER Nee FENICHEL	Mindl	
FISHELBERG	Zigmund	

FENICHEL	Moshe	
IRGANG Nee KURTZ	Gusta	
SÜSSKIND	Slata	Killed in Fulda.
SÜSSKIND	Natalia	Killed in Fulda.
SÜSSKIND	Teofilia	Killed in Fulda.
BLAUNER	Leib	
BLAUNER	Lea	
BLAUNER	Chaskel	
BLAUNER	Rachela	
BLAUNER	Pinkas	
BLAUNER	Ada	
HABER	Fredek	
HABER	Hanka	
HABER	Chilus	
BLAUNER	Natan	
BLAUNER	Cyla	
BLAUNER	Esterka	
BLAUNER	Maria	
EISEN	Mosiek	
EISEN	Honda	
EISEN	Celinka	
BLAUNER	Romek	
SUESSKIND	Jacob	
SZANCER	Karolina	murdered in Zbylitowska Góra; widow of Artur
RINGELHEIM	Kazimierz Herman	born Tarnów 1911 to Teodor and Ernestyna nee SZANCER
SZYFMAN Nee FLAUMENHAFT	Ryvka (Regina)	born 16-Dec-1888 in Tarnów; last heard from 1941. Married to GIMPEL/Gustav.
GAENGER Nee FLAUMENHAFT	Paula (Paulina)	born 23-May-1890 in Tarnów. Married to Max. Returned to Tarnów around 1939.
FLAUMENHAFT	Samuel	born 25-Nov-1891 in Tarnów; deported back to Polan 10-May-1938. Last seen alive Sep-1942.
FLAUMENHAFT	Golda Mire (Gizelle)	wife of Samuel
FLAUMENHAFT	Paul	son of Samuel, born in Tarnów 31-Jul-1919. Died Mauthausen-Gusen camp 1944.
FLAUMENHAFT	Leo	son of Samuel, born 1918. Died Mauthausen-Gusen camp 1944.
JACUBOWICZ Nee FLAUMENHAFT	Sara (Selma)	born 24-Feb-1894 in Tarnów. Wife of Nathan. Last known alive on transport list to Auschwitz from Berlin in 1943, declared dead in 1945.
KLEINFINGER Nee FLAUMENHAFT	Rachel	born 10-May-1896 in Tarnów. Wife of Salomon (Szlama). Last known alive on transport list to Auschwitz from Berlin in 1943, declared dead in 1945.
HALTRECHT Nee FLAUMENHAFT	Leah (Lotte)	born 14-Jan-1898 in Tarnów, wife of Nathan. Deported from Wuppertal, Germany on 28-Oct-1938 to Zbaszyn, declared dead 1945. Possibly died in Ozarow, Poland.
MELLIMGER	Maria	born 17-Jan-1900 in Tarnów, single. Last known alive on transport list to Auschwitz from Berlin in 1943, declared dead .1945
PINKUS Nee MELINGER	Jochewet	born 1902 in Tarnów, wife of Chaim. Deported to Auschwitz from Berlin between 1939-1945.
THALER	Batia	seamstress, wife of Avigdor

THALER	Avigdor	furrier
THALER	Mania	daughter of Avigdor
TRINKENREICH	Extended Family	
TILLES	Extended Family	
UNGER	Moses (Moniek, Moshe)	born Tarnów 1896, died St. Valentin Dec.1944; owned shop Moses UNGER at Walowa 28, mechanic for Madritsch; father of Romek (Ron) Unger (survivor)
UNGER	Jeremiasz (Yirmiyahu)	Father of Moshe, born Tarnów c. 1870, died in Tarnów c. 1940, buried in cemetery
UNGER	Rifka	Mother of Moshe, born Tarnów c. 1870, died in Tarnów, c. 1940
UNGER NEE RUCKEL	Leah (Lotka)	Wife of Moshe. Born in Nowy Sacz 1900. Worked for Madritsch in Tarnów and Plaszow. Died at Auschwitz August 1944
UNGER	Menashe	Brother of Moshe, born in Tarnów c. 1897, died in Tarnów Ghetto c. 1941
UNGER	Mania	Wife of Menashe died in Tarnów Ghetto c. 1941
UNGER	Josef	Son of Menashe, born in Tarnów 1930, died c. 1942.
UNGER (MAIDEN NAME)	Toby	Sister of Moshe, born Tarnów 1890, died in Tarnów during Action c. 1942
UNGER (MOTHER'S MAIDEN NAME)	Josephine	Daughter of Toby, born Tarnów 1922, died c. 1942
UNGER (MOTHER'S MAIDEN NAME)	David	Son of Toby, born Tarnów 1924, died c. 1942
EDER	Hirsch	Brother-in-law of Leah UNGER, born Tarnów 1887. Owned cosmetic shop at Walowa 28. Shot as member of Judenrat June 1942
EDER NEE RUCKEL	Michal	Wife of Hirsch sister of Leah UNGER. Born in Nowy Sącz 1894/5, died in Tarnów Ghetto1942
EDER	Abraham	Son of Hirsch born in Tarnów 1921, died in Tarnów Ghetto 1942.
EDER	Jonah	Son of Hirsch born in Tarnów 1924, died in Tarnów Ghetto 1942.
RUCKEL	Moniek	Brother of Leah UNGER, born Nowy Sacz 1907, died Tarnów Ghetto 1942.
UNGER	Markus	
UNGER	Etie	wife of Markus
UNGER	Chiel	son of Markus
UNGER	Taube	daughter of Markus
UNGER	Markus	b.1898 Tarnów, married Etta Kipfel from Warsaw. Died Auschwitz.
UNTERBERGER	Izak Weiser	born 1902, son of Tobias Guttman UNTERBERGER & Rachel Beile (Beila Ruchla) WEISER (wife #1)
UNTERBERGER	Mendel	
UNTERBERGER	Mendel Yosel	born 1907, son of Tobias Guttman UNTERBERGER & Frejda (Beile) Balsam (wife #2)
UNTERBERGER	Naftali Hirsch/Hirsz Weiser	born 1906, son of Rachel Beile (Beila Ruchla Weiser (wife #1)
UNTERBERGER	Rechel Balsam	born 1914 in Tarnów, daughter of Tobias Guttman UNTERBERGER & Frejda (aka Beile) Balsam (wife #2)
UNTERBERGER	Frejda (Beile) Balsam	2nd wife of Tobias Guttman UNTERBERGER
UNTERBERGER	Sarah	
UNTERBERGER	Serla Balsam	born 1925, daughter of Tobias Guttman UNTERBERGER & Frejda Balsam (wife #2)
UNTERBERGER	Tobias Guttman	Born 1876, son of Mendel UNTERBERGER (Marjem Pesli/Pessel KORN, possible mother)

UNTERBERGER	Zalmen Zeger	Born 1933, son of Tobias Gutiman UNTERBERGER & Susko Zeger (wife #3).
WEITZ	Bentzion	
WEITZ NEE STRUM	Miriam	Wife of Bentzion
WEITZ	Chana	Daughter of Bentzion & Miriam
WEITZ	Tzvi Hersh	Son of Bentzion & Miriam
WIMISNER	David Ha Cohen	
WIMISNER NEE FENICHEL	Mina	Wife of David.
PIPERSBURG	Moritz	
PIPERSBURG		Child of Moritz.
PIPERSBURG		Child of Moritz.
WYMISNER	Genya	
WYMISNER	Dora	
WYMISNER	Vilik	
WYMISNER	Hella	
WYMISNER	Eva	
WYMISNER	Sara	
WYMISNER	Gisela	
WYMISNER NEE HOLLENDER	Clara	Wife of David WYMISNER
W MISNER	Genya	
WYMISNER	Lusha	
WYMISNER	Chaim Rosa	
WYMISNER	Cheshik	
WYMISNER	Genya	
ZALCMAN	Hanna	
ZAUDER	Ignace	
ZAUDER	Gisela	
ZEILENDER	Dr. Adolph	murdered at Tarnów train station
ZEILENDER NEE SHTERN	Frida	wife of Adolph, murdered at Tarnów train station
ZEILENDER	Dolly	daughter of Adolph and Frida, murdered at Tarnów train station
ZEILENDER	Rafael	son of Adolph and Frida, murdered at Tarnów train station
ZWECHER	Hersh	
ZWECHER NEE HELLWING	Tilce	wife of Hersh
ISLER NEE ZWECHER	Ella	daughter of Hersh and Tilce

TARNOW NECROLOGY SUPPLEMENT – UPDATED JULY, 2021

SURNAME OR MAIDEN NAME	APPEARS UNDER THESE BLUE NAMES
ABEND	ABEND FISCH
AFFENKRAUT	GEWÖLB

ALLINA	KORNMEHL
ALSTER	SUSSKIND
AMSTER	ABEND
ASHMAN	ASHMAN
AUSSENBERG	AUSSENBERG NEE STEINER
BARBASCH	BARBASCH
BARDACH	BARDACH
BEGLAS	LESER
BERGMAN(N)	HIRSCH; SUSSKIND
BIEDER	FINK NEE RIEMER
BIRSTENBINDER	KWADRATSTEIN (QUADRATSTEIN) NEE STERNHEIM
BLAUNER	SÜSSKIND
BLONDER	BLONDER
BLUMENKRANZ	JAKUBOWICZ; SUSSKIND
BOHRER	SUSSKIND
BRANDMANN	BRANDMANN
BRANDSTADTER / BRANDSTATTER	BRANDSTADTER (BRANDSTATTER)
BRATTER	BRATTER
BRIGG	BRIGG
CELNIK	CELNIK
CYZER	KALFUS
DAAR	DAAR
DEBEL	HIRSCH
DEGEN	GRUN
CIAMANT	DIAMANT
DOMINITZ	BARBASCH
DROBNER	GAST/DROBNER
DYM	SCHIFF
EDER	UNGER
EICHENBAUM	FRISCH
EISEN	BARBASCH; SÜSSKIND
EISENBACH	MENER
EISLAND	EISLAND

EKSTEIN	LESER
ENDE	ENDE
ENGELBERG / ENGELBURG	ENGELBURG
ENGELHARDT	ENGELHARDT; KORNMEHL
FABER	ENGELHARDT
FABER	GELB
FALLEK	LUST
FALLMAN / FELMAN	FALLMAN / FELMAN; LEDERBERGER
FEDERGRÜN	BARBASCH
FEIGENBAUM	GRABER
FELSEN	DIAMANT
Fenichel	GOLDMAN; LEIBEL NEE Fenichel; SUSSKIND; WIMISNER
FEUER	FEUER
FEUERSTEIN	GOLDMAN; ISRAELER
FINGERHUT	SCHIFF
FINK	FINK NEE RIEMER
FISCH	FISCH
FISCHLER	LESER NEE HOROWITZ
FISHELBERG	SUSSKIND
FLAUMENHAFT	BRIGG; OWIDE; SZYFMAN NEE FLAUMENHAFT
FLEISCHER	JAKUBOWICZ
FLOR	SALAMON
FOLKMAN	ASHMAN
FORSTENZER	EISLAND
FRANK	REICH
FREIMAN	CELNIK
FRIES	HUTNER
FRISCH	FRISCH
FROHLICH	CELNIK
FUNARSKA	PILCER
GAENGER	SZYFMAN NEE FLAUMENHAFT
GARN	EISLAND
GAST	GAST/DROBNER; SUSSKIND
GASTWIRT	GASTWIRT

GELB	GELB
GELBWACHS	ISRAELER
GELERNTER	KALFUS
GENGER	LESER
GEWÖLB	GEWÖLB
GOETZ	GOETZ
GOLDBERG	GOLDBERG
GOLDFARB	ISRAELER
GOLDMAN	BARBASCH
GOTLIEB	FINK NEE RIEMER
GRABER	GRABER
GREEN	SPITZEN
GROSS	SCHWEIT
GROSSBARD	MARGULIES
GRUN	GRUN
GRÜNBERG	RAND
GRUNFELD	GRUNFELD
GRUSZOW	GRUSZOW
HABER	SCHREIBER; SPITZEN; SÜSSKIND
HALTRECHT	SZYFMAN NEE FLAUMENHAFT
HAUT	BARBASCH
HELLWING	ZWECHER
HERBST	GRABER
HERMELE	SUSSKIND
HILLER	HILLER
HIRSCH	GRUSZOW; HIRSCH
HOLLANDER / HOLLENDER	HILLER; LESER; WIMISNER
HONIG	EISLAND; GEWÖLB
HORNIK	JAKOB
HOROWITZ	LESER NEE HOROWITZ
HUTNER	HUTNER
HUTTER	SCHREIBER
ICKOWICZ	ICKOWICZ
INGBER	INGBER

IRGANG	SUSSKIND
ISENBERG	FINK NEE RIEMER
ISLER	ISLER; ZWECHER
ISRAELER	ISRAELER
IZAK	IZAK
IZRAEL	HABER
IZRAEL	SPITZEN
JACUBOWICZ / JAKUBOWICZ	JAKUBOWICZ; SZYFMAN NEE FLAUMENHAFT
JAKOB	JAKOB
KAHANE	INGBER
KALFUS	KALFUS
KAMPF	KAMPF
KANAR	BRANDSTADTER (BRANDSTATTER)
KARTAGENER	HIRSCH
KESTENBAUM	BRATTER
KLAPHOLZ	SOMMER
KLAUSNER	KWADRATSTEIN (QUADRATSTEIN) NEE STERNHEIM; LUBASCH; SCHÖNBERG NEE KORZENNIK
KLEIN	BARBASCH; GRABER; SUSSER
KLEINFINGER	SZYFMAN NEE FLAUMENHAFT
KLEINHÄNDLER	BARBASCH
KOCH	SUSSKIND
KOENIGSBUCH	KOENIGSBUCH
KOHANE	BARBASCH; INGBER
KORN	JAKUBOWICZ
KORNHEISER	IZAK
KORNMEHL	KORNMEHL
KORZENNIK	SCHÖNBERG NEE KORZENNIK
KRIESER	ISRAELER
KRISHER (KRISCHER)	KWADRATSTEIN (QUADRATSTEIN) NEE STERNHEIM
KUBIE	OWIDE
KUDLER	GEWÖLB
KÜNSTLICH	KÜNSTLICH
KUPFER	LADNER

KURTZ	JAKOB; SUSSKIND
KWADRATSTEIN / QUADRATSTEIN	KWADRATSTEIN (QUADRATSTEIN) NEE STERNHEIM
LADNER	LADNER
LAM/LEM	LESER
LANDERER	ISRAELER
LANGER	LEIBEL, NEE Fenichel
LAUBER	BARDACH
LEDER	KORNMEHL; SCHREIBER
LEIBEL	LEIBEL NEE Fenichel; RAND
LENKOWICZ	BARBASCH
LESER	BARBASCH; LESER
LEUCHTER	PILCER
LEZER	LEZER
LICHTIG	IZAK
LIEBE	BLONDER
LINZENBERG	LEIBEL, NEE Fenichel
LION	BARBASCH
LUBASCH	LUBASCH
LUFTIG	LESER
LUST	LUST
LUSTBADER	LUSTBADER
MANTEL	SPITZEN; SUSSKIND
MARFELD	MARFELD
MARGULIES	BARBASCH; MARGULIES
MELLIMGER	SZYFMAN NEE FLAUMENHAFT
MENER	MENER
MESSINGER	SOMMER
MIRE	OWIDE
MONSDORF	SPITZEN
MÜLLER	BARBASCH
NEUGEBOREN	SCHREIBER
OSTERWEIL	SPITZEN
OWIDE	OWIDE

PADWE	BARBASCH
PARNES	LESER
PICK	BARBASCH
PILCER	PILCER
PINER	OWIDE
PINKUS	SZYFMAN NEE FLAUMENHAFT
PIPERSBURG	WIMISNER
PLANER	ENDE; LUBASCH
PLAWKER	STORCH
PRESSER	LUSTBADER
RACHMIL	FINK NEE RIEMER
RAICHMAN	OWIDE
RAUCHWERG	ASHMAN
RAND	RAND
REDNER	REDNER
REICH	REICH
REINHOLD	SCHIFF
RICK	OWIDE
RICKS	KORNMEHL
RIEMER	FINK NEE RIEMER
RINDER	RINDER
RINGELHEIM	SZANCER
ROSENBAUM	GRUN
ROSENBLATT	BARBASCH
ROSENBLUM	CELNIK; IZAK
ROSENBLUTH	LESER NEE HOROWITZ
ROSENFELD	BARBASCH
ROSENZWEIG-LEDERBERGER	LEDERBERGER
ROSNER	KOENIGSBUCH; KORNMEHL
ROTH	ROTH
ROTHKOPF	SCHMERZ
ROTHSTEIN	BRANDMANN
RUBIN	RUBIN; SCHIFF
RUCKEL	UNGER

RUDNER	IZAK
SALAMON	SALAMON
SAMET	RUBIN
SCHACHTER	CELNIK
SCHIFF	SCHIFF
SCHLESINGER	SCHLESINGER
SCHMERZ	SCHMERZ
SCHMIDT	ENGELBURG
SCHMUCKLER	BARBASCH
SCHNOLL	SPITZEN
SCHÖNBERG	SCHÖNBERG NEE KORZENNIK
SCHÖNWETTER	BARBASCH
SCHREIBER	BARBASCH; SCHREIBER
SCHWARTZREICH	SCHWARTZREICH
SCHWARZ/SCHWARC	BARBASCH; SCHWARZ
SCHWEID/SCHWEIT	ASHMAN; SCHWEIT
SCHWEITZER	SCHWEITZER
SEGAL	LESER
SEIDEL	SPITZEN
SEIDEN	BARBASCH
SHTERN	ZEILENDER
SHTEUER (HOLZER)	LEZER
SMIGA	BARBASCH
SOKOLER	BRIGG; STURMWIND NEE SOKOLER
SOLENDER	SOLENDER
SOMMER	SOMMER
SPANGELET/SPANGLET	BARBASCH; KWADRATSETIN (QUADRATSTEIN) NEE STERNHEIM; LESER NEE HOROWITZ; SPITZEN
SPANIER	SPANIER
SPIELMAN	SPIELMAN
SPITZEN	SPITZEN
SPITZER	BARBASCH
SPRUNG	FINK NEE RIEMER
STEIN	LESER

STEINER	AUSSENBERG NEE STEINER
STEINHORN	LESER
STERN	SOMMER
STERNHEIM	KWADRATSTEIN (QUADRATSTEIN) NEE STERNHEIM
STEUER (SZTOJER)	SUSSKIND
STIEGLITZ	SCHIFF
STORCH	STORCH
STORM	OWIDE
STRUM	SPITZEN; WEITZ
STURM	LEIBEL, NEE Fenichel
STURMWIND	STURMWIND NEE SOKOLER
SÜSS	BARBASCH
SUSSER	SUSSER
SUSSKIND	SCHMERZ; SUSSKIND
SÜSSKIND/SUESSKIND	SÜSSKIND
SZANCER	SZANCER
SZYFMAN	SZYFMAN NEE FLAUMENHAFT
TEMPLER	SCHIFF
THALER	THALER
THORSCH	BRANDMANN
TILLES	TRINKENREICH
TISCH	GOLDMAN; HIRSCH
TOPPEL	BARBASCH
TRAUM	FINK NEE RIEMER
TRINKENREICH	TRINKENREICH
TURKELTAUB	SCHWEITZER
TURTELTAUB	HIRSCH; KOENIGSBUCH; KORNMEHL
UNGER	LEIBEL, NEE Fenichel; UNGER
UNTERBERGER	UNTERBERGER
URABIN	ISRAELER
VIND	SCHWARZ
VOLKMAN	ASHMAN
WACHSKERZ	BARBASCH
WEINMAN	OWIDE

WEISER	KALFUS
WEISS	SUSSKIND
WEISSMAN	RUBIN
WEITZ	WEITZ
WESTREICH	BARBASCH; LEIBEL, NEE Fenichel
WIKLER	BARBASCH
WIMISNER/WYMISNER	SUSSKIND; WIMISNER
WIND	SCHLESINGER
WINTER	KORNMEHL
WITTLIN	BARBASCH
WOLF	ISRAELER
WULKAN	JAKOB
WYMISNER / FALLMAN	FALLMAN / FELMAN
ZALCMAN	ZALCMAN
ZAUDER	ZAUDER
ZEILENDER	ZEILENDER
ZINS	BARBASCH
ZWECHER	ZWECHER
ZWIEBEL	SCHIFF
ZYLBERMAN	HUTNER

NAME INDEX

A

Abend, 242, 392, 396, 415
Aberdam, 8, 9, 10, 28, 30, 48, 242
Abraham, 242
Abramovich–Arnon, 240
Abramovicz-Arnun, 162
Abramowicz, 407
Abramowitz, 242
Abramowitz-Horowitz, 356
Achler, 243
Ackerman, 356
Ader, 356
Adler, 97, 218, 242, 292, 356
Adrowoncz, 146
Affenkraut, 397, 415
Afner, 356
Afte, 356
After, 30, 356
Aftergut, 395
Agatstein, 242
Ajzenbach, 293
Ajzner, 296
Alban, 181, 244, 356
Allina, 402, 416
Alster, 412, 416
Alter, 49, 50, 52, 161
Altman, 244
Alwajs, 306
Alwajz, 306
Alweis, 356
Alweiss, 244, 245
Amaiz, 244
Amster, 392, 416
Amsterdam, 356
Anisfeld, 244, 356
Anker, 244, 356
Ansky, 356
Apel, 55, 56
Appel, 253, 356
Appelman, 338
Apple, 244
Appleboim, 244, 245
Apsler, 245
Arak, 69, 71, 105, 245, 356
Arantz, 356
Argand, 142, 245, 356
Arimawitz, 356
Arimovic, 245
Armian, 245
Armien, 356, 357
Arnold, 357
Arnstein, 357
Aronovich-Rockman, 182, 183
Arshitzer, 357
Arszicer, 30
Arziser, 357
Arzt, 357
Ashkenazi, 245
Ashman, 392, 416, 417, 421, 422, 423
Asterwajl, 63
Asterweil, 357
Aszchenazi, 49
Aszer, 218
Auerbach, 357
Ausaibel, 243
Ausenberg, 348
Aussenberg, 392, 416, 423
Auver, 357
Averdam, 357
Avida, 243, 357
Avinger, 357
Avsiskin, 357

B

Baber, 357
Badner, 245, 357
Baer, 357
Bagen, 245
Bajczer, 128
Bajtrag, 292
Balsam, 245, 246, 250
Balzam, 358
Banat, 358
Banch, 358
Banek, 212, 213
Bank, 246
Baran, 30, 358
Baranowitz, 358
Barbasch, 392, 416, 417, 418, 419, 420, 421, 422, 423, 424
Bardach, 246, 394, 416, 420
Bardoff, 324
Barfenig, 314
Barganicht, 358
Barivitz, 358
Barnsztajn, 181
Baron, 47, 80, 246, 249, 250, 369
Bartfeld, 246
Batist, 245, 294, 358
Bau, 221, 245
Baum, 241, 245, 358
Bayer, 246
Bazlar, 245
Bazler, 197, 358
Bebelsky, 248
Beck, 248, 250, 358
Becker, 358

Beder, 248, 298
Beeber, 250
Beeder, 250
Beglas, 416
Begleiter, 392
Beim, 246
Beitch, 358
Beitcher, 246
Beller, 150, 248
Ben Gurion, 11, 358
Berchiye, 36
Berel, 248
Berger, 235, 248
Berglas, 404
Bergman, 3, 42, 43, 58, 60, 75, 88, 89, 90, 91, 92, 100, 105, 107, 108, 109, 111, 126, 186, 233, 248, 249, 294, 328, 358, 412, 416
Bergmann, 399
Bergstein, 228, 302
Berkelhamer, 301, 358
Berkelhammer, 248, 249
Berkowitz, 248
Berman, 358
Berner, 248
Bernfeld, 248, 306
Bernknopf, 248
Bernshtater, 11
Bernstein, 248, 358
Bester, 118, 358
Betail, 248
Bethajl, 301
Betrebenis, 358, 359
Betribnis, 206, 218, 224
Betrivnis, 248
Betrubniss, 213, 302
Bezkes, 309
Bialik, 80, 359
Bibelman, 28
Biber, 296
Biberberg, 246, 334
Biberstein, 246
Bieder, 396, 416
Biederman, 359
Biegeleisen, 246
Bielatowicz, 74
Bienenshtock, 240
Bienenstock, 94, 234
Bier, 412
Bierman, 246
Bild, 246
Bilfeld, 246
Bilow, 246
Binenstock, 246, 249, 295, 359
Binensztok, 327
Birenbaum, 246
Birenstein, 247
Birer, 247, 359
Birkan, 359
Birken, 247
Birken–Kirsztmal, 224

Birken–Krisztal, 218
Birman, 234, 294
Birnbaum, 301, 359
Birstenbinder, 402, 416
Bistrisky, 359
Bitner, 359
Bitner-Friedman, 359
Blache, 139, 140, 141, 142
Blajwajs, 148, 149, 218, 299, 338, 346
Bland, 247, 359
Blat, 39, 298, 354
Blauner, 247, 250, 296, 413, 416
Blazer, 40, 47, 48, 49, 55, 247, 297, 359
Bleicher, 248, 359
Bleichfeld, 248
Bleiweiss, 229, 230, 234, 235, 247, 248, 250, 359
Blitz, 248, 359
Bloch, 39, 65, 81, 230, 247, 359
Bloch-Mertz, 359
Block, 62, 121
Blond, 229, 270, 300, 352
Blonder, 247, 326, 359, 394, 416, 420
Blonsky, 247
Bloomer, 360
Blotner, 247
Blumenfeld, 247, 360
Blumenkranz, 94, 360, 401, 412, 416
Blumenstein, 249, 330, 351
Bluner, 360
Blutman, 360
Bochenek, 146, 150
Bodek, 245
Bodin, 246
Boduch, 150
Bogan, 250
Bohrer, 412, 416
Bookbinder, 246
Borduch, 146
Borganicht, 67
Borgenicht, 39
Bór-Komorowski, 180
Borman, 249
Bornstein, 246
Bornsztajn-Ross, 181
Borstin, 360
Boterfas, 360
Boykowitc, 54
Brach, 360
Brachfeld, 249, 360
Bram, 249
Bramberg-Vitkowsky, 360
Brand, 50, 98, 133, 249, 292
Brandmann, 394, 416, 421, 423
Brandst Adter, 394
Brandst Atter, 394
Brandstadter, 416, 419
Brandstatter, 328, 394, 416, 419
Brandsteter, 360
Brandsztatter, 28, 29, 30
Branstetter, 249

Bratter, 394, 416, 419
Brau, 360
Braun, 191, 220, 360
Braunfeld, 249
Braunstein, 249
Brener, 47, 408
Brezel, 360
Bridre, 182
Brig, 249, 360
Brigg, 394, 416, 417, 422
Brigg-Flaumenhaft, 394
Briland, 249
Broah, 360
Brod, 250
Broder, 249, 360
Brodheim, 249
Bronstein, 242, 360
Broveh, 249
Brown, 20
Brownfeld, 336
Bruckner, 249, 360
Bruder, 249
Buber, 61
Buch, 150
Bucholc, 349
Buna, 310
Buchholtz, 246
Burg, 246

C

Cahane, 360
Camet, 360, 361
Casher, 361
Celler, 229
Celnik, 394, 395, 416, 417, 421, 422
Cesear, 278
Cetar, 278
Chiechodowsky, 278
Chiut ?,, 361
Choczner, 263
Chodorov, 8
Chomet, 1, 49, 52, 74, 104, 110, 191, 206, 230, 232, 239, 240, 324, 372
Chomet Shlomeh, 372
Chust, 24
Ciamant, 416
Cimet, 128
Cinz, 30
Ciołkosz, 63
Citronenbaum, 278
Cizer, 326
Comet, 24, 324
Cooperblulm, 280
Cooperman, 280, 361
Coopfer, 280
Cymerman, 128
Cymet, 138
Cyzer, 401, 416
Czoban, 264

D

Daar, 220, 395, 416
Damast, 361
Dankowicz, 28
David, 254, 361
Debel, 398, 416
Degen, 254, 398, 416
Dener, 254
Diamant, 395, 416, 417
Dickstein, 254
Dindas, 254
Dintenfas, 361
Dintenfass, 230
Dintenpas, 254
Dirdalowa, 240
Doar, 361
Dom, 253
Domast, 254
Dominitz, 254, 392, 416
Domler, 254, 283
Dor Dreisiger, 254
Dorf, 254
Dorlich, 254
Dorman, 254
Dornfest, 410
Dorst,, 361
Drelich, 254
Dresner, 254
Drezner, 361
Dringer, 254
Drobner, 396, 416, 417
Drucker, 254, 361
Duczik, 25
Dym, 407, 416
Dyrdałowa, 208, 209, 210, 211, 212
Dzikówer, 161
Dzshikavs, 361

E

Ebersztark, 159, 165
Ebner, 361
Eched, 361
Ecker, 272, 273
Eckstein, 107
Ecksterman, 361
Edelstein, 272, 361
Eder, 50, 130, 134, 272, 361, 414, 416
Ehrenberg, 272, 361, 407, 408
Ehrenfreund, 272, 361
Ehrenprise, 361
Ehrlich, 272, 273, 361
Eichenbaum, 396, 416
Eichenholtz, 243, 244
Eichenholz, 362
Eichenwald, 243
Eichhorn, 97, 98, 243, 362
Einhorn, 163, 244, 362
Einshpruch, 103
Einspruch, 362

Einziger, 407
Eirom, 245
Eisen, 243, 362, 392, 413, 416
Eisenbach, 243, 405, 416
Eisenberg, 19, 243
Eisland, 395, 416, 417, 418
Ejzenberg, 28, 30
Ekstein, 272, 362, 404, 417
Elenberg, 362
Elend, 272, 362
Eliash, 272
Ellenbogen, 411
Ende, 395, 417, 421
Ender, 272, 344, 362
Engel, 272, 273, 362
Engelberg, 362, 417
Engelburg, 272, 395, 417, 422
Engelhard, 272, 273
Engelhardt, 330, 396, 401, 417
Engelhart, 19, 62, 65, 362
Engelman, 325
Englander, 253, 272, 273, 302, 330, 362
Etinger, 30
Etkes, 362
Ettinger, 272
Evershtark, 272
Ezrachi, 232
Ezrahi, 240

F

Faber, 120, 121, 126, 127, 148, 273, 277, 330, 336, 362, 396, 397, 417
Fabian, 273, 362
Facher, 181
Fagelfang, 273, 362
Fagi, 38
Faigenabaum, 274
Fajenbaum, 335
Fajer, 328
Fajg, 38
Fajgenbaum, 26
Fajngold, 337
Falkman, 196
Fallek, 405, 417
Fallman, 396, 402, 417, 424
Faner, 362
Fargash, 277
Farnem, 274
Farnes, 362
Farshiram, 274
Farshirm, 277
Farshtendik, 276
Farshtenzer, 274
Fassel, 362
Fast, 120, 273, 362
Fastring, 362, 363
Faust, 22, 49, 50, 363
Febus, 30, 385
Feder, 277

Federgrün, 417
Federgrün, 392
Fedever, 363
Fefer, 158, 363
Feffer, 276
Feig, 363
Feigenbaum, 363, 397, 398, 417
Feiner, 275
Feines, 363
Feingold, 125
Feir, 363
Feirstein, 363
Feitel, 363
Feivel, 274, 363
Feivels, 363
Felber, 276, 363
Feld, 240, 276, 277, 363, 406
Feldbaum, 276, 363
Feldbloom, 363
Feldgreve(r?), 363
Feldgrever, 276
Feldman, 396
Feldmaus, 276
Feldstein, 97, 363
Felenc, 130
Fellenz, 129
Feller, 276
Felman, 396, 417, 424
Felsen, 395, 417
Fenichal, 9
Fenichel, 424
Fenichel, 98, 260, 276, 282, 332, 363, 397, 403, 412, 413, 415, 417, 420, 423
Fenig, 276, 363
Fenik, 276
Fenster, 363
Ferber, 276
Ferenc, 331
Ferentz, 277
Fersztman, 158
Feuer, 396, 417
Feuerstein, 397, 399, 417
Fier, 274
Fiereisen, 363
Filerstarf, 363
Finder, 150, 274
Fineberger, 274
Fingerhut, 408, 417
Fingerman, 343
Fingerman–Friman, 94
Fink, 274, 363, 396, 416, 417, 418, 419, 421, 422, 423
Finkelstein, 274, 363
Fireaizen, 274
Firestein, 274, 275
Fisch, 396, 415, 417
Fischler, 404, 417
Fish, 274, 275, 364
Fishbein, 275
Fishelberg, 275, 412, 417
Fishler, 275, 364

Fishman, 275, 364
Fisz, 331
Flancer, 62, 65
Flanzer, 364
Flatau, 364
Flaum, 275
Flaumenhaft, 275, 394, 406, 413, 417, 418, 419, 420, 421, 423
Flaumenhaft, 275
Fleck, 276
Fleischer, 275, 331, 401, 417
Fleisher, 18, 78, 81, 275, 364
Flejszer, 182
Fletscher, 276
Flink, 234, 275, 334
Flor, 275, 407, 417
Flugajzn, 298
Flugejzen, 128
Flur, 364
Fluzer, 364
Fogel, 277
Fogelhut, 273
Fogler, 273
Folkman, 120, 179, 197, 392, 417
Folksman, 149
Forstenzer, 395, 417
Fox, 274
Fracht, 47
Frajlich, 330
Frank, 121, 196, 276, 406, 417
Frankel, 277
Fredek, 63
Freeman, 333, 364
Freilich, 364
Freiman, 277, 343, 395, 417
Freinkel, 412
Freireich, 277, 364
Frelich, 277
Frenkel, 120, 364
Freund, 3, 13, 24, 40, 60, 69, 116, 144, 157, 167, 172, 175, 181, 184, 186, 191, 206, 217, 364
Fridman, 163, 334
Fried, 277
Friedberg, 364
Friedlander, 364
Friedler, 277
Friedlich, 277
Friedman, 21, 276, 277, 364
Fries, 364, 365, 399, 406, 417
Fries-Epstein, 364
Friman, 94
Frimes, 365
Fris, 62, 64
Frisch, 365, 396, 416, 417
Frish, 277
Frishman, 365
Frishtak, 277
Frohlich, 394, 395, 417
Fuder, 332
Funarsak, 406
Funarska, 406, 417

Fus, 365
Fuzio, 151
Fyrek, 148, 150, 152

G

Gaa, 129
Gabay, 35, 36
Gabbay, 35, 36, 37
Gaenger, 413, 417
Galicer, 63
Gal-Stein, 365
Gans, 197, 365
Ganz, 251
Garden, 365
Garlitzer, 365
Garlizer, 365
Garn, 395, 417
Garnreich, 229
Garzaiman, 252
Gast, 251, 306, 396, 412, 416, 417
Gastwirt, 396, 417
Gastwirth, 251, 365
Gatz, 10
Gavralovitch, 250
Gawelczyk, 212, 213
Gelb, 251, 294, 365, 396, 417, 418
Gelbwachs, 399, 400, 418
Gelbwax, 251, 365
Geldtzeler, 252
Geldwirt, 30
Gelernter, 234, 251, 253, 304, 312, 319, 365, 401, 418
Geller, 234, 235, 271, 353
Geminder, 252
Genger, 403, 418
Gershon, 365
Gerstein, 188
Gersten, 252, 365
Gerstner, 365
Gertler, 365
Gertner, 252, 365
Geshiv, 365
Getsler, 140
Gettinger, 251
Gctzler, 252, 365
Gevelb, 251
Geviazda, 253
Gewelb, 47, 365
Gewirc, 49
Gewirtz, 49, 251, 366
Gewolb, 397
Gewölb, 415, 418, 419
Gimpel, 149, 413
Ginger, 251
Giniger, 366
Ginsberg, 61
Ginzberg, 153, 253
Giser, 251
Glas, 366
Glass, 251, 366

Glassman, 366
Glatzner, 251
Glazer, 251, 366
Glazner, 366
Gleicher, 8, 251, 366
Glick, 251
Glickman, 253
Glik, 366
Glinik, 251, 346
Goetz, 397, 418
Goldberg, 30, 63, 120, 142, 176, 250, 366, 392, 397, 418
Goldberg-Klimek, 175, 176
Goldfarb, 190, 250, 366, 400, 418
Goldfinger, 98, 229, 250
Goldhamer, 30, 366
Goldklang, 253
Goldman, 25, 203, 234, 235, 334, 366, 392, 397, 408, 417, 418, 423
Goldman-Brodie, 35
Goldschmidt, 250
Goldstaff, 250
Goldstein, 250, 366
Goldstern, 366
Goldsztajn, 170, 172
Goldwachs, 366
Goldwaser, 28
Goldwasser, 250, 366
Goldzeller, 366, 367
Golwasser, 250
Gorlitzer, 251
Göth, 139, 140
Gotlieb, 367, 396, 418
Gotlob, 250
Gottleib, 238
Gottlieb, 3
Gottlob, 145, 153
Graber, 397, 398, 417, 418, 419
Grabshrift, 367
Graizman, 252
Gralitzer, 252, 367
Gras, 182
Grasman, 367
Graz, 327
Greber, 367
Greem, 253
Green, 252, 253, 367, 411, 418
Greenbaum, 253, 367
Greenberg, 253, 367
Greenberger, 253, 367
Greenboim, 253
Greeneviza, 253
Greenfeld, 253, 367
Greenhut, 253, 367
Greenkraut, 253
Greenspan, 253, 367
Greenstein, 253, 367
Grim, 172
Grinbaum, 47, 49
Grinberg, 302
Grinewize, 197

Grinfeld, 98
Grinszpan, 332
Gris, 308
Gros, 319
Grosbard, 29, 317
Grosman, 318
Gross, 252, 282, 410, 418
Grossbard, 340, 405, 418
Grossbart, 252
Grossman, 252
Gruca, 186
Gruder, 367
Grun, 398, 416, 418, 421
Grünberg, 406, 418
Grunfeld, 398, 418
Grunoff, 118, 126, 129, 132, 133, 139
Grunow, 149, 164
Gruschov, 252
Grushow, 367
Gruszow, 128, 398, 418
Grzimek, 143
Gustek, 150
Guter, 49, 251, 253, 367
Gutinower, 304
Gutman, 251
Gutter, 302
Gutter–Bergstein, 226
Gutwirth, 251
Gzashiv, 67

H

Haar, 256
Haber, 63, 98, 254, 257, 296, 306, 345, 367, 368, 409, 411, 413, 418, 419
Haberman, 254, 368
Hackbarth, 131
Hackenholt, 187
Hadas, 232
Hager, 49, 161
Hajman, 28, 70, 74
Halbershtam, 158
Halberstam, 47, 49, 106, 165, 255, 368
Halbersztam, 47, 165
Haler, 131
Halpern, 255, 368
Haltrecht, 413, 418
Hamer, 368
Hammer, 255
Hammerschlag, 255
Handelsman, 368
Handler, 19
Haptka, 33
Hauser, 254
Hausman, 255, 368
Hausner, 255
Haut, 254, 255, 368, 392, 418
Hayman, 69
Hazelberg, 234, 342
Heiberg, 256

Heinberg, 256
Helin, 257
Heller, 67, 257, 368
Hellwing, 415, 418
Hendler, 63, 67, 121, 189, 249, 257
Henenberg, 257
Henig, 257
Herbst, 257, 368, 397, 418
Herbstman, 257
Hercbaum, 30
Hercberg, 307
Hercig, 30
Hercl, 330
Hercman, 65
Herel, 257
Hermele, 412, 418
Hershkovitz, 368
Hershkowitz, 257
Herszkowic, 14
Herskowicz, 295
Hertz, 368
Hertzberg, 257, 368
Hertzig, 56
Hertzman, 257, 268, 368
Hertzog, 47
Herzig, 257, 368
Herzl, 61, 368
Herzman, 354, 368
Herzog, 167, 257, 368
Hess, 368
Heydrich, 192
Hilfstein, 368
Hiller, 398, 418
Himelfarb, 369
Hirsch, 256, 257, 398, 399, 416, 418, 419, 423
Hirschfeld, 256, 316
Hirschhorn, 35, 256
Hirsh, 134, 369
Hirshenhorn, 369
Hirshfeld, 369
Hirshhorn, 369
Hirsz, 306
Hirszenhorn, 309
Hirszfeld, 126
Hitner, 256
Hitter, 256
Hiziger, 256
Hochberg, 257, 369
Hochberg Marianska, 172
Hochberger, 255
Hochhajzer, 255
Hochman, 369
Hochner, 255
Hodes, 256, 369
Hodorov, 314
Hoenig, 234
Hofert, 369
Hoffman, 256, 257
Hoffmeister, 256
Hofmajster, 212, 213

Hofman, 47
Hofmeister, 369
Hofsteter, 369
Holender, 47, 126, 128, 185, 305, 306, 348
Holer, 255
Holes, 256
Holeshitzer, 255
Holland, 255
Hollander, 255, 369, 398, 403, 418
Hollender, 415, 418
Holtzapel, 369
Holtzer, 255, 369
Holzer, 121, 404, 422
Honig, 120, 255, 256, 290, 308, 320, 342, 369, 395, 397, 418
Horn, 369
Hornik, 400, 418
Horovitz, 35
Horowicz, 157, 158, 159, 160, 162, 164
Horowitz, 49, 50, 51, 157, 162, 163, 166, 256, 370, 404, 417, 418, 421, 422
Hoter, 256
Hulem, 370
Hules, 370
Huter, 370
Hutner, 399, 417, 418, 424
Hutter, 409, 418
Hyman, 370

I

Ickowicz, 294, 399, 418
Iklerf, 139
Ilkow, 129
Imber, 36
Ingber, 244, 399, 418, 419
Inlender, 244
Insler, 63, 244
Iram, 244
Irgang, 413, 419
Irum, 293
Isaac, 245, 370
Isenberg, 396, 419
Isler, 240, 399, 415, 419
Israel, 243, 245
Israelavich, 370
Israeler, 399, 400, 417, 418, 419, 420, 423, 424
Israelovitch, 243
Israelowitz, 98
Iwanski, 148, 149, 150
Izak, 120, 243, 400, 419, 420, 421, 422
izrael, 411
Izrael, 148, 411, 419

J

Jacob, 370, 400
Jacobowitz, 370
Jacubowicz, 413, 419
Jakimowitz, 370
Jakob, 400, 418, 419, 420, 424
Jakubowicz, 30, 321, 400, 401, 416, 417, 419

Jarmula, 213, 214
Jartner, 370
Jasne, 370
Jek, 129, 132, 133, 139
Jekel, 370
Jekele, 370
Jeri, 370
Jochnowicz, 322
Joris, 370
Juliosh, 97

K

Kac, 220
Kaczik, 180
Kahan, 370, 371
Kahana, 265, 35, 3510
Kahane, 399, 419
Kahler, 279
Kaitch, 281
Kaizer Wilhelm, 65
Kalb, 352, 371
Kalfus, 343, 401, 416, 418, 419, 424
Kalman, 335
Kalpos, 279, 282
Kaminer, 26
Kamm, 75, 282
Kamp, 294
Kampf, 63, 279, 401, 419
Kanar, 394, 419
Kanareck, 279
Kaner, 234, 279, 299
Kant, 279
Kapelansky, 371
Kapelner, 279, 326
Kapelushnik, 36
Kapler, 279
Kartagener, 398, 419
Kasif, 7, 232, 240
Kastura, 139
Katz, 56, 98, 265, 280, 338, 322, 371
Katzenberg, 338
Katzner, 283
Kaufman, 19, 47, 279, 371
Kegel, 282, 285
Keitelman, 281
Keler, 28
Keller, 26, 30, 109, 282, 371
Kellman, 371
Kellner, 371
Kelner, 49, 282
Kenig, 282
Kenigberg, 327
Kenner, 80, 182, 371
Kerner, 282, 371
Kessler, 139, 142
Kestenbaum, 282, 394, 419
Kestenberg, 313
Ketz, 282
Khumit, 191

Kiel, 281
Kielbasa, 208
Kimchi, 80
Kimel, 371
Kipfel, 414
Kippel, 280
Kirsch, 280
Kirshenbaum, 280, 371
Kisten, 280
Kitay, 281
Kitsch, 371
Klagsbald, 407
Klahr, 281
Klajn, 335
Klajner, 28
Klajnhendler, 28, 120
Klapholc, 140, 218, 224
Klapholtz, 22, 239, 281, 282
Klapholz, 63, 67, 336, 410, 419
Klar, 63, 75, 355
Klaubauf, 282
Klausner, 3, 232, 281, 371, 402, 405, 409, 419
Klefel, 371
Klein, 281, 282, 372, 392, 397, 412, 419
Kleinberger, 281, 372
Kleiner, 282
Kleinfinger, 413, 419
Kleinhandler, 103, 372
Kleinhändler, 392, 419
Kleinhendler, 281
Kleinkopf, 281
Kleinman, 281
Kleinpisal, 281
Klener, 47
Klepel, 282
Kligman, 372
Klitovski, 8
Kloch, 148, 150
Klopholtz, 372
Kluger, 281, 372
Knabel, 282
Knecht, 337
Knecht Zeidman, 282
Knobloch, 282, 335
Koad-Atstein, 372
Koch, 141, 279, 282, 372, 412, 419
Koenigsbuch, 401, 419, 421, 423
Kogan, 372
Kohane, 392, 399, 419
Kohn, 229
Kolb, 279
Komet, 110, 265, 324, 372
Komlos, 308
Konarek, 372
Kook, 310
Koperman, 19
Koplanski, 1
Korc, 3381
Koretz, 97, 372
Korn, 50, 182, 183, 243, 280, 282, 306, 372, 400, 414, 419

Kornblitt, 280
Korndeich, 372
Kornhauser, 280, 372
Kornheiser, 400, 419
Kornila, 372
Kornilo, 20, 21, 22, 63, 116, 148, 149, 206, 209, 217, 218, 224, 232, 240, 280, 292, 326, 336, 337, 339
Korn-Lenkovich, 183, 184
Kornmehl, 372, 401, 402, 416, 417, 419, 420, 421, 423, 424
Kornmehl Winter, 401, 402
Kornmel, 372
Kornreich, 280, 324, 372, 373, 394
Korpos-Nager, 373
Kortz, 280
Korzennik, 409, 419, 422
Kose, 279
Kostman, 279
Kostura, 148
Kotruvan, 129
Kowalik, 148, 149
Kramer, 373
Kranish, 283
Krantz, 282, 373
Kranzler, 282
Krapner, 41
Krassel, 80
Krauser, 338
Krauter, 411
Kreiger, 282
Kresch, 282
Krieger, 373
Krieser, 400, 419
Krietzer, 373
Kriezler, 282
Krimeski, 78
Krischer, 402, 419
Krisher, 282, 402, 419
Krisztal, 149
Krokner, 282
Krumholc, 121
Krumholtz, 282
Krumhulc, 65
Krzisztopowicz, 148, 150
Kubozu, 182
Kubie, 406, 419
Kudler, 397, 419
Kunstlich, 402
Künstlich, 419
Kupfer, 402, 419
Kupferwasser, 373
Kurc, 30
Kurtz, 373, 400, 413, 420
Kutnowski, 305
Kwadratsetin, 422
Kwadratstein, 280, 402, 416, 419, 420, 423
Kwadratsztajn, 41
Kwiatkowska, 171, 172

L

Labendz, 151
Ladner, 64, 265, 299, 373, 402, 419, 420
Lajbgorn, 321
Laker, 373
Lam, 403, 420
Lamensdorf, 265
Landau, 373
Landerer, 399, 420
Landman, 206, 265, 266, 373
Langer, 121, 266, 268, 323, 373, 403, 420
Langsam, 373
Lashkowitz, 266
Laskowitz, 373
Last, 266
Lau, 373
Laub, 150, 265, 332, 395
Lauber, 218, 265, 394, 420
Laufban, 373
Laufer, 120, 265, 323, 373, 374
Lauterbach, 265, 374
Laynman, 39
Lazar, 374
Lazarowitc, 54
Lebencrown, 267
Lebenkorn, 235, 326
Leder, 267, 401, 410, 420
Leder Ricks, 401
Lederberger, 374, 402, 417, 421
Lederberger-Kresch, 402
Lederer, 403
Lefel, 267
Lefelholtz, 267, 374
Leffel, 374
Leffelholtz, 374
Lehman, 374
Lehrer, 343
Lehrfeld, 374
Lehrhaupt, 374
Leib, 266, 374
Leibel, 80, 137, 247, 266, 374, 375, 403, 406, 417, 420, 423, 424
Leibl, 98, 241
Leibler, 306
Leichter, 266
Leiner, 375
Leinwand, 266, 267, 375
Leisten, 266
Leister, 267
Lem, 403, 420
Lemberger, 267, 375
Lemel, 267
Lengovich, 183
Leniek, 54
Lenkavich, 183
Lenkowicz, 393, 420
Lenonid, 325
Leon, 375
Lerer, 268

Lerfeld, 267, 268
Lerhauft, 196
Lerhaupt, 30, 120
Lerman, 267, 294
Lerner, 128, 148, 150, 267, 375
Lerr, 268
Leser, 393, 403, 404, 416, 417, 418, 420, 421, 422, 423
Leuchter, 406, 420
Levanoni, 22, 94
Levenstein, 375
Levine, 375
Levinger, 267
Levniavsky, 375
Levniowski, 267
Levy, 337
Lewinger, 97
Lewinowski, 211, 212
Lezer, 148, 149, 267, 404, 420, 422
Lezerin, 34
Libor, 129, 151
Licht, 268
Lichtblau, 267, 268, 375
Lichtbloy, 229
Lichtenger, 268
Lichter, 375
Lichtig, 267, 375, 400, 420
Lichtik, 267, 375
Lichtinger, 213, 267, 375
Liebe, 394, 420
Lieber, 266, 367, 375
Liebeskind, 265
Lieblich, 266, 375
Lifshitz, 267
Linhard, 267
Linkowitz, 362, 375
Linzenberg, 403, 420
Lion, 266, 393, 420
Lipiner, 267
Lipinski, 150
Lir, 146
Lirer, 267
Lis, 375
Lisowska, 180
Liss, 267, 375
List, 64
Lit, 151
Lorenc, 145, 153
Lubasch, 405, 419, 420, 421
Lubash, 266
Lubianiker, 375
Ludmer, 375
Luftig, 404, 420
Lumbe, 185, 186
Lust, 405, 417, 420
Lustbader, 405, 420, 421
Lustgold, 266
Lustgrarten, 266
Lustig, 150, 266, 375
Lustik, 121, 142, 376

M

Madritsch, 133, 134, 140, 203, 207, 208, 209, 215, 414
Madshevitsky, 376
Mahler, 268, 270, 308, 376
Maibruch, 268
Mais, 270
Malchiel, 232
Maler, 312
Malkisher, 268
Malter, 47
Maltz, 376
Malutki, 120, 125
Man, 62, 63, 65, 317
Mandel, 268, 376
Mandelbaum, 268, 376
Mandelshtam, 78
Mandsein, 376
Mane, 376
Mangel, 269, 376
Manheim, 268
Manheimer, 150, 252, 376
Manheit, 268
Mankes, 376
Mann, 263, 268, 376
Mansdorf, 149, 172, 269, 270, 345
Mantel, 269, 411, 412, 420
Marcus, 376
Marder, 269, 376
Mardkovitch, 269
Marfeld, 405, 420
Margases, 376
Margolies, 376
Margolit, 19
Margolius, 269
Margoshes, 269
Margulies, 393, 405, 418, 42
Margulis, 340
Markfeld, 269
Markus, 269, 394, 395
Marmer, 376
Marmoor, 67
Marmor, 269
Maschler, 269
Maszler, 28, 30, 31, 177, 178, 197
Maurer, 268, 376, 391
Mayer, 268
Mayerhof, 268
Mazel, 376
Mazes, 376
Me'at–Ezrahi, 103
Meher, 376
Mehr, 47, 270
Melach, 270
Melinger, 270, 377, 413
Meller, 377
Mellimger, 413, 420
Meltzer, 377
Menase, 377
Menashe, 357, 377

Mendel, 313
Menderer, 49, 133, 270, 377
Mendlinger, 377
Mener, 405, 416, 420
Merc, 29, 33
Merel, 269, 270
Merl, 328
Mertz, 270, 377
Merz, 92, 107
Meshel, 270
Mesinger, 326
Mesner, 312
Messinger, 140, 270, 410, 420
Mestel, 377
Meszel, 300
Metel, 403
Meth, 240
Mett, 269
Metzendorf, 270
Metzger, 270, 377
Metzker, 293
Meves, 270
Meyerhoff, 377
Michalewicz, 14, 220, 222, 225, 229
Michelowitz, 377
Mifelev, 377
Miler, 128
Miller, 149, 172, 269, 377
Mingelgreen, 269, 270
Mink, 66
Mintz, 269, 377
Mintzer, 269, 377
Mira, 327
Mire, 405, 406, 420
Mireh, 269
Mitler, 206
Mitz, 269, 377
Mitzenmacher, 377
Mokadi, 377
Molutki, 164
Monderer, 269
Mondschein, 268
Monsdorf, 411, 420
Montefiori, 377
Mor, 268
Mordkowicz, 327
Morgenbesser, 269
Morgenstern, 377
Mosel, 268
Moshel, 269
Moskatenblit, 377
Mosner, 269, 346, 347, 354
Mossler, 378
Mozel, 11
Mozes, 268
Müller, 420
Müller, 393
Muskatenblit, 98, 280
Mutz, 111

N

Nachman, 270, 378
Naftali, 49, 378
Naiger, 378
Najhaus, 329
Nathan, 271
Nat, 347
Natt, 270, 271
Nauberg, 352
Nauman, 335
Navamiast, 271
Navatni, 378
Nebensal, 378
Neiberg, 270
Neifeld, 271, 378
Neigasser, 270
Neiman, 270, 271, 378
Neistat, 378
Neker, 378
Neugeboren, 409, 420
Nichthauser, 378
Nigar, 9, 11
Nisenfeld, 348
Nissenfeld, 271
Nizinsky, 270, 333
Nogaser, 378
Nordau, 61
Novak, 177, 270
Nowak, 120
Nusboim, 234

O

Ober, 242
Oberlender, 242
Ochler, 378
Ofner, 62, 244
Ofsler, 344
Omanski, 8, 20
Omansky, 378
Opfelbaum, 321
Oppermann, 118, 126, 129, 132, 139
Organd, 121
Ornsztajn, 30
Orszicer, 47, 245
Osterwajl, 126
Osterweil, 244, 292, 411, 420
Osterwejl, 121
Ostrogski, 54
Ovisibel, 378
Ovshitzer, 245
Owide, 405, 406, 417, 419, 420, 421, 423

P

Pacher, 273
Padaver, 273
Padwe, 393, 421
Paionk, 150
Palman, 273

Palten, 129
Parnes, 404, 421
Pasternack, 274
Pasternak, 378
Pastrong, 274
Patasmacher, 379
Patt, 211
Pearlstein, 276
Peretz, 61, 385
Perlberg, 180
Perlberger, 276, 379
Perlstein, 379
Pfefer, 197
Philippson, 24
Pick, 393, 421
Piechowicz, 145
Pilarsdorf, 274
Pilcer, 30, 33, 406, 417, 420, 421
Pilcerowa, 406
Pilzner, 131, 157
Piner, 406, 421
Pinkus, 413, 421
Pinna, 8
Pinsker, 61, 379
Pinter, 274
Pintshoski, 22
Piontek, 146, 150
Pipersburg, 415, 421
Pishawa, 54
Pishowa, 55
Plachte, 379
Plachteh, 275
Planer, 395, 405, 421
Plashen, 275
Platner, 275
Plato, 275
Plawker, 411, 421
Plemtser, 275
Plocki, 137
Poder, 274
Polanecky, 273
Polish King Stanislaw August, 27
Pomerantz, 98, 273, 277, 330, 379
Poss, 274
Post, 268, 273
Postrong, 206
Potaschmacher, 273
Potaschmann, 250, 273, 277, 282
Potashman, 336
Preminger, 379
Presser, 405, 421
Price, 277
Primerman, 178, 180
Primus, 277
Pris, 20, 65, 331
Pris-Chour, 80
Prowizer, 277
Przybitek, 150
Pshezlaver, 158
Pyrek, 146

Pyrkowa, 146

Q

Quadratstein, 402, 416, 419, 420, 422, 423

R

R' Abaeli Hirsh, 8
R' Menahem Hillel, 111
Raab, 283
Rabbi Elazar, 36
Rabbi Yehuda Leib haKohan Maimon, 44
Rachmiel, 379
Rachmil, 396, 421
Radek, 379
Radwan, 283
Radziwill, 54
Ragle, 379
Raichman, 406, 421
Rajch, 121
Rajchman, 345
Rajn, 293
Rajnbach, 341
Rajnback, 341
Rajnkraut, 312
Rajnsztajn, 301
Rajs, 197
Rak, 308
Ramzowa, 151
Rand, 283, 325, 344, 379, 406, 418, 420, 421
Rapapart, 379
Rapaport, 30, 213, 284, 285, 323, 379
Rappaport, 379
Rappel, 403
Rastel, 379
Rauch, 379
Rauchwajg, 340
Rauchwerg, 392, 421
Raush, 283
Rausz, 221
Reb Aron, 56
Reb Chaim, 56, 160
Reb Eliezer, 157, 158, 159, 160, 161, 163, 164, 165
Reb Ezra, 56
Reb Mekhl, 56
Reb Sholem-Dovid, 162, 163, 164, 165
Reb Yehiel-Meirl, 164, 165
Reb Yehosha, 50
Reb Yitzhak, 56
Rebhan, 284
Rebhon, 182, 284
Reder, 284
Redner, 406, 421
Reich, 284, 285, 298, 379, 406, 417, 421
Reichman, 284
Reifen, 284
Rein, 284, 379, 380
Reinbach, 285
Reiner, 284
Reinhold, 284, 380, 407, 408, 421

Reiss, 130
Reiver, 270, 284
Remer, 285
Renert, 380
Rennert, 285
Resler, 310
Ressler, 20, 284, 285
Rice, 284
Rick, 284, 406, 421
Ricks, 401, 421
Riemer, 396, 416, 417, 418, 419, 421, 422, 423
Riger, 380
Rik, 47
Rimer, 284
Rimler, 322
Rinder, 47, 284, 406, 421
Ringelheim, 380, 413, 421
Ringleblum, 183
Riter, 284
Ritter, 185
Rochverg, 283, 285
Rodner, 19
Roich, 229
Rokeach, 190
Rokh, 380
Rommelman, 164
Rommelmann, 129, 132, 139, 144, 145, 147, 148, 149, 152, 172
Ropczicer, 50
Ropshitzer, 161
Rosemarin, 380
Rosen, 283, 285, 304, 380
Rosenbaum, 283, 380, 398, 421
Rosenberg, 283, 343, 380
Rosenblat, 380
Rosenblatt, 283, 341, 393, 421
Rosenblit, 283, 380
Rosenblum, 394, 395, 400, 421
Rosenbluth, 404, 421
Rosenbusch, 112, 283
Rosenbush, 380
Rosenfeld, 380, 393, 421
Rosengarten, 259
Rosensztok, 283, 285
Rosental, 283
Rosenthal, 380
Rosenzweig, 283, 285, 380, 402, 421
Rosenzweig-Lederberger, 402, 421
Roskes, 177, 178, 380
Rosner, 283, 401, 421
Rot, 283, 342, 329
Rotenberg, 64, 181, 283
Roth, 234, 380, 406, 408, 421
Rothkopf, 409, 421
Rothstein, 394, 421
Rottenberg, 9
Rovel, 3548
Rovner, 283
Rozenbaum, 130, 134
Rozenberg, 132, 182, 340

Rozenberger, 400
Rozenblat, 340
Rozenbush, 9, 121
Rozengarten, 309
Rozensztok, 343
Rozner, 47, 49
Rubashav, 380
Rubel, 284
Ruben, 189
Rubenstein, 234
Rubin, 11, 22, 30, 284, 285, 340, 380, 406, 407, 408, 421, 422, 424
Rubinfeld, 352
Rubinstein, 284
Ruckel, 414, 421
Ruczicka, 186
Rudner, 400, 422
Rudnicki, 35, 37
Rudnitzki, 380
Rumeld, 380
Rutenberg, 62
Ruvin, 30, 165

S

Sacher, 354
Sachwald, 271, 343, 380
Safir, 28, 30, 34, 176
Sagan, 381
Salamon, 271, 353, 407, 417, 422
Saldinger, 381
Salholc, 306
Sali, 381
Salit, 133
Salomon, 305
Salpeter, 271, 381
Saltz, 381
Sambar, 271, 273
Samet, 407, 422
Sanzer, 49
Sapir, 271, 329, 381
Sapir-Ringel, 381
Sauerstram, 381
Savader, 381
Schachar, 83, 84
Schachter, 395, 422
Schanzer, 285
Scharf, 407
Schechter, 121, 288, 290
Schenkel, 177
Scheps, 286
Scherner, 204
Schiff, 232, 286, 289, 348, 407, 416, 417, 421, 422, 423, 424
Schiffer, 286
Schildkraut, 234, 266, 288, 290
Schiling, 290
Schiller, 288
Schindel, 350
Schindler, 203, 208, 397
Schiper, 36

Schlaff, 287
Schlangenkopf, 287
Schlenger, 289
Schlesinger, 287, 408, 422, 424
Schmerz, 409, 421, 422, 423
Schmidt, 288, 381, 395, 422
Schmuckler, 393, 422
Schmukler, 288, 290
Schneider, 288, 290, 381
Schneps, 288, 290
Schnepps, 315
Schnoll, 411, 422
Schnur, 288, 411
Schönberg, 409, 419, 422
Schönwetter, 393, 422
Schreiber, 290, 393, 409, 410, 418, 420, 422
Schwarc, 410, 422
Schwartz, 121, 252, 286, 354, 381
Schwartzbard, 289
Schwartzkachel, 285
Schwartzkichel, 285
Schwartzreich, 410, 422
Schwarz, 82, 84, 393, 410, 422, 423
Schweber, 286
Schweid, 392, 422
Schweit, 410, 418, 422
Schweitz, 285
Schweitzer, 410, 422, 423
Schwimmer, 286
Schwinger, 286
Segal, 404, 422
Seidel, 411, 422
Seiden, 381, 393, 422
Seidenverg, 381
Seinfeld, 36
Seinwel, 382
Seis, 382
Selenfreund, 382
Selinger, 263, 382
Shabatinski, 382
Shachar, 82
Shacher, 285
Shachner, 285
Shafan, 9
Shalit, 285, 382
Shamrot, 285
Shanhoff, 22
Shantzer, 382
Shap, 382
Shapira, 285, 290, 382
Shapiro, 310, 382
Sharfstein, 382
Sharov, 290
Shedlesker, 288
Shedlisker, 229, 382
Sheif, 382
Sheifer, 382
Sheitelavsky, 382
Shenaug, 288
Shenbach, 290

Shenberg, 288, 382
Shenfeld, 288, 383
Shenirer, 288
Shenkel, 288, 383
Shenveter, 288
Shenvetter, 383
Sher, 289, 290
Sherman, 289
Shezer, 383
Shidler, 286
Shifer, 55, 56, 80
Shilai, 288
Shildkraut, 383
Shiller, 383
Shinagel, 286
Shindel, 286, 289, 290
Shipman, 286
Shitzer, 383
Shivitz, 288
Shlam, 383
Shlang, 207
Shlangenkapf, 383
Shlisel, 287
Shmarak, 383
Shmelkis, 383
Shmolberg, 290
Shneur, 34
Shnor, 103
Shnur, 383
Shoenenfeld, 383
Sholdenfrai, 383
Shornshtein, 285
Shpan, 241
Shpangelet, 290
Shpatz, 289
Shpeizer, 97
Shpet, 290
Shpielfogel, 289
Shpielman, 113
Shpiler, 290
Shpitzin Sztrom, 290
Shporn, 3
Shpringer, 290
Shpritzer, 290
Shpyzer, 67
Shreiber, 22
Shteier, 286
Shtern, 415, 422
Shteuer, 404, 422
Shtiglitz, 287
Shtil, 287
Shtramer, 287
Shtrobing, 98
Shtub, 286
Shturm, 286
Shudmak, 383
Shulbaum, 285
Shulerer, 285, 383
Shwager, 383
Shwanenfeld, 108

Shwartz, 403
Shweber, 383, 384
Shweidt, 285
Siedlisker, 347
Sigman, 261
Silber, 262
Silberberg, 10
Silberfenig, 11, 262
Silberman, 262
Silbershatz, 262
Silberstein, 262
Silbiger, 262, 384
Silbing, 313
Silver, 384
Silverberg, 384
Silverfenig, 384
Silverman, 384
Silverstein, 384
Sima, 356, 384
Simcha, 384
Simcheh, 271
Sinagel, 384
Sinai, 384
Singer, 3, 102, 236, 262, 384
Siroka, 385
Sisler, 385
Skowronsky, 385
Slobetsky, 80
Slowik, 150
Smiga, 393, 422
Smolenskin, 385
Sobelson, 385
Sofer, 385
Sokman, 271
Sokoler, 271, 394, 411, 422, 423
Sokolov, 385
Soldinger, 30, 109
Solender, 271, 410, 422
Solnik, 333
Solomon, 385
Somerman, 385
Somerstein, 385
Sommer, 385, 410, 419, 420, 422, 423
Sosne, 385
Souder, 278
Souderer, 278
Spadek, 385
Span, 385
Spangelet, 289, 385, 393, 404, 411, 422
Spanglet, 402, 422
Spanier, 410, 422
Spanoff, 385
Sparn, 385
Speigel, 289
Speiser, 289
Speizer, 19, 385
Spenadel, 290, 385
Sperber, 290
Sperling, 290
Spiegel, 385

Spielman, 290, 385, 411, 422
Spiller, 385
Spinrod, 290
Spira, 408, 410
Spitz, 386, 407, 412
Spitzen, 411, 418, 419, 420, 422, 423
Spitzer, 386, 393, 422
Spizman, 386
Spodek, 271
Sprai, 386
Springer, 386
Spritzer, 386
Sprung, 396, 422
Srebbel, 386
Sroka, 151, 240, 271
St. Krol, 145, 153
Stamberger, 286
Starel, 289
Stark, 286
Starkman, 286, 386
Staszowski, 271
Steigler, 287
Stein, 20, 287, 386, 404, 422
Steinbeck, 386
Steiner, 287, 289, 386, 392, 416, 423
Steinhauer, 287, 386
Steinhorn, 404, 423
Stern, 287, 410, 423
Sternheim, 402, 416, 419, 420, 422, 423
Sternlicht, 287
Steuer, 392, 412, 423
Stieglitz, 408, 423
Stiglitz, 386
Stockfish, 386
Storch, 411, 421, 423
Storm, 405, 423
Straim, 386
Stram, 386
Strasberg, 386
Strassberg, 289
Straus, 129, 386
Strauss, 287
Stricker, 287
Strum, 411, 415, 423
Sturm, 22, 403, 423
Sturmwind, 411, 412, 422, 423
Suberman, 386
Suesskind, 413, 423
Sukman, 329, 386
Süss, 394, 423
Susser, 412, 419, 423
Sussheim, 386
Susskind, 412, 416, 417, 418, 419, 420, 423, 424
Süsskind, 409, 413, 416, 418, 423
Swarch, 83
Swartz, 19
Szajner, 47
Szancer, 14, 30, 32, 220, 413, 421, 423
Szapira, 44
Szarf, 407

Szenkel, 120
Szenkl, 15
Szer, 323, 353
Szicer, 26
Szif, 126, 348
Szifer, 218, 224
Szilder, 348
Szildkraut, 351
Szindelhajm, 303
Sziper, 33, 120
Szisler, 182
Szit, 151
Szjanfeld, 180
Szlenger, 352
Szlisl, 47
Szmukler, 182
Sznur, 30, 327
Szotland, 51
Szpajzer, 126, 196, 197
Szpan, 78, 79, 230
Szpangelet, 335, 350
Szperber, 352
Szpicen, 335
Szpigel, 30
Szpiler, 177, 178, 180
Szpindler, 177, 180
Szpinrad, 302
Szpira, 30, 157, 165, 240
Szpiro, 49
Szporn, 5, 167, 229, 233, 234, 235, 236, 289, 346
Szprung, 354
Szrajber, 335
Szrobing, 287
Sztajn, 346
Sztajner, 305
Sztajnfeld, 338
Sztamberger, 349, 350
Szteinbok, 287
Szteinhorn, 287
Sztiglic, 47
Sztil, 303
Sztojer, 412, 423
Sztorm, 349
Sztram, 120
Sztraus, 182, 320
Sztrasberg, 321
Sztreng, 150
Sztrom, 287, 289, 312, 335
Sztrum. 328
Sztub, 120
Sztum, 141
Szwanenfeld, 30, 220
Szwarc, 47, 60, 62, 63, 65, 81, 82
Szwarcbard, 33
Szyfman, 413, 417, 418, 419, 420, 421, 423

T

Tajtelbaum, 323
Tajtlbaum, 47, 351
Taler, 320
Taller, 263, 264
Tan, 386
Tarn, 30
Tartakower, 33
Taub, 263, 332, 387
Taube, 103
Taubeles, 226, 263
Taubenfeld, 263
Taubenshlag, 387
Taubensig, 387
Tauber, 263
Teder, 387
Teichler, 264
Teichner, 392
Teitel, 264
Teitelbaum, 157, 158, 264, 387
Telerman, 298
Teller, 264
Tellerman, 235, 264
Temmer, 264
Templer, 47, 264, 387, 407, 423
Tenenbaum, 319, 387
Tennenbaum, 264
Terle, 387
Tesse, 387
Thaler, 413, 414, 423
Thorsch, 394, 423
Tifenbron, 264
Tifenbruch, 316
Tiferbruch, 326
Tilles, 414, 423
Timberg, 264, 387
Tinger, 264
Tirkel, 185, 218, 224
Tisch, 134, 264, 397, 398, 423
Tish, 387
Tishatkas, 324
Tisz, 197, 200
Titsch, 207, 208, 210
Tochferderber, 263
Tochsherer, 264
Toder, 263
Toibeles, 387
Tomm, 263
Toppel, 393, 423
Torn, 263
Tornheim, 20
Tram, 134
Tratner, 264
Traum, 19, 128, 130, 387, 396, 423
Treller, 387
Trinc, 28
Trinczer, 130, 134
Trinkenreich, 414, 423
Trintscher, 387
Trintsher, 264
Trom, 264
Trop, 264
Truvig, 387

Tsajchner, 347
Tsettel, 333
Tshech, 387
Tshechanavsky, 387
Tsidon, 315
Tuchsherer, 387
Turkeltaub, 410, 423
Turkow, 169, 172
Turnheim, 263
Turteltaub, 398, 401, 423
Turtletaub, 263
Twerski, 165

U

Uber, 97, 404
Ulman, 243
Uman, 77
Umanski, 62, 77, 78
Unger, 35, 47, 49, 50, 52, 157, 158, 159, 162, 163, 164, 165, 181, 243, 245, 331, 403, 414, 416, 421, 423
Unterberger, 414, 415, 423
Urabin, 399, 423
Urmian, 62
Utzinger, 149

V

Vachtel, 20
Vandstein, 82
Veg, 260
Veit, 259
Vestraykh, 39
Vind, 410, 423
Volk, 258
Volken, 310
Volkman, 392, 393, 394, 423
Von Malotky, 177
Vorschim, 407
Vulcan, 261

W

Wachs, 259
Wachskerz, 393, 423
Wachskurtz, 387
Wachtal, 148
Wachtel, 68, 69, 75, 121, 149, 257, 387
Wagner, 203
Wajc, 312, 326
Wajchert, 195, 196, 200, 203, 204, 205, 206
Wajcman, 311
Wajnrib, 311
Wajnrub, 311
Wajs, 63, 65, 126, 133, 185
Wajsberg, 132
Wajzer, 172, 173, 306, 309, 327
Wajzers, 173
Waks, 350
Wakselman, 78
Wakskritz, 304

Wakspres, 47, 49
Wald, 35, 261, 387
Waldman-Ginter, 387
Walk, 387
Wall, 388
Wallach, 258, 388
Wallafsky, 388
Walstock, 388
Wander, 258
Wandersztajn, 65
Wandstein, 258, 388
Wandsztajn, 63
Warenhauft, 259
Warhaftick, 388
Warowitz, 259
Waserlauf, 185
Waserman, 128
Wasersztrom, 258
Washitz, 62, 388
Wasnitzer, 388
Wasser, 388
Wasserfel, 258
Wasserkurtz, 261
Wasserlauf, 258
Wasserman, 258, 261, 388
Wasserreich, 261
Wasserstein, 258
Waxman, 258, 388
Waxpress, 258, 259
Waznitzer, 257
Wczostek, 150
Wczotek, 148
Webtchyu, 81
Wechsler, 100
Weg, 388
Weidenberg, 259
Weider, 259, 388
Weikselbaum, 259
Weil, 259, 388
Weimisner, 253
Weinberg, 259, 388
Weinberger, 259, 329, 388
Weindling, 259, 388
Weiner, 260
Weinfeld, 259, 388
Weingarten, 388
Weinig, 388
Weinman, 388, 406, 423
Weinmann, 406
Weinreb, 388
Weinrib, 259
Weinstein, 78, 259, 307
Weinstock, 102, 261, 388
Weintraub, 259, 325, 388
Weisenberg, 260, 388
Weiser, 229, 259, 401, 414, 424
Weisman, 98
Weiss, 75, 94, 247, 259, 260, 388, 389, 412, 424
Weissberg, 260
Weissbloom, 389

Weissen, 389
Weisser, 389
Weiss-Kellner, 388
Weissman, 260, 389, 407, 424
Weissmann, 408
Weistreich, 260
Weitz, 260, 389, 415, 423, 424
Weitzman, 389
Weitzner, 389
Weizer, 234
Weksler, 11, 17, 26, 30, 47, 309
Wellner, 389
Weltsch, 260
Weltsh, 389
Wenger, 3, 260, 344, 389
Wermut, 261
Wermuth, 97
Werner, 261, 332
Werobel, 261
Werteimer, 261
Wertzel, 389
Westrain, 260
Westreich, 260, 389, 393, 403, 424
Wexler, 260, 261, 389
Wexner, 390
Wideman, 259
Wider, 121, 177, 185
Wider-Rozenberg, 184
Wieder, 112
Wierzbicki, 9
Wiesenfeld, 390
Wietshner, 260
Wikler, 394, 424
Wild, 260, 296, 390
Wildstein, 97, 103, 259, 260, 390
Wildsztain, 309
Wilenberg, 46
Wilf, 260
Wilk, 260
Wimisner, 260, 412, 415, 417, 418, 421, 424
Wind, 49, 260, 390, 408, 409, 424
Winer, 167
Winter, 401, 402, 424
Wirth, 188
Wisznowitz, 260
Witmaier, 30
Witte, 390
Wittlin, 394, 424
Wittmayer, 47
Wittmeyer, 390
Witztom, 260
Wolf, 257, 390, 399, 400, 424
Wolff-Silberfenig, 11
Wolfowitz, 258
Wolfson, 390
Woolf, 390
Wortzel, 390
Woszczina, 151
Wozniak, 146, 150
Woznicer, 261

Wroclawski, 261
Wrubel, 47, 390
Wrubel–Ankori, 47
Wulkan, 400, 424
Wunder, 129
Wurcel, 220
Wurm, 261, 407
Wurtzel, 259
Wymisner, 396, 415, 424

Y

Yablonski, 265
Yachnawicz, 265
Yakobowicz, 264, 265
Yakov, 264
Yarmush, 265
Yechiel, 265
Yekel, 265
Yisrael, 94
Yortner, 98

Z

Zaberski, 82
Zagersztrom, 62
Zaiden, 315
Zainvell, 262
Zajdenwerg, 306
Zajdman, 170, 172
Zalcman, 349, 415, 424
Zaltz, 19, 261
Zamler, 261
Zandhouse, 261
Zangen, 390
Zanin, 390
Zarker, 263
Zauder, 415, 424
Zauersztorm, 120
Zavader, 263, 270, 273
Zaverstrom, 261
Zavorstrum, 64
Zawader, 312
Zayden, 39
Zebald, 263
Zech, 278
Zei(?)er, 390
Zeichner, 278
Zeiden, 261
Zeidenwerg, 262
Zeilender, 415, 422, 424
Zeisel, 390
Zeizler, 278
Zeller, 279, 390
Zelnick, 278, 279
Zelt, 278, 279
Zemel, 20, 97
Zemir, 279
Zetel, 278
Zettel, 390
Zevelle, 263

Zichmer, 390
Zidman, 337
Ziegfried, 121
Zielanka, 262
Zigeltuch, 278
Zigfried, 261
Zigler, 261
Zilberfenig, 8, 314
Zilberman, 316, 320, 331
Zilberphenig, 313
Zilberstein, 325
Zilmberman, 263
Zimand, 390
Zimetbaum, 278, 390
Zimmerman, 19, 278, 390, 391
Zinaman, 391
Zinger, 13, 140, 302, 307, 318, 345
Zins, 391, 394, 424
Zinz, 278

Zis, 317
Ziskind, 148, 149, 234, 263, 317, 344
Ziss, 234, 262
Zisser, 262
Zist, 334
Zitranenbaum, 391
Zohar, 355
Zomer, 67, 261
Zowder, 102
Zucker, 278, 391
Zuckerman, 61
Zughaft, 218, 278
Zwecher, 278, 415, 418, 419, 424
Zweibel, 278, 391
Zweig, 278
Zwickelberg, 278
Zwicker, 391
Zwiebel, 407, 424
Zylberman, 399, 424

APPENDIX

RIGHTEOUS GENTILES FROM TARNOW

A partial list of the righteous gentiles with a short version of their rescue stories. Compiled and written by Jill Leibman Kornmehl. Information courtesy of Yad Vashem, the Tarnow Yizkor Book and hidden survivors and their descendants, including the Schlesinger, Mittler, Weksler and Freireich families.

Dyrdał-Kiełbasa, Maria. Maria was a single woman who rescued an infant, Eleonora Lindenberg. Eleonora (later Elisheva Patt) survived the war and moved to Israel in 1957. On October 18, 1966, Yad Vashem recognized Maria Dyrdał-Kiełbasa as Righteous Among the Nations.

Walęga, Danuta Janina. Danuta was a single woman who hid 4-year-old Lea Blumenkranz. However, neighbors began suspecting that Lea was Jewish and blackmailers began threatening her. Walęga traveled by train to the town of Przemyśl with Lea hidden in a suitcase. She enrolled Lea, under a false identity, in a children's institution run by Catholic nuns where Walęga paid for Lea's upkeep until the area was liberated by the Russian army. On August 12, 1975, Yad Vashem recognized Janina Filozof (née Walęga) as Righteous Among the Nations.

Zaczkiewicz, Bronisław. Bronislaw was a railroad employee. During the occupation, he helped shelter Leah (Łucja) Freireich on the Aryan side of town. Bronisław dug a hole in the cellar and hid Łucja there from April 1942 until the liberation in January 1945. During this entire period, Bronisław obtained food, clothing, and medicine for her. The couple married after the war and remained in Tarnow. Bronisław cared for the Freireich family graves in the Tarnow Jewish cemetery until his death. On August 11, 1992, Yad Vashem recognized Bronisław Zaczkiewicz as Righteous Among the Nations.

Poetschke, Jerzy. Jerzy knew Blanka Goldman (later Drillich) before the war when he had been a lodger in her parents' home in Tarnow. Goldman was hidden by the Poetschke family during the war. The neighbors were told she was a relative from Poznan and a hiding place inside the home was prepared for her. Blanka survived the war and moved to Australia. On November 26, 1995, Yad Vashem recognized Jerzy Poetschke as Righteous Among the Nations.

Madritsch, Julius. Madritsch was born in Vienna and was an expert in textiles. Madritsch opened a branch of his factory next to the Tarnow ghetto. This factory employed some 800 workers who worked under humane conditions. A factory car, which was used for the delivery of materials, was also used to smuggle food into the ghetto. He helped Jews get out of the Tarnow ghetto, letting them join the Jewish workers who walked from the ghetto to the factory without being counted. Ron Unger and Margot and Chaskiel Schlesinger worked for Madritsch in Tarnow. On February 18, 1964, Yad Vashem recognized Julius Madritsch as Righteous Among the Nations.

Dagnan Family. The Dagnan family mill in Tarnow sheltered 9 Jews in an attic crawl space behind a hidden wall. All of them survived the Holocaust including Israel Unger and his brother as well as sisters Anna and Cesia Weksler. Israel Unger moved to Canada and the Weksler sisters moved to Israel.

Gawelczyk, Bronislawa and Julian. The friendship between Hofmeisters, owners of a haberdashery store in Tarnów, and the Gawelczyks, began many years before the war. During the final liquidation of the Tarnow Ghetto, the Hofmeisters asked the Gawelczyks to save their one-year-old daughter, Sara. They looked after little Sara and treated her as a daughter. When the neighbors began suspecting they were hiding a Jewish girl, the Gawelczyks moved with Sara to the village of Rzedzin. Sara moved to Israel after the war. On January 31, 1966, Yad Vashem recognized Bronisława and Julian Gawelczyk as Righteous Among the Nations.

Banek, Josef. Josef Banek and his daughter, Irma, lived in Tarnow. They hid five Jewish fugitives from 1942-1945 within a bunker under a shed situated in Józef's garden or in Józef's house. The hidden included: (Abraham) Chaim Betrübniss, his wife- Dora and their daughter, Ingeborg (Inge) as well as Barbara Lichtinger (Sabina) and Samuel Rapaport. All were smuggled out of the sealed Tarnów ghetto. On the January 27, 1993, Yad Vashem recognized Josef Banek and his daughter Irma (Józefa), as a Righteous Among the Nations

Strzalkowski, Kazimierz. During the war, Kazimierz Strzałkowski lived in Tarnów. Beginning in September 1942, he sheltered four members of the Mittler family (Maurycy, Franzeska and children Lila and Sigmund) in his home. In one of the rooms in his house, he built a double wall and the Mittler family hid behind the wall until January 1945. The Mittlers moved to South America. On February 24, 1981, Yad Vashem recognized Kazimierz Strzałkowski as Righteous Among the Nations.

Wesołowski, Halina and Jerzy. The Wesolowskis resided in Tarnów. During World War II, they hid pediatrician Dr. Augusta Mandel and her family in their home.

Mikowski, Franciszek and Stefania. The couple hid Cesia Honig-Ritter who was born in Tarnów, in 1926. Assembling for an Aktion, two of Cesia's friends pulled her out of the group. Cesia's father had worked during the war at a saddle factory and become acquainted with Franciszek Mikowski. Her father told her to seek help from him and Cesia arrived at his door asking for shelter. Tarnow became unsafe for the family because Cesia had no papers and Franciszek left for his home village. When the local priest threatened him for hiding a suspected Jewish girl, he moved once more to his wife's village. Cesia immigrated to the US after the war.

Post War Lists of Jewish Residents

Page 448

EMPLOYEES OF THE JEWISH COMMITTEE IN TARNOW AND THEIR FAMILY MEMBERS REGISTERED WITH THE JEWISH COMMITTEE OF TARNOW, POLAND 1946

(Entrees include name, birth year, parents' name and address).

Courtesy of the Jacob Rader Marcus Center of the American Jewish Archives, Cincinnati, Ohio at "americanjewisharchives.org"

Page 449-450

JEWISH CHILDREN REGISTERED WITH THE JEWISH COMMITTEE OF TARNOW, POLAND 1946

(Entrees include name, birth year, parents' name and address).

Courtesy of the Jacob Rader Marcus Center of the American Jewish Archives, Cincinnati, Ohio at "americanjewisharchives.org"

Page 451-454

JEWISH RESIDENTS WHO ARE EMPLOYED AND REGISTERED WITH THE JEWISH COMMITTEE OF TARNOW, POLAND 1946

(Entrees include name, birth year, parents' name and address).

Courtesy of the Jacob Rader Marcus Center of the American Jewish Archives, Cincinnati, Ohio at "americanjewisharchives.org"

Page 455-456

JEWISH SICK WHO ARE UNABLE TO WORK AND REGISTERED WITH THE JEWISH COMMITTEE OF TARNOW, POLAND 1946.

(Entrees include name, birth year, parents' name and address).

Courtesy of the Jacob Rader Marcus Center of the American Jewish Archives, Cincinnati, Ohio at "americanjewisharchives.org"

```
CENTRALNY KOMITET ŻYDOW POLSKICH          Województwo Krakowskie
    Warszawa-Praga, Szeroka 5             Komitet Żydowski w Tarnowie.
  Wydział Ewidencji i Statystyki
```

Wykaz pracowników Komitetu Żydowskiego w T a r n o w i e

L.P.	Nazwisko i imię	Rok ur.	Imiona rodziców	zajm.stan.	Obecny adres
1	Betrubnis Abraham	1903	Samuel i Beila	kasjer	Sowińskiego 8
2	Bleiweis Uszer	1907	Mojżesz i Matel	aprowizator	Goldhamer
3	Bloch-Merzowa dr.	1892	Zygmunt i Klara		Mickiewicza 6
4	Braun Chanina	1906	Jeruchim i Cecylia	Dentysta	Brodzińskiego 3
5	Freireich Anna	1914		kier.stoł.	"
6	Goldberg Halina	1923	Leib i Ruchla	urzędniczka	Goldhamera 1
7	Gross Nechuma	1913	Daniel i Jochwet		" "
8	Kryształ Franciszka	1910	Izak i Rozalia	sekretarz	Targowa 10
9	Kohn Markus mgr.	1907	Aron i Rachela	Człon.Komit.	Sienna 8
10	Klapholz Edward	1902	Józef i Jetti	Kom.Rewizja	Paderewskiego
1	Kohane Chaja	1909	Peretz i Chana	prac.stoł.	Brodzińskiego
2	Korniło Józef	1903	Szymon i Czarna	dentysta	" 3
3	Lauber Samuel	1915	Henio i Blima	urzędnik	Widok 15
4	Manheimer Norbert	1910	Markus i Toni	Kom.Rewiz.	Brodzińskiego
5	Rosenblat Mila mgr.	1907	Eliasz i Fryda	zast.przew.	Paderewskiego
6	Rubin Wanda mgr.	1912		Człon.Komit.	Piłsudskiego
7	Rauch Leizer	1905	Hersz i Tauba	" "	Goldhamera 7
8	Rosenblüth S. dr.	1909	Chaim i Regina	Kom.Rewiz.	Sienna 8
9	Rubin Bronisław dr.	1899	Aleksan.i Erna	lekarz	Paderewskiego
20	Schiffer Chaim	1912	Hersz i Pesla	przewodnicz.	Sowińskiego 8
1	Schildkraut Naftali	1908	Leib i Jetti	prac.stoł.	Goldhamera 1
2	Stern Leo	1904	Joel i Fryda	" "	"
3	Sauerstrum Dawid	1917	Izrael i Regina	stóż nocny	"
4	Weissbrot Rózia	1920	Abraham i Sara		"
5	Zeller Jonas	1911		Kom.Rewiz.	Bandrowskiego
6	Zughaft Helena	1920	Abe i Bronisława	urzędniczka	Piłsudskiego

Wykaz rodzin pracowników Komitetu Żydowskiego w T a r n o w i e

1	Betrubnis Dora	1913		żona	Zielona 19
2	" Inga	1930		córka	" "
3	Kohn Adela	1914		żżona	Sienna 8
4	" Rela	1937		córka	" "
5	Klapholz Ita	1937		"	Paderewskiego
6	Zeller Feiga	1916		żona	Bandrowskiego

Wykaz dzieci zarejestrowanych w Żydowskim Kom. w T a r n o w i e

L.P.	Nazwisko i imię	Rok urodz.	Imiona rodziców	Obecny adres
1	Brater Natan	1945	Dawid i Lieba	Krasińskiego 9
2	Bezen Leon	1945	Emanuel i Gusta	Krakowska 63
3	Blau Resia	1940	Dawid i Helena	Nowodąbrowska 3
4	Blumenkranz Lila	1937	Emil i Erna	Sienna 8
5	Bursztyn Anna	1931		Legionów 18
6	Daar Lila	1938	Abraham i Róża	Goldhamera 1
7	Ekstein Gita	1931	Leon i Róża	" "
8	Fenichel Abracham	1936	Izrael i Amalia	Pierackiego 10
9	Gruschów Cesia	1940	Chaim i Frania	Krakowska 2
10	Garnreich Dania	1945	" Dwojra	Krasińskiego 9
1	Geld Aleksander	1941	Maks i Cyla	Goldhamera 1
2	Grünszpan Michał	1942	Eli i Cypa	Starodąbrowska
3	Genendelbanm Jakub	1944	Abraham i Berta	Goldhamera 1
4	Gotzler Basia	1942	odebrane od aryjczyków	" "
5	Feinstadt Teodor	1945	Abraham i Antonina	" "
6	Hofmeister Sara	1941		Mickiewicza 6
7	Hauser Ignacy	1932	Maurycy i Helena	Krakowska 63
8	Jachimowicz Samuel	1932	Majer i Rachela	Brodzińskiego 8
9	" Salomon	1935	" "	" "
20	Kohn Rela	1937	Markus i Adela	Sienna 8
1	Korn Tadeusz	1945	Mozes i Rajza	Legionów 18
2	Klapholz Ita	1937	Edward i Regina	Paderewskiego 12
3	Krieger Marek	1939	Maurycy i Anna	Lotników 20
4	Krzywda Jan	1931	odebrany od aryjczyków	Goldhamere 1
5	Lichtblau Edward	1939	Leon i Gizela	Lotników 20
6	Landau Giza	1932	Erna	Mickiewicza 6
7	Linder Lila	1943	Dawid i Mira	Goldhamera 1
8	Mittler Marlena	1933	Maurycy i Franciszka	Krakowska 2
9	" Zygmunt	1937	" "	" "
30	Müller Aleksander	1944	Mojżesz i Fredla	Goldhamera 1
1	Mann Michał	1932	Todrys i Syma	Legionów 18
2	Mansdorf Józef	1931	Salomon i Helena	Żydowska 12
3	Orner Estera	1938	Chaim i Felicja	Goldhamera 1
4	Riemer Norbert	1913	Herman i Francisz.	Legionów 18
5	Reichman Henryk	1935	Salomon i Chana	Goldhamera 1

Wykaz dzieci zarejestrowanych w Żydowskim Kom. w Tarnowie

L.P.	Nazwisko i imię	Rok urodz.	Imiona rodziców	Obecny adres
36	Rosner Estera	1944	Chune	Goldhamera 1
7	Rosenbaum Helena	1945	Ignacy i Dora	Sprawiedliwości
8	Steinkoler Edzia	1944	Husen i Runia	Krupnicza 13
9	Silberman Hanka	1936	Mozes i Basia	Goldhamera 4
40	Schönweter Zofia	1938	Izrael i Sala	Drukarska 21
1	" Manek	1932	" "	" "
2	Süskind Artur	1939	Jakub i Mina	Żydowska 12
3	Seidenberg Emil	1938	Ludmiła	Rogojskiego
4	Spielman Edyta	1936	Henryk i Mina	Legionów 5
5	" Maria	1943	Mojżesz i Irena	" "
6	Stiebel Perla	1945	Josef i Mela	Goldhamera 1
7	Sprechman Monek	1945	Izrael i Lotka	Nowodąbrowska
8	Tesse Monek	1936	Bernard i Erna	Krakowska 2
9	Unger Kalman	1936	Dawid i Minda	Żydowska 12
50	" Izrael	1938	" "	" "
1	Wonger Bolesław	1945	Kamila	Św. Anny 9
2	Weg Sara	1944	Stanisław i Dora	Chyszowska 1
3	Weiss Karolina	1942	Wowek i Dora	Goldhamera 1
4	Wronowicz Bronisława	1935	Regina	Krupnicza 13
5	Weld Zuzanna	1936	Zofia	Drukarska 21

Wykaz kształcącej się młodzieży

1	Betrübnis Inaga	1930	gimn.	Abraham i Dora	Zielona 19
2	Pessel Ewa	1927	uniwer.	Chanan i Maria	Goldhamera 7
3	Goldman Blanka	1924	Gimn.		Sanguszki
4	Korniło Halina	1929	"	Józef i Regina	Brodzińskiego
5	Roth Ida	1925	"	Herman i Małka	Goldhamera 1
6	Schmukler Ruta	1930	"	Chaim i Sabina	" 7
7	Simche Henryka	1923	uniwer.		Piłsudskiego 2
8	Steigler Ryszard	1922	"		" "
9	Ssabeles Maryla	1929	gimn.	Jakub i Rozalia	Limanowskiego
10	Wider Lila	1927	"	Emil i Maria	Krakowska 2
1	Zielonka Bronisław	1922	uniwer.		Goldhamera 1

Wykaz pracowników Spółdzielni zarejestrowanych w Żyd.Kom.w Tarnowie

L.P.	Nazwisko i imię	Rok ur.	Imiona rodziców	Zawód	Obecny adres
1	Abend Ida	1926	Szyja i Regina	krawczyni	Goldhamera 1
2	Adler Bernard	1895	Szymon i Rózia	krawiec	" "
3	Birken Józef	1910	Izak i Rozalia		Targowa 10
4	Braun Henryk	1906	Jeruchim i Cecylia	dentysta	Brodzińskiego 3
5	Beer Alter	1911	Izrael i Rywka		Goldhamera 1
6	Berkelhamer Adolf	1910	Szaja i Frida	krawiec	Krupnicza 13
7	" Herman	1920	" "	"	" "
8	Buchenbaum Bronia	1927	Mozes i Estera	"	Goldhamera 1
9	Blaksbalk Sala	1910	Izrael i Chaja	"	" "
10	Balsam Mendel	1909	Chaim i Sabina	"	" "
1	Bizgajer Sabina	1917	Hirsz i Salomea	"	Krakowska 23
2	Blatt Abraham	1911	Henryk i Feiga	"	Nowodąbrowska 1
3	Buchholz Bernard	1911		"	" "
4	Bass Rózia	1893		"	Rogojskiego 16
5	Blau Lajka	1921	Józef i Sara	"	Brodzińskiego 32
6	Eksterman Abraham	1904	Mordko i Debora	szewc	Wałowa 5
7	Erlich Hela	1915	Mojżesz i Maria	krawczyni	Goldhamera 1
8	Feiner Jakób	1899	Jakub i Chana	"	" "
9	Fischer Anna	1922	Wolf i Blima	"	Wekslarska 7
20	Fried Mojżesz	1907	Arjan i Hania	"	Goldhamera 1
1	Fisch Ichel	1909	Józef i Dora	"	" "
2	Fischbaum Ele	1902	Izrael i Perla	"	" "
3	" Roza	1913	Jankiel	"	" "
4	Fischer Herman	1921	Schulim i Blima	"	" "
5	Fromowicz Roman	1914	Izak i Lea	"	Wekslarska 19
6	" Dawid	1912	Maks i Estera	"	" "
7	Fajerstein Izrael	1909		szewc	Wałowa 5
8	Fromowicz Dawid	1912	" "	blacharz	Krupnicza 13
9	Fessel Maria	1895			Goldhamera 7
30	Gross Natan	1898	Gitla i Józef		Sprawiedliwości
1	Genendelman Berta	1914	Bernard i Lea	krawiec	Goldhamera 1
2	Gruschow Chaim	1912	Susel Rikla	"	Krakowska 2
3	Garnreich Jakub	1907		"	Krasińskiego 9
4	Glück Lea	1904		"	Brodzińskiego 32
5	Goldberg Karola	1921	Aron i Matla	"	Goldhamera 1

Wykaz pracowników spółdzielni zarejestrowanych w Żyd.Kom.w Tarnowie

L.P.	Nazwisko i imię	Rok ur.	Imiona rodziców	Zawód	Obecny adres
36	Grober Pinek	1913	Jakób i Sara	krawiec	Brodzińskiego 32
7	Goldberg Paulina	1915	Maks i Cyla	"	" 3
8	Hirschhorn Jakub	1917	Pesach i Ksawera	"	Folwarczna 6
9	Haber Rachela	1917	Izak i Beila	"	Goldhamera 1
40	Hirsch Bernard	1904	Gimpel i Rywka	"	" "
1	Izrael Regina	1922	Wigdor i Sara	"	" "
2	" Jakub	1912		szewc	" 4
3	Jassy Janek	1910		"	Pierackiego 21
4	Jassy Berta	1908	Józef i Fanny	aptekar.	Limanowskiego
5	Jochniwicz Majer	1917	Leib i Bronka	Krawiec	Goldhamera 1
6	Kuczyński Mordka	1912		szewc	Folwarczna 6
7	Korn Leib	1913	Dawid i Rachela	"	Goldhamera 4
8	Korniło Józef	1903	Szymon i Czarna	dentysta	Brodzińskiego 3
9	Klapholz Edward	1902			Paderewskiego 12
50	Kohn Marek mgr.	1907		adwokat	Sienna 8
1	Kamm Regina	1912	Mozes i Mina	krawiec	Krupnicza 13
2	" Salomon	1907	" "	"	Mickiewicza 6
3	Klein Hela	1917	Samuel i Regina	"	Tatas 5
4	Kracer Regina	1920	Chaim i Stefania	"	Goldhamera 1
5	Krieger Tema	1930	Zygmunt i Fela	"	Polna 5
6	" Anna	1903	Georg i Maria	"	Lotników 21
7	Lederer Frania	1925	Barnel i Idessa		Goldhamera 7
8	Lefolhölz Szymon	1888	Hirsz i Sabina		Rogojskiego 16
9	Lengel Chilel	1904			Brodzińskiego 3
60	Lust Jakub	1905			Goldhamera 1
1	Linder Dawid	1914	Mojżesz i Mina	krawiec	" "
2	Landau Józef	1904	Baruch i Roza	"	Mickiewicza 6
3	Lenkowicz Natan	1904		"	Goldhamera 1
4	Merz Franciszka dr.	1892	Zygmunt i Klara	lekarz	Mickiewicza 6
5	Manheimer Norbert	1910	Markus i Toni		Brodzińskiego 27
6	Majbruch Jakub	1920	Feiwel i Rachela	krawiec	Ogrodowa
7	Mandel Kiwa	1908	Eisig i Elka	"	Goldhamera 1
8	Milchman Pesach	1910	Chaim i Pesia	"	Piłsudskiego 12
9	Pfeffer Chaim	1902		szewc	Krakowska 23
70	Polanecki Józef	1924	Oskar i Maria	krawiec	Legionów 18

Wykaz pracowników spółdzielni zarejestrowanych w Żyd.Kom.w Tarnowie

L.P.	Nazwisko i imię	Rok ur.	Imiona rodziców	Zawód	Obecny adres
71	Perlberger Helena	1913	Pinkas i Cyla	krawiec	Goldhamera 1
2	Platner Markus	1906	Jakub i Sara	"	" "
3	Riemer Herman	1904	Naftali i Lea	szewc	Lotników 18
4	" Pinkas	1910	" "	"	" "
5	Regenbogen Adolf	1896		blacharz	Piłsudskiego 12
6	Rotstein Maria	1895	Leon i Paulina		Kołątaja 9
7	Rosenblüth Simon dr.	1909	Chaim i Regina	lekarz	Sienna 8
8	Rubin Bronisław dr.	1899	Aleksander i Erna	"	Piłsudskiego 21
9	Reich Kalman	1909	Abraham i Feiga		Goldhamera 4
80	Rosenbaum Izak	1911			Sprawiedliwości 6
1	Rubinowa Wanda mgr.	1912		adwokat	Piłsudskiego 21
2	Rudner Doba	1914	Abraham i Regina	krawiec	Goldhamera 1
3	Rosenblatt Rozalia	1912	Aszer i Rachela	"	" "
4	Rosenfeld Genek	1913	Simon i Feiga	"	Drukarska 10
5	Roth Sara	1923	Herman i Małka	"	Rogojskiego 16
6	Rotstein Sabina	1918	Samuel i Maria	"	
7	Rosenbaum Frania	1916	Szyja i Sara	"	Brodzińskiego 3
8	" Pinek	1907	Salomon i Małka	"	" "
9	" Moszek	1908	" "	"	" "
90	Rosdeuscher Samuel	1908		"	Goldhamera 7
1	Ritter Mendel	1916	Chaim i Cyla	"	Krupnicza 13
2	Rauch Leizer	1905	Hersz i Tauba	"	Goldhamera 7
3	Reich Lea	1913	Sender i Perla	"	" "
4	Schifrin Benzion	1918		szewc	Wałowa 33
5	Schächter Jakub	1906		blacharz	Piłsudskiego 12
6	Schoo Natan	1908			Goldhamera 1
7	Sturm Adolf	1919	Akiwa i Rozalia	krawiec	Żydowska 7
8	Steinkoler Nussen	1913	Leib i Golda	"	Krupnicza 13
9	" Runia	1921	Hersz i Rywka	"	" "
100	Schuss Abraham	1917	Mendel i Hinda	"	Pierackiego 21
1	Schiff Sabina	1910	Józef i Etel	"	Goldhamera 1
2	Schönbach Sabina	1924	Lazar i Rachel	"	Tertila 25
3	Sommer Hinda	1915		"	Folwarczna 6
4	Schiff Janina	1912	Józef i Etel	"	Goldhamera 1
5	Schwalb Estera	1916	Markus i Ita	"	" "

Wykaz pracownoków spółdzielni zarejestrowanych w Żyd.Kom. w Tarnowie

L.P.	Nazwisko i imię	Rok ur.	Imiona rodziców	Zawód	Obecny adres
106	Spitzen Chaim	1916	Izrael i Feiga	krawiec	Mickiewicza 6
7	Sporn Chaim	1922	Salomon i Fani	"	Piłsudskiego 22
8	Staszewska Sala	1920		"	Folwarczna 6
9	Sussman Salomon	1910	Eisig i Feiga	"	Goldhamera 1
100	Süsskind Marjem	1926	Majer i Ernestyna	"	" 4
1	Schuldenfrei Saul	1911	Hersz i Małka	"	Widok 15
2	Taubeles Rozalia	1893	Józef i Fanny	aptekarka	Limanowskiego
3	Tiefenbrun Lieba	1920	Rozalia i Samuel	krawiec	Krupnicza 13
4	Weinstock Józef	1920		"	Goldhamera 1
5	Weisman Regina	1923		"	" "
6	Werner Anna	1901	Izrael i Rywa	"	
7	Wronowicz Regina	1903		"	Krupnicza 13
8	Waks Szaja	1912	Sussman Gitla	"	Goldhamera 1
9	Zelt Mania	1902	Szaja i Rywka	"	" 4
120	Zeller Jonas	1911		"	Bandrowskiego 22
1	Apfelbaum Ascher	1910	Józef i Helena	"	Krakowska 23
2	Susskind Mina	1915			Żydowska 13

Wykaz chorych i niezdolnych do pracy zarejestr.w Żyd.Kom.w Tarnowie

L.P.	Nazwisko i imię	Rok urodz.	Imiona rodziców	Obecny adres
1	Bassowa Róża	1893	Abraham i Jetta	Rogojskiego 16
2	Bassler Abraham	1902	Izrael i Rozalia	Goldhamera 1
3	Bardach Róża	1889	Benjamin i Etla	Rogojskiego 16
4	Blau Sara	1908	Josef i Sara	Brodzińskiego 8
5	Bochner Feiga	1876	Mojżesz i Gitla	Goldhamera 1
6	Fisch Peretz	1897	Efraim i Matla	" 4
7	Finder Chana	1878	Salomon i Sara	" 18
8	Flaumenhaft Henia	1925		Mickiewicza 6
9	Fürst Ida	1920	Jakub i Berta	Krupnicza 13
10	Gold Adela	1911	Alter i Sara	Goldhamera 1
1	Goldberg Blima	1918	Blima	" "
2	" Simon	1908	Ascher i Felicja	" "
3	Goldman Cyla	1898		" "
4	" Hania	1929	Majer i Cyla	" 4
5	Gralitzer Juda	1896	Chaim i Gitla	" "
6	Hollender Regina	1860		Rogojskiego 16
7	" Sabina	1876	Wolf i Hinda	Goldhamera 7
8	Jachimowicz Tema	1885	Aron i Bajla	" 1
9	Karp Berko	1885	Motel i Szaja	Starodąbrowska 33
20	Kochane Chaja	1909	Perec i Chana	Goldhamera 1
1	Lauber Mina	1910	Natan i Tauba	" "
2	Laub Jakub	1926	Markus i Mina	" "
3	Last Szaja	1907		" "
4	Lenkowicz Natan	1904		" 4
5	Löfelholz Szymon	1888	Hirsz i Sabina	Rogojskiego 16
6	Mansdorf Salomon	1881		Żydowska 11
7	Puter Henryk	1905		Goldhamera 1
8	Rotstein Maria	1895	Leon i Paulina	Kołłątaja 9
9	Riemer Lea	1873		Legionów 18
30	Rosdeutscher Osjasz	1903	Jakub i Chaja	Goldhamera 1
1	Ruck Rachela	1908		" "
2	Schiff Sabina	1910	Józef i Etel	" "
3	Schlesinger Dora	1932	Chanine i Paula	Mickiewicza 6
4	Schneps Abraham	1885		Goldhamera 1
5	Silber Sil	1886	Mozes i Golda	Bernardyńska 25

Wykaz chorych i niezdolnych do pracy zarejestr. w Żyd.Kom. w Tarnowie

L.P.	Nazwisko i imię	Rok urodz.	Imiona Rodziców	Obecny adres
36	Speiser Regina	1890	Abraham i Chana	Wałowa 27
7	Sperber Chaja	1873		Bandrowskiego 12
8	Spielman Abraham	1860		Legionów 5
9	" Fryda	1882		" "
40	Strobinger Ewa	1892	Zygmunt i Helena	Rogojskiego 16
1	Weitz Fryda	1888		Krakowska 63
2	Wolf Sala	1915	Chaim i Sala	Broduińskiego 32
3	Wolkenfeld Giza	1924	Abraham i Cypora	Goldhamera 1
4	Zeller Fela	1916		Bandrowskiego 12
5	Ziegfried Doba	1882	Abraham i Estera	Rynek 19

Tarnow Photos

Pre War Pictures

The main mikvah was designed in the Moorish style and opened in 1904. It had 3 floors, with the mikvah in the basement. Smaller mikvahs existed elsewhere in Tarnow. Courtesy of Yad Vashem.

Rabbi Alter Horowitz and his disciples in Tarnow. Rabbi Horowitz was the last chief rabbi of the Hasidic Dzikówer-Ropshitzer dynasty. Courtesy of USHMM archives.

Building of the Safa Berura School on Sw. Anny Street. Safa Berura was a progressive Jewish coed private school where students learned Hebrew, Latin and secular subjects. Courtesy of Audrey Unger Reich.

Jewish Orphans' home. The orphans were taken to Buczyna forest and brutally killed in June, 1942. Courtesy of Yad Vashem.

Left: Hashomer Hazair group in 1930s. Courtesy of the Tarnow Yizkor book.

The Samson Zionist sports club table tennis team in Tarnow. Courtesy of Henry Sommer.

Tarnow town hall in the main plaza of the Rynek. Courtesy of Stanislaw Siekierski.

The inside of the majestic Jubilee (New) Synagogue on Nowa Street. Completed in 1908, it was the largest synagogue in Tarnow. Courtesy of D. Czechowski.

Above: Staff of Jewish Hospital before the war. Courtesy of Silvia Nath.
Right: Bus depot in 1930. The Sanz yeshiva with its domed windows is in the middle in back. Courtesy of Adam Bartosz.

During the War

Nazis destroying Old Synagogue in September 1939. Courtesy of Dariusz Czechowski.

Inside of the destroyed New Synagogue. Courtesy of Dariusz Czechowski.

Hospital staff in the Tarnow Ghetto. Third from right Dr. Szaja Handler, later on "Schindler's List". Courtesy of Lili Haber.

Jews with armbands in the Rynek (market square). Armbands were mandated in November, 1939. Courtesy of Dariusz Czechowski.

Dr. Henryk Faber, a doctor in the Jewish Hospital, with his daughter, Francziska, in the Tarnow Ghetto. Courtesy of Arie Avigor.

German soldiers standing on the ruins of the Old Synagogue after it was destroyed in 1939. Courtesy of Dariusz Czechowski.

Jewish shopkeeper and child wearing armbands at their stall in the marketplace. Courtesy of Dariusz Czechowski.

Two men in conversation. Circa 1940. Courtesy of Yad Vashem.

Stores with Jewish stars on their doors located near the Old Synagogue. Author unknown.

Religious man with armband, 1941. Courtesy of Yad Vashem.

New Synagogue in 1939 after the Nazis third attempt at destruction. Courtesy of D. Czechowski.

Jewish residents and stall merchant in the Tarnow Ghetto in 1940. Courtesy of Chris Webb private archives.

POST WAR PICTURES

Jewish children in Tarnow post war. Courtesy of Helen Cammarata.

Goldberg family at the monument in the cemetery, circa 1950s. Courtesy of Helen Cammarata.

Gates of the Jewish Cemetery in 1990, before they were donated to the USHMM. Courtesy of A. Bartosz.

Former Jewish Hospital building. Courtesy of Audrey Unger Reich.

Jewish Cemetery, 1990. Courtesy of Pawel Topolski.

Former restaurant with Yiddish signs still visible on its walls. Courtesy of Pawel Topolski.

Abraham Ladner with ark in the synagogue in his home in Tarnow, circa 1980. Courtesy of P. Topolski.

Beit Tahara in the cemetery, 1988. Courtesy of Adam Bartosz, personal archives.

Dedication of the monument in the cemetery, 1946. Courtesy of Sylvia Nath.

Memorial plaques donated by survivors placed on a wall in the back of cemetery. Courtesy of Yad Vashem.

Former Talmud Torah School (religious elementary school) building on Sienna Street. Courtesy of Yad Vashem.

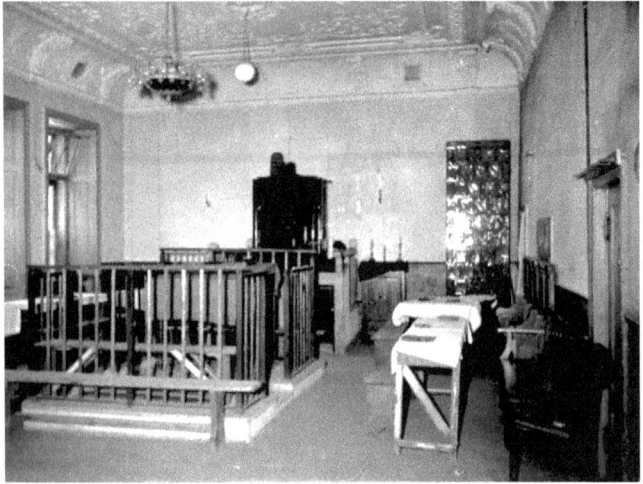

First post war synagogue on Goldhammera Street. Courtesy of Yad Vashem.

Zydowska Street in the former Jewish neighborhood. Courtesy of Yad Vashem.

Monument to 800 Jewish children murdered in Buczyna Forest near Tarnow in 1942. Courtesy of Izabela Sekulska.

The Bima, the only remaining element of the destroyed Old (Stara) Synagogue, on Zydowska Street in the 1940s. Courtesy of Yad Vashem.

The monument in the cemetery installed after the war. It was a column from the destroyed New Synagogue with the top sheared off. Courtesy of Yad Vashem.

Jewish cemetery in the 1990s. Courtesy of Pawel Topolski.

Remnant of the Chadushim Synagogue, one of many synagogues in Tarnow, destroyed in 1939. Courtesy of D. Czechowskiego.

Jewish children who were hidden during the war, gather at the monument in the cemetery, circa 1948. Courtesy of A. Gal.

Szancer steam mill, opened in 1846. Henryk Szancer was known for his many charitable contributions and as a member of the Town Council. Courtesy of S. Siekierski.

Gates at the entrance to the former Old Synagogue on Zydowska Street. Courtesy of Jill Kornmehl.

www.ingramcontent.com/pod-product-compliance
Lightning Source LLC
Chambersburg PA
CBHW082006150426
42814CB00005BA/243